Rethinking Moundville and Its Hinterland

Florida Museum of Natural History: Ripley P. Bullen Series

UNIVERSITY PRESS OF FLORIDA

Florida A&M University, Tallahassee
Florida Atlantic University, Boca Raton
Florida Gulf Coast University, Ft. Myers
Florida International University, Miami
Florida State University, Tallahassee
New College of Florida, Sarasota
University of Central Florida, Orlando
University of Florida, Gainesville
University of North Florida, Jacksonville
University of South Florida, Tampa
University of West Florida, Pensacola

Rethinking Moundville and Its Hinterland

Edited by Vincas P. Steponaitis
and C. Margaret Scarry

Foreword by Henry T. Wright III

University Press of Florida
Gainesville · Tallahassee · Tampa · Boca Raton
Pensacola · Orlando · Miami · Jacksonville · Ft. Myers · Sarasota

Copyright 2016 by Vincas P. Steponaitis and C. Margaret Scarry
All rights reserved
Published in the United States of America

This book may be available in an electronic edition.

First cloth printing, 2016
First paperback printing, 2019

24 23 22 21 20 19   6 5 4 3 2 1

Library of Congress Cataloging-in-Publication Data
Names: Steponaitis, Vincas P. | Scarry, C. Margaret.
Title: Rethinking Moundville and its hinterland / edited by Vincas P.
Steponaitis and C. Margaret Scarry ; foreword by Henry T. Wright III.
Description: Gainesville : University Press of Florida, [2016] | 2016 |
Series: Florida Museum of Natural History : Ripley P. Bullen series |
Includes bibliographical references and index.
Identifiers: LCCN 2015035907 | ISBN 9780813061665 (cloth : acid-free
paper) | ISBN 9780813068039 (pbk.)
Subjects: LCSH: Moundville (Ala.)—Antiquities. | Excavations
(Archaeology)—Alabama—Moundville. | Indians of North
America—Alabama—Moundville—Antiquities. | Mississippian
culture—Alabama—Moundville.
Classification: LCC E78.A28 R48 2016 | DDC 976.1/43—dc23
LC record available at http://lccn.loc.gov/2015035907

The University Press of Florida is the scholarly publishing agency for the
State University System of Florida, comprising Florida A&M University,
Florida Atlantic University, Florida Gulf Coast University, Florida
International University, Florida State University, New College of Florida,
University of Central Florida, University of Florida, University of North
Florida, University of South Florida, and University of West Florida.

University Press of Florida
2046 NE Waldo Road
Suite 2100
Gainesville, FL 32609
http://upress.ufl.edu

In Memoriam
Christopher Spalding Peebles
(1939–2012)

Contents

List of Figures   ix
List of Tables   xiii
Foreword   xv
Preface   xix

1. New Directions in Moundville Research   1
   Vincas P. Steponaitis and C. Margaret Scarry

2. Social Archaeology of Monumental Spaces at Moundville   23
   Vernon James Knight Jr.

3. Long-Term Trends in the Making and Materialization of Social Groups at Moundville   44
   Gregory D. Wilson

4. Mound X and Selective Forgetting at Early Moundville   54
   John H. Blitz

5. Was There a Moundville Medicine Society?   74
   George E. Lankford

6. The Distribution of Hemphill-Style Artifacts at Moundville   99
   Erin E. Phillips

7. Moundville Palettes—Prestige Goods or Inalienable Possessions?   121
   Vincas P. Steponaitis

8. Rural Settlement in the Black Warrior Valley   134
   Scott W. Hammerstedt, Mintcy D. Maxham, and Jennifer L. Myer

9. Late Prehistoric Social Practice in the Rural Black Warrior River Valley   162
   John F. Scarry, H. Edwin Jackson, and Mintcy D. Maxham

10. Domestic and Ritual Meals in the Moundville Chiefdom   187
   H. Edwin Jackson, C. Margaret Scarry, and Susan Scott

11. Crafting Moundville Palettes   234
   Jera R. Davis

12. Moundville as a Ceremonial Ground   255
   C. Margaret Scarry and Vincas P. Steponaitis

   References   269
   List of Contributors   301
   Index   305

Figures

1.1. The Moundville site   2
1.2. The Black Warrior Valley, encompassing Moundville and its immediate hinterland   4
1.3. Radiocarbon dates for the West Jefferson and Moundville I phases, showing their probability distributions and means   10
1.4. Radiocarbon dates for the Moundville II, Moundville III, and Moundville IV phases, showing their probability distributions and means   11
1.5. Phase sequences in the Black Warrior Valley   12
2.1. Schematic map showing Moundville's bilateral symmetry   24
2.2. Four interpretive models of partitioned monumental space around a central plaza   27
3.1. The Moundville site, showing excavated areas discussed in the text   45
3.2. Plan of Residential Group 9 featuring the location of Moundville I structures superimposed by a Moundville II–III cemetery   48
3.3. Detailed plan of the cemetery from Residential Group 9, highlighting the burial of male aged 50+, with associated burial furniture   50
4.1. The Moundville site, showing the location of Mound X   62
4.2. Mound X study area with the location of the 2004 excavation units   64
4.3. Plan of excavations at Mound X   65
4.4. Mound X palisade lines and refilled 1983 excavation trench exposed below plow zone, view north, 2004   66
4.5. North profile at western portion of Mound X   67

5.1. Known distribution of medicine lodges related to the Midé Society 77
5.2. The Red Lake scroll, a mnemonic chart of the ritual flow of the Midewiwin among the Ojibwa 85
5.3. A detail from the Red Lake scroll 87
5.4. Owls depicted in Midewiwin bark scrolls 88
5.5. Two temples from the Lower Mississippi Valley and a Midé lodge 89
5.6. Conjectural elevation and archaeological plan of greathouse on the summit of Mound E at Moundville 93
5.7. Conjectural elevation and archaeological plan of earthlodge on the summit of Mound V at Moundville 95
5.8. Moundville owl effigies 96
6.1. Hemphill-style bottles 101
6.2. Five main themes of the Hemphill style 101
6.3. Stone palettes 103
6.4. Stone pendants 104
6.5. Copper gorgets 106
6.6. Mean richness, all Moundville II–III burials containing datable artifacts compared with those containing Hemphill-style artifacts of each genre 110
6.7. Spatial distribution of excavation areas with Moundville II–III phase burials, burials possessing Hemphill-style pottery, burials with stone palettes, burials with stone pendants, and burials with copper gorgets 112
6.8. Spatial centroids of burials with Hemphill-style artifacts by genre, compared with the centroid of all Moundville II–III burials 113
6.9. Venn diagram showing the rarity of burials with more than one Hemphill genre 117
7.1. Typical stone palettes from Moundville 123
7.2. Cross sections of typical Moundville palettes 124
7.3. The centering theme in stone and copper 125

7.4. Palettes with engraved designs on reverse face   126

7.5. Palettes exhibiting clear impressions of wrappings or containers   130

8.1. Sites in the Black Warrior Valley   135

8.2. Black Warrior Valley Survey (BWVS) transects and Moundville Coal Degasification Field (MCDF)   138

8.3. Surveyed well pads in the Moundville Coal Degasification Field (MCDF)   139

8.4. Late Woodland period sites in the combined MCDF-BWVS study area   140

8.5. Mississippi period sites in the combined MCDF-BWVS study area   141

8.6. Known site clusters   149

8.7. Estimated annual sherd deposition rates, corrected for differential sherd preservation   156

9.1. The Black Warrior Valley, showing the locations of sites discussed in this chapter   164

9.2. Wiggins site, Feature 1, profile and plan   169

9.3. Wiggins site, Feature 1, engraved carinated bowl   170

9.4. Grady Bobo site, Feature 10, profile and plan   171

9.5. Grady Bobo site, Feature 10, engraved beaker   171

9.6. Grady Bobo site, Feature 10, bone tools   174

9.7. Wiggins site, Feature 1, Moundville Incised vessel fragments showing variations in the execution of incised designs   178

10.1. The Black Warrior Valley, showing sites with plant and animal assemblages included in this study   189

10.2. The Moundville site, showing localities with plant and animal assemblages included in this study   190

10.3. Abundance of hickory and acorn shell from Moundville I contexts at hamlets, Hog Pen mound, and Moundville   202

10.4. Abundance of maize cupules and kernels, and the kernel-to-cupule ratio from Moundville I contexts at hamlets, Hog Pen mound, and Moundville   204

10.5. Abundance of maize cupules and kernels, and the kernel-to-cupule ratio from Moundville I contexts on the Riverbank, North of Mound R, and the mounds at Moundville   208

10.6. Abundance of hickory and acorn shell from Moundville through time   209

10.7. Abundance of maize cupules and kernels, and the kernel-to-cupule ratio from Moundville through time   214

10.8. Abundance of hickory and acorn shell from late Moundville III contexts at Moundville and White   215

10.9. Abundance of maize cupules and kernels, and the kernel-to-cupule ratio from late Moundville III contexts at Moundville and White   216

10.10. Abundance of anatomical units for deer from Moundville II and III assemblages in Mound Q at Moundville   221

10.11. Abundance of major faunal taxa at Oliver, Grady Bobo, Wiggins, Gilliam, and White   222

10.12. Abundance of anatomical units for large mammals from Moundville II and Moundville III contexts in Mound Q at Moundville   222

10.13. Abundance of anatomical units for deer from White and Mounds G and Q at Moundville   224

11.1. Stone palettes from the Black Warrior Valley   235

11.2. Map of excavations at Pride Place   237

11.3. Stages of experimental palette production   244

11.4. A sample of the experimentally produced diskette preforms and finished diskettes   245

11.5. Replicated debitage   245

12.1. Comparison of a Mississippian site cluster in the Black Warrior Valley with an eighteenth-century Indian town   262

Tables

1.1. Phase Boundaries in the Moundville Chronology 8
6.1. Frequency of Burials with Hemphill-Style Artifacts 107
6.2. Frequency of Burials with Hemphill-Style Artifacts by Age Group 108
6.3. Frequency of Burials with Hemphill-Style Artifacts by Sex 109
6.4. Frequency of Burials with Hemphill-Style Artifacts by Context 110
8.1. Nonmound Sites by Topographic Zone 142
8.2. Sites by Distance to Water 143
8.3. Sites by Soil Type 144
8.4. Sites by Distance to Mound 145
8.5. Nonmound Sites by Distance to Moundville 147
8.6. Sites by Distance to Nearest Nonmound Site 148
8.7. Distribution of Sites by Survey Area and Period 151
8.8. Sherd Counts from the UMMA, BWVS, and MCDF Assemblages 152
8.9. Sherd Counts for Model Phase Assemblages 154
8.10. Estimated Rates of Sherd Deposition by Temporal Unit 157
9.1. Birds from Grady Bobo 173
9.2. Birds from Gilliam 176
10.1. Plant Assemblages from the Black Warrior Valley, Moundville I–Early Moundville II Phases 188
10.2. Plant Assemblages from the Black Warrior Valley, Late Moundville II–Moundville III Phases 191

10.3. Faunal Assemblages from the Black Warrior Valley, Moundville I–Moundville III Phases   192

10.4. Plants Identified at Sites in the Black Warrior Valley, Moundville I–Moundville III Phases   197

10.5. Standardized Counts of Plants, Moundville I–Early Moundville II Phases   199

10.6. Ratios of Maize Kernels to Cupules   205

10.7. Standardized Counts of Plants, Late Moundville II–Moundville III Phases   210

10.8. Fauna from Mound Q at Moundville, Moundville II–Moundville III Phases   218

10.9. Unusual Animals from Mounds G and Q at Moundville   227

11.1. Ground-Stone Debris, Tools, and Craft Items from Pride Place and Moundville   239

11.2. Archaeological Correlates of Sandstone and Palette Crafting   243

11.3. Size-Grade Data of Experimental and Archaeological Sandstone Debitage Assemblages   246

Foreword

In many ways this volume is the legacy of research begun at Moundville in the 1960s by Christopher Spalding Peebles, who died unexpectedly in Bloomington, Indiana, on April 16, 2012. Chris left behind a rich and complicated record of scholarship, one that is difficult to understand, not the least because he did not have the time to complete a synthetic overview of what he had accomplished. Nonetheless, it is possible to integrate the many perspectives within which he worked, and such an integration makes it clear why he was so pleased with the papers given in his honor at the Society for American Archaeology meetings in Atlanta in 2009, which have been revised and supplemented to constitute this volume.

I first met Chris Peebles in 1965 at the Central States Archaeological Societies meeting in Champaign-Urbana. He had finished his bachelor's work at Chicago in both anthropology and philosophy and was moving on to graduate work. While at Chicago, he had worked with Lewis Binford at the Carlyle Reservoir in Illinois, learning completely new methods of surface survey, excavation, and settlement analysis. Several of us drove from Chicago to the meetings, talking heatedly about archaeology, Hopewell and Mississippian societies, and our understanding of chiefdoms at that time. Chris was, to my surprise, very cautious, drawing on southeastern ethnohistory to criticize models derived from Polynesia, and most circumspect about what he might learn from the mortuary record of Moundville, an effort he was already planning. During the rest of his career, Chris used his understanding that the archaeological and ethnohistorical records of the Southeast form a continuous cultural record with great elegance. The contact period did not provide "analogies" for the past but were a later phase of dynamic cultural traditions for which any explanatory propositions must account.

Chris did graduate work with Albert Clanton Spaulding at the University of California at Santa Barbara. His dissertation studies were undertaken at the great Mississippian center at Moundville, Alabama, under the tutelage of the doyen of Alabama archaeology and director of excavations at Moundville during the 1930s, David L. DeJarnette. Chris acquired an immense respect for the pioneers of southeastern archaeology from DeJarnette and from his meticulous study of primary sources. During this period we met rarely, and my knowledge of this period of deep immersion in the WPA-era records of excavations at Moundville and related sites comes primarily from later conversations. He greatly respected the fact that nineteenth-century pioneers like Clarence B. Moore not only saw things we could not but saw them from the point of view of another era.

As was customary in the 1960s and 1970s, Chris took teaching positions at Florida Atlantic University and the University of Windsor while working on his dissertation. Using tools learned from Binford and Spaulding, particularly such multivariate techniques as cluster analysis, he began to sort out the structure of mortuary dimensions on which the burials at Moundville could be ordered. In the era of huge mainframe computers and the entry of programs and data with punched paper cards, this was slow work. He visited Ann Arbor frequently, and we had many arguments about the extent to which these were dimensions of cultural variability in Spaulding's sense versus clusters based on gender, class, and sodality. Although he never again had access to such a large and comprehensive sample of burials, he never ceased to puzzle over the issue of dimensional structure.

Chris joined the Museum of Anthropology and the Department of Anthropology at the University of Michigan in Ann Arbor in 1974 and began a revival of Michigan's program in the archaeology of the Great Lakes region, simultaneous with an expanded program of research in west-central Alabama. The Alabama research of the 1970s was carefully designed to fill gaps in our knowledge of the evolution of complex social and political networks the middle reach of the Black Warrior River valley. Chris was very generous in helping colleagues and students to work on different aspects of the Moundville cultural system. He encouraged studies of the large collection of ceramics at Moundville, from the points of view of manufacture, exchange, and symbolic embellishment. With these understandings, with a broad understanding of Mississippian ceramics developed at Harvard and Michigan, and with nonparametric multidimensional scaling approaches to the ceramics from sealed contexts at Moundville,

Vin Steponaitis was able to develop a five-phase ceramic chronology that elucidated the foundation and transformations of Moundville itself. This chronology in turn was used by Tandy Bozeman to reanalyze the archeological survey collections—redating the smaller settlements with only one or two artificial mounds up and down the valley—and writing a developmental narrative of the sustaining area around the great center. Modern excavations at some of the small centers, undertaken by Paul Welch and others, documented the movement of raw materials and crafted goods between smaller and larger settlements. The plant remains from these settlements and from his salvage excavations at Lubbub Creek, studied by Margaret Scarry and others, provided a firm understanding of gardening and plant collecting during Mississippian times. Studies of the rich collection of human remains from Moundville and related states by Mary Lucas Powell, Pat Bridges, Margaret Schoeninger, and others provided unparalleled insight into nutrition and health in a Mississippian society. Some of these studies implied a serious modification or rejection of ideas Chris had put forward in earlier papers, but no one was happier than he with these new understandings. He addressed himself to basic reporting of the work at Lubbub Creek and the effort to integrate the vast amounts of data generated by the work at Moundville and Lubbub Creek. During this time he also began a thorough reconsideration of his own philosophical roots, reading widely in such philosophers and social theorists as Maurice Merleau-Ponty, Antonio Gramsci, and Pierre Bourdieu. These changing philosophical perspectives are manifest in some of his later papers and would doubtless have grounded the synthesis he intended to write.

In 1985 Chris took a post in the Glenn Black Laboratory of Archaeology and the Department of Anthropology at Indiana University at Bloomington, where he remained after his formal retirement in 2009. It was his intention to continue the laboratory's research at Angel Mounds in southern Indiana, but his energies were diverted by organizational problems and by the need to use his own vast experience with database construction and analysis to help his university build its information-technology capacities. He kept a close eye on the new work at Moundville by Jim Knight and others, and he spoke when we last met of their accomplishments and of the possibility of synthesizing the Moundville evidence in a completely new way. Alas, this was not to be. New work did begin at Angel in 2005, and this continues under others. He found Angel to be very different from

Moundville, a product of different processes than other Mississippian centers, and one that would be amenable to the new perspective he was developing. This too was not published at the time of his passing.

The chapters that follow carry Chris's work at Moundville and related sites in new directions, many of which no one could have envisioned in the 1960s. Chris took copious notes on the presentations and had nothing but praise for the original presentations. I am sure he would be no less pleased with the final versions published herein.

Henry T. Wright III

Museum of Anthropological Archaeology
University of Michigan, Ann Arbor

Preface

Back in 1998, Jim Knight and one of us edited a synthesis called *Archaeology of the Moundville Chiefdom*. Its preface noted that Moundville research was moving at such a rapid pace that the book could only capture a moment "in flight"; it further predicted that "an additional resynthesis" would soon be necessary (Knight and Steponaitis 1998: xix). Happily, that prediction was right. Archaeological work in the Moundville region continued at a rapid pace with new excavations, regional surveys, and analyses of extant collections. This volume takes stock of the "flight paths" over the last two decades and hints at some directions present and future work is taking us. We believe the solid foundation of past research set the stage for a flurry of new interpretations that draw heavily on both archaeological evidence and ethnohistorical models, the latter firmly rooted in the Native cultures of the American South. The result is a richer, more detailed understanding of the people who inhabited both Moundville and its immediate hinterland.

Yet another impetus for this volume was the retirement of our teacher and mentor Christopher S. Peebles, a leading figure in Moundville archaeology. To mark this event we organized a session in his honor at the 2009 annual meeting of the Society for American Archaeology in Atlanta. The papers presented in that symposium, "Rethinking Moundville and Its Hinterlands," were the starting points for the chapters in this volume.

One of the pleasures of working at Moundville is the collegiality and intellectual stimulation offered by senior and junior colleagues, who are passionate about their research and bring diverse viewpoints to bear on our mutual interests. Some authors in this volume are Chris Peebles' students or their contemporaries who were directly influenced by him. Other authors are younger scholars, students of Chris's students. The latter are numerous and flourishing, and we could include only a subset of their work here, but we are confident that the future of Moundville archaeology is in excellent hands and that further syntheses will be forthcoming.

We are grateful to the participants of the SAA symposium and the authors in this volume for their insightful contributions and their patience as this volume took shape. We also thank Jon Marcoux and an anonymous reviewer for their careful, critical reading of the manuscript; Brett Riggs and Paul Welch for their help with the maps that appear herein; and Judy Knight and Meredith Morris-Babb of the University Press of Florida for their enthusiasm and sound advice. The Graham Archaeological Research Fund at the University of North Carolina at Chapel Hill provided essential support for the completion of this book.

1

New Directions in Moundville Research

VINCAS P. STEPONAITIS AND C. MARGARET SCARRY

Between the start of the second millennium AD and the onset of European colonization, the American South was home to a set of Indian cultures that are now called Mississippian. These people inhabited the South's many river valleys and organized themselves into polities that the early Spanish explorers described as *provincias,* or provinces, and which were headed by *caciques,* or chiefs (Clayton et al. 1993). Such polities appear to us nowadays as geographical clusters of archaeological sites, which are separated from other, contemporary clusters by uninhabited areas (Hally 1993). The most important sites within these clusters are also marked by large pyramidal mounds, built of earth, which were platforms for such buildings as chiefly residences, temples, and lodges that served political and religious ends. Hundreds of these mound sites were built and used across the South during Mississippian times, but only a few stood out in the number of earthworks and the scale of their monumental construction. One of these was Moundville, the second-largest Mississippian center ever built, whose regional history is the subject of this book.

Located in the Black Warrior Valley of west central Alabama, Moundville was marked by at least 29 pyramidal mounds arranged around a plaza (figure 1.1). This site was clearly a major political and religious center, not only for the people living in its region but also for the wider Mississippian world. Its chronology and history are reasonably well understood, at least in broad outline (Knight and Steponaitis 1998). Moundville began around AD 1100 as a dispersed settlement with two small mounds. Not long after AD 1200, it experienced a burst of construction that transformed it into a major center. Most of the mounds were built at this time, as was a large, bastioned fortification wall, made of thousands of logs,

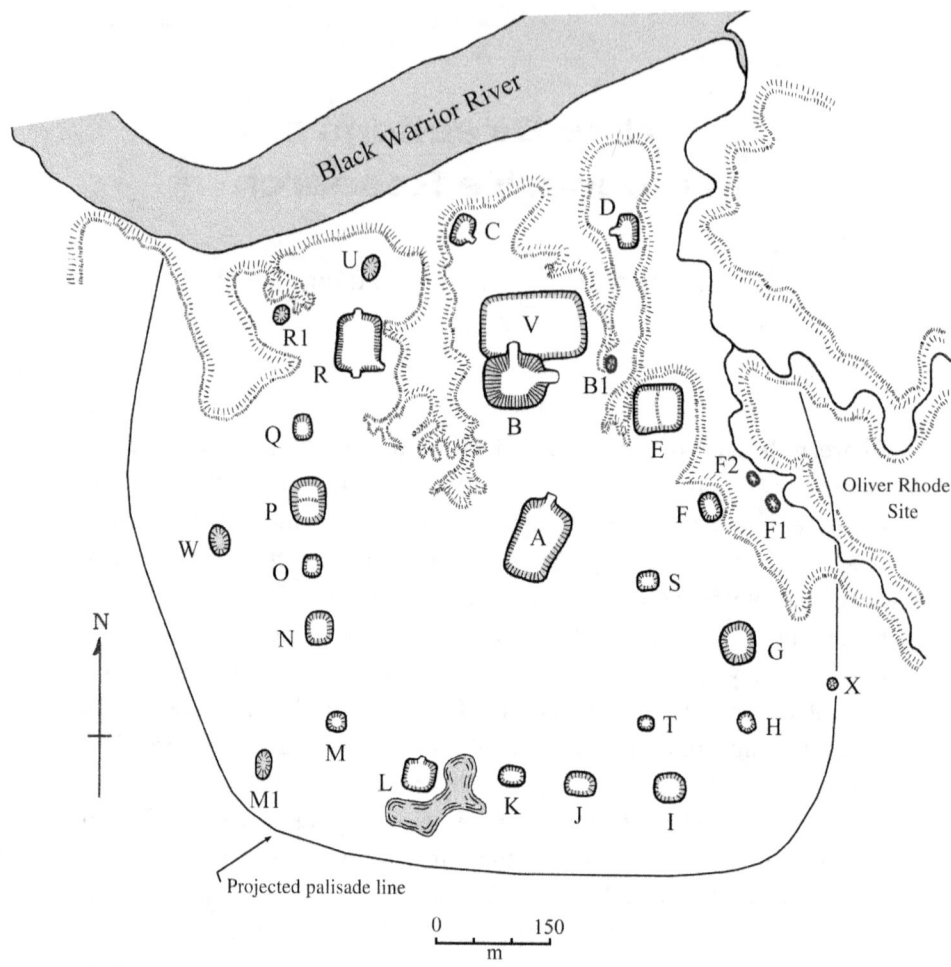

Figure 1.1. The Moundville site.

which protected the site on the sides away from the river. Initially the site had a substantial resident population, which presumably provided the labor for this construction. At about AD 1300, however, the character of the site changed dramatically. Much of the resident population dispersed into the countryside, the fortifications were dismantled, and Moundville became a "necropolis," a place of ritual where the dead were brought from outlying settlements for burial. Indeed, many of Moundville's residential neighborhoods were turned into cemeteries, which were used by the same social units that had once lived there (Wilson 2010). During this time the site was inhabited mainly by the social elite—chiefs, priests, and their retainers. Literally thousands of people were buried at Moundville during the fourteenth and fifteenth centuries. After AD 1450 the level of activity began to decline, and by AD 1650 the site was abandoned.

At its peak Moundville was far and away the largest site in the region, but there were also many contemporary settlements scattered along a 50-km stretch of the Black Warrior Valley just below the Fall Line at Tuscaloosa (figure 1.2). These other settlements, which constituted Moundville's immediate hinterland, were of two kinds. Some were small, local centers marked by a single pyramidal mound; at least 14 such sites are currently known (Welch 1998). The second category comprised hundreds of small sites without mounds, which are generally called "farmsteads" or "hamlets." These smaller residential sites tend to occur in geographical clusters, each associated with a local center (Myer 2002a, 2002b). Many people lived in these outlying settlements, particularly when Moundville itself was a necropolis. The subsistence economy was based on farming, with maize as the principal crop. Craft production of various items, including ritual paraphernalia, took place not only at Moundville, but also in the hinterland (e.g., Marcoux 2007; Sherard 1999; Wilson 2001).

The classic, long-standing interpretation of this evidence is that Moundville was the center of a chiefdom—a polity that was politically centralized but lacked the elaborate bureaucracy that is typical of states (Peebles and Kus 1977; Wright 1977). Beginning in the 1970s, Peebles' pioneering analysis of funerary evidence showed that Moundville's social organization was hierarchical, with marked social distinctions that were visibly expressed in mortuary rituals (Peebles 1974; Peebles and Kus 1977). Settlement studies published soon thereafter argued that the distinction between Moundville and the local centers was a political hierarchy, and that the spatial distribution of these centers was well suited for the movement of tribute from the hinterland to the paramount center (Peebles 1978; Steponaitis 1978). Later studies found direct evidence of such tribute or "provisioning" of foodstuffs at Moundville (Scarry and Steponaitis 1997), examined the circulation of craft items within the polity (Welch 1991), and refined the conclusions of earlier burial and settlement studies in myriad ways. Much of this work culminated in a 1998 volume called *Archaeology of the Moundville Chiefdom*, which presented a new synthesis of Moundville and its region (Knight and Steponaitis, eds. 1998).

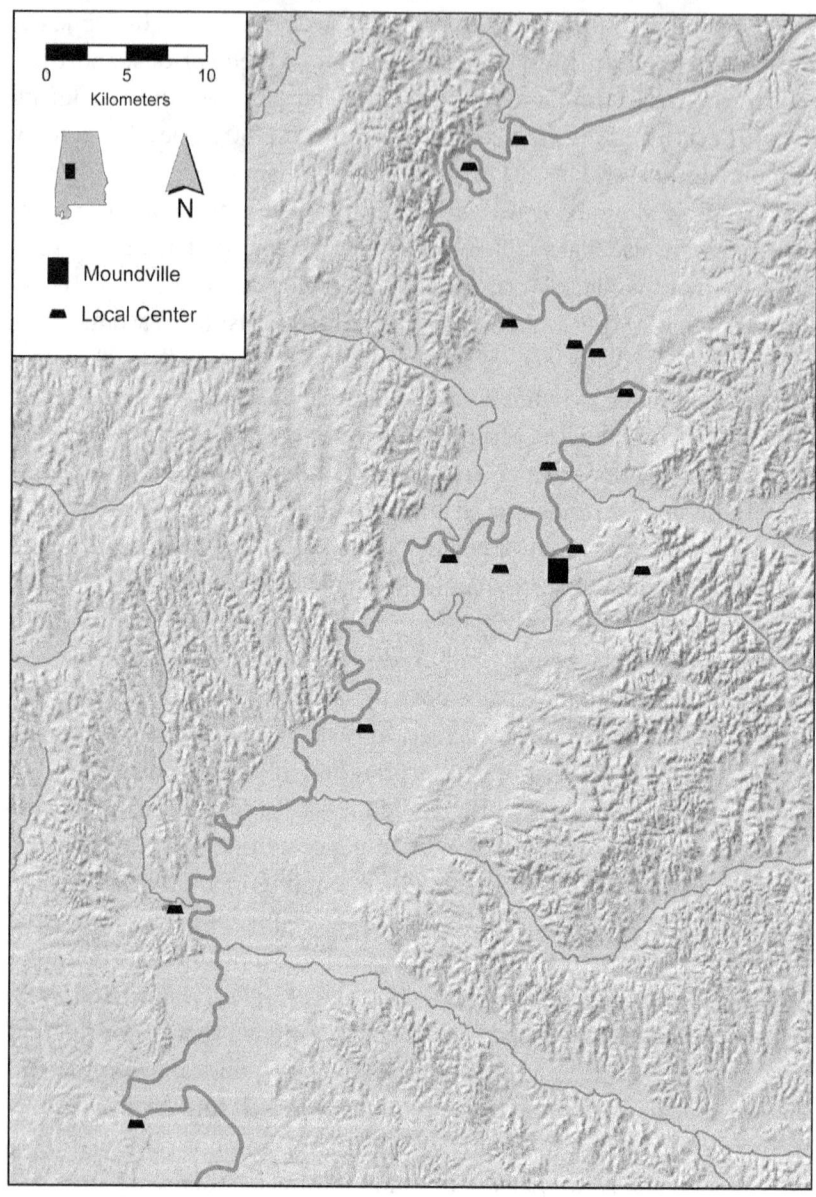

Figure 1.2. The Black Warrior Valley, encompassing Moundville and its immediate hinterland.

Our purpose in this book is to draw together some strands in the enormous amount of research that has taken place at Moundville since that 1998 synthesis was published. Despite the criticism that the term *chiefdom* has endured in recent years (e.g., Pauketat 2007), we still find it useful in describing the kind of "middle-range" societies that Moundville represents. We accept many of the criticisms that have been made—particularly that chiefdoms have sometimes been "essentialized" into a rather rigid, idealized category, based on Polynesian examples, which can prevent one from recognizing the variability in social forms that appear in the archaeological record. The answer to this criticism, in our view, is not to throw away the term, as some would have us do, but to recognize that it encompasses a great deal of variability, which can become an object of study in itself. In other words, the concept of a chiefdom still retains value as a descriptive and comparative tool, so long as one does not define the category too rigidly or assume too much about the range of social features it entails. Ultimately, the variability in chiefdoms is a matter that must be explored empirically with archaeological evidence, not assumed a priori.

This is the spirit, we believe, that has animated much of the recent research at Moundville, and that the chapters in this book exemplify. Indeed, one can see a clear trend in the way Moundville studies have evolved over the past four decades. The initial reconstructions of Moundville as a chiefdom were based on the simplified, neo-evolutionary taxonomies of Service (1962) and Fried (1967) and relied heavily on ethnographic analogies with Polynesia (Peebles and Kus 1977; Steponaitis 1978). Since then, the trend has been toward increasingly nuanced interpretations that rely on better archaeological data and more directly on analogies with historical Indian cultures in the American South—societies not far removed, in either time or space, from the archaeological case at hand. The resulting interpretations have not been unduly constrained by neo-evolutionary assumptions and have given us a much richer, more detailed understanding of Moundville and the people who lived there.

In the remainder of this chapter, we discuss several lines of research on Moundville that have played out over the past two decades, not only to review what has been done since the 1998 synthesis, but also to lay the groundwork for the subsequent chapters herein. We see four major themes in this recent work. Described in the briefest of terms, these are (1) chronology, (2) mounds and social memory, (3) iconography and religious practice, and (4) Moundville's hinterland. Let us now consider each of these themes in turn. Together, they lead us to a new perspective on Moundville, which is discussed at the end.

Chronology

Moundville's internal chronology was first worked out in the 1970s and consisted of five ceramic phases: West Jefferson (AD 900–1050), Moundville I (AD 1050–1250), Moundville II (AD 1250–1400), Moundville III (AD 1400–1550), and Alabama River (AD 1550–1700). The West Jefferson phase was first recognized at outlying sites in the upper reaches of the Black Warrior drainage (Jenkins and Nielsen 1974; O'Hear 1975). The Moundville I–III phases were defined at Moundville itself, based on stratigraphic evidence and a gravelot seriation (Steponaitis 1980, 1983a). And the Alabama River phase was recognized in an analysis of ceramic assemblages from both central Alabama and the Black Warrior Valley (Cottier 1970; Sheldon 1974). During the 1990s the last phase was renamed to Moundville IV, to differentiate the protohistoric ceramic assemblages in the Black Warrior Valley from those in neighboring regions (Little and Curren 1995). Continuing excavations at Moundville and surrounding areas in the 1990s and 2000s yielded additional ceramic stratigraphy, which resulted in some minor adjustments to the ceramic varieties diagnostic of each phase, but the sequence of phases remained remarkably intact (Knight 2010).

One major change to the chronology in recent years has been the addition of a new unit, the Carthage phase, just before the West Jefferson phase (Jenkins 2003). Like the latter, the Carthage phase has a ceramic assemblage dominated by plain, grog-tempered sherds; but, unlike West Jefferson, its pottery has much higher frequencies of cord marking and limestone tempering. In absolute dates, the Carthage phase is roughly estimated to last from AD 600 to the start of West Jefferson times.

The second major change has been a significant shift in the absolute dates associated with some of the phases, particularly at the early end of the original sequence. This refinement was a direct result of the accumulation of new radiocarbon dates from Moundville (Knight 2010), the increasing use of stable-isotope corrections and tree-ring calibrations for such dates, and the easy availability of software for statistically pooling and analyzing dates using Bayesian techniques (e.g., Bronk Ramsey 1995, 2009).

In a widely cited but unpublished paper, Knight, Konigsberg, and Frankenberg (1999) used these advances to reestimate the boundaries of the five original phases. They relied on a large corpus of new radiocarbon dates that, when added to those previously available, yielded a total of 107 samples dated by radiocarbon, three by paleomagnetism, and two by thermoluminescence. Their statistical analysis of these dates entailed the following steps:

- All the radiocarbon dates were corrected for isotopic fractionation. Samples for which the $^{13}C/^{12}C$ ratios were unknown (mostly on those submitted prior to 1990) were corrected using the average value in the dataset as a whole. This estimated correction had the effect of shifting uncalibrated dates 40 years later than the original determination.
- The corrected radiocarbon dates were then calibrated for changes in atmospheric carbon, using the most recent tree-ring curves. This calibration had the greatest effect on dates around AD 1000, generally pushing them about a century later.
- Each date was assigned to a single phase in the sequence, West Jefferson through Moundville IV, based on its archaeological context.
- The dates assigned to each phase were then examined statistically for anomalies, using Bronk Ramsey's (1995) agreement index. Thirty-eight dates, about a third of the total, were identified as outliers and eliminated from further consideration.
- To estimate the most likely boundaries between phases, the remaining dates were subjected to the Gibbs Sampler, a statistical algorithm that estimates a target distribution (in this case, for a phase boundary) by repeatedly sampling from a set of prior distributions (the radiocarbon dates). Two additional constraints were imposed on the model based on prior assumptions: (1) that adjacent phases did not overlap, and (2) that the Moundville IV phase ended before the start of French colonization in 1699. This analysis was accomplished using an early version (2.18) of Bronk Ramsey's (1995) OxCal program.

The Gibbs Sampler yielded a probability distribution for each phase boundary, and these results are summarized in table 1.1. Compared to the original estimates, the West Jefferson phase was shortened and shifted

Table 1.1. Phase Boundaries in the Moundville Chronology

Phase Boundary	Original Estimates[a]	Knight et al. Estimates[b]		Current Estimates[f]	
		Mean[c]	Range[d]	Mean[g]	Range[h]
Moundville IV end	1700	1690[e]	1686–1699	1690	1683–1699
Moundville III–IV	1550	1520	1480–1550	1520	1466–1545
Moundville II–III	1400	1400	1381–1409	1390	1383–1417
Moundville I–II	1250	1260	1242–1267	1250	1237–1271
West Jefferson–Moundville I	1050	1120	1098–1140	1120	1104–1149
West Jefferson start	900	1020	990–1055	1070	1021–1109

[a] After Steponaitis 1983a: figure 23.
[b] Derived using the Gibbs Sampler algorithm in OxCal version 2.18; after Knight et al. (1999).
[c] Rounded to the nearest decade.
[d] Plus or minus one standard deviation from the mean.
[e] Estimated here as the midpoint of the one-standard-deviation range, rounded to the nearest decade. Knight et al. (1999: figure 7) set this boundary at 1650, without explanation. We assume that their earlier date is based on external archaeological evidence, not the statistical procedure.
[f] Derived using the Markov chain Monte Carlo (MCMC) algorithm in the current OxCal version 4.2, using exactly the same dates, with the same outliers eliminated, as Knight et al. (1999). The dates themselves come from numerous theses and publications (Bozeman 1982: 62; Curren 1984: 241; Jenkins and Nielsen 1974: 155–58; Knight 2010: tables 4.13, 5.7, 6.6, 6.13, 6.20; Scarry 1986: 150, 164; Scarry 1995: 92–93; Steponaitis 1983a: 104, 126; Walthall and Wimberly 1978: 118, 120; Welch 1986: 53; Welch 1998: table 7.1).
[g] Rounded to the nearest decade.
[h] Plus or minus one standard deviation from the mean.

about a century later, the Moundville I phase was also shortened to accommodate this shift, and the remaining three phases stayed roughly where they had been, with only minor adjustments to their boundaries.

In assessing these results, one must keep two caveats in mind. First, the dates for adjacent phases show a great deal of overlap (figures 1.3, 1.4). This does not necessarily mean that the estimated boundaries are wrong, but it does provide grounds for caution. In other words, the Gibbs Sampler identifies the most likely boundaries given the available data, but these boundaries are not the only plausible ones. As additional data accumulate and statistical methods evolve, the estimates could well change. Indeed, running the same set of dates through the current version of OxCal (4.2), which uses a related but different sampling algorithm (Bronk

Ramsey 2009), yields a somewhat different result.[1] The most likely start of the West Jefferson phase is pushed five decades later, and the start of the Moundville II phase moves a decade earlier (table 1.1; figures 1.3, 1.4).

It is also important to recognize a difference in the way the Gibbs Sampler or any related technique determines boundaries in the middle of the sequence, as compared to the ends. In the middle, phase boundaries have dates on *both* sides, which constrain the algorithm from two directions simultaneously and yield estimates that, in essence, balance these opposing probabilities. At each end of the sequence, on the other hand, dates exist on only *one* side of the boundary. As a result, these boundaries are much less constrained by the available dates, and may be more prone to error. This problem is undoubtedly why Knight et al. (1999) imposed an external (albeit reasonable) constraint of 1699 on the terminal date of the Moundville IV phase. Because of idiosyncrasies in the calibration curve, many of the Moundville IV dates have distributions that extend far beyond 1699 (see figure 1.5). Absent that external constraint, the Gibbs Sampler would have pushed the "best fit" terminal date well into the eighteenth century—a result that would be implausible, because we know from historical evidence that the Black Warrior Valley was abandoned by that time (Knight 1982). Again, this observation does not invalidate the algorithm but simply reminds us that its results, like those of any statistical procedure, should be taken with a grain of salt.

For present purposes, we are inclined to adopt the phase boundaries estimated by the current iteration of OxCal for the middle of the sequence, but to modify the date at the beginning (figure 1.5). We feel the start of the West Jefferson phase is not well enough dated to accept the AD 1070 estimate at face value. Rather, we prefer to adopt a more conservative, rounded estimate of AD 1000 instead, at least until more Late Woodland dates become available. It is worth noting that this rounded date is still within one standard deviation of the best estimate in the 1999 OxCal results. As for the end of the sequence, the Black Warrior Valley may well have been largely vacant by the mid-seventeenth century, based on the lack of historically documented sites and the rarity of European trade goods (Knight 1982; Knight and Steponaitis 1998: figure 1.2). Even so, for present purposes we see no harm in adopting a terminal date of AD 1690, as estimated from the radiocarbon evidence alone.

In sum, our best current estimates for the temporal spans of the phases in the local chronology are Carthage, AD 600–1000; West Jefferson, AD

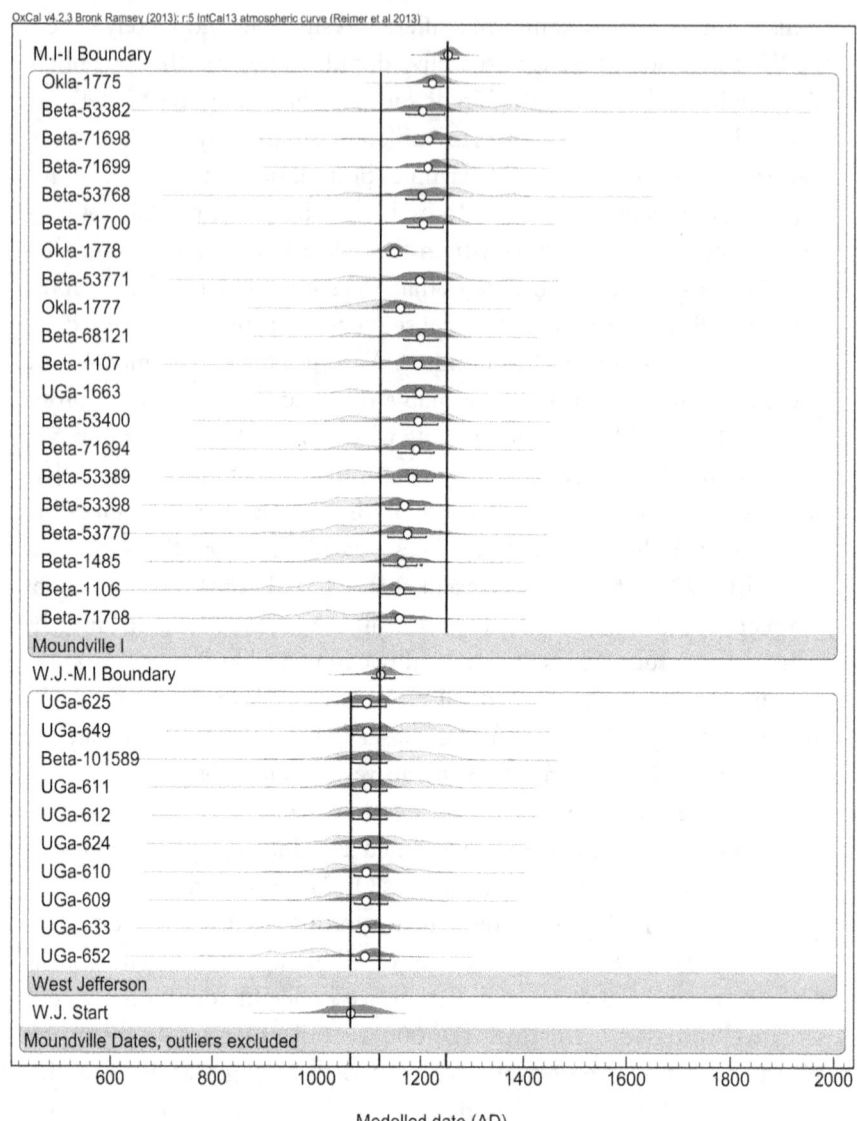

Figure 1.3. Radiocarbon dates for the West Jefferson and Moundville I phases, showing their probability distributions and means. The most likely phase boundaries are shown as vertical lines (see Table 1.1). Key: the posterior probability distributions are shown in dark gray, the means of these distributions appear as circles, and the prior probabilities appear in light gray. Posterior probabilities and phase boundaries were calculated with the Markov chain Monte Carlo (MCMC) algorithm implemented in the current version of OxCal (4.2).

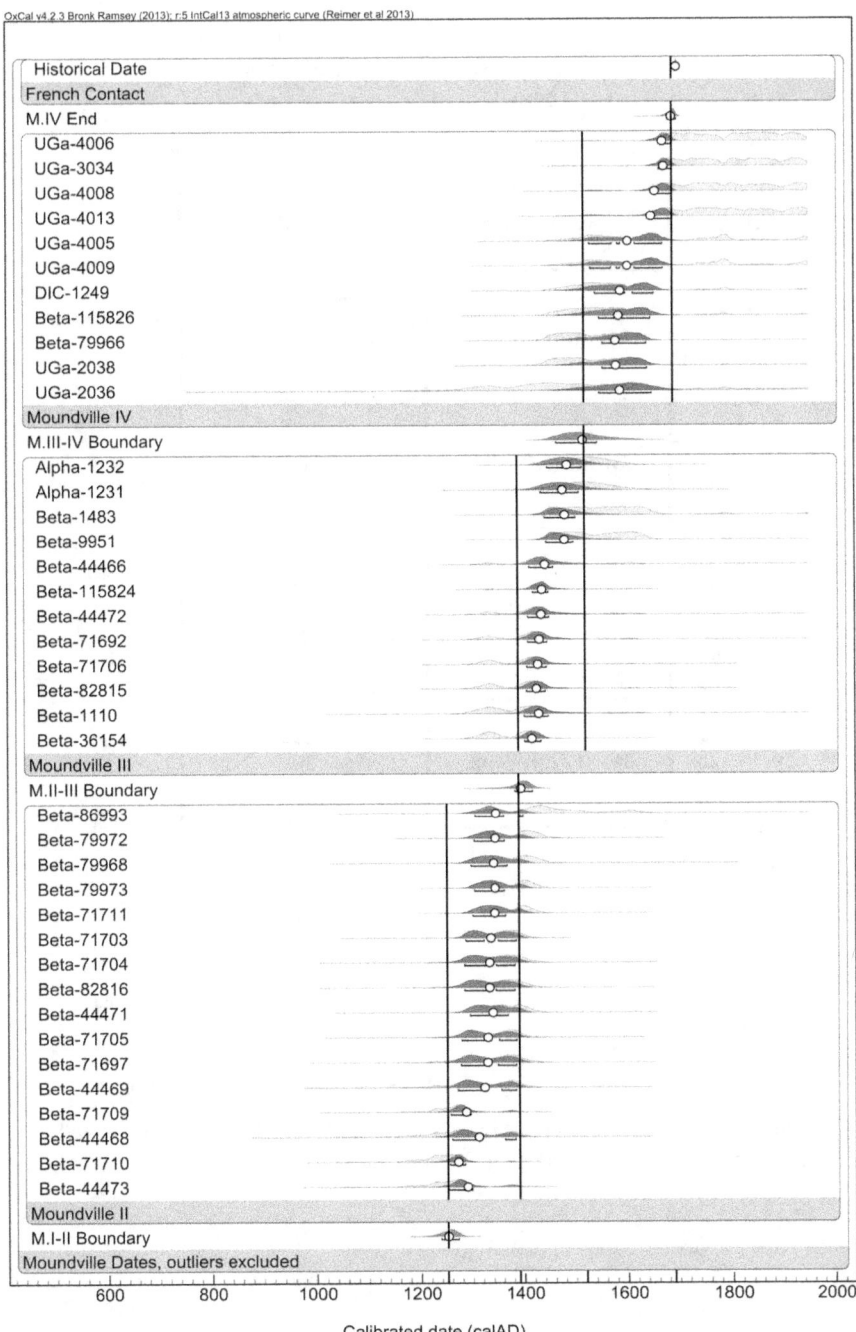

Figure 1.4. Radiocarbon dates for the Moundville II, Moundville III, and Moundville IV phases, showing their probability distributions and means. The most likely phase boundaries are shown as vertical lines (see table 1.1). See figure 1.3 for key.

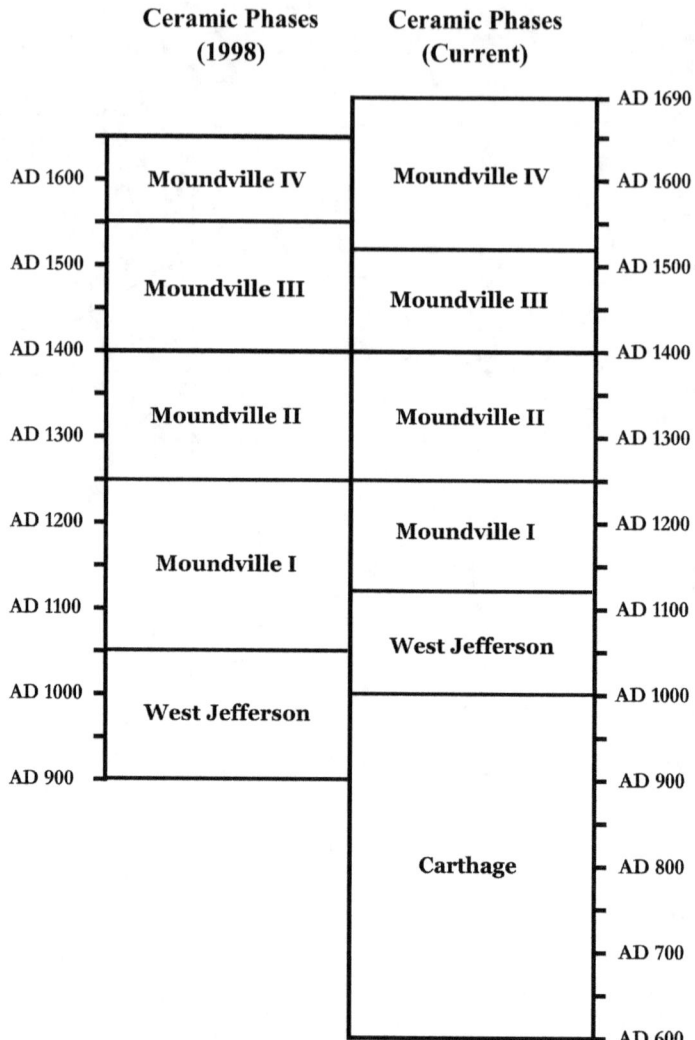

Figure 1.5. Phase sequences in the Black Warrior Valley: (*left*) the sequence in 1998 (after Knight and Steponaitis 1998); (*right*) the current sequence.

1000–1120; Moundville I, AD 1120–1250; Moundville II, AD 1250–1400; Moundville III, AD 1400–1520; and Moundville IV, AD 1520–1690.[2]

Mounds and Social Memory

From 1989 until 2002, Knight directed a long-term project investigating the history and function of the monumental earthworks at Moundville, which in many ways revolutionized our understanding of the site. By the mid-1990s, two major insights had already been gleaned. One was that most of the mound construction happened in a single extended burst during the thirteenth century AD (Knight and Steponaitis 1998). Another was that the overall layout of the mounds was planned at the outset, and that this layout constituted a "sociogram," in other words, a diagrammatic representation of the social order that existed at the time the construction took place (Knight 1998). Knight postulated a distinction between the mounds on the site's central axis, which were linked to the chiefdom's central institutions, and those along the plaza's periphery, which were used by local kin groups. The plaza-periphery mounds were arranged in pairs, reflecting a difference in function. Knight suggested that the larger mound in each pair supported an elite residence, and the smaller one served a mortuary function. Testing and refining this model served as an overarching framework that guided the project's research in subsequent years, culminating in two monographs (Knight 2009, 2010), as well as a series of articles and reports (Gage and Jones 2001; Jackson and Scott 2003; Knight 2004; Markin 1997), several master's theses (Astin 1996; Barry 2004; Gage 2000; Mirarchi 2009; Ryba 1997; Taft 1996), and a dissertation (Lacquement 2009).

In chapter 2 of the present volume, Knight reviews the major findings of his mound excavations and revisits the idea of Moundville as a sociogram. He evaluates four alternative models of the social arrangements that may have been expressed in the site's layout and concludes that his original model still fits the data, albeit with some adjustments. In his current view, the plaza-periphery mounds were likely associated with kin groups or "houses," which were ranked relative to each other but were in many respects autonomous. The functions of individual mounds were highly variable, as were the activities that took place on their summits. The latter included crafting ritual objects of copper and stone, preparing and consuming food, burying the dead, and bone handling unconnected with mortuary rituals. Although the pairing of the mounds was still evident, a simple "residential" versus "mortuary" dichotomy did not adequately capture their variability, and there was no evidence at all of the mortuary temples so often described in ethnohistoric accounts. All in all, Knight suggests that this variability reflects a ritual complementarity and interdependence among kin groups, like that sometimes seen ethnohistorically in Indian tribes from the South and Great Plains—a kind of organic solidarity (in Durkheim's sense) that created social cohesion.

Building on the notion of a sociogram, Wilson examines the spatial structure of Moundville's residential areas and cemeteries in chapter 3. He shows how, early in the site's sequence, off-mound residences were arranged in clusters that corresponded to kin groups. Later in time, when Moundville became a necropolis, the residences were abandoned, but their former locations became cemeteries, presumably used by the same kin groups that once lived there. Wilson's analysis points to the persistence and continuing importance of these kin groups throughout Moundville's history and provides an interesting example of how nonelite groups used spatial order and ritual to create social memory and maintain their identity over many generations.

The theme of social memory as inscribed in spatial order is further explored by Blitz in chapter 4. Focusing on Moundville's "big bang," when the site's grand plan was first laid out, Blitz shows how the creation of this new sociogram simultaneously entailed the erasure of the more modest layout that preceded it. He argues persuasively that this erasure was not inadvertent, but rather a deliberate example of "selective forgetting," as one social order was replaced by another.

All in all, these studies have yielded many new insights on how Moundville's spatial configuration served as an arena in which power, identity, and social memory were actively created and negotiated throughout the site's history. In so doing they provide an appropriate backdrop for the next line of research to be discussed, which deals with iconography, religious practitioners, and ritual objects.

Iconography and Ritual Practice

Moundville has long been known for its representational art, so it is perhaps not surprising that a great deal of research since 1998 has focused on iconography. Much of this new work has been done under the auspices of the Mississippian Iconography Workshop, a group of scholars who meet annually and have thus far published a pair of edited volumes (Lankford et al., eds. 2011; Reilly and Garber, eds. 2007). As a charter member of this group, Lankford has been particularly influential in shaping our understanding of Moundville's imagery. He persuasively showed that much of the representational art at Moundville relates to stories about the "Path of Souls," that is, the journey taken by souls after death (Lankford 2004, 2007c, 2011a). It is no coincidence that this imagery was produced mostly in the fourteenth and fifteenth centuries AD, when Moundville was a necropolis, a place where the dead were brought for burial from throughout the region. He also argued that Moundville's distinctive imagery—with its emphasis on serpents, felines, and the swastika, or "swirl cross"—was oriented mainly to the Beneath World, the portion of the layered Mississippian cosmos that lay below the Middle World of humans and could be entered through caves and water (Lankford 2007b, 2011b). The political and ritual implications of these iconographic themes are not difficult to imagine. As Steponaitis and Knight (2004: 180) have said:

> It is reasonable to speculate that at least some of the priests and chiefs who lived at Moundville had a special connection with the Beneath World. It is also possible that Moundville itself may have been seen as a propitious point of entry to the Path of Souls. . . . In either case, such beliefs would have provided powerful ideological support for the social and political power wielded by Moundville's elite residents.

So who were these priests and chiefs? Building on his previous work, Lankford examines an interesting hypothesis in chapter 5: that Moundville was home to a medicine society, analogous (or perhaps ancestral) to the Midé Society and similar groups known ethnohistorically from the western Great Lakes and eastern Plains. These were sodalities of shamans and priests who had spiritual powers used in healing and mortuary ritual, and who had close connections to the Beneath World. Their ritual activities took place in specially constructed lodges, often involved shell beads, and invoked the help of animal spirits, prominent among which were owls. Lankford argues that the wooden "greathouse" on Mound E and the earthlodge on Mound V had features characteristic of such lodges and may have been used in similar ways. He also notes the presence of owl effigies in the earthlodge and elsewhere on the site. Although his evidence is more suggestive than conclusive, Lankford's detailed examination of this hypothesis takes us far beyond the generic references to "elites" so common in the literature, to a detailed, ethnographically grounded consideration of *who* the ritual practitioners at Moundville may have been. He also highlights the important role that medicine societies may have played at Moundville and other Mississippian sites (cf. Byers 2006, 2013).

Another set of recent studies, closely related to the iconographic work just discussed, has looked at two other aspects of the imagery at Moundville: the formal, stylistic attributes of representation (Gillies 1998; Knight 2007; Lacefield 1995; Schatte 1997) and the geological sources of raw materials on which the imagery appears (Gall and Steponaitis 2001; Steponaitis and Dockery 2011; Whitney et al. 2002). Taken together, these lines of research resulted in the definition of the Hemphill style, a distinctive mode of representation associated with items crafted locally in the Moundville region (Knight and Steponaitis 2011). In chapter 6, Phillips looks at four different genres of Hemphill-style objects—engraved pots, stone palettes, stone pendants, and copper gorgets—and how these were distributed among the people buried at Moundville. She finds that engraved pottery and stone pendants were buried with individuals of all ages and both sexes; that copper gorgets were buried with all ages but only males; and that stone palettes were typically buried with adults, mostly males, who were accompanied by an unusually rich assortment of other grave goods. She argues that the pottery, pendants, and gorgets represent ascribed religious identities, which in the case of gorgets was a gender-specific, male identity. The palettes, on the other hand, represent an achieved identity, probably that of a religious practitioner. By providing a richness of detail on how and by whom specific categories of Hemphill-style objects were used, Phillips brings us a step closer to understanding the functions of such objects, which in the past have simply been generically lumped under the heading of "status items" or "prestige goods."

Steponaitis takes an even closer look at the function of such objects in chapter 7. Focusing specifically on stone palettes, he argues that these were religious objects—portable altars that were kept in sacred bundles. This argument has two implications. First, ethnographic accounts clearly show that bundles were used only by people who had the spiritual power and religious training to do so properly. The unusual abundance of palettes in Moundville burials therefore suggests that this site was a center for the religious practices that involved these objects. Second, bundles could never be exchanged or given away as gifts. Rather, acquiring a bundle involved apprenticing oneself to an established practitioner, from whom one could learn the knowledge needed to use it. Thus, the presence of Moundville palettes at distant sites, a pattern well documented archaeologically, implies that Moundville was also a place of pilgrimage, where individuals from distant towns would come to acquire religious knowledge and then would return home with the bundled palettes that were a tangible sign of that knowledge and the spiritual power it entailed.

These studies, and several others undertaken since 1998 (e.g., Davis 2008; Marcoux 2007; Wilson 2001), have taken us far beyond Welch's (1991) seminal notion of Moundville as a prestige-goods economy, in which a chief's power depended on the ability to control local craft production and long-distance trade as a way to acquire socially valuable objects that could be given to followers as gifts. Although craft production did take place at Moundville (Knight 2004, 2010; Markin 1997), there is little evidence that such activities were centrally controlled or managed. Moreover, as suggested in chapter 7, many of the elaborate items that circulated over long distances in the Mississippian world were probably religious objects that could not be used as gifts to buy political loyalty (also see Steponaitis and Dockery 2011; Steponaitis et al. 2011). Possessing such objects undoubtedly contributed to an individual's power but did so in ways that were spiritual and ideological, rather than economic.

Moundville's Hinterland

The social and political changes that led to the emergence of Moundville as a paramount center and to its ultimate demise also wrought changes in its hinterland communities. Archaeological investigations conducted prior to the mid-1990s had determined the chronological placements of the 14 single-mound centers, demonstrated that most were built on locations that had previously held West Jefferson villages, discovered that the resident populations at the outlying centers were quite small, and documented that the majority of the population living in the hinterlands resided at small dispersed sites generally construed as farmsteads (Bozeman 1982; Welch 1998). These lines of evidence were woven together to create a model of the Moundville polity in which a paramount chief at Moundville held ultimate political authority and controlled access to prestige goods. Subordinate chiefs, who were presumably close relatives of the paramount or drawn from cadet lineages, lived at the single-mound centers, overseeing ceremonies, acting as intermediaries between the paramount and the rural population, and facilitating the flow of provisions from the hinterlands to Moundville. People living at the small rural sites were cast as farmers, who procured and produced food for themselves, as well as provisions for the elite. These rural folks had limited if any access to prestige goods and looked to their chiefs for ritual services (Peebles and Kus 1977; Knight and Steponaitis 1998; Scarry and Steponaitis 1997; Welch 1991, 1998). This model provided the backdrop and framed interpretations for many of the chapters in the 1998 synthesis (Knight and Steponaitis, eds. 1998).

Several excavation and survey projects completed since 1998 expand our understanding of the nature and distribution of Moundville's hinterland communities. They also challenge some of the tenets on which the 1998 model was built. Rees' (2001) excavations at Fosters Landing, a mound and village center thought to date to Moundville IV, disclosed an earlier Moundville II mound stage. This should remind us that while single-mound centers with only Moundville I material are likely securely dated, mounds thought to have been constructed later in the polity's reign may have earlier stages—as they do at Moundville (Knight 1998). In 1995 Scarry and Scarry (1997) conducted small excavations at 1Tu570, a West Jefferson village; Grady Bobo (1Tu66), a West Jefferson village and Moundville I rural site; and Wiggins (1Tu768), a Moundville I hamlet. In 1999 and 2000, they conducted larger excavations at Grady Bobo. Work at these sites documented, among other things, evidence for feasting and ritual at small rural sites, indicating that some at least were more than simple farmsteads. Maxham (2000, 2004) used this evidence to argue for agency and construction of community identity not directly connected to or directed by chiefs. In 1998 and 1999, excavations were conducted by Johnson at Pride Place (1Tu1), a Moundville III village (Davis 2008, this volume; Johnson 1999, 2001; Johnson and Sherard 2000). Pride Place is located just below the Fall Line at Tuscaloosa near an outcrop of the fine-grained sandstone from which Moundville palettes were made.

Two larger-scale survey and testing projects contributed much-needed data about the distribution of nonmound sites in Moundville's hinterland. Hammerstedt and Myer systematically surveyed two 4.8-km (3-mi) transects spanning the width of the Black Warrior Valley and conducted test excavations at three nonmound sites (Hammerstedt 2000, 2001; Hammerstedt and Myer 2001; Myer 2002a, 2002b, 2003). This work provided crucial information about the locations of rural settlements with respect to natural resources as well as to Moundville and the single-mound centers. The excavations at the nonmound sites produced further evidence of ritual and crafting at rural communities (Jackson 2003a, 2003b; Myer 2003). The second project consisted of surveys and test excavations (mostly conducted by the University of Alabama and PanAmerican Consultants) on hundreds of well pads that were part of the Moundville Coal Degasification Field. These pads were distributed over 265 sq km of the Black Warrior Valley and its adjacent uplands. The work covered areas not surveyed by Hammerstedt and Myer and provided valuable data on upland sites (Maxham 2004).

Four chapters in this volume use the additional excavation and survey data to refine our understanding of settlement patterns and offer new perspectives on site functions and relationships within and between communities.

In chapter 8, Hammerstedt, Maxham, and Myer summarize and synthesize the results of the two survey and testing projects. They analyze the locations of rural sites with respect to natural features—topography, water source, and soil type—as well as the placement of sites vis-à-vis distance to Moundville, single-mound centers, and other nonmound sites. In so doing, they demonstrate continuity in land use from West Jefferson through Moundville IV times. Not surprisingly, people living in rural settlements selected locations with ready access to water sources and deep, well-drained soils. People also chose to live near one another, creating clusters of nonmound sites around single-mound centers. The authors also delineate demographic shifts in the hinterlands through time. Rural population declined during Moundville I, when Moundville itself was a large community, and later rebounded as the resident population at Moundville declined. Notably, people moved back to areas that were long occupied, rather than dispersing to new settlement clusters.

Social practices at hinterland communities are examined by Scarry, Jackson, and Maxham in chapter 9. They present evidence from three rural hamlets to show that religious objects and regalia were crafted, and communal rituals were held, at places distant from the mound centers. They argue that rural folk were more than farmers, and that not all rural sites were farmsteads. Instead, these people exercised agency and created identity apart from the purview of Moundville's elites.

Jackson, Scarry, and Scott synthesize the data on plant and animal foods in chapter 10. They argue that rural communities provisioned people living at Moundville and the single-mound centers but also suggest that the flow of food may have followed kinship paths in addition to being paid as tribute to the elite. They also identify consumption of special foods, particularly meat, in ritual contexts at Moundville and hinterland sites.

In chapter 11 Davis documents the rural production of ritual objects, specifically the stone palettes previously discussed in chapters 6 and 7. Davis uses experimental archaeology and evidence from Pride Place to show how the palettes were made and what tools were used at each stage in their manufacture. The palettes may have been crafted by specialists, not necessarily the same people who used them in rituals. Ultimately the palettes took on complex "lives" and meanings over the span of their use.

New Perspectives on Moundville

The insights derived from the past two decades of work in the Black Warrior Valley—many of which inspire the chapters in this book—cause us to rethink the nature of Moundville. How do we accommodate our more detailed and nuanced understanding of the sociogram at Moundville, the erasure of earlier monuments to make way for a new social order, the associations of residential neighborhoods and later corporate cemeteries with mound pairs, and the complementarity of ritual activities associated with the various mounds? How does the recognition of Moundville as a religious center and place of pilgrimage affect our interpretations of its political organization and leaders? What was the nature of the relationships between Moundville and the single-mound centers with their clusters of rural hamlets?

We address these questions in chapter 12 with a new model for Moundville's organization, which draws heavily on the archaeological work of our colleagues and the ethnohistory of the Native South. Our model builds on the idea, presented by Knight in chapter 2, that Moundville was planned according to the logic of a ceremonial ground where ritual practitioners held sway. Most southern Indian societies had two crosscutting structural elements with distinct social roles, namely towns and clans. Towns were corporate entities, marked by a defined area of settlement and led by secular chiefs. Clans, on the other hand, were exogamous, matrilineal groups, which crosscut towns, linking people within a tribe or polity to one another. Clan priests held sacred knowledge and came to the fore during ritual performances, in which different clans played complementary roles. When people gathered at ceremonial grounds, they arrayed themselves by clan, rather than by town affiliation. We speculate that Moundville was constructed at a time when clan priests gained precedence over town chiefs and that its monumental sociogram was inspired by the layout of more ephemeral ceremonial grounds. That is, Moundville was built when people from multiple towns came together under the leadership of clan priests, thereby forming a community that was different from a conventional town. In so doing, they used a familiar spatial logic for organizing people from disparate communities. We further suggest that towns continued to exist and were represented by the outlying mound sites with their clusters of rural settlements. Presumably, the town chiefs lost some of their authority during the ascendency of the clan priests, but over time, as people moved away from Moundville and back to the hinterlands, towns and their chiefs regained political power.

There is much to be learned from continued work on Moundville and its hinterland. Future excavations as well as continued analyses of extant collections are sure to add to and amend our current understandings. Nonetheless, the present chapters, which range from detailed analyses of material objects to broader syntheses and applications of new theoretical frames, offer many new perspectives. To our minds, they also make the lives and activities of this region's people more tangible and connected to what we know from local ethnohistory and ethnography. At the same time, we believe that Moundville continues to be an important case for understanding the middle-range societies we call chiefdoms. Our interpretation of Moundville and its organization has come a long way from the Polynesian archetype of the conical clan ruled by a paramount chief.

Acknowledgments

We are grateful to Vernon J. Knight for providing the radiocarbon dates used in this chapter, and for his advice on their reanalysis. Daniel Amrhein was very helpful in explaining the fine points of OxCal and the statistical procedures used herein. We also wish to thank Jon Marcoux and an anonymous reviewer for their thoughtful suggestions.

Notes

1. All the Oxcal 4.2 runs reported here excluded the same outliers previously identified by Knight et al. (1999). The outlier routine as currently implemented yields different results, not nearly as plausible, so we decided to use exactly the same set of "good" dates as in the previous study. This approach also has the effect of making the results of the two sampling algorithms more easily comparable.

2. Building on the work of Jenkins (1978, 2003), Paul Jackson (2004) has argued that West Jefferson and Moundville I represent overlapping, rather than sequential phases. His evidence consists of two late radiocarbon dates associated with grog-tempered pottery from the Cane Creek site (1Wa140) in Walker County: AD 1240 ± 80 (Feature 56) and AD 1130 ± 100 (Feature 76), both uncalibrated. He also cites a previously reported date from the Jones Ferry site in Tuscaloosa County of AD 1140 ± 70 on a probable West Jefferson feature (Welch 1998: 154–55, table 7.1). When calibrated with OxCal 4.2, the means of all three dates fall within the Moundville I phase as currently defined, but the 2σ confidence intervals for two of them (Cane Creek Feature 76 and Jones Ferry) also overlap substantially with the West Jefferson phase. The one date that does not overlap (Cane Creek Feature 56) came from an isolated cooking pit that contained only a single, plain, grog-tempered sherd of a type that continued being used in early Moundville I times (Knight and Steponaitis 1998:12). In other words, none of these dates by themselves invalidate the chronology used here. That said, we have no quarrel with the idea that the inhabitants of Cane Creek, located in the hills nearly 100 km north of Moundville as the crow flies, may have had a predominantly grog-tempered ceramic assemblage around AD 1200. Our chronology works for the lower Black Warrior drainage, and we would not be the least bit surprised if the ceramic sequence in the Cane Creek area were different.

2

Social Archaeology of Monumental Spaces at Moundville

VERNON JAMES KNIGHT JR.

Milner (1998: 10) has commented, in respect to the great Mississippian ceremonial center of Cahokia, that its past interpreters have held to quite firm opinions about the social meaning of the site and its hinterlands. He regrets that "this fixity of opinion is all out of proportion to the scant attention directed toward evaluating models of sociopolitical organization using the considerable information so laboriously collected in numerous surveys and excavations." The same might be said of other Mississippian centers to the south of Cahokia.

If we can speak of a social archaeology of Moundville, then one of its key elements surely lies in interpreting the spatial arrangement of its mounds. It seems reasonable to assume that this spatial arrangement is in some sense a broadcast statement of social or political relationships. If so, taking Milner's comment to heart, we might proceed by examining alternative models about the nature of the corporate groups (or persons?) that sponsored individual mounds or categories of mounds. In fact, several such models have already been proposed, each deriving from a different ethnographic analogy. If we can adequately spell out the archaeological correlates of such models, then their evaluation hinges on which of them best accord with our field data.

In this chapter, then, I shall outline several interpretive models of Moundville's mound arrangement, hoping thereby to clarify the question. I will stop short of answering that question, or at least answering it definitively; my intent is to make the point that its solution is an empirical problem, not merely a theoretical one. In the course of the chapter, I will take the opportunity to review newly available field data from the mounds at Moundville. I will also review three related concerns: chronological change, evidence of feasting, and labor requirements for building the mounds and plaza.

Moundville's Mound-and-Plaza Arrangement

It is necessary first to describe in summary terms the spatial qualities of the mound-and-plaza arrangement at Moundville (for more extensive discussion, see Knight 1998, 2010; Peebles 1971):

- The site presents itself as a large aggregate of mounds of multiple forms in a compact arrangement, giving the definite impression of intentional design (figure 2.1). There once were, at minimum, 32 earthen mounds by my current count.[1]

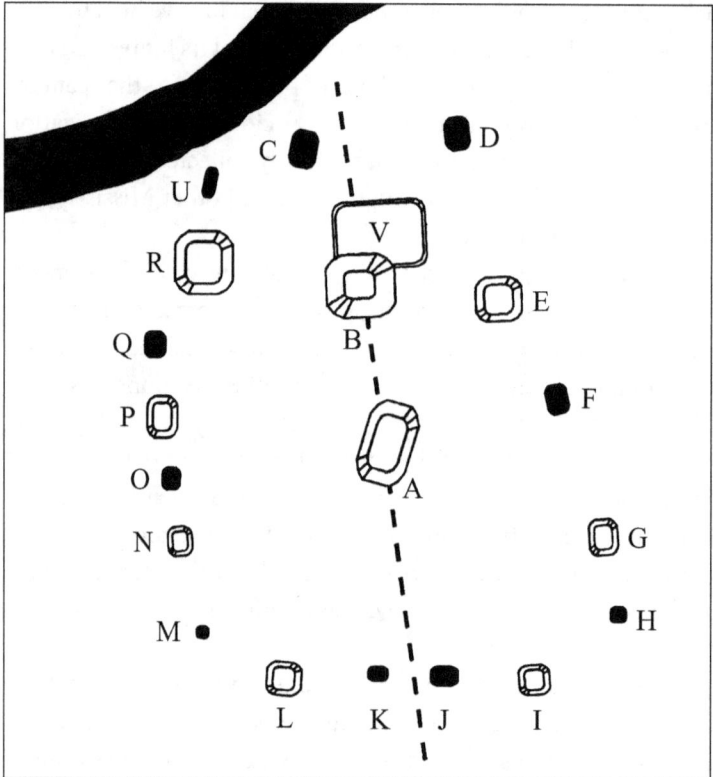

Figure 2.1. Schematic map showing Moundville's bilateral symmetry, the largest mounds (A, B, and V) located on the center axis, alternation of mounds containing burials (*darkened*) with those not containing burials (*light*), and the diminishing size of mounds without burials moving southward (smaller mounds are omitted for clarity).

- Central to the configuration is a large, unitary quadrilateral plaza.[2]
- The three largest mounds at the site by volume—A, B, and V—are positioned along a center axis that divides the site bilaterally into roughly symmetrical east and west halves. Conjoined mounds B and V, their margins oriented to the cardinal directions, occupy the north-central position on the plaza, and of these the larger, Mound B, may be considered the primary mound at the site. Mound A, oriented to a different azimuth than the remainder, occupies the center of the plaza. All are quadrilateral flat-topped mounds.
- Arrayed around the margins of the plaza is a tightly spaced ring of smaller quadrilateral flat-topped mounds, each with sides oriented to the cardinal direction. These I refer to as the "plaza-periphery group."
- Within the plaza-periphery group, there is a rigid alternation between large mounds lacking human burials and smaller mounds containing them. Although the smaller mounds contain human burials, they are in no sense dedicated mortuary, or burial, mounds; burials within them originate from use-surfaces, they tend to be few, and they tend to occupy marginal positions on the summits (Moore 1905: 241–43).
- The mounds lacking human burials in the plaza-periphery group decrease regularly in size moving southward, both clockwise and counterclockwise around the plaza from Mound B at center-north.
- Pairs of similar mounds of the plaza-periphery group appear to occupy corresponding positions on the east and west sides of the plaza, contributing to the impression of a bilateral symmetry (Peebles 1971: 82).
- Two quadrilateral flat-topped mounds, C and D, are situated away from the plaza on isolated terrace remnants bordered by steep ravines on the north side of the site. Both contain lavishly accoutred human burials (Moore 1905).
- Two small mounds of unknown purpose, S and T (not shown in figure 2.1; see figure 1.1), are situated apparently within the margins of the plaza on the east side.
- A number of additional small mounds are situated in places external to the dominant mounds of the plaza-periphery group. Most

are poorly understood. Some may not originally have been flat-topped mounds, at least one (Mound W) may have the character of an accretional "midden mound" (Johnson 2005), one (Mound X) predates the plaza and palisade (Blitz 2007, this volume), and some (especially Mounds M1 and U) have yielded sufficiently large numbers of burials to suggest that they are legitimate mortuary mounds.

Moore (1907: 404) understood the big mounds on Moundville's center axis as qualitatively different from the rest, being connected, he supposed, to the primary religious cults, while the mounds of the plaza-periphery group he believed were merely residential. Recent measurements show that the three central mounds account for over half of the mound building at the site by volume (Lacquement 2009: table 2.1). Analysis of cores from central Mounds A and V shows that they went up rapidly in very large episodes of work.

In its elementary conjunction of one or more very large mounds, a unitary plaza, and a ring of smaller plaza-periphery mounds, Moundville's layout is comparable to a number of other Mississippian centers, among them perhaps most notably the Winterville site in the Lower Mississippi Valley (Brain 1989; Moore 1908: 595) and the St. Louis Mound Group (Pauketat 1994: figure 4.1) farther north. Points of comparison might also be made with the palisaded center of the Cahokia site (Fowler 1989: 198–201).

Four Readings of the Mound Arrangement

Figure 2.2 schematically depicts four competing models of monumental space in a plaza-periphery arrangement, each potentially applicable to Moundville. In keeping with our description of Moundville, each diagram incorporates a notion of rank order of the segments decreasing from top to bottom with exceptional monumental space positioned on the center axis. The number of segments is arbitrary.

In the first (a), which is closely related to descriptions of ramage organization in chiefdoms advanced by Sahlins (1958: figure 1) and Service (1962: 145–55), all monuments belong to persons of noble birth who are related to one another, and whose relative rank depends on genealogical distance from a paramount chief. Thus, the spatial order is a reflection of

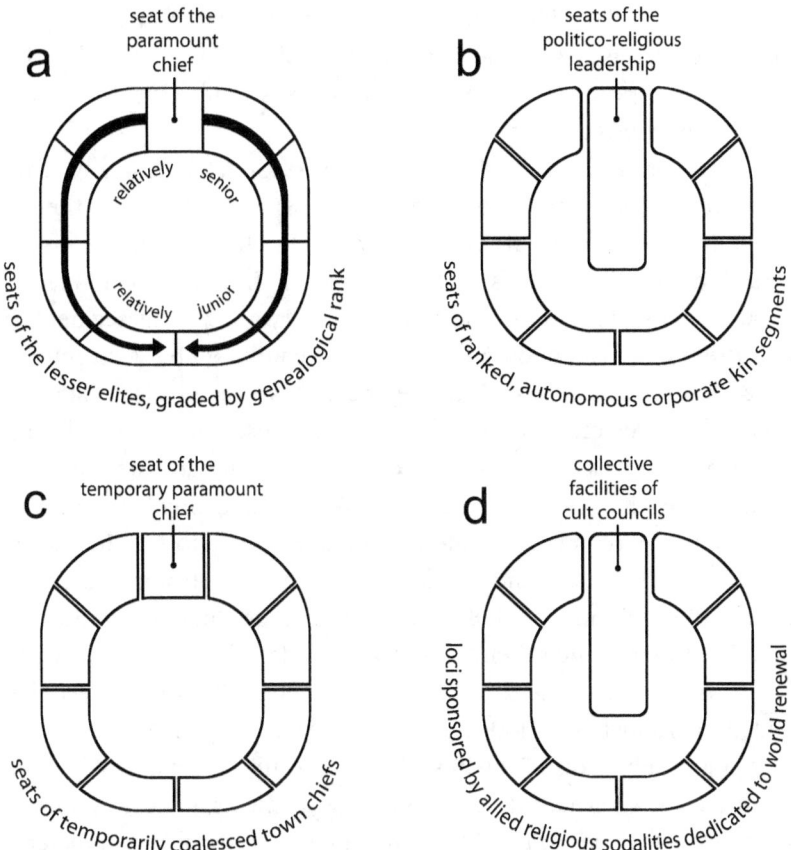

Figure 2.2. Four interpretive models of partitioned monumental space around a central plaza. Each model rests on a different ethnographic analogy: (*a*) peripheral monuments as the seats of lesser elites all related genealogically to a paramount chief; (*b*) peripheral monuments as expressions of ranked, autonomous corporate kin groups; (*c*) peripheral monuments representing the coalescence of towns; (*d*) peripheral monuments as loci sponsored by religious sodalities.

the familiar cone-shaped genealogy (Kirchhoff 1959). And while each of these elite persons might occupy a named social status, each might also represent a cadet lineage, perhaps with a corresponding lineage house. Ramage-type organizations have been suggested for Mississippian societies (e.g., Hatch 1976), even as the typical form (Widmer 1994; see also Knight 1990). Specifically with reference to Moundville, Welch (1996: 87–88) suggests the possibility, in contrast to (b) as described below, that "all mounds 'belonged' to high-ranking kin among the paramount chief's own kin group." As is illustrated by the article from which Welch's quote was extracted, this general view of monumental space is much in keeping with a "power perspective" emphasizing social stratification and chiefly control over goods and labor.

In the interest of full disclosure, I am on record as having advocated the second model, labeled (b) in figure 2.2 (Knight 1998). In it there is a fundamental tension between a centralized political authority, as expressed in the axial mounds, and a segmentary structure as exhibited by the surrounding mounds of the plaza-periphery group. This segmentary structure is one of autonomous, structurally equivalent but conceptually ranked kin groups. Although the segments have been called "clans" by others, I have personally resisted that label, because clans among the historic tribes of the southeastern United States were broad hereditary categories rather than corporate entities capable of amassing labor. I rather conceive of the segments in question as comparable to the lineages of the historic Chickasaw and Muskogee, which were strongly corporate (Knight 1990). Swanton (1928b) called these units "house groups," and I have elsewhere called them "corporate subclans," because each was a local subset of one of the so-called clans (Knight 1998). More research is needed to productively model how such lineages might have functioned demographically and socially in such an environment. In a related manner, one could alternatively envision these segments as Levi-Straussian "social houses" (Levi-Strauss 1982), emphasizing material and immaterial estates, fictive kinship, and a fusion of unilineal with affinal transmission of estate goods and titles. Brown (2007) sees "social houses" of this kind as potentially structuring spatial dimensions of mound burial at the Mississippian site of Etowah in Georgia.

In the third model (c), individual monuments are seen as the symbolic embodiment of distinct political units that have, in the case of Mississippian multiple-mound centers, coalesced. John Blitz (1999) sees these centers as the product of a dynamic "fission-fusion process" in which the constituent units were "towns" comparable to those of the historic Creek and Choctaw. In this view, during times demanding mutual security, formerly autonomous town populations "would abandon their old centers and establish new mounds at a single site to create a powerful multiple mound chiefdom" (Blitz 1999: 587). In such situations constituent towns might have been ranked as senior or junior, based on such factors as relative stability or status as newcomers, just as in historic southeastern tribal confederacies. The largest mounds at such sites may be viewed as "linked to the principal chief and a high-rank faction, [that] may represent the collective labor of all social segments at the site, perhaps as a form of tribute or sumptuary rule to acknowledge the ranked social order" (Blitz 1999: 586). As in this view mounds in general embody chiefly authority, the smaller mounds at the big centers presumably were the residences of chiefs of the constituent towns. Sites with one or two mounds in the hinterlands of these large sites do not represent subordinate administrative centers, but rather periods of fissioning and decentralization. Blitz and Lorenz (2006) apply this idea to the multiple-mound Rood's Landing site and smaller mound sites on the Chattahoochee River in Georgia. Although the model's application to Moundville is not as explicitly developed in print, it clearly could be. Blitz (2008: 67–68) more than hints at this possibility as he describes a scenario in which a number of the secondary mound sites in Moundville's hinterland were established by rival chiefs upon the loss of political power by Moundville's paramount.

The view expressed in (c) echoes a common thread in Mississippian studies in which platform mounds and their histories are seen as the materialization of the political authority of town chiefs and their lineages (e.g., Anderson 1994; Hally 1996; Williams 1995). Thus, from a "platforms-as-chiefs" point of view (Wesler 2006), the periodic addition of mantles to these mounds ritually embodies the accession to power of new hereditary chiefs. As for envisioning the smaller, peripheral mounds at large centers as the residences of community leaders, we find a comparable idea in Fowler's account of Cahokian organization of monumental space. Fowler (1989: 198) believes the political elite at Cahokia acted from within the central palisaded precinct containing Monks Mound, and he identifies the numerous mounds external to that precinct as "the residences of lesser functionaries" who controlled coalesced subordinate communities.

In the fourth model (d) the constituent social units are neither kin-based nor residentially based. They are instead religious sodalities, special-purpose corporate groups conceived on the model of the secret societies of the historic Central Plains tribes. Thus, a multiple-mound Mississippian center materializes an alliance of autonomous cults. Further, because mound building is a ritual act of world renewal (cf. Knight 1989a), these are sodalities specifically dedicated to world renewal.

The sodality-alliance model has been developed in great detail by Martin Byers, explicitly for Cahokia (2006) and more recently for Moundville

(2013). He draws inspiration from the seeming complementarity of age-graded cult sodalities vis-à-vis clan organization in structuring social relations among the Osage and Hidatsa. In applying it to Moundville, Byers paints an extraordinarily detailed picture of how voluntary alliances of Hidatsa-like religious sodalities could produce the known archaeological record. For our purposes we need only make note of a few of its features. First, Moundville never had a sedentary population. Its numerous "houses" were not permanent homes, but rather "hostels" for transient, visiting ritual participants. Labor to build the mounds was recruited by the constituent cults, whose base locales were, generally speaking, in Moundville's hinterlands. Mounds, as loci for world-renewal rites, were presided over not by resident elites but by nonresident "priestly artisans" drawn from the participating cults. The number of collaborative cults and the number of mounds was not necessarily congruent; cults could collaborate in the construction of a common monument, especially in central collective monuments (Mounds A and B). All Moundville burials were at least secondary, and its collective burial locales were in constant use from the initial establishment of the ritual center. Because networks of cult affiliations were open systems, polity boundaries were nonexistent (Byers 2013: 619–27, 637, 649–50, 693, 813).

Byers (2006: 240–60) is critical of hierarchical accounts of Mississippian social systems portrayed as bounded polities, and especially of those who treat kinship as the only relevant structural dimension governing monumentality (as in models [a] and [b]). His account is by far the least hierarchical of the four models I present here. By this logic large Mississippian mound groups do not represent conventional chiefdoms. Beyond Byers' specific model I must agree that the potential roles of sodalities in Mississippian systems have been very much overlooked. Lankford's chapter in this volume expands the exploration of this topic for Moundville.

While this concludes my outline of the four models diagramed in figure 2.2, we might as well add a fifth possibility: that some monumental landscapes at Mississippian sites might reveal combinations of several or even all of the structural principles cited above. Exactly such a position has been articulated for Cahokia by Hall (2007) in a review of Byers' work on Cahokia.

It seems to me that solving the problem outlined here lies at the heart of understanding Moundville's evolutionary significance. It is also a key to understanding the purpose of the dozen or so single-mound Mississippian sites found in Moundville's immediate hinterland (Welch 1998). Let us see, then, what light might be shed on this by new evidence from Moundville's mounds.

Evidence from Mound Excavations

For many decades the only available information on the content of Moundville's mounds resided in the early reports of Clarence B. Moore's (1905, 1907) excavations. Moore's digging was explicitly in search of burials, with little attention to stratigraphy or artifacts other than grave goods. Most of Moore's excavations were also relatively superficial, penetrating no more than a meter or so into the summit platforms.

The resulting shortage of modern data on the mounds is now mitigated to some extent, partly as a result of new excavations. My own fieldwork undertaken between 1989 and 2002 involved the excavation of trenches into the flanks of five mounds of the plaza-periphery group (Mounds E, F, G, Q, and R), test excavations into the summit of one other mound (Mound A), and extensive horizontal excavations on the summits of three mounds (Mounds E, Q, and V). I have reported the results of this work elsewhere (Knight 2009, 2010). I have also summarized earlier trenching by others into seven additional mounds (Mounds H, I, J, K, L, M, and P), and have described separate Depression-era collections made under obscure circumstances from five mounds (Mounds A, B, E, P, and R) (Knight 2010). Aside from the above, Astin (1996) has reported on excavations in Mound M, Ryba (1997) has described the architecture on Mound E, Johnson (2005) and Barrier (2007) have reported on materials from Mound W, Mirarchi (2009) has reported on materials from Mound V, and Blitz (2007, this volume) has reported on his excavations in Mound X. In addition, Gage (2000; Gage and Jones 2001) has described 48 solid cores extracted from summit to subsoil in Mounds A, E, L, M1, Q, R, and V, while Lacquement (2009) has investigated artificial plaza leveling adjacent to several mounds. As a result of this recent flurry of interest in Moundville's earthworks, there are now useful data on stratigraphy, artifact assemblages, biocultural remains, and radiometric dates for a number of contexts from several periods of Moundville's history (e.g., Jackson and Scott 2003; Knight 2004; Markin 1997; Taft 1996).

A Duality of Mound Categories?

My own research addressed two hypotheses. The first, based on Moore's data, was that the alternating plaza-periphery mounds with and without burials would prove to belong to two categories. The smaller mounds with burials would be revealed as mortuary temple mounds, with summit buildings corresponding to the temples documented in southeastern ethnohistoric sources. The larger mounds without burials would prove to be elite residence mounds (Peebles 1971: 82). As the activities on these two kinds of mounds would be categorically different, I predicted that there would be a corresponding dichotomy in patterns of artifacts and biocultural remains.

I have found, however, that there is no such dichotomy. In our excavations of two smaller mounds containing burials, Mounds F and Q, we found little corresponding to temples as described ethnohistorically in the Southeast. Colonial-period temples were private sanctuaries housing the bones of deceased chiefs and their close kin, reliquaries for sacred objects and carved images, storerooms for war honors accrued by the chiefly line, and shelters for perpetual sacred fires. They were guarded by temple priests, whose meals were brought to them by others (for a summary, see DePratter 1983). In contrast, in Mound Q, where we conducted horizontal summit excavations, we found crowded arrangements of very lightly framed buildings—impermanent and frequently replaced—with unusual features such as conjoined rooms and subfloor storage pits. I interpret these seemingly transient buildings as temporary residential quarters associated with dense flank middens revealing a very diverse mix of ritual and quotidian activities that accumulated episodically over a long period of time. These activities included two that are undocumented in the relevant ethnohistoric sources on temples: first, the skilled crafting of display goods in sheet copper, tabular stone, and wood; and second, bone handling in a nonmortuary context, as evidenced by finely crushed bits of human crania and extremities mixed in general midden and feature fills throughout. Human burials were present, but rare and seemingly peripheral to everything else. More generally, because the shrine figures associated with temples elsewhere in the Mississippian world have never been found anywhere at Moundville, I now rather doubt that "temples" in a conventional sense were ever in use there (cf. Brown 2001; Smith and Miller 2009).

In our excavations of mounds without burials (E, G, and R), the ones hypothesized as "elite residence mounds," we did find evidence that the mounds were lived on and that their inhabitants generated debris of the sort we tend to associate with exclusive activities: pottery assemblages having large numbers of engraved bottles bearing religious art, artifacts of copper and galena, and faunal and botanical remains that reveal in several ways the special nature of the meals consumed there. Nonetheless, we found little that might be considered as confirming a uniformity of use, and much that contradicts such a uniformity. For example on Mound E, where we conducted large-scale horizontal excavations on the summit, we found architectural components that included a highly surprising "greathouse," of Cahokian inspiration. The interior spaciousness of this 14-m-×-16-m greathouse, together with the expansive dimensions (19 × 30+ m) of a heavily walled, open compound adjacent to it, evokes accommodations for collective activities beyond the merely domestic. Moreover, summit contexts on Mound E yielded evidence of skilled lapidary work in greenstone, sandstone, and quartz crystal, plus evidence of nonmortuary bone handling, neither of which were found in flank middens associated with Mounds G and R, likewise mounds without burials, but comparable to evidence found in Mound Q of the presumptive opposite category.

This lack of patterning along the predicted dichotomous lines can be traced for a number of mound-top activities (see Knight 2010: 358–60). Radiocarbon-dated assemblages useful in tracking this variability were secured from the following: late Moundville II phase contexts in Mounds F, G, and Q; and Moundville III phase contexts in Mounds E, G, Q, and R. These contexts date, importantly, to the latter portion of Moundville's history during which, according to our current model (Knight and Steponaitis 1998), the site was a vacant ceremonial center and regional necropolis, occupied primarily by political and religious functionaries and their families.

Among these contexts we were able to confirm that mortuary ritual was confined to Mounds F and Q. Nonmortuary bone handling was, in contrast, confined to Mounds E and Q. Ritual gear such as stone palettes, tabular stone pendants, terraced-rim bowls, and figurines were most closely associated with Mounds E, F, and Q. Elaborately engraved pottery bottles, especially those bearing religious representational art, were most closely associated with contexts on Mounds F and G. Pigments and other minerals associated with the decorative arts were salient in assemblages on Mounds F and Q. Lapidary crafting was especially in evidence on Mounds E and R. Coarse woodworking as evidenced by polished greenstone tools was most closely associated with Mounds F and R, while fine carving using blades struck from nonlocal chert cores was most prominent on Mounds F and G. Access to exotic stone was most in evidence on Mounds F, G, and Q, although the only clear evidence of flaked-stone tool manufacture was on Mound R. Conspicuous consumption in the form of discarding relatively whole mammal bone with little regard for marrow extraction was seen on Mound G and to a lesser extent on Mound Q (for the associated quantifications, see Knight 2010: 353–57 and Jackson and Scott 2010: 343–44).

Most of these distinctions are relative rather than categorical, and some activities were much the same throughout, as indicated by comparable inventories of service and utility pottery. Nonetheless, what stands out is a seeming complementarity rather than a uniformity of the more specialized activities. In sum, as to my first hypothesis, our assemblage data show no simple dichotomy corresponding to "temple mounds" versus "elite residence mounds," but rather what I interpret as a much more complex complementarity of specialized mound-summit activity that crosscuts mounds with and without human burials.

Coordinated Initial Construction?

My second hypothesis bears directly upon an assumption embedded in all four of the spatial models I have reviewed. That assumption is that the central mounds and the mounds of the plaza-periphery group represent a planned, coordinated allocation of space that can be read as a sociogram of elementary relationships among constituent individuals or groups. That is, the layout we see today is not the product of an incremental addition of mounds over time. Thus, my hypothesis states that initial construction of these mounds was both coordinated and early in the site's history.[3]

Thus, in my excavations I placed emphasis on obtaining stratigraphic data from flank trenching, obtaining radiocarbon dates—preferably multiple—from each important context excavated, elaborating and refining the pottery chronology (see Steponaitis 1983a), studying older mound collections in search of chronologically diagnostic pottery, and refining the absolute chronology of the phase periodization.

A shortcoming of the flank-trenching approach is that in very few cases could the trenches penetrate as far as the earliest construction levels. Gage's (2000; Gage and Jones 2001) program of solid coring in several mounds, already mentioned, ameliorates this problem to some degree. Nonetheless, at present we have only two cases, Mounds E and F, for which we now possess multiple radiocarbon dates for the earliest core constructions. In both cases these core constructions date from the middle to late thirteenth century, late Moundville I to early Moundville II in our phase chronology. In other cases (Mounds G, Q, and R), we have well-dated upper mound stages dating to either the late thirteenth or fourteenth century, with some number of undated construction stages beneath. Mound M lacks radiocarbon dates, but a flank midden on the stratigraphically earliest construction stage can be dated on the basis of diagnostic pottery to the early-to-middle thirteenth century, the late Moundville I phase. Similarly, sherds excavated from the fill in Mound A date no later than late Moundville I. In all other mounds for which we have older collections (Mounds B, H, I, J, K, L, and P), there is a strong showing of late Moundville I phase pottery diagnostics (Knight 2010: table 9.1).

Although these data are of variable quality, taken together I see them as confirming initial construction of the central and plaza-periphery mounds on all sides of the plaza at a time corresponding to the late thirteenth century, ca. AD 1250–1300. This timing is within the broad range of an earlier estimate (Knight and Steponaitis 1998: 14–17), although a little later than previously suspected, due in part to our use of a new calibrated chronology.

Before returning to an evaluation of our four models of spatial organization, let us briefly review some intermediary concerns that have direct bearing on how we envision Moundville's monumentality.

Discussion: Chronological Concerns

My description of complementarities of mound assemblages on the plaza periphery is a synchronic one. However, because recent research has devoted much effort to describing historic changes at Moundville, some transformational in character (Knight and Steponaitis 1998; Wilson 2008), one should not mistake my portrait as a static picture of relationships that held for the duration of the functioning center. The data, in fact, point to change over time. When our late Moundville II phase mound contexts are compared with the corresponding contexts from the Moundville III phase, we find that the intensity of special activities is generally greater for the earlier period (for the data, see Knight 2010: table 9.2). Thus, the patterning of elite activities I have identified is more strongly expressed in the fourteenth century than in the early fifteenth, an observation that accords with other signs of dissolution: a decline after AD 1400 in long-distance exchange, abandonment of many of the plaza-periphery mounds, and cessation of the practice of burying high-status individuals in mounds (Knight and Steponaitis 1998: 19–21).

To repeat, our mound contexts showing the best integrity and preservation date to the late Moundville II and Moundville III phases. Steponaitis and I (1998) have characterized this stage of Moundville development as that of a functioning paramount chiefdom, with the Moundville site itself in the role of a ceremonial center and necropolis, with resident functionaries living mainly on mounds and with a dependent population largely resident elsewhere in outlying communities. It is in the context, then, of a relatively depopulated monumental landscape that we must make sense of most of the mound data in hand.[4]

Discussion: The Question of Feasting

As some sort of communal organization has been suggested for Moundville at points in its history (King 2001; Trubitt 2000), it is appropriate to ask if there is evidence of communal feasting at the site. We know that such feasting, on a large scale, is well documented at Cahokia (Pauketat et al. 2002), and closer to our immediate concern, feasting has been suggested as a key social mechanism on platform mounds in Mississippian west central Alabama as well (e.g., Blitz 1993). However, in my mound excavations, we found no evidence for feasting as might be manifested in the bulk accumulation and consumption of high-yield foods and an emphasis on large cooking and serving vessels. Instead, pottery vessel assemblages from mounds were highly diverse (Taft 1996), and our better-preserved faunal assemblages meet the expectations of domestic meals consumed by social elites: "prime cuts of venison, little butchering debris, low levels of bone processing, the importance of turkey, a generally diverse bird assemblage, and carnivore taxa" (Jackson and Scott 2010: 347; Jackson et al., this volume), together with rare taxa such as bison, shark, and peregrine falcon that were no doubt there for nondietary reasons. To my knowledge, data indicative of feasting so far have not been identified in any of the excavated off-mound contexts either.

Discussion: Labor Requirements

Lacquement's (2009) quantitative research on the human energy required for mound building and plaza leveling at Moundville concludes that the major construction stages within large mounds on the central axis of the site were beyond the organizational capacity of any specific social unit in a segmentary structure. He concludes that the labor to build these monuments in a timely manner must have drawn collectively from most, if not all, social segments resident in Moundville's hinterlands. By itself this finding would not appear to contradict any of the four models I have described, because each leaves room for collective construction of facilities of common cause, which might include not only the axial mounds A, B, and V, but also the palisade surrounding the site. Lacquement does, however, embrace a more specific model, in which the plaza-periphery mounds represent autonomous corporate kin groups in a segmentary structure (that is, model [b] in figure 2.2). In so doing, he concludes that ordinary kin groups would have been perfectly capable of constructing any of the mounds of the plaza-periphery group, unaided.

Bearing on Competing Models of Monumental Space

So the question stands: which of the competing models of monumental space outlined in the first part of this chapter find support in the recent accumulation of field data? Rather than dwelling on the full implications of each model in turn, I use my remaining space to emphasize a few key points of connection between models and data.

To begin, our data reveal no evidence of centralized economic control. Display goods were being produced and consumed by people living on a variety of mounds around the plaza periphery, without any apparent central coordination. To the degree that goods, food, and labor were being extracted from primary producers living in outlying settlements, the locus of coordination was each individual social segment represented in the monumental sociogram. If this is correct, the political economy was diffuse, and the managerial hand of a paramount chief is nowhere in view.

Among the models we are reviewing, this apparent economic autonomy seems most consistent with those labeled (b), (c), and (d) in figure 2.2, that is to say, the models in which social segments retain a significant degree of autonomy. It seems less consistent with model (a), which is structured as a graded hierarchy of elites related by kin ties to an apical paramount chief. In that model, everything and everyone stands in a hierarchical relation to a single office, and ultimately to a single person.

That said, it is immediately apparent that our data contain a large blind spot, which is Mound B, the dominant mound and presumptive seat of a paramount chief if indeed such a person held sway at Moundville (see Payne 2002). Because we have no data from the presumptive apex of the system, we cannot say whether artifact assemblages deriving from that apex were quantitatively or qualitatively different from those found in the plaza-periphery mounds. Excavations in Mound B should be a priority for future research, focusing on the location and sampling of flank middens consisting of debris cast down from the summit of Moundville's tallest mound.

Second, although production on plaza-periphery mounds was diffuse in a general sense, production of specific goods was more focused. The locally made goods needed in politics and ritual—blades of special imported chert, nonutilitarian stone axes, paint palettes, stone and copper pendants, beads, and copper-clad wooden objects—were not made on every mound. As already stated, I regard this as a pattern of complementarity, as might be generated by a Maussian web of reciprocal obligations, one encouraging a kind of specialization of production among community segments. Ongoing social obligations of this sort promote solidarity and counter fissioning.

Which of our four models warrant that sort of complementarity of production? On the one hand, it is difficult to see the sense in which the models labeled (a) and (c) might do so, and for opposite reasons. Model (a) is not a segmentary system, and its units are not autonomous; whereas in (c) the social units, here representing separate towns, are perhaps too autonomous to permit any specialization and interdependency of production to develop. On the other hand, in models (b) and (d), interdependency of production is perhaps more plausible. In the case of (b), corporate kin groups are already both autonomous and interdependent in culturally defined ways (see Kelly 2006); whereas for (d) such an interdependency of religious sodalities would effectively embody what Spielmann (2002) calls a "ritual economy" such as we see in operation ethnographically among the Osage and Omaha of the central Plains (Hall 2006).

A special feature of the sodality model (d) that may have direct archaeological implications is that its segmentary units are explicitly religious organizations of the kind that might well generate art. As noted, Byers' model is based ethnographically on the religious sodalities of the central Plains tribes. Some of these secret societies had supernatural patrons such as the Thunder Beings, the horned Water Monster, and the mystic powers associated with ghosts or the celestial bodies. Initiates manipulated sacred poles, pipes, pigments, scalp locks, and shells and were entitled to wear special emblems and regalia (see, e.g., Fletcher and La Flesche 1911: 486–581; Fortune 1932). These seem precisely the kinds of images that constitute the stable themes of local art in the Hemphill style at Moundville (Knight and Steponaitis 2011), and it seems conceivable to me that similar societies of initiates and their lodges might have been engines driving the production of much of Moundville's representational art.

If so, and if platform mounds were in fact the seats of religious sodalities, we might expect to find a correspondence between specific artistic themes such as the winged serpent, crested bird, or raptors, and specific mounds. This notion can be put to the test, as sherds from engraved pottery vessels bearing such representational art were routinely used, broken, and discarded on mounds. Some 105 sherds with identifiable representational themes occur in our mound assemblages. But an examination of the distribution of these themes by mound reveals no correlation. Instead, these subjects are more or less freely distributed across all of the mounds investigated (Knight 2007: 160–61). Thus, it seems that if Moundville's religious images were associated with major sodalities, then the social entities represented by plaza-periphery mounds crosscut that organization.

The model (b) in which mounds are the seats of ranked corporate kin groups has in its favor a specific ethnohistoric analogy with the layout of a traditional Chickasaw camp square, as given to Speck (1907) by his informant Ca'bi'tci. This camp layout featured a four-sided plaza with named, corporate lineage groups (not clans, but subclans) arrayed around the margins in a rank order clockwise and counterclockwise from center north. It exhibited a bilateral symmetry with respect to a north–south axis, and a common facility, a council fire, in the center of the plaza. I have written at length on the goodness of fit and other merits of this analogy (Knight 1998), which I still find striking in relation to the specific mound-

and-plaza arrangement at Moundville as outlined above. I am thus still on record as favoring this model.

Conclusions

I have offered for consideration four competing models of monumental space, each potentially applicable to the Moundville site as an organization of monuments on a plaza-periphery layout. These models emphasize different, complementary facets of group identity in traditional village societies: political rank, kinship, residence, and voluntary association. While I did not expect, and cannot deliver, a definitive solution, I hope to have clarified the question and to have made the point that each of these models has different implications with respect to the information revealed by excavation. Available data, especially on mound chronology, the size and number of construction stages, summit architecture, artifact assemblages, and biocultural remains, are now in a state where a proper weighing of such alternatives can productively take place. In this light, I see weaknesses in the models I have labeled (a), (c), and (d) that I do not think are shared by model (b), one that places emphasis on ranked, corporate kin-based community segments as responsible for mound building on the plaza periphery. I have also suggested that neither feasting nor temples played major roles at the center, and that its organizational features were not static over time.

For a long time I have been struck by the lack of fit between what we know of Moundville, on the one hand, and a "power perspective" of centralized control by a paramount chief (e.g., Earle 1997), on the other. The evidence for a much more diffuse political environment is convergent. We might start with the multiplicity of the mounds themselves, densely arrayed in partitioned space around the plaza, and what that says about the distributedness of labor.[5] Fancy goods were made and used at the site, but not in quantities sufficient to drive a system of "wealth finance" of chiefly control—that is to say, a prestige-goods economy (Marcoux 2007). Richly furnished high-status burials are found at Moundville, but not concentrated in any single place. They are instead found in many places around the plaza periphery, as in Mounds C, D, H, O, and U, and indeed in places far removed from mounds, as in the isolated Rhodes locality (Moore 1905; Peebles 1979). Locally made religious imagery is associated with indications of high status, but not exclusively (Phillips 2006, this volume); that imagery is strikingly devoid of human beings as subjects, such as mythic heroes that elsewhere may have chartered individualistic, elite statuses (King 2007: 130–31; see also Keyes 1994). To this list we can now add a diffuse, pluralistic pattern of production of special goods used in politics and ritual, together with a potential complementarity in their loci of production on distinct mounds that calls to mind an organic solidarity of reciprocal exchange. Further, we can add the presence of collective facilities, as opposed to private domestic architecture, on at least one mound of the plaza-periphery group.

What, then, do we make of the large mounds on the center axis of the site, those which in all probability drew on numerous social segments for labor in their construction? And what do we make, especially, of Mound B, the dominant mound? In this chapter I have pointed out the need for new excavations in Mound B, but in the interim we must at least ponder the possibility that a despotic leader governed from that high perch. Would a despot have permitted competitive mound building and reciprocal exchange of valued goods among autonomous social segments operating openly within sight? Not likely. Aggrandizers tend to suppress competing organizations that subvert the hierarchical ethos and siphon goods and labor away from central control (Kowalewski 2006: 120).

Given what is now known, I cannot agree that Moundville, even after AD 1300 (see Knight and Steponaitis 1998: 17–21), was ever a "fully entrenched apical hierarchy" (Beck 2003: 653). Instead, I now tend to see Moundville as politically pluralistic and consensual from the beginnings of regional coalescence to its collapse. I predict that central council facilities will ultimately be found—and the place to look for them is Mound A, in the center of the plaza. That is, then, yet another research priority, and one that might be aided greatly by remote sensing.

Acknowledgments

My 1989–2002 mound excavations herein cited were supported by the University of Alabama Department of Anthropology, the Alabama Museum of Natural History, the University of Alabama Research Grants Committee, and the National Science Foundation (grants 9220568 and 9727709). Further, I am indebted to Chris Peebles, who first got us thinking about the interpretive potential of the regularities and symmetries of Moundville's mounds.

Notes

1. Much of the older literature on Moundville mounds reports smaller numbers. Moore (1905) listed 20 earthworks that he considered mounds (lettered A–T), and that number is often cited, but there were, and still are, clearly more of smaller size. The count of 29 given by Knight and Steponaitis (1998: 2–3) is conservative and includes only confirmed mounds now given names. Some 32 mounds (the number I have adopted here) are identified on an April 1930 topographic map of the site, while the number specified by Jones and DeJarnette (1936) is 34. A sketch map prepared by Nathaniel T. Lupton in 1869 (Steponaitis 1983b: figure 2) shows additional mounds northwest of Mound R and southeast of Mounds H and I whose locations on modern maps are unknown.

2. Pauketat (2007: 120) sees potential significance in the apparent trapezoidal, rather than strictly rectangular, form of the Moundville plaza, comparing its shape to that of the palisade at the early Mississippian Cool Branch site on the Chattahoochee River in Georgia.

3. Hints of an early, coordinated timing of plaza-periphery construction at Moundville were aired in the 1980s (e.g., Knight 1989b). Based on Moore's data and a seriation of the burials, Steponaitis (1983a: 156–60) had previously argued for a more incremental model of site growth culminating in the Moundville III phase (see Knight and Steponaitis 2007).

4. Earlier radiocarbon-dated mound assemblages of value exist as well. Particularly informative are the materials from our relatively expansive horizontal excavations of the Stage II summit features of Mound Q, which date to the early Moundville II phase (after ca. AD 1250). The only flank midden we encountered from this period is from the north side of Mound G (Stage I), from which the recovered assemblage is small. Also dating to the last decades of the thirteenth century is the earliest construction stage in Mound F (Stage I), from which we have a moderately large assemblage, the only such material from a well-documented initial construction stage. Unfortunately, there are indications that most of the fill from this context as well as the artifacts are redeposited from slightly earlier middens, thus compromising their utility. In sum, these earlier mound components, although not to be overlooked, are rather incommensurate and do not allow the sort of comparative analysis we have done with the later components. Materials recovered in the early 1970s from a flank midden on Mound M, reported by Astin (1996), seem to be our best direct evidence of late Moundville I phase mound construction on the plaza periphery. My own excavations also encountered minor Moundville I phase middens, features, and artifacts from beneath Mounds E, G, and R. As they are nonmound materials, we are not concerned with them here.

5. A set of intriguing contrasts can be made with the Etowah site (King 2003), Moundville's contemporary in northwest Georgia during the Wilbanks phase. Etowah, despite its size, has only three major mounds, and the majority of mound-building labor was invested in the largest of these, Mound A. Etowah's Mound A is both taller and more massive than Moundville's counterpart, Mound B. There are further indications of comparative nucleation at Etowah, including the concentration of high-status burials in only one mound, a relative exclusivity in religious symbolism, and an iconography

that King (2007: 131) describes as marking "a shift to individualistic themes." In contrast, Brown (2007) sees evidence of pluralism rather than apical hierarchy manifested in Etowah's mortuary Mound C, even to the point of doubting whether Etowah was in fact a "chiefdom." Brown's vision of a basically pluralistic society at Etowah resonates, of course, with my own for Moundville. In questioning the long-dominant view that Etowah was an apical chiefdom, Brown offers no opinion on who might have lived on its principal mound, Mound A.

3

Long-Term Trends in the Making and Materialization of Social Groups at Moundville

GREGORY D. WILSON

The Moundville site has a highly structured spatial plan—a point made long ago by Peebles (1971, 1979) and later developed by Knight (1998, 2010, this volume). On a macro-community level, Knight (1998, this volume) has interpreted the rectangular distribution of paired earthen monuments at the site as indicating the presence of a number of ranked, corporate kin groups (figure 3.1). My ongoing research has documented evidence that Moundville community members employed a similar socio-spatial logic to establish their kin-based identities on a subclan or lineage level through the construction of spatially discrete residential groups (Wilson 2008: 87–90). Moreover, I also found that these residential groups were later replaced by small burial clusters that I interpreted as kin-group cemeteries (Wilson 2008: 90–92, 2010).

Collectively, these patterns lend themselves to the conclusion that Moundville consisted of a carefully structured arrangement of clans and subclans. This model of community organization is even more compelling in that it corresponds so closely with the ethnohistorically documented kinship systems and community patterns of American Indian groups who once occupied neighboring portions of the interior Southeast (Knight 1990: 10; Speck 1907; Swan 1855: 262; Swanton 1922, 1928a: 115–16, 1928b: 204–6; Wilson 2008).

On the basis of this highly structured community plan, it may be tempting to conceptualize Moundville in structuralist theoretical terms. Structural-functionalist perspectives emphasize the inherent stability and cohesion of societies. Accordingly, the different segments that constitute a society are viewed as well-integrated building blocks with particular

Figure 3.1. The Moundville site, showing excavated areas discussed in the text. Residential groups along the Moundville Roadway are labeled numerically, RG1–RG10. Key to abbreviations for excavation areas: NR, North of Mound R; ECB, East of the Conference Building; PA, Picnic Area.

socioeconomic functions that serve to reproduce the social whole (see Yaeger and Canuto 2000: 2). Moreover, individuals are not viewed as significant in and of themselves but only in terms of their position in patterns of social relations, and their associated behaviors in reproducing those relations. Such a perspective downplays the historical and political importance of social inequalities, conflicts, and hybridity, as well as the role of agency and social practice in generating broader relationships (Brumfiel 1992).

I have adopted a practice-based theoretical perspective as an alternative to the structuralist approach just discussed (Bourdieu 1977; Giddens 1984). From a practice-theory perspective, social structure is not independent of or causally prior to the practices and interests of individuals and small groups. In addition, social relations and social entities are not viewed as inherently stable but as requiring constant maintenance to perpetuate. In theorizing agency, some anthropologists have also emphasized the importance of material culture in stabilizing broader social networks (Latour 1992; Law 1991: 173–76; Whitridge 2004). Thus, social groups manufacture and manipulate buildings, monuments, and portable items in the attempt to make certain social relations and identities more durable.

Small-scale Mississippian social groups in the Black Warrior Valley appear to have been surprisingly durable despite important political economic changes in the region (see Wilson 2008: 130–37, 2010). Determining the relationship between the actions and interests of these social groups and an overarching kinship system is of key importance to understanding their durability and their role in shaping Mississippian society in the Black Warrior Valley. To address this issue I will provide a diachronic summary of Moundville's community organization. In so doing I will highlight the different strategies that small-scale social groups employed to produce and maintain their corporate identities and socioeconomic claims over the course of several centuries.

The data for this investigation come from the Alabama Museum of Natural History's excavation of the Moundville Roadway. The Roadway excavations were conducted in 1939 and 1940 at the Moundville site within a winding corridor, 15 m (50 ft) wide and 2.4 km (1.5 mi) long, that was to be disturbed by the construction of a road that now encircles portions of the plaza and areas east, west, and south of the mounds (see figure 3.1). In conjunction, several large block excavations occurred prior to the construction of an entrance building and site museum. These excavations uncovered the archaeological remains of hundreds of Mississippian buildings and associated architectural features, a total of 289 burials, and over 100,000 artifacts (see Peebles 1971, 1979).

The early Moundville I phase corresponds with the beginning of Mississippian culture in the Black Warrior Valley. Two low earthen mounds were built on the Moundville terrace at this time (Blitz 2007, this volume;

Steponaitis 1992). Large-scale excavation and widespread subsurface testing, however, have revealed that this area was only lightly occupied in the early twelfth century AD (Knight and Steponaitis 1998: 13; Scarry 1995, 1998; Steponaitis 1998). The earliest Mississippian domestic structures at the Moundville site are widely scattered and have relatively short occupation spans (Wilson 2008). Thus, despite Moundville's emerging political and ceremonial importance, there is little evidence of the well-structured community order that defined later occupation at the site.

An analysis of over 200 excavated buildings at the Moundville site has revealed a sizable population increase around AD 1200, at the beginning of the late Moundville I phase (Wilson 2008). Moundville's expanded population settled into numerous spatially discontiguous residential groups—most of which consisted of an estimated 10 to 20 structures (figure 3.2; Wilson 2008; Wilson et al. 2006). The spatial distribution of these residential groups roughly corresponds with broader clan-based social divisions at the site as represented in the arrangement and size of earthen monuments. Indeed, based on the spatial proximity of numerous building clusters to discrete mound pairs, each clan unit at Moundville included multiple subclan residential groups.

These newly established residential groups were larger and more formally organized than the dispersed Mississippian households of the early Moundville I phase (Wilson 2008). Methods of architectural construction became more standardized, and buildings were arranged to create pathways and small courtyards (Scarry 1998). The members of some residential groups also built large, special-purpose buildings that may have been used for ceremonial purposes or as the residences of lineage leaders (see figure 3.2; Peebles 1979: 927–28; Wilson 2008; Wilson et al. 2006).

The initial creation of these spatially discrete residential areas and the in situ rebuilding of domestic structures suggest a conscious attempt on the part of Moundville community members to delineate a corporate kin-group identity. These persistent identity claims by small residential groups correspond with the construction of Moundville's mound-and-plaza complex, an act that has been interpreted as an attempt to stabilize the social relations among a number of ranked corporate subclans (Knight 1998). Thus, the late Moundville I founding of the Moundville community entailed considerable coordinated effort and labor expenditure in the form of earthmoving, monument building, and architectural construction. The

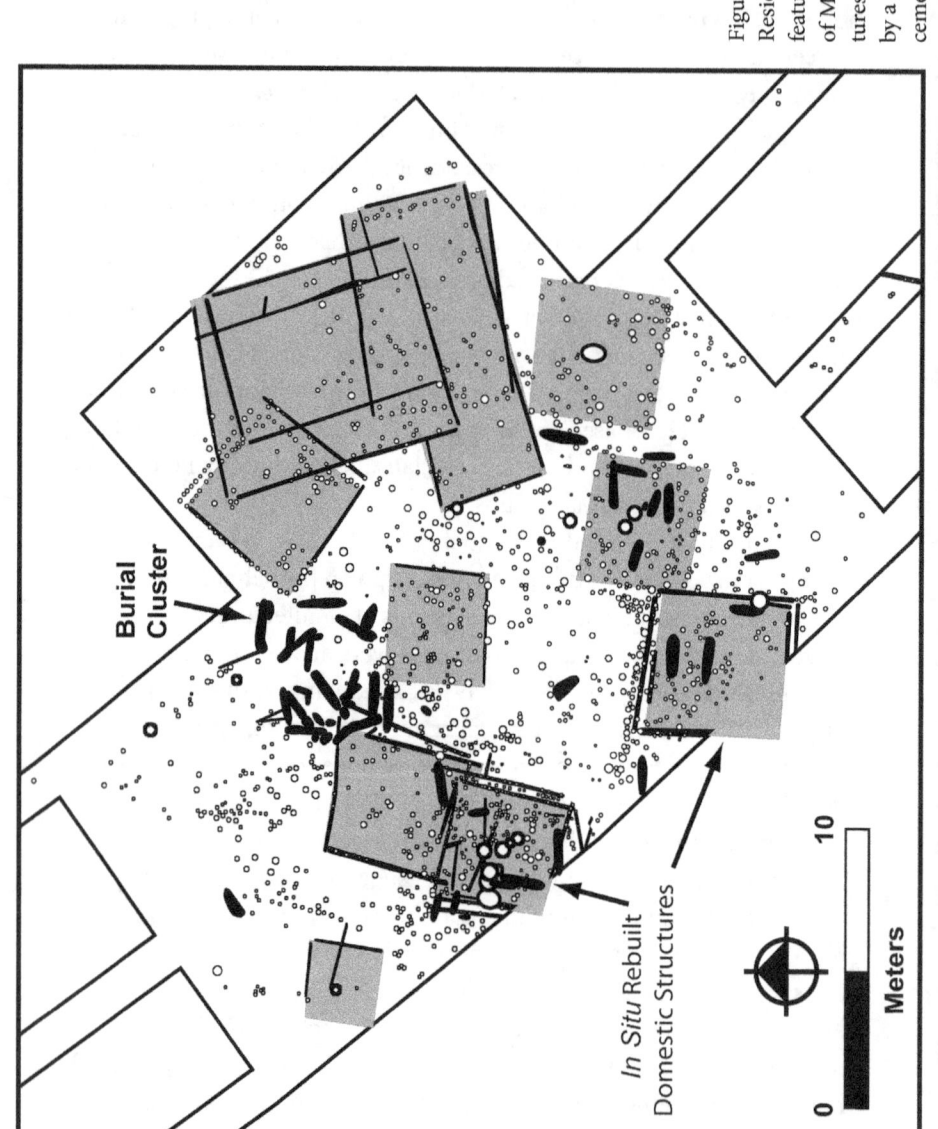

Figure 3.2. Plan of Residential Group 9 featuring the location of Moundville I structures superimposed by a Moundville II–III cemetery.

Moundville sociogram and the segmentary kin-based community order it embodied were literally created by these practices and cannot be separated from these initial acts of construction and persistent rebuilding.

In the last decades of the thirteenth century, most of Moundville's occupants dispersed into the rural countryside of the Black Warrior Valley (Hammerstedt et al., this volume; Knight and Steponaitis 1998; Maxham 2004; Steponaitis 1998). By AD 1300 the site was no longer a nucleated residential center, occupied only by small groups of elites and religious specialists. Over the course of the next two centuries Moundville was used as a vacant ceremonial center and necropolis, where much of the regional populace buried their dead (Knight and Steponaitis 1998; Wilson et al. 2010).

The motivation behind this outmigration is currently a matter of debate. In one scenario this demographic shift is interpreted as a distancing strategy in which the political elite stake an exclusive claim to Moundville's mound-and-plaza ceremonial complex (Beck 2003; Knight and Steponaitis 1998). Alternatively, this population exodus is portrayed as a result of Moundville's political decentralization, during which polity members were drawn away by aspiring elite competitors elsewhere in the Black Warrior Valley (Blitz 2008: 67–68). In either scenario this large-scale settlement shift would have dramatically changed the ways that Mississippian household members negotiated everyday socioeconomic relationships. Indeed, it seems these changing circumstances influenced late Mississippian groups in the region to devise new spatial practices by which to materialize their positions in the social order.

After AD 1300 Moundville was a place strongly defined by mortuary ritualism. Various kinds and sizes of cemeteries were created in both mound and off-mound locations throughout the site (Peebles 1979). Based on the prevalence of elaborate mortuary furniture (e.g., copper artifacts, freshwater pearls, marine-shell beads, etc.), at least some of the cemeteries placed in mounds were associated with Moundville's political elite (Moore 1905, 1907; Peebles 1974; Peebles and Kus 1977). With few exceptions, it appears that off-mound cemeteries were primarily associated with the nonelite, based on the paucity of mortuary accoutrements. Most off-mound cemeteries consist of small rectilinear clusters of burials arranged around a small central open space (figure 3.3). Additional burials are typically scattered around the outer perimeter of these clusters (Wilson et al. 2010). A seriation of mortuary vessels reveals that many of

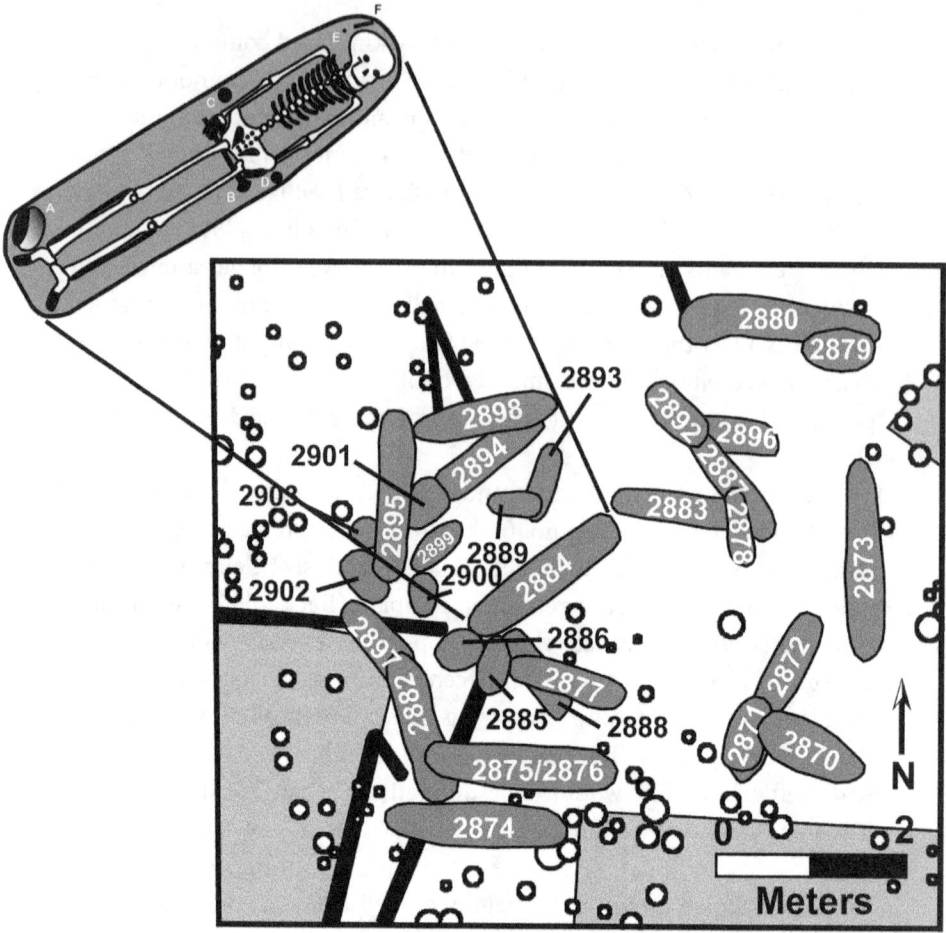

Figure 3.3. Detailed plan of the cemetery from Residential Group 9, highlighting the burial of male aged 50+ years, with associated burial furniture. Artifacts in Burial 2884: (*a*) Carthage Incised, *var. Summerville* jar; (*b*) greenstone spatulate celt; (*c*–*d*) stone discoidals (gaming stones); (*e*) marine shell bead; (*f*) bone hair pin.

these off-mound cemeteries were used for as long as two centuries (Steponaitis 1983a). The presence of numerous superimposed burials in the central portions of these cemeteries provides further evidence that they had a long history of use (Wilson et al. 2010).

Perhaps the most notable feature of off-mound cemeteries is their placement in community space. The vast majority of these mortuaries were placed directly on the midden-covered architectural remains of earlier residential groups (Wilson 2008). Very few burials in the Moundville Roadway are located outside the spatial limits of these residential groups.

I have interpreted this careful and consistent positioning of cemeteries as an attempt by late Mississippian kin groups to establish social continuity with ancestral kin space at Moundville (Wilson 2008, 2010; Wilson et al. 2010).

A closer examination of a particular residential and cemetery group located along the northwest portion of the Moundville Roadway provides a more detailed understanding of how late Mississippian groups created social and spatial connections with the past. This residential-cemetery palimpsest is composed of a group of ten early Mississippian structures that was subsequently superimposed by 57 Mississippian burials (see figure 3.2). Thirty-six of the 57 burials are arranged in a small rectilinear cluster. The remaining 21 burials are dispersed immediately to the south.

A seriation of mortuary vessels and a careful examination of feature superimposition reveal that this cemetery had a long history of use (Steponaitis 1983a, 1998; Wilson et al. 2010). It appears that the cemetery was initiated with the burial of an adult male immediately after the early Mississippian residential occupation of the location ended (see figure 3.3). This individual was over 50 years of age at time of death and was buried with artifacts of social and ceremonial importance, including a long-stemmed greenstone spatulate celt and two discoidals (gaming stones). Over the next two centuries, a small rectangular cemetery was literally built around this individual, likely an ancestral kin member of some political importance.

Thus, like many others, this late Mississippian group returned to Moundville long after they ceased living at the site, to bury their dead. In doing so they intentionally chose to establish their cemetery in the exact location of a spatially circumscribed early Mississippian residential area. This late Mississippian group also referenced their past through the careful placement of graves around the remains of a prominent ancestor. It is particularly noteworthy that this individual is old enough to have been alive during the early part of the eleventh century and perhaps even lived in the residential group area in which he was later buried. The strategic placement of graves around such an individual could have greatly contributed to social and spatial continuity with the past.

Cross-cultural studies of mortuary ceremonialism have revealed that agricultural groups that exercise hereditary control over land often affirm their corporate status and lineal property claims through the creation and strategic placement of corporate kin-group cemeteries (Goldstein 1980;

McAnany 1995; Saxe 1970). The political and economic logic of this kind of spatial practice may explain aspects of Moundville's community organization, which appears to have been formally laid out in a way to embody social-group membership on several different scales.

Thus, like the construction of paired mounds and the in situ rebuilding of domestic architecture, the use of spatially discrete cemeteries may have strategically assisted kin groups in establishing connections to corporate space at Moundville and to the socioeconomic claims that followed from such corporate ties. This is not to imply that there was always direct continuity among the kin groups occupying residential groups and those that later claimed these places to bury their dead. The regional settlement changes following Moundville's population outmigration no doubt entailed political and economic changes that impacted regional inhabitants on the household level. Some kin groups may have fragmented, while others ceased to exist entirely. There may have also been instances where the ancestral spaces and heredity claims of one group were contested or co-opted by others. Such outcomes would be consistent with anthropological understandings of kin-based political dynamics in middle-range societies around the world (Comaroff 1978; Ogilvie 1971: 12–13; Sahlins 1958: 146; Turner 1957: 86). The important point here is that late Mississippian social groups in the Black Warrior Valley used Moundville's early Mississippian history of kin-based spatial occupation to define their social identities and interests long after they relocated to Moundville's rural countryside.

An important implication of these mortuary practices is that small-scale kin groups played a prominent role in defining Moundville's community organization long after the site ceased to be used as a residential center (Wilson 2010). These patterns provide evidence that politically charged decisions and relationships regarding community, religion, and ceremonialism were broadly negotiated among different Mississippian kin groups at a time when we have the best archaeological evidence for the entrenchment of an elite ruling class in the form of elaborate mortuary ceremonialism and the production of iconographically decorated objects thought to reference a legitimizing elite ideology.

The organizational changes at Moundville highlight the different ways in which kin groups defined and redefined their corporate status and identities over the long term. Moundville wasn't always a sociogram. A segmentary, kin-based community order on the scale of Moundville's wasn't always in place in prehistoric west central Alabama. Toward the end of the twelfth century, Mississippian groups began changing their everyday routines and periodic ritual practices in ways that produced the social and spatial order embodied by the late Moundville I community at the Moundville site. These new practices can be viewed as the negotiation of social identities, rights, and resources that heralded a new regional political order. From a practice-theory perspective, the spatially delimited nature of mound construction, house building and rebuilding, and mortuary ritual were not passive expressions of a shared Mississippian political culture and kinship system, but the ongoing attempts of different groups to produce and stabilize particular social relations—sometimes in the face of sweeping regional changes. The actions and interests of these Mississippian groups assured that Moundville remained an important place on the southeastern landscape over the course of several centuries.

Acknowledgments

I am grateful for the research support provided to me by faculty members in the Department of Anthropology at the University of North Carolina, Chapel Hill. Specifically, I would like to thank Vincas Steponaitis, C. Margaret Scarry, John Scarry, R. P. Stephen Davis, and Brian Billman. Also, thanks to Vernon Knight who has been an important mentor throughout the years. A special thanks to my graduate school peers (Tony Boudreaux, Kandace Hollenbach, Jon Marcoux, Mintcy Maxham, Chris Rodning, Tiffiny Tung, and Amber VanDerwarker), now all gainfully employed elsewhere. This research was greatly facilitated by the support of the Office of Archaeological Services at Moundville. Finally, I acknowledge Christopher Peebles for his many contributions to Moundville archaeology, particularly his earlier research on the Moundville Roadway excavation maps, notes, and artifacts.

4

Mound X and Selective Forgetting at Early Moundville

JOHN H. BLITZ

> The struggle of man against power is the struggle of memory against forgetting.
>
> —Milan Kundera (1999), *The Book of Laughter and Forgetting*

In this chapter, I explore a social contradiction found in Mississippian and other emergent complex societies at times when political and social integration coalesced, formal offices of leadership were established, and mound-center polities were founded. Based on what is known about the forms of legitimization in nonstratified social formations (Friedman 1998; Leach 1954; Sahlins 1958), assertions of rank, status, and privilege by constituent corporate groups at Mississippian mound centers were probably closely tied to competing and contradictory claims about origins, land-use rights, descent, and events in the mythic past of ancestry (Anderson 1994: 87–93; Knight 1986; Peebles and Kus 1977). Certainly, such claims played an important role in the legitimization of elites among native southeastern peoples in the early historic period (Knight 1990). Therefore, archaeologists might expect that when large mound-center polities formed, materializations of the past such as pottery styles, house forms, and venerable monuments would be retained and promoted as valued ideological resources. Often, however, these traditional things were treated as cultural liabilities to be rejected, denied, and replaced with new styles, new forms, and new monuments. This tension between past and present, exacerbated by the inequality of corporate groups, generated social contradictions that could threaten the stability of the new political order. I propose that one way this contradiction was resolved in these societies was through acts of selective forgetting. I illustrate this proposed contradition and resolution with archaeological examples from prehistoric Moundville, in particular focusing on platform mounds as iconic symbols that commemorated and sanctified a social group's status at Mississippian centers (Knight, this volume). A review of investigations at Mound X, one of the first mounds constructed at Moundville, suggests that group claims on the past, memorialized by construction and maintenance of a mound, could be challenged or erased by mound destruction: a Mississippian example of selective forgetting as "repressive erasure" (Connerton 2008).

Culture Change, Collective Identity, and Social Memory

Archaeologists concerned with culture change in early complex societies can draw on two important concepts to understand how the past might be a resource or a burden during periods of rapid social transitions: collective identity and social memory. Collective identity may be defined as the idea of uniqueness, belonging, and unity shared by members of social groups (Snow 2001). Classic anthropological observations about middle-range societies document how group affiliation through collective identity was achieved by ramping up the scale and intensity of group rituals that linked non-kin in dependent relationships of obligation and gift-giving, fostered a more inclusive integration, and increased community solidarity (Durkheim 1995; Fortes 1953; Mauss 2000). Group affiliation through collective identity may also be communicated through the forms, styles, and decorations of objects and the ways these objects were made, used, and displayed (Appadurai 1986); this renders collective identity an ideological construct accessible to archaeologists (for a Mississippian example, see Alt 2002). Archaeologists can apply these insights to understand how collective identity played an integrative role that helped counter factionalism in prestate communities or polities by permitting individuals and groups to feel vested in a larger social world beyond family and kin. When central-place polities formed in a region, localized groups aggregated into large communities of unrelated people. Efforts to institutionalize the new social forms and increase the scale of political integration generated an imperative to produce new collective identities that could transcend localized group loyalties, counter kin-group factionalism, and mask or deflect tensions generated by emerging differences in rank and power. In Mississippian polities, platform mounds and plazas were the material result and provenience of these new integrative actions.

One way collective identity is fostered and maintained is through social memory (also known as collective memory or cultural memory), which refers not to subjective or idiosyncratic individual remembering, but to the socially constructed memory shared by a group (Halbwachs 1992; Olick and Robbins 1998). Social memory is usefully defined as the "construction of a collective notion about how things were in the past" (Van Dyke and Alcock 2003: 2). Shared perceptions of the past are used by communities, groups, and leaders to justify how and why people do things in certain ways in the present (Connerton 1989; Halbwachs 1992; Hobsbawm and Ranger 1983). Competing social groups appeal to the idealized sanctity of social memory to construct charter myths that imbue the group with a sense of unity, legitimate claims of resource ownership, and rationalize inequality. Values, perceptions, and beliefs may remain abstract to people unless given objective reality in the form of material things (Childe 1956: 86–90; DeMarrais et al. 1996). A common way that social memory can be given an objective reality is to build it into the spaces and landscapes where people live and act (Connerton 1989). Once in place, material things become references that inform the construction of identity in the present (Olick and Robbins 1998: 122–26; Lowenthal 1985: 41). Because various physical media may transmit social memory, a current approach in archaeology is to assess how the construction and spatial organization of bounded community space materialized social memory in the built environment (Alcock 2002; Ashmore 2002; Bradley 1998; Joyce 2003, 2004; Meskell 2003), including the houses, plazas, fortifications, and mounds of Mississippian centers (Beck et al. 2007: 842–44; Pauketat and Alt 2003; Wilson 2008, 2010).

Wilson (2010, this volume) has traced how social memory was built into Moundville's landscape of mounds, houses, and cemeteries to affect "place-based identity politics." For example, when the multiple-mound polity at Moundville formed, a new spatial distribution of domestic houses appeared as a radical departure from the traditional ways houses were built and distributed in earlier times. These "residential groups" were clusters of 8–12 houses widely separated from neighboring clusters. Wilson (2010: 5, 10) identifies the social memory expressed in residential groups as an example of sociologist Paul Connerton's (1989) "incorporated memory," which is "embodied in and transmitted through routinized bodily practices," and performed without introspection, a concept Wilson sees as similar to Bourdieu's habitus. According to Wilson, the new spaces of domestic living replicated social memory at the scale of continuous and patterned daily activities, and localized aspects of ideology and identity in quotidian routines. Later in Moundville's history, after the fortified town became a depopulated ceremonial center, the abandoned residential group locations became small cemeteries, and burials were interred at the places where the domestic houses once stood. Wilson interprets the reuse of Moundville residential groups as cemeteries as an example of Connerton's (1989) "inscribed memory," actions undertaken with the express intent of communicating memory. In this case, inscribed memory took the form of "commemorative ceremonies in which domestic groups re-presented their history in a ceremonial capacity" (Wilson 2010: 13). A group's claim to ancestral affiliation with Moundville was conveyed through burial of the dead at the location of abandoned residential groups, and social memory was remade (Wilson 2010: 14–15) (for a similar example of abandoned house locations reused as cemeteries in a Mississippian community, see Boudreaux 2007: 60).

In addition to cemeteries, palisades, and plazas, platform mounds were perhaps the most distinctive projects that Mississippian communities undertook as materializations of inscribed social memory (Wilson 2010: 7–9). Platform mounds were the places where various expressions of social relations and meaning intersected. Polity formation required the forging of new understandings about leadership and rank among competitive factions. The remaking of the site plan materialized these new understandings by establishing a highly visible, symbolically charged landscape of monumental mounds unlike anything in the past experience of the inhabitants. Many archaeologists discuss how platform mounds materialized various meanings related to territory, rank, authority, and community (Anderson 1994; Blitz 1999; Blitz and Lorenz 2006; Hally 1996; Pauketat and Alt 2003). As Knapp and Ashmore (1999) put it, monument construction transforms the cultural landscape, "fixing social and individual histories in place." Because Mississippian platform mounds are interpreted as corporate-group facilities, the presence of multiple mounds at a polity center implies the presence of multiple constituent corporate groups. The masses, spatial arrangement, and use-lives of mounds are thought to mirror the relative size, status, and history of the constituent groups and their leadership at such sites (Blitz and Livingood 2004). The interpretation of site layout as a "sociogram" is well developed at Moundville (Knight 1998, 2004; Peebles 1971), even if there are differing interpretations as to how the social groups affiliated with mounds were organized (Blitz 2008; Knight 2010, this volume).

The preceding discussion points to three important connections among polities in middle-range societies, collective identity, and social memory: (1) polity formation required new forms of collective identities at the scale of community and polity; (2) social memory is basic to the production of collective identity; and (3) social memory and collective identity are ideological constructs with material referents. Given these linkages, when archaeologists find that the built environment and material culture at polity centers such as Moundville were reorganized, rebuilt, or replaced, it may be inferred that societal changes occurred that required new social memories and collective identities.

A social contradiction was created by polity formation: claims of rank and privilege based on a mythic past had to be reconciled to the new memories and new identities of a different social order. There was a disjunction between a venerated past and a reinvented present. If the past was an important ideological resource of legitimization for competing social groups as polity centers were established, then it would seem that idealized collective identities forged from local, traditional, and familiar practices would be valued. Materializations of this ideology should emphasize continuity with the past, not just through individual and group affiliation with mnemonic monuments such as platform mounds, but through the replication of traditional material culture such as community plans, pottery styles, and house forms. However, with the initial creation of large regional centers, what archaeologists often find are rapid and significant discontinuities with the past: new community plans and the rejection of traditional material culture such as pottery styles and house forms in favor of new ones, and this was certainly true for Moundville (Blitz 2008; Knight and Steponaitis 1998; Wilson 2008).

The new cultural practices and collective identities of polity formation disrupted the maintenance of traditional social relations and motivated the agents of innovation to replace the social memories of an inconvenient past. For new social memory to replace old social memory, the emotional hold of an established ideological framework must be relinquished or subsumed, but how can people give up deep-seated values and practices? The contradiction between the new lived experience and tradition would be resolved only if some form of forgetting opened up a cognitive "space" that could be filled with new social memory (Connerton 2008;

Lowenthal 1985: 205). In other words, production of social memory necessitates forgetting. While not ignoring the many specific causal forces that stimulated polity formation, a focus on social memory provides a useful interpretive framework, once it is understood that memory and forgetting are inseparable components of historical process (Olick and Robbins 1998: 126–30). For these reasons archaeologists must identify material expressions of forgetting in the archaeological record.

Selective Forgetting and Repressive Erasure

Selective forgetting is a term used in clinical psychology to define how individual memories are allowed to fit a person's understanding of the world and his or her own place in it by selectively relinquishing those memories that do not validate these perceptions. In social memory studies, this aspect of individual forgetting has been applied to collective phenomena shared by members of a social group. There are various forms of forgetting, with different social impacts and agents (Connerton 2008). Here I will use *selective forgetting* as a covering term for the forms of forgetting that suppress or remake specific memories to promote an alternative dominant narrative, a basic strategy in the production of ideology (Olick and Robbins 1998). Some forms of forgetting are initiated at the family and kin-group level, but because changes to legitimization ideologies are central to the contradictory uses of the past discussed above, we are most concerned here with a form of selective forgetting initiated by political agents, which Connerton (2008: 60) labels "repressive erasure."

Repressive erasure is an attempt by political agents to obliterate or remove all memory of a political or ideological rival in the competition for power; it is "employed to deny the fact of a historical rupture as well as bring about a historic break" (Connerton 2008: 60). There are two variants of repressive erasure, depending on whether the target of memory removal is an individual or an ideology. *Damnatio memoriae* (condemnation of memory) refers to a punishment in Roman law, which decreed that, after the death of powerful or influential individuals who had rebelled against the state, all images of the persons were to be destroyed and their names removed from inscriptions. Cross-culturally, archaeologists can identify *damnatio memoriae* by the discovery of defaced or destroyed monuments depicting the names or images of leaders. Examples from antiquity include the removal of one pharaoh's image and name from monuments by successors in ancient Egypt (Redford 1984: 206; Reeves 2001: 94, 167) and the smashing and burial of the colossal-head statues of Olmec rulers in Formative period Mesoamerica (Diehl 2004: 119). A modern example of *damnatio memoriae* is the retouching of group photographs to remove images of officials liquidated as "enemies of the state" in Stalinist Russia (King 1997). A second form of repressive erasure is iconoclasm, the destruction of sacred objects or monuments by those who are motivated by politics or religion. Examples from antiquity include the uprooting of menhirs in Neolithic France (Balter 1993), the heretic Akhenaten's directives to destroy images of Amun and replace them with those of Aten in ancient Egypt (Reeves 2001: 155), and the toppling of Easter Island moai statues (Flenley and Bahn 1992: 150). More recently, Taliban iconoclasts destroyed the Buddhas of Bamiyan in Afghanistan (Bearak 2001).

Mound X: An Archaeological Example of Selective Forgetting as Repressive Erasure

The brief review above underscores why, in times of rapid sociopolitical change such as succession to chiefly office, contestation of rank among competing factions, or the formation of polities, the past could be either a resource or a burden. Material representations of the past, such as platform mounds, are sites of social memory production and, potentially, subjects for selective forgetting. Excavations at Mound X have revealed surprising evidence of this contradiction between a symbol of the past and the changing ideological orientation of a new political order at Moundville. I contend that this contradiction was resolved through selective forgetting as repressive erasure. Before presenting this evidence, we must place Mound X in the larger sweep of Moundville's dynamic social history. The construction and use of Mound X spanned a critical time in Moundville's early formation, when populations in the region exhibited the consequences of Mississippianization, manifested in a fusion of Woodland and Mississippian styles and forms in material goods and cultural practices (Blitz 2008; Jenkins 2003). In the early Moundville I subphase (ca. AD 1120–1200), Moundville's site plan of multiple mounds, large plaza, and palisade fortifications was not yet established. The site was a small community of widespread houses dispersed for a kilometer or more along a flood-free terrace above the Black Warrior River. Inhabitants came together for rituals at two small platform mounds: Mound X, a low rise positioned just outside the later mound-plaza arrangement, and 1Tu50, a larger mound about 900 m to the north (Knight and Steponaitis 1998; Scarry 1998; Steponaitis 1992). The construction of these two mounds signals that the institutionalization of social rank and some degree of political integration was in place prior to Moundville's later site plan of multiple mounds, plaza, and palisade.

Early Moundville I occupations have a "hybrid" house style that combined the Terminal Woodland house forms of sunken floors or single-set posts with the new Mississippian wall-trench construction methods (Lacquement 2007; Scarry 1998; Wilson 2008). Pottery with grog temper and cord marking, also with Woodland antecedents, persisted as a minority ware (Jenkins 2003). Around AD 1200, events transformed the site. The residential population grew rapidly. Use of the house forms and pottery attributes that originated in Woodland times ended, replaced by exclusively Mississippian forms such as wall-trench houses and pottery in a recognizable Moundville style and a more homogeneous material expression of a new collective identity. In a relatively short span of time, an enormous construction project created a planned mound-plaza arrangement enclosed by a palisade wall, houses clustered in residential groups, and a large mound-center polity was founded (Knight and Steponaitis 1998). With the initiation of this new social and political order, the older mounds X and 1Tu50 were abandoned.

Mound X is an inconspicuous 1-m-high rise in the eastern portion of the site, positioned outside the tight arrangement of nearby mounds along the plaza periphery (figure 4.1). The mound does not appear on any early site maps, although an aerial photograph from the 1930s shows a marked discoloration in the soil at this location (Blitz 2007: figure 3). The presence of Mound X went undetected until 1983, when Joseph Vogel and Jean Allan encountered a swath of dense white clay while excavating a long segment of the site's palisade. The plow zone was removed over a 35-×-15-m area, exposing a clay mound remnant, dark organic deposits of ash and artifacts related to mound and premound activities, and palisade lines (Blitz 2007: figures 4–7). The horizontal extent of these features was photographed and mapped, but the features were not excavated. A shallow trench 35 m long and 1 m wide was dug across the exposed white clay mass. Examination of the resulting profile suggested to the excavators that the palisade trenches superimposed and intruded into the mound remnant. No further excavation took place, few artifacts were collected,

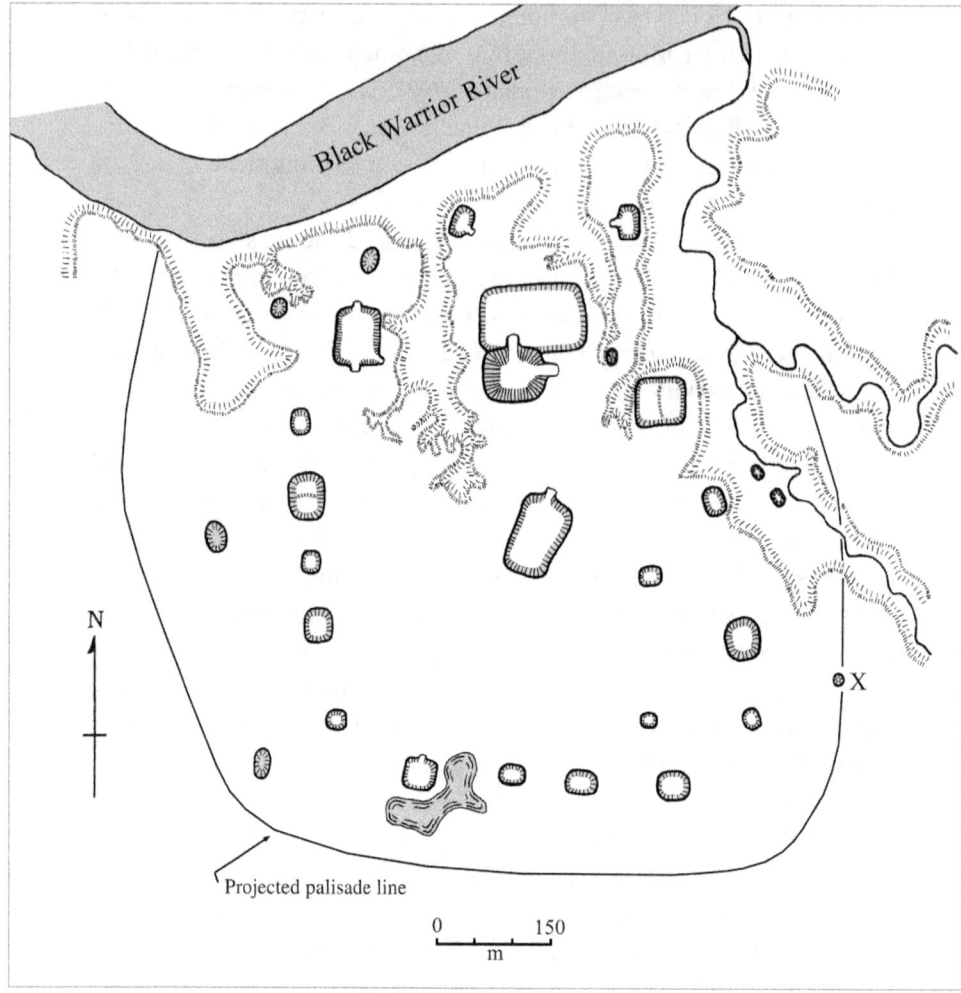

Figure 4.1. The Moundville site, showing the location of Mound X.

and only a brief description was published (Vogel and Allan 1985). The remnant mound was labeled X, the next unassigned letter for a mound at the site. The chronological placement of the palisade and Mound X remained ambiguous, however, in part because no report of the investigation was written, and the chronological subdivision of the Moundville I phase was not available at the time of excavation. Only later, after extensive investigations confirmed that construction of Moundville's spatial arrangement of multiple mounds, plaza, and palisade commenced around AD 1200, did the chronological implications of the superposition of the palisade over Mound X become clear: Mound X must date earlier in time. Commenting on this unusual situation, Knight and Steponaitis (1998: 16) proposed that Mound X had been "decommissioned" at the time when the new site plan was initiated.

Investigation of Mound X resumed in 2004 (figure 4.2). This time the goal was to identify a context in which aspiring elites and followers came together in a ritual format, in this case a platform mound, and to attempt to recover material evidence of associated activities that may have supported the institutionalization of leadership and rank just prior to the founding of Moundville's large polity (Blitz 2007: 5). The low relief of Mound X suggested that this goal was obtainable while adhering to the necessity of low-impact, small-scale archaeology at the protected site. In addition, it was essential to date the mound more securely and determine the precise relationship between the palisade lines and the mound. Within the study area indicated in figure 4.2, ground-penetrating radar delineated the strange elliptical shape of the remnant mound, apparently due to postdeposition destruction and alteration, and the gradiometer survey identified probable features (Blitz 2007: figures 11–12). With the remote-sensing results as a guide, a grid of 2-×-2-m units was placed to find the probable features and to intersect the unexcavated mound deposits exposed in 1983.

Figure 4.3 illustrates the excavation plan, showing the location of the 2004 units superimposed over the white-clay mound remnant and associated deposits exposed and mapped when the plow zone was removed in 1983. We delineated the mound edge in several places, visible as horizontal bands of contrasting soil deposits (Blitz 2007: figure 19). When we cut down into the clay construction stages and mound fill, it became clear that the mound had been severely truncated in the past. There were at least two substantial construction stages of contrasting white and reddish-brown clays obviously derived from different sources (Blitz 2007: figure 21). The mound stages yielded relatively few artifacts; more were secured from the dark, organically stained deposits along the mound periphery and from a submound occupation. In addition to burnished and unburnished potsherds, the mound deposits produced local and nonlocal chert tools and debitage, worked sandstone and greenstone, mica, a stone palette fragment, and evidence of a "pigment complex" (Knight 2004: 317) of crude sandstone slabs, abraded ferruginous chunks, and more refined fragments of pigment, all residues from red paint production. None of

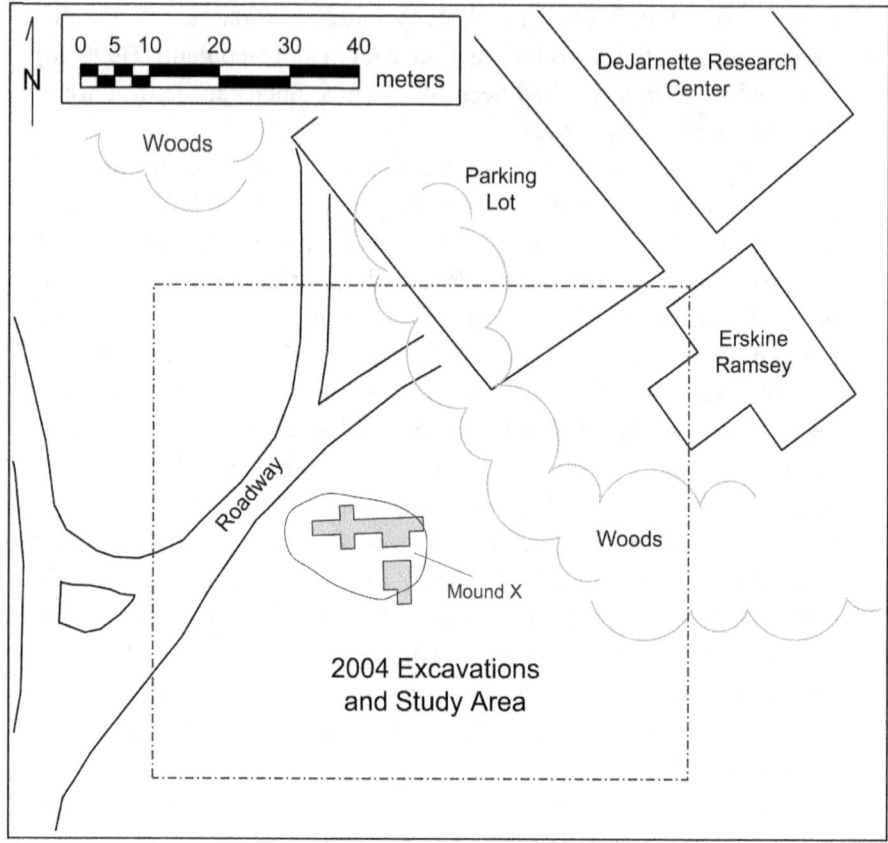

Figure 4.2. Mound X study area with the location of the 2004 excavation units (*shaded*).

these materials are exclusive to mound contexts at Moundville (Thompson 2011). As the Mound X excavation results are presented in greater detail elsewhere, it is the relationship between the palisade and the mound that most concerns us here.

Once the two palisade lines observed in 1983 were relocated (figure 4.4), we emptied the old trench that crosscut the palisade line at a right angle, and cut back the section wall to expose a fresh profile (figure 4.5). As can be seen in a 4-m-long profile view, the palisade lines are superimposed over the western portion of the mound stages and intrude into them. Diagnostic pottery recovered from the intrusive palisade trenches, Mound X, and the submound deposits date exclusively to the Moundville I phase, with ceramic attributes of the early Moundville I subphase present in the potentially mixed palisade trench and mound fill, as well

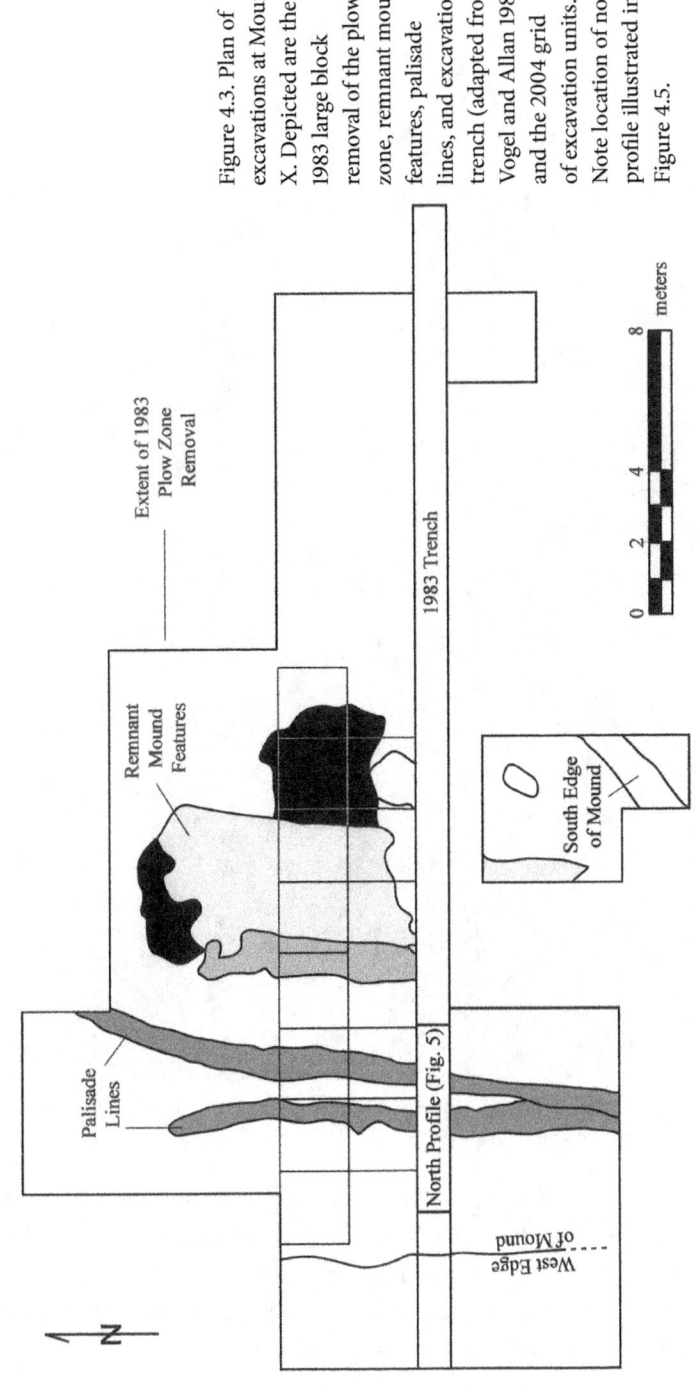

Figure 4.3. Plan of excavations at Mound X. Depicted are the 1983 large block removal of the plow zone, remnant mound features, palisade lines, and excavation trench (adapted from Vogel and Allan 1985) and the 2004 grid of excavation units. Note location of north profile illustrated in Figure 4.5.

Figure 4.4. Mound X palisade lines and refilled 1983 excavation trench exposed below plow zone, view north, 2004.

as in the sealed submound deposits. To reiterate, dating elsewhere at the site places palisade lines in late Moundville I (Scarry 1998); nothing from the Mound X palisade segment suggests otherwise. The 2004 excavations confirmed what was previously suspected: use of Mound X was terminated by late Moundville I times, the subphase that marks the initiation

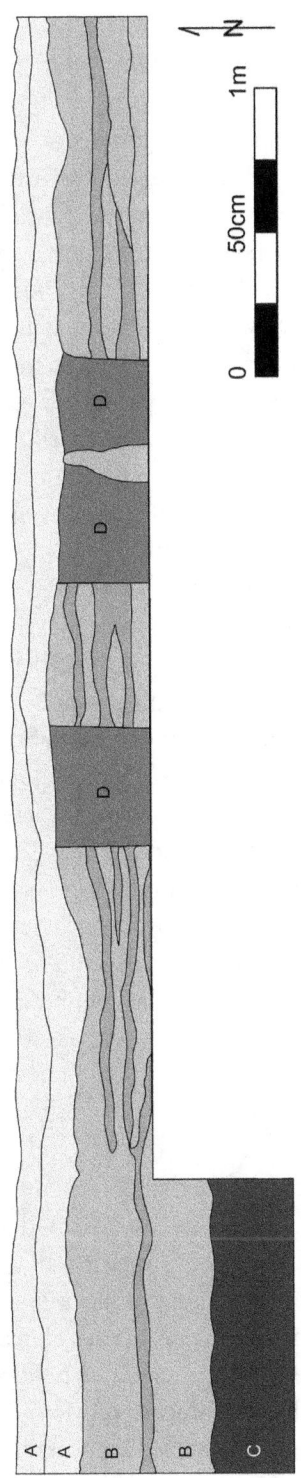

Figure 4.5. North profile at western portion of Mound X: (*A*) truncated and disturbed surface of Mound X; (*B*) mound construction episodes; (*C*) submound surface; and (*D*) palisade lines.

of the massive mound-plaza-palisade building effort that accompanied formation of the large polity.

It is clear from Vogel and Allan's investigations that the palisade lines that intersected Mound X were part of an extensive fortification wall that originated far beyond the mound. The Mound X palisade lines were not an integrated part of the mound's architecture, but a separate building project intentionally superimposed on the existing mound. Unlike some communities in antiquity where walls were permanent fixtures, Mississippian mounds and buildings were not constructed to abut fortification walls (Stout and Lewis 1998: 173–75). The palisade lines went right over Mound X, leaving most of it exposed outside the wall. This is highly unusual and requires explanation. Perhaps the people who used Mound X moved inside Moundville's walls and established a new mound in the new multiple-mound site plan. However, everything we know about the symbolism of Mississippian mounds suggests that people would be reluctant to abandon their mound. The readily observable fact that Mound X was already in place prior to the construction of the other mounds should have conferred an advantage for the affiliated group's assertions of origins and land-use rights as a "document" of prior claims, but only if the past was a valued resource. Furthermore, there is no apparent reason why either the route of the palisade or the placement of the later mounds could not have easily incorporated Mound X into the overall plan, but this did not happen. The location of Mound X, about 100 m east of the mound-plaza periphery, stands out as separate from the ordered arrangement of other mounds at the site. If the Mound X group did not move inside the walls, then it seems likely that the Moundville community excluded these people from a prominent position in the new social order.

Discussion

I contend that the transformation of Mound X from a sacred monument of a corporate group to an inconspicuous rise obscured by palisade walls is an archaeological example of repressive erasure, an intentional act of selective forgetting. Because platform mounds like Mound X were corporate-group symbols with the mnemonic properties of inscribed memory, and because repressive erasure is implemented by political agents (Connerton 2008: 69), it is likely that the erasure of Mound X was directed by the leadership of rival corporate groups. It appears that the Mound X group lost out in the struggle for rank and place at Moundville, and the mound was abandoned. Perhaps the divisive memories of the event were not conducive to the creation of the new collective identity that appeared with Moundville's emergent polity and necessitated selective forgetting. Consequently, Mound X was the target of repressive erasure, made feasible by the small size of the mound. Because platform mounds were revered symbols of social groups, the erasure of Mound X may have been an act of iconoclasm directed at a sacred object. Platform mounds were also directly linked to individuals of high rank as a provenience, symbol, and context for group leadership, and so the erasure of Mound X may have been an act of *damnatio memoriae* aimed at a specific person. Of course, the division between object, symbol, and person in many cultural contexts is very permeable. In this case the point is moot, because differentiation between these two variants of repressive erasure is not possible.

The identification of selective forgetting as repressive erasure in the archaeological record requires careful attention to context. There should be evidence of intentional efforts by political agents to remove, destroy, or obliterate. Not all forms of selective forgetting are repressive erasure (Connerton 2008: 69–70). For example, it is unlikely that the continuous additions of major construction stages to platform mounds represent repressive erasure. The cyclic refurbishing and expansion of platform mounds was a project in the production of social memory; world renewal and revitalization are the primary themes (Knight 1986). However, the addition of major construction stages is thought correlated with shifts in political leadership or corporate-group status (Anderson 1994: 126–29; Hally 1996: 95–97). Tensions, rivalries, and counterclaims about the legitimacy of the new leadership may have been resolved by the addition of a new mound stage; thus, each construction event had the potential to alter or edit social memory (Pauketat and Alt 2003). Such reinterpretations of social memory may be signaled by changes in the form, size, or spatial arrangement of mound summit buildings with the successive addition of stages (e.g., Pauketat 1993; Schnell et al. 1981). Each construction stage validated the new status of the corporate group or its leadership and promoted a new social memory; thus, the addition of mound stages was a claim of continuity through investment in a sacred and highly visible symbol, not the discontinuity of repressive erasure.

Mound abandonment, marked by termination rituals or a final capping of occupation summits, brought the continuous cycle of chiefly leadership and the associated social memory to an end (Hally 1996: 95–97); these closing acts may be examples of repressive erasure. Nonliterate social groups may retain and cultivate social memory that commemorates affiliation with important places long after abandonment (e.g., Colwell-Chanthaphonh and Ferguson 2006), but such memories are unlikely to pass through the generations without alteration by selective forgetting, because understandings of the past are conditioned by the ever-changing social circumstances of the present (Connerton 2008). Abandoned mounds and ancient sites were ideological resources on the landscape, highly visible, and available for refurbishing, revitalization, and the reinvention of social memory (Bradley 1998). Reoccupation and reuse of the abandoned special place, such as a mound or former house sites, was a common Mississippian practice (Blitz 1999); these acts were claims of continuity that initiated production of new social memory. Reoccupation and reuse need not imply any continuity of memory or ownership based on historical reality, as is demonstrated by the centuries-long temporal spans of cultural discontinuity between occupation episodes for some platform mounds (Blitz and Lorenz 2006: 93–94). Mississippian mound reoccupations are best interpreted as efforts to legitimate and document claims to localized ancestors, resources, and territory. Like the reuse of residential-group locations for cemeteries, mound reuse was an effort to inscribe memory on a visible sacred place to assert a claim of continuity (Blitz and Lorenz 2006: 95–96). The termination of Mound X, however, was selective forgetting as repressive erasure to ensure discontinuity and obliteration.

Space does not permit a review of the archaeological evidence for selective forgetting as repressive erasure at other late prehistoric sites in the Eastern Woodlands, but some well-known phenomena should be mentioned as possible examples: the smashed and burned sacred objects deposited in termination rituals at Ohio Hopewell ceremonial centers (Case and Carr 2008: 308–9), the breaking and hasty burial of the Etowah stone idols representing a pair of male and female beings (King 2003: 154–55), and the dismantling of massive wooden-post monuments at Cahokia (Young and Fowler 2000: 91, 276). One possible example of repressive erasure is particularly widespread: the construction of plazas over places formerly occupied by houses as part of the rapid reordering of social space that accompanied polity formation (e.g., Pauketat 2004: 76–78). Because plaza formation hides all reference points of prior use, plazas sever continuity with the past and inscribe new memory. This is the case at Moundville, where evidence is accumulating that the plaza was created by filling and leveling large areas, concurrent or close in time to the construction of the multiple-mound arrangement and palisade. Recent subsurface survey, shovel test pits, and small excavation units in the plaza have confirmed the presence of house remains and habitation debris beneath the plaza at scattered locations dating to early Moundville I, the time just prior to plaza construction (Lacquement 2009; Steponaitis et al. 2009; Thompson 2011; Thompson and Blitz 2009). With polity formation, families abandoned their former places of residence as domestic houses were obliterated and replaced by a new public space.

It is important to stress, however, that social memory and forms of forgetting have different agents and unfold at different rates. House forms, house distribution, pottery styles, and other aspects of domestic material culture changed during the Moundville I phase of polity formation. The causes of these domestic-level changes in material culture and ways of living were multiple and complex, and I will not attempt to parse them here. But much of the incorporated memory of households living in residential groups at Moundville was generated by incremental practice at the family and kin-group level over a span of several decades; traditional objects and practices such as pottery styles and house forms were replaced by new ones at a gradual, multigenerational pace. This kind of selective forgetting may be similar to Connerton's (2008: 64) "structural amnesia," in which people remember and value only those things that are socially important. As the new collective identity took hold at Moundville, these older practices were slowly relinquished. Household-level incorporated memory supported the conservative maintenance of tradition through practice and is best interpreted as resistance and resilience by family and kin group in the face of change instigated by political agents (Wilson, this volume). In contrast, the examples of inscribed social memory materialized by the mounds, plaza, and palisade of Moundville's site plan and the accompanying selective forgetting as repressive erasure were intentional and rapid acts directed by elite actors at the polity level. These acts reflect agent-driven efforts to advance a new ideology, alter or end traditional practice, rearrange social relations, and propel societies in new and different directions. For these reasons, the archaeological correlates of forgetting that accompanied such sweeping changes, such as the repressive erasure of Mound X, should not be dismissed as trivial curiosities.

Conclusion

The Moundville polity could not have come about without contradictions in the social uses of the past as competing corporate groups and leaders sought to create, legitimate, and strengthen their claims of rank. To resolve these contradictions, traditional practices were discontinued, and projects of inscribed social memory and selective forgetting were implemented by corporate groups and their leadership to naturalize the social inequities of the new order. As a large polity formed at Moundville, some people did not continue to build their houses at the location of the new plaza or continue to use established sacred places like Mound X. The termination of Mound X by repressive erasure suggests that ownership of a venerable piece of real estate or monument as a document of the sacred past was insufficient to ensure a place in the new order. In the relatively short, decade-scale time span that established the multiple-mound community plan, negotiations and decisions were made about who moved and who stayed, and what materializations from the past were kept or replaced. Families and corporate groups were made to understand that they could not do some of the important and valued things they had done in the past. Successful implementation of the new social order required the wielding of power by influential agents, actions that are detectable by archaeologists in the short-term, episodic, and bounded provenience of architectural construction, or destruction, as in the case of Mound X. At Moundville, I interpret the discontinuation of some traditional forms of material culture, the burial of domestic houses beneath the fills of a massive public plaza, and the erasure of Mound X as the archaeological correlates of selective forgetting to change social memory—a tactic in efforts to institutionalize unequal social relations and find ways to materialize the ideology of a new social order.

Acknowledgments

An earlier version of this paper was presented in the symposium "Neighborhood, Community, and Polity: Alternative Interpretations of Mississippian Societies," organized by John Blitz and Greg Wilson at the 72nd Annual Meeting of the Society for American Archaeology, Austin, Texas, in 2007. My thanks go to Vin Steponaitis and Margie Scarry for the invitation to contribute to this volume. Investigations at Mound X were undertaken as part of the Early Moundville Archaeological Project directed by the author and supported logistically by the University of Alabama Department of Anthropology and UA Museums, and financially by a grant from the University of Alabama College of Arts and Sciences. Finally, I wish to express my gratitude to Chris Peebles, who introduced me to the archaeology of Moundville. Thank you, Chris, for teaching me that archaeology could be something more than a chronicle of artifacts.

5

Was There a Moundville Medicine Society?

GEORGE E. LANKFORD

The site of Moundville has been linked in recent years to a specialized mortuary role. In their reassessment of more than a century of archaeological exploration of the site, Knight and Steponaitis (1998) concluded that, for many decades after the high point of its habitation around AD 1200, Moundville continued to be a place of interment far greater than its living population warranted. They suggested that Moundville became some sort of necropolis in its lengthy final stage before abandonment. Using a completely different approach—analysis of an iconographic cluster of Moundville ceramic designs—I completed a study in 1996 in which I found that a significant number of graphic motifs at Moundville were related to the myths and beliefs of the journey of souls after death (Lankford 2007a, 2007c).

The fact that two separate and different studies produced a focus on specialized mortuary activity at Moundville calls for further consideration. The hypothesis advanced by Knight and Steponaitis suggests that Moundville experienced a social transformation from vibrant community at a large and complex mound site to a sparsely populated sacred area for mortuary rites and burials—a necropolis. That putative transformation needs some explanation of its dynamics and the structures involved, particularly if other sites can be identified as having experienced a similar transformation. How does a thriving community become a necropolis?

In the past few years of work by scholars focused on the Mississippian art known by various names in the past, such as the Southeastern Ceremonial Complex, it has become increasingly clear that the regional centers where such imagery appears were far from passive recipients of other people's creations. The local nature of art forms becomes emphasized with every new study, it seems, and I have personally elected to follow the path suggested by Knight—that we would do well to retire the terminology of overarching concepts, so that we can focus on the regional evidence (Knight 2006).

Even so, the examination of widely known icons embedded in the corpus of local art forms continues to raise the complex issue of diffusion. When identical or related images and art forms appear in different locations, by what process did they come there? Their functions and meanings may be localized, but they still bear witness to linkage with locations farther away. At the very minimum, stimulus diffusion was at work in the larger Mississippian world, whatever the means of transmission.

When it comes to mortuary symbolism and rituals, this issue of diffusion seems an important question to pursue, if only because the societal treatment of death is likely to be a universal concern. If it is correct that Moundville was transformed into a necropolis, it could have been a unique occurrence, but it seems just as likely that there were relevant ideas and stories floating around in the Mississippian sphere that were available for adoption, reaction, rejection, or adaptation.

The hypothesis examined in this paper can be simply stated:

In Mississippian times (ca. AD 1300?) a sodality of shamans organized around health and death issues arose in the upper Mississippi–Great Lakes area and diffused over a wide area, even as far as Moundville. Through unknown mechanisms of diffusion, it took root in a variety of societies, taking the form of a medicine lodge, an organization of religious specialists with ritual activities, mythological charters, and artistic symbols such as owl effigies. At Moundville this lodge became a matrix for the elaboration of symbolism into a variety of art forms, including Hemphill Engraved ceramic decoration focused on a set of mortuary designs related to the lodge's emphasis. While other sodalities may also have flourished at the site, the mortuary focus predominated in Moundville's final centuries, and the lodge may be considered a vital part of the site's transformation into a necropolis.

Assessing such a complex set of hypotheses about prehistoric social development is difficult, especially in regard to finding relevant ethnographic sources. One very famous and well-studied example of a mortuary sodality provides material for study, and it is known to have been widely diffused. More specifically, the Midewiwin of the Central Algonkian and Siouan peoples seems worth examining for ideas and practices that could have spread to Moundville. This study attempts to make the case for such a relationship.

Why the Midewiwin?

At first glance, selecting the Midewiwin for examination in thinking about Moundville seems a strange choice, for its hearth in the Great Lakes region is far from central Alabama, and there is a general consensus that it has its roots in the somewhat alien cultural realm of the Central Algonkian peoples such as the Ojibwa, Pottawatomie, and Menomini. Yet a map of the occurrence of the Midewiwin and related forms of the medicine lodge reveals an important trait—it was diffused over a wide area and across linguistic boundaries (figure 5.1). Scholars of the phenomenon are not in complete agreement about the participants in the diffusion, because only the Ojibwa name or one or two traits is not adequate for identification, given the likelihood of local adaptation. Some forms, especially among the Siouan-speakers, bear names such as "Shell Society" and "Pebble Society" (Omaha) and "medicine lodge" (Winnebago). A recent listing of tribal groups that are believed to have had the Midewiwin or Midewiwin-like societies was compiled by Weeks (2009: 4). Among Algonkian speakers, he names "the Cree, Fox, Illinois, Kickapoo, Menominee, Miami, Ottawa, Pottawatomie, and Sauk, and possibly the Delaware, Penobscot, and Shawnee"; among Siouan speakers, he lists "the Dakota, Ioway, Kansa, Omaha, Otoe, Ponca, and Winnebago." Other disputed possibilities include the Pawnee, Mandan, Hidatsa, and Osage, but they have not been charted here.

This distribution is particularly interesting from the viewpoint of Moundville studies, because it includes a number of people who are known to be part of the group manifesting the production and use of Mississippian religious art, especially the ancestral Chiwere and Dhegiha Siouan-speakers, who are likely to have roots in the Cahokian phenomenon of a millennium ago. Since the southeastern Muskogean-speaking peoples were participants in the distribution of Mississippian iconographic art and share some important mythic traditions with the Mississippi Valley tribes, the existence of a social structure known to have been diffused in

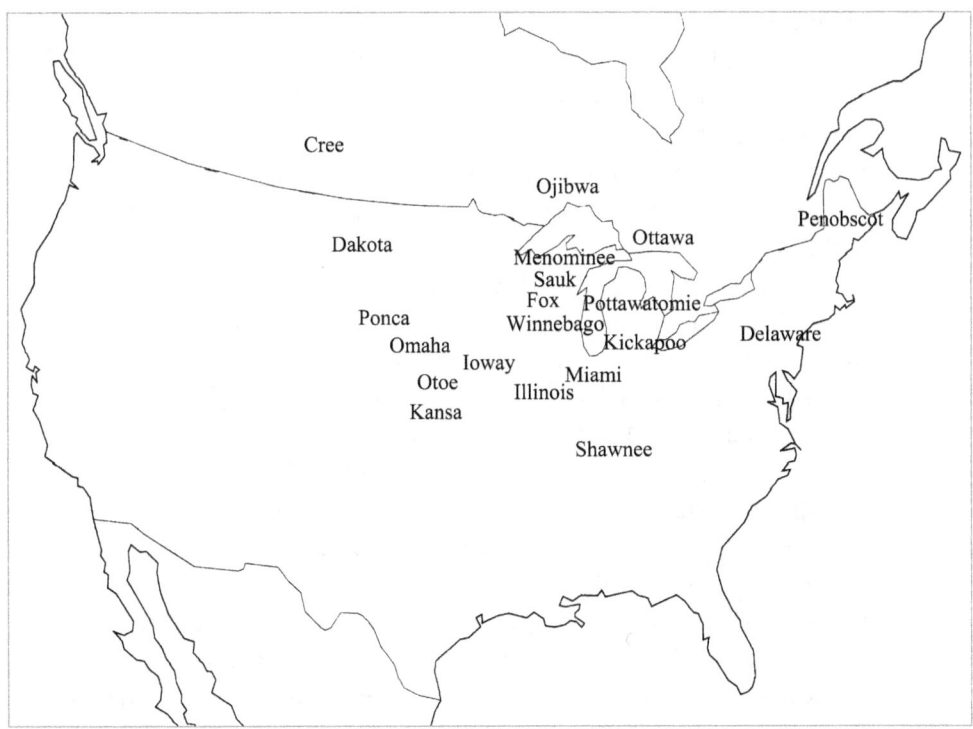

Figure 5.1. Known distribution of medicine lodges related to the Midé Society (based on Weeks 2009: 4).

the latter group raises the question of whether it was also presented to the southeasterners for their adoption.

So what was the Midé Society? The Midewiwin ("Midé Society") deals with some of the very issues that appear to be embedded in the Moundville iconographic art—healing power and death. The Midé Society is inherently interesting, not only because it was a diffused social phenomenon, but also because it seems an improbable creation. It was a sodality of shamans ("Midé"), a phrase that seems almost paradoxical. In religious studies, anthropologists have long been accustomed to contrasting shamans and priests, both in their psychology and in their social roles. Shamans are usually presented as individuals who have received special powers directly from the cosmic Powers by visions and out-of-body travel. These gifts made them the healers and seers of society, usually acting individually, somewhat like doctors in private practice. By contrast, priests are usually understood to be ritual functionaries who preserve the corporate traditions and control the public ritual activities to ensure accuracy and social cohesion. A sodality of priests has the important task of maintaining quality control in the religious life of the society. It was this conceptual conundrum—the paradox of individualistic shamans joining a society of the likeminded—that has provoked a variety of scholarly interpretations of the Midewiwin.

Fascinating as this paradoxical quality is, though, the importance of the Midé Society for broader study lies in the fact of its diffusion. As a model of the mechanisms of diffusion of prehistoric art and iconography, the Midewiwin provides a much-studied example of an early diffusion.

Even though the Midé Society is well known, it will be helpful to summarize the major characteristics, focusing on the classic presentation of the Ojibwa version by Hoffman (1891). One of the functions filled by the medicine lodge was to serve as an academy (Landes 1968: 42). Those who wished to become members of the lodge applied for instruction and initiation in a sequence of four (some say eight) stages of complexity and power. They paid for the privilege with a significant amount of goods, a cost that kept most people at the first or second degree. The initiation consisted of private instruction followed by a semipublic set of rituals in which the creation myths were recited and the initiate was "killed" by being "shot" with small shells (*megis*), propelled from an otter-skin medicine pouch, and resurrected with the ability to cough up the shell that killed him. With each degree the initiate's powers were understood to increase in specific ways, and so the series of rituals also functioned in the tribe to identify the power levels and prestige of the practitioners. The general public was allowed to watch at least part of the initiatory rites, thus creating a societal understanding of the shamanistic traditions and practices. From the public's view, the rites had considerable entertainment value, for the lodge members participated in both the death-and-resurrection rituals and the ancient shamanistic "jugglery" of making animal skins move, of handling hot objects, and so on. This sort of presentation led Hoffman (1891: 151) to offer a somewhat cynical characterization of the lodge: it gives "a certain class of ambitious men and women sufficient influence through their acknowledged power of exorcism and necromancy to lead a comfortable life at the expense of the credulous." Hoffman was aware of the fact that in many Ojibwa communities almost all of the leadership of the town were members of the Midé Society, regardless of their other roles, although their Midé positions may not have reflected their social ranking.

How Old Is the Midé Society?

Before we can even begin to examine the dynamics of the medicine-society movement, two issues need to be addressed: (1) the age of the Midé Society and (2) the dual nature of the medicine society's composition.

How old is the Midewiwin? Did it exist in Mississippian times? If not, then the issue of Midé influence on Moundville is irrelevant. Hoffman did not raise the question, for he assumed that it was "traditional" among the Ojibwa, as represented by their charter myths. It was Keesing (1939), an ethnographer of the Menomini tribe, who opened the debate by arguing that the Midewiwin began as a revitalization movement and thus had a recent origin. Hickerson (1962: 404), on the basis of his ethnographic study of the Ojibwa, accepted the late dating: "the Midewiwin of the Chippewa and contiguous central Algonquian peoples was not an aboriginal ceremonial, but developed in post-contact times." The reason for its development, Hickerson hypothesized, was a seventeenth-century change in the social and political organization of the proto-Ojibwa: "a new tribal unity which stemmed from the coming together and integration of once discrete autonomous kindreds" (Hickerson 1962: 404–5).

This late dating for the creation of the Midé lodge gives the impression that Hickerson saw that institution as part of a revitalization movement, as Keesing argued, but Hickerson was at pains to deny that interpretation. He contrasted his view with that of Keesing, who "viewed the Mitawin [Midewiwin] as a nativistic cult, arising as a response to European encroachment. I saw in it a reflex of the development of tribal solidarity" (Hickerson 1962: 405). Hickerson's argument even provided a location—the large village of Chequamegon on the southern shore of Lake Superior, "the largest and most important of all the historic Chippewa settlements" (1963: 72). Further, he suggested a date for the new organization: it developed in the two decades from 1660 to 1680 and emerged "as a full-blown ceremonial at about the turn of the eighteenth century" (1963: 76).

Hickerson's view found acceptance among later interpreters of Central Algonkian history, but there is also a tradition of dissent. The issue is still unresolved after decades, largely because the supporting evidence for either side is so sparse. The major documentary evidence for the earlier existence of the Midewiwin comes from the observations of a Huron medicine society in 1636 by Jean Brébeuf and in 1645–1646 by Paul Ragueneau (Thwaites 1896–1901: 10: 207, 209, 30: 23), and an account of an undated seventeenth-century Illinois–Miami medicine society by Pierre Deliette (Pease and Werner 1934: 369–71). Hickerson accepted the possibility that these were indeed sightings of medicine societies, but only "among the economically more advanced tribes of the eastern woodlands in the seventeenth century" (Hickerson 1963: 75).

Ultimately, the basis for Hickerson's hypothesis of a late-seventeenth-century origin of the Ojibwa Midé Society is an argument from silence:

> Not a suggestion exists in the writings of the Jesuits or of Perrot, who knew those peoples as no one else knew them, that in the seventeenth century there were organized medicine cults. On the other hand, the weight of evidence from source material indicates that medicinal and magical practices were in the hands of shamans, individual practitioners. (Hickerson 1963: 76)

Hickerson's position thus seems to recognize the possibility of early medicine societies, for he recognized that the medicine lodge, whenever founded, "incorporated, as its main external expression, medicinal practices rooted in the aboriginal past" (Hickerson 1962: 405). The issue thus became one of distinguishing between the two structures. Hickerson saw a threefold standard:

> Three features distinguish it from earlier shamanistic practice: (1) The regular recurrence of the celebration; (2) an organized priesthood; and (3) the incorporation of a tribal tradition. These three features, in the light of the sociopolitical changes in Chippewa organization discussed above, may be seen to provide a basis for an annual tribal gathering, for a solution to the problem of authority in the new tribal group, and for the tribal solidarity of the discrete kin-groups now combining under a single political authority. (Hickerson 1963: 76)

These three traits fit nicely with his hypothesis of the Midewiwin's role of creating a societal structure, but there are some questions that need to be raised about them. First, the "regular recurrence" of the ceremonies seems in some cases to have been an annual one, but there are also indications that they could be called by any member wanting to be the host. There were also four degrees of ceremony, and each would likely be called on the basis of need—the fourth-degree ritual was apparently seldom performed. Then, too, the town inhabitants who were not members were permitted to be spectators only. The solidarity function of the lodge seems weak. Second, the "organized priesthood" is problematic, because the ceremonies were conducted by the various hosts, who were selected anew for each occasion. It may be that Hickerson was focusing more on the ceremonial function of the Midé lodge, reasoning that there was a "priestly" role manifested in the very sponsoring of a public ritual. Third, the "incorporation" of a tribal tradition probably refers to the use of foundation myths as part of the Midewiwin, but that is a standard feature of all bundle holders—they preserve and tell the charter myths of the people, their society, and their sodalities. It is difficult to identify the medicine lodge as unique or even unusual in this way.

Moreover, the idea that these three traits can serve to distinguish the presence of the medicine lodge seems debatable, for it is not clear how they would be observed, particularly by European newcomers. Hickerson expressed that ambiguity by suggesting that even Raudot's 1710 observation of a proto-Chippewa Midé cult is questionable: "even in that description, lacking in detail as it is, we are not yet certain that it was the full-fledged Midewiwin" (Hickerson 1962: 418).

In a more recent assessment of the medicine society, Schlesier disagreed with Hickerson's explanation of its origin. His major argument is that Hickerson had misread the nature of the late seventeenth-century events impacting the Great Lakes tribes. Instead of Hickerson's model of an evolutionary change in the context of fur trade and acculturation to the European presence, Schlesier offered a view of the times as disastrous for the Indians, due to massive population loss by disease and warfare, together with forced migrations and realignments—precisely the conditions usually understood to provoke revitalization movements. He thus agreed, "It was both 'nativistic' and 'revivalistic,' to use Hickerson's terms" (Schlesier 1990: 9–11). In this reassessment of the Midé Society, Schlesier accepted Hickerson's late dating (except that he saw the sodality as fully formed by the 1660s rather than the 1680s), which fits well with his argument that the lodge was an excellent example of a revitalization movement.

A major conceptual problem with Keesing's and Schlesier's categorizing the Midewiwin as a revitalization religious movement, however, is that some of the salient characteristics of such religious organizations seem to be missing. There is no identifiable "prophet," for example. No reformer with a new vision appears in the origin legendry, unless the minority representation of "Cutfoot" as the recipient of the Midewiwin lore is a weak memory of a prophet (Landes 1968: 110–11, quoted in Angel 2002: 56–57). Certainly there is no historical prophet recorded for the seventeenth- and eighteenth-century Ojibwas. Nor does there seem to be much defining of Ojibwa religion and life in contrast to the European worldview offered by the French and Jesuits, although Schlesier sought to identify traces of that opposition in the restriction of the Path of Souls to Midé members (Schlesier 1990: 11).

In 2002 yet another interpretation of the Midewiwin was offered. Angel portrayed the society as an early development in Ojibwa life, expressing traditional shamanic understanding and being innovative only in institutionalizing the practice of medicine as a demonstration of core beliefs and values (Angel 2002). He affirmed Schlesier's reading of the seventeenth century as a time of upheaval and stress for the Ojibwa, but he rejected the argument that the Midewiwin was founded as a revitalization movement. Instead, Angel reaffirmed the position that the Midé Society was a sodality whose history reflected the changes being incorporated "into the basic structure of the Ojibwa worldview. The result was not a radical break with the past, but was, instead, part of a gradual adaptation process, which had been going on long before the arrival of Europeans" (Angel 2002: 73). Angel ultimately concluded that the questions of the date, location, and circumstances of the creation of the Midé Society cannot be answered with the available evidence, but he emphasized the continuity of the beliefs and practices of the Midewiwin from precolonial times.

One result of this brief survey of some of the key studies of the Midewiwin is the lack of chronological clarity. Despite the popular notion that it has a seventeenth-century origin, with many interpreters adopting the categorization of it as a response to European contact, that is by no means a necessary conclusion. Students of the movement are ranged on both sides of the debate. A nonexhaustive listing of those who argue for precolonial origins must include the following: Hoffman (1891), Warren (1984), Kinietz (1940), Johnston (1976, 1982), Howard (1977), Benton-Banai (1988), Deleary (1990), Angel (2002), and Weeks (2009). Those who see it as a revitalization movement include: Hickerson (1962, 1963), Landes

(1968), Dewdney (1975), Blessing (1977), Harrison (1982), Vecsey (1984), Grim (1983), and Schlesier (1990).

In some cases it is hard to escape the conclusion that the two poles of the discussion, a seventeenth-century date and response to European presence, have become a circular argument, each pole supporting the other. Today that seems a weaker stance than it used to be, because the possibility of *prehistoric* organizations and movements that exhibit characteristics of historic revitalization movements has been fruitfully explored (Harkin 2007). That revitalization-causing movements necessarily require threat from technologically superior societies has been questioned, raising the possibility of broadening the understanding of the causes of such movements or even creating a new category of religious patterns.

An important addition to the discussion of the age of the Midewiwin has recently been offered by Weeks (2009). In a lengthy study he expanded the evidentiary base for the determination of the age of the Midewiwin, adding to the historical documents the categories of origin stories, archaeological sites, and iconography. With a dozen prehistoric archaeological sites and two radiocarbon dates (AD 1560 ± 70 [cal 1434–1629] and AD 1320 ± 75), he made a post-contact dating for the origin of the Midewiwin appear unlikely (Weeks 2009: 32; also see Crane and Griffin 1963: 233; Kigoshi et al. 1969: 320). His conclusion sets the new proposition for the dating debate: "When taken together, analyses of the four data sets, including colonial documents, origin narratives, archaeological excavations, and rock paintings, seem to be roughly in agreement that the hypothesis of prehistoric Midewiwin origins is the most probable" (2009: 724–25).

Although the actual age of the Midewiwin remains to be established, the possibility of a medicine lodge in Mississippian times now appears reasonable. That raises anew the issue of how such a sodality would be recognized by archaeologists and ethnographers. It seems a minimal standard to set as identifying marks of the Midé Society such concrete characteristics as a physical lodge structure, well described in later ethnography, and the practice of shooting with shells and the otter pouch, with death and resurrection as the dramatic result, a clear extension of traditional shamanism into medicine lodge ritual-as-performance. The latter might be seen in the ground as medicine bags and small shells from exotic sources or small polished stones (as described for the Pebble Society of the Omahas). Neither of these characteristics—the lodge structure or the use of shells and pouch—is clearly described in the ethnographic literature until long after the medicine lodge must have been in existence, and Weeks found that despite wide belief that the trait unites the various forms of historic medicine lodges, only 31 percent of the accounts actually identify the shooting-rite trait as present (Weeks 2009: 5, 716). Even so, a further trait (albeit nonmaterial) that might be an indicator of the medicine lodge's presence is the tale of the "Bead Spitter," an enigmatic story that features a societal leader (chief? priest?) who spits shells in a ritual context (see Lankford 2007a: 107–13 for an examination of this story). Another possible indicator of a lodge is the use of owl images (discussed below).

An Additional Complexity: Two Lodges

One further complexity in establishing the origin and diffusion of the medicine society has been little explored by the interpreters. Hoffman's classic study of the Ojibwa Midé Society makes it clear that he was aware of an extraordinary fact about the organization: it had a dual form. When one of the members died, the standard way of replacing the deceased was a special ritual procedure in which the family-chosen successor was validated by visiting the spirit powers and even the deceased himself. In this process the Midé lodge membership assumed a different ritual posture and affiliation, becoming members of the "Ghost Lodge." In some Ojibwa villages they built a new lodge for the ritual, one that was oriented north–south rather than the standard east–west alignment of the Midé lodge (Hoffman 1891; Landes 1968). A likely explanation of this architectural feature is that the east–west movement of the Above World marks the road of life, whereas the north–south direction is for death. It appears that the concept is more than metaphor, for it reflects an empirical reality: the north–south direction of the Milky Way, which was believed to be the Path of Souls (Lankford 2007a: 201–25, 2007c). When the mortuary ritual was completed, the north–south lodge was abandoned in favor of the traditional east–west "road of life." The separateness of the Ghost Lodge from the Midewiwin is visually indicated in some of the birch-bark scrolls that contain the ritual diagrams for the medicine lodge. In one, the Red Lake Scroll, the Ghost Lodge ritual mnemonic is drawn alongside the Midé four-degree ritual sequence, but with no connection between them (figure 5.2).

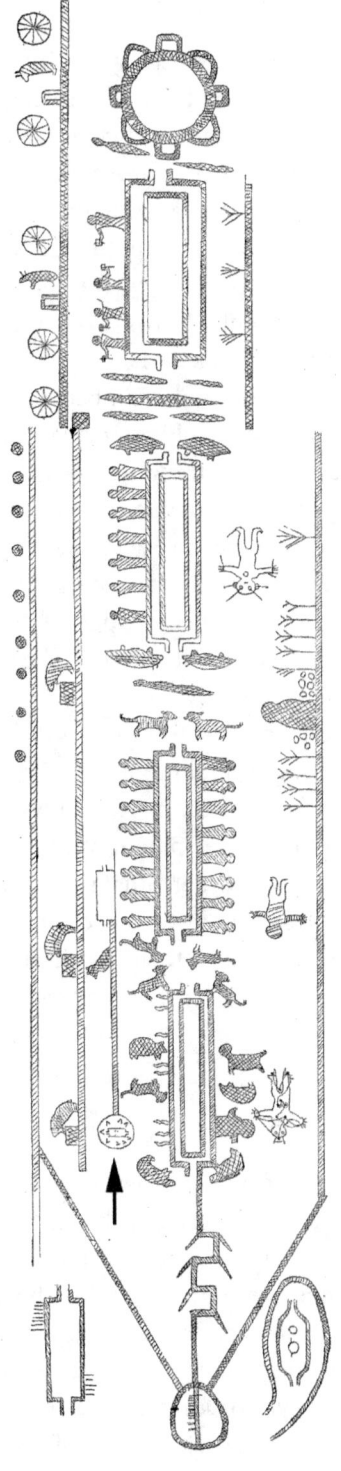

Figure 5.2. The Red Lake Scroll, a mnemonic chart of the ritual flow of the Midewiwin among the Ojibwa (after Hoffman 1891: Plate 3a). The arrow points to the separate Ghost Lodge marker (see Figure 5.4c).

While this Ghost Lodge structure is clearly a case of alternate ritual posture for a single organization, it may have a more complex ancestry than just a ritual nuance developed in the practice of the Midewiwin. In recent studies of the "Orpheus" myth in North America, a double diffusion process has been suggested as an explanation of a peculiarity in the pattern (Brumbaugh 1995; Hultkrantz 1957; Lankford 2007a: 217-23). The text as collected in the late nineteenth century—the charter myth of the Ghost Dance revitalization movement—shows a continental diffusion, but with the Plains tribes strangely weak or lacking the death myth. It has been suggested by both Hultkrantz and Brumbaugh that the historical movement drew its materials from an older mortuary tradition in the Eastern Woodlands. This hypothesis is strengthened by the existence in the east of two different oicotypes of the myth of the journey to the realm of the dead—the Orpheus quest and the men who take the journey as an adventure (Lankford 2007a: 215-23). A third form might be an unknown narrative as told in the Ghost Lodge that became part of the Midé Society and may not have been collected as a public myth in the tribes that had the society—hence, the Plains omission.

While this is a big hypothesis to draw from just a diffusion study of myth, it has the virtue of resolving several problems in the prehistory of mortuary ritual in eastern North America. It also suggests another possibility in the reconstruction of the development of the Midewiwin: the Ghost Lodge may have been an even earlier ritual structure that became embedded in the Midewiwin, resulting in the obscuring of its separate trajectory through time. If this is correct, then it indicates that the two phenomena need to be dated separately, for they may have quite different histories.

An Additional Character: The Owl

In the modern American Indian world the belief in witches is persistent and widespread. The general understanding is that witches are people who have the power to cause illness or death to other humans, and in many groups this belief is coupled with the belief that this power can be either unconsciously or consciously used. In the latter case, the witch is a practitioner of spells and is generally known or suspected to have sought the power and training deliberately in order to cause harm. This character of the witch is a logical extension of the basic concept of shamanistic heal-

Figure 5.3. A detail from the Red Lake Scroll. The dark figure in the center represents the powerful adept who has hidden himself in isolation in the forest in order to use his second- or third-degree power for bad purposes (Hoffman 1891: Plate 3a).

ing: if a person can gain enough spiritual power to heal illnesses, then that person can also use it to hurt or kill. The difference will lie in the personality and goals of the individual person of power.

The Midé Society, as an organization of people of power, was well aware of the danger of the misuse of that power. One of the Ojibwa scrolls even graphically offered a reminder to the shamans by portraying one second-degree holder as withdrawn into the woods and living in the dark (figure 5.3). The danger of witchcraft was pointed out as a cautionary warning for all Midé.

Belief in witchcraft is such an inherent part of the logic of the Midewiwin that diffusion does not even have to be invoked to explain why it is so widespread. So, too, the symbol of the witch's patron spirit, the owl, seems subject to independent invention, simply because the owl is the avian predator of the night. The widespread belief that the owl is both patron spirit and alternate form of the witch is thus an additional belief to be expected in the witchcraft complex.

An unexpected part of the complex, though, is the owl's role in the positive side of the power organization. Since the owl is identified as an important source of spiritual power, it should come as no surprise to find the owl present in both medicine lodge and Ghost Lodge ritual and belief. Hennepin observed that "some of them have a lean Raven, which they carry always along with them, and which they say is the Master of their Life; others have an Owl, and some again a Bone, a Sea-Shell, or some such thing" (quoted in Hoffman 1891: 152; note the shaman speaking to his owl guide in the scroll image in figure 5.4a).

In the Ojibwa scrolls the owl is portrayed as a patron of all four of the degree rituals. One of the distinguishing marks of the physical lodge is the presence of a post erected on the center line of the lodge, on top of which

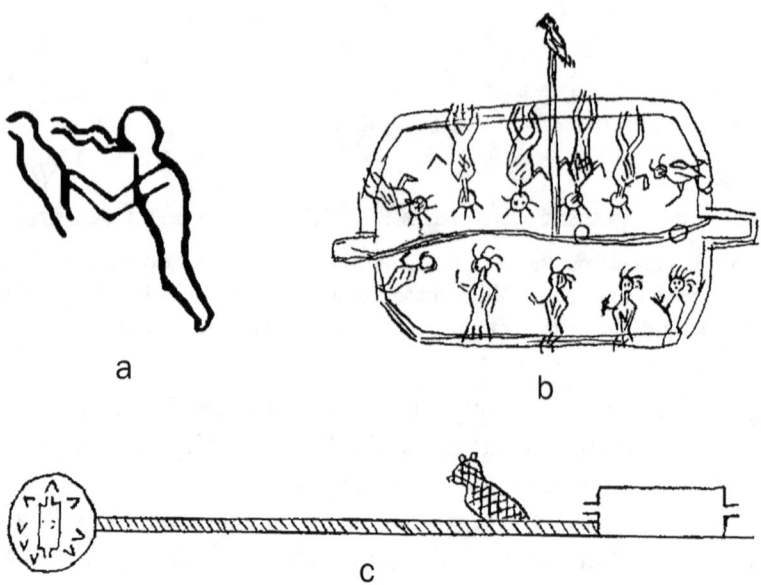

Figure 5.4. Owls depicted in Midewiwin bark scrolls: (*a*) a society member speaking to an owl spirit guide (Hoffman 1891: 293); (*b*) a sketch of a first-degree lodge from a Midé birch-bark scroll, Ojibwa's Record (Hoffman 1891: plate 8); (*c*) an owl guide on the path from the medicine lodge at right to the Ghost Lodge at left, as shown on the Red Lake Scroll (Hoffman 1891: Plate 3a).

is a patron of that particular degree rite. The first-degree lodge has a single post bearing an owl (figure 5.4b). The successive-degree lodges have two, three, and four posts, but in every lodge construction, at least one post is surmounted by the owl (Hoffman 1891: 181–82).

This distinctive feature calls to mind the early historic drawings of Lower Mississippi Valley temples with their birds on posts rising above the roofline, a feature not explained in ethnographic notes (figure 5.5). If the surviving illustrations from the Acolapissa and Natchez were mortuary temples (which the Natchez temple was known to be [Swanton 1911]), then a connection with the medicine lodge would seem even more likely, since the owl who is patron of the Midewiwin also serves as psychopomp and spiritual adviser in the Ghost Lodge's journey to the realm of the dead (see figure 5.4c).

In an ethnographic survey of the functions of the owl in Indian thought, Wilson (1950) found that owls served as personal guardian spirits, soothsayers, protectors of the dead, weather predictors, teachers of medicinal knowledge, givers of power, and friends of humans. Among

Figure 5.5. Two temples from the Lower Mississippi Valley and a Midé lodge: (*top*) Natchez temple in 1725 as depicted by Le Page du Pratz (1758: 3: 55); (*middle*) Acolapissa temple painted by DeBatz in 1732 (Bushnell 1927: 3–4, Plate 1); (*bottom*) a third-degree Midé lodge as shown on the Red Lake Scroll (Hoffman 1891: plate 8).

the ethnographic notes gathered from the tribes with known medicine lodges, Wilson listed these practices:

> Ojibwa medicine men placed a stuffed owl near them when they were preparing their medicine that it might "see if they do it right" (Densmore 1928: 326).
>
> Among the Menominee the owl sits "by the burial place of the dead to see that their resting place is not disturbed" (Hoffman 1896: 91). The Menominee Owl Dance was "founded upon the legend that it was the owl that gave the first gift of medicine to the Indians by which they were able to secure success in all their undertakings" (Densmore 1932: 194). "The Menominee warrior placed the skins of two kinds of owls in his war bundle" (Densmore 1932: 196).
>
> The owl carried into war in a sacred bundle by the Fox Indians bestowed these blessings: "He will be able to cross deep and wide rivers without obstruction and be able to heal the wounded" (Michelson 1921: 12).

At the end of his survey of owl ethnography, Wilson concluded that "in many sections the owl is a portentously sacred bird," and that "a kindly, beneficent aspect of the owl is frequently met with, thus dispelling the idea that the American Indian generally looked upon this creature as a bird of ill omen and evil influence" (Wilson 1950: 344).

Wilson's survey is a helpful correction of the impression that the owl is solely a malevolent power in the Indian worldview. This positive perspective helps to explain why owls have so frequently been encountered in Mississippian archaeological contexts. They were commonly manufactured in the Cumberland and Mississippi Valleys as pottery effigy bottles, rim effigies on pottery bowls, and carved-stone figures (e.g., Cox 1985: 34, Plate 2; Hathcock 1988: 112–17; Miller 1992; Moore and Smith 2009). They were used in stuffed form in rituals such as the Midewiwin (where they were placed on posts in the lodge) and deposited in sacred bundles as both stuffed effigies and as skins.

This larger view of the owl as a spirit patron and central figure in the medicine lodge makes it tempting to include the owl, especially the ceramic versions, as an additional marker indicating the former presence of a medicine lodge or shaman. Unfortunately, distinguishing between owl images as indicators of lodge versus individual shaman usage seems unlikely, unless specific types of owl figures can be linked to known lodge sites. At present, the ethnographic data do not distinguish medicine-lodge use, but the distribution of ceramic owl effigies, when studied and plotted by type, may fit with the known or suspected distribution of medicine lodges. That would be an important conclusion. Such a research project is beyond the scope of this chapter, but the data collection for an owl distribution study is under way (Kevin Smith, personal communication, 2008).

What about Moundville?

The primary goal of this paper is to present the case for some manifestation of a medicine lodge at Moundville in Mississippian times. The entire discussion thus far has made few references to Alabama, because the problem of the prehistoric existence and nature of a medicine lodge is itself a complex one that called for first consideration. The focus on the Midewiwin began in a concern to identify models of mechanisms that could explain the prehistoric diffusion of ritual practices and iconographic art over great distances. In this study so far, the phenomenon of an organized society of shamanic healers has been explored in regard to its nature, history, and possible origin. Unfortunately, the survey has revealed little of the dynamics of the diffusion process itself. The bare memory that "we received this ceremony from" remains unsupported as to precise mechanisms—marriage, amalgamation, apprenticeship, and other hypotheses. Yet the diffusion did occur.

What has been discovered in this exploration can be summarized as a few propositions:

1. A clear model of a medicine society that survived into historical times is the Midewiwin, and related lodge forms from the Central Algonkian and Siouan tribes.
2. Despite efforts to see its origin among the Ojibwa as postdating European contact, evidence from oral tradition, historical documents, archaeology, and iconography presents a compelling case that the medicine lodge tradition dates from Mississippian times or even earlier. Such a case can be made even if Hickerson was correct in seeing this tradition as a recent construct or adaptation in Ojibwa life.
3. Identifying the Midewiwin in the ethnographic accounts is not simple, because of the ambiguity of the authors' notes and the

difficulty of specifying what constitutes a set of legitimate markers of diffused medicine lodges after local adaptation has wrought its changes.

4. An important hindrance is the realization that the Midewiwin contains both the healing lodge and the mortuary lodge, which may indicate two separate traditions that have been brought together at some point into a single organizational structure. The possibility that the Ghost Lodge has a separate history makes the question of medicine lodge origins very complex indeed, for it suggests that separate bundles of traits could have diffused without the rest of the cult complex, including art and myth.

5. The ethnological markers for the former presence of a Midé lodge are *megis* shells, otter-skin pouches, rituals of death and resurrection by means of shooting shells, and possibly the "Bead Spitter" myth incorporating that ritual. The Ghost Lodge mythic correlate is the "Orpheus" story that seems to be a charter for mortuary belief and practice. The presence of any of these markers, however, was likely governed by local adaptation, and thus no single trait can be considered a sine qua non for the medicine lodge.

6. The archaeological markers for the existence of a medicine lodge are few in number: shell beads (of limited use, since they are ubiquitous in Mississippian life), lodge patterns in the ground (difficult to identify as medicine lodges if they do not follow the historical Ojibwa Midewiwin pattern), ceramic owl effigies (although it seems impossible to distinguish individual shamanic use from Midé–Ghost Lodge ritual use), and bundles containing owls, otter skins, shells, or related lodge artifacts. The posts on the center line of the lodge may be an important marker, seen as postmolds archaeologically.

In the light of these propositions, was the medicine lodge at Moundville? There are only a few vague hints of the possibility. Peebles (1978: 377–78) has reported the existence of a large structure adjacent to Mound Q, and Knight has excavated possible lodge structures on Mound E and Mound V. Master's theses provided early reports on what was found. Ryba (1997) described the footprint of Structure 3 on Mound E, which has the unusual characteristic of four large posts in a line down the center of the building (figure 5.6). She compared the floor plan with other structures

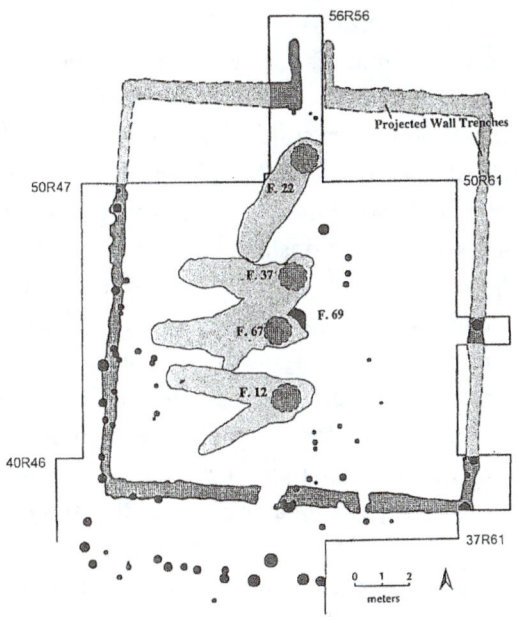

Figure 5.6. Conjectural elevation and archaeological plan of greathouse on the summit of Mound E at Moundville: (*top*) reconstructed elevation that suggests the massive posts along the central axis of the building protruded above the roof and supported bird effigies (Ryba 1997: figure 13); (*bottom*) archaeological plan of greathouse, showing the massive internal posts with insertion trenches (Ryba 1997: figure 5).

found in southeastern archaeological sites, and she concluded that the closest resemblance was found at Cahokia in Illinois (Ryba 1997: figure 26). That led her to create the speculative reconstruction shown in figure 5.6, which includes poles above the roof bearing bird effigies inspired by historic drawings of the Acolapissa and Natchez temples. Knight reaffirmed her connection of Moundville to Cahokia, referring to "greathouse architecture at Cahokia, a connection of considerable interest" (Knight 2010: 230). He finds that the "Cahokian affinity is so strikingly specific . . . that one might well attribute to the Moundville architect a firsthand, intimate schooling in the principles of Midwestern structure design." Rather than the angular appearance drawn by Ryba, he suggests the structure had "a dome-shaped roof built on a flexed-pole frame bent over the ridge pole, thatched without the use of wall daub and possibly mat-covered. It would have looked much like the Acolapissa temple sketched by De Batz in Louisiana in 1732" (Knight 2010: 230).

The structure on Mound V, a low mound immediately north of Moundville's highest mound (B), has a square footprint and postmolds signifying a four-post lodge structure similar to known earthlodges (figure 5.7). Mirarchi's thesis compared the Mound V structures with other similar sites in the Southeast, but he was not able to reach strong interpretive conclusions about relationships and functions (Mirarchi 2009). His reconstruction of the building and its footprint show two intriguing details that may relate to medicine lodge traditions farther north: tunnel portals on both east and west sides, with another structure on the east that may be oriented north and south. Whether the directional aspects of these structures have medicine lodge significance can only be speculation, but as excavations continue, other public building structures are likely to emerge, offering more evidence for assessing whether some are lodges for sodalities.

Owls, another possible indicator of medicine lodge tradition, are present at Moundville (figure 5.8). Moore reported finding only two owl effigies. One was from Mound F, and the other was from Mound Q (Moore 1905: 193, 215). Since Moore's time, additional owl effigies have appeared in Moundville archaeological excavations. Two rim effigies were pictured in a pictorial volume of prehistory: one from south of Mound D, and one that lacks a specific provenience (Krebs et al. 1986). Knight has recovered two more from excavations at Mound E, as well as a miniature owl figurine from his investigations of an earthlodge at Mound V (Mirarchi

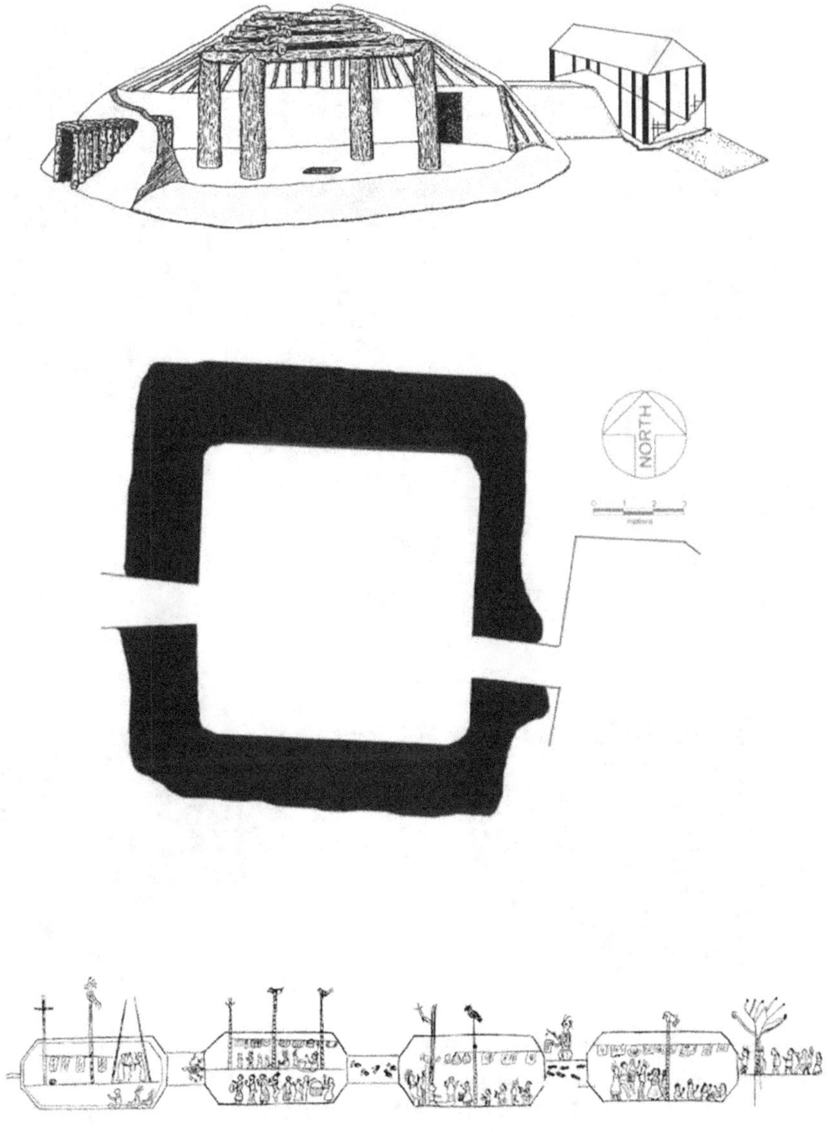

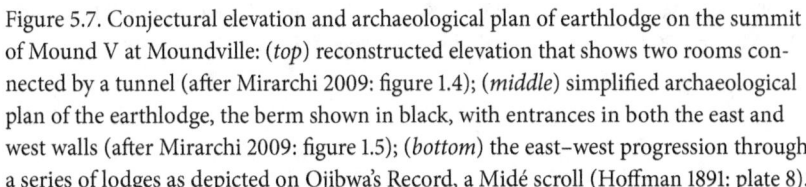

Figure 5.7. Conjectural elevation and archaeological plan of earthlodge on the summit of Mound V at Moundville: (*top*) reconstructed elevation that shows two rooms connected by a tunnel (after Mirarchi 2009: figure 1.4); (*middle*) simplified archaeological plan of the earthlodge, the berm shown in black, with entrances in both the east and west walls (after Mirarchi 2009: figure 1.5); (*bottom*) the east–west progression through a series of lodges as depicted on Ojibwa's Record, a Midé scroll (Hoffman 1891: plate 8).

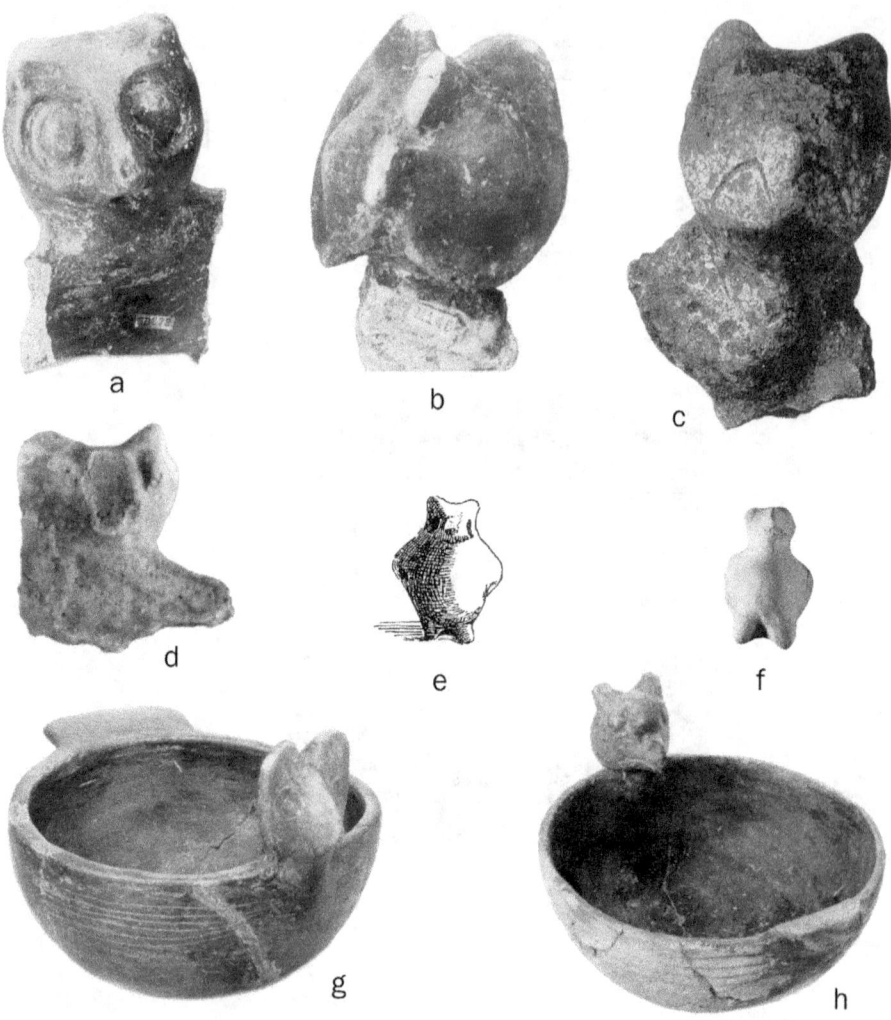

Figure 5.8. Moundville owl effigies: (*a–d*) pottery rim adornos, from bowls; (*e–f*) ceramic free-standing effigies, each about 3 cm tall; (*g–h*) pottery bowls with rim adornos. (Collections: *a*, AMNH, SD272; *b*, AMNH, Mi45; *c*, NMAI, 17/2797; *d*, AMNH, 41.1230.1; *e*, NMAI, 17/2799; *f*, AMNH, Mound V; *g–h*, AMNH. Images: *a–b*, Krebs et al. 1986: 57; *c*, Moore 1905: figure 138; *d*, Knight 2010: figure 5.33l; *e*, Moore 1905: figure 99; *f*, Mirarchi 2009: figure 3.31; *g*, Krebs et al. 1986: 78; *h*, Krebs et al. 1986: 88)

2009: figure 3.31). One was found near Mound R (John Blitz, personal communication, 2014). Recent excavations in the south plaza have discovered two more (Jera Davis, personal communication 2011). In his recent book on the mound excavations at Moundville, Knight summarized what is known about ceramic effigies there. Dividing the forms into bowl rim adornos, effigy-shaped vessel bodies, and head medallions, he noted that owls are restricted primarily to the rim adornos (Knight 2010: 49). The body effigies feature mostly frog and fish characteristics, while the medallions consist of human heads. The 14 rim adornos from Mound Q include humans and birds, three of which are owls (Knight 2010: 142–43). A similar collection of effigy ceramics was found at Mound E: 22 frog and fish vessels, and 11 rim adornos, only two of which are owls (Knight 2010: 215–16). These few examples suggest that more owl effigies will be discovered in the soil of Moundville, but they give no reason to expect a different pattern or percentage.

Knight's conclusion regarding the effigy ceramics generally does not offer support for the hypothesis that the owl images at Moundville are indicators of a medicine lodge. "This fundamental similarity across contexts adds up to a convincing demonstration against the function of these pottery effigies as totemic markers of clans, moieties, sodalities, or any other such restricted social groups" (2010: 215–16). The role of these owl effigies remains uninterpreted. However, unlike some of the Hemphill Engraved ceramics that seem to bear mortuary designs and are found in burial contexts, the owls do not appear to be burial offerings. One Moundville archaeologist has commented that his "general impression is that owl-effigy bowls occur very rarely, if ever, in Moundville burials" (V. P. Steponaitis, personal communication 2009; note the absence of owl-effigy bowls in Steponaitis 1983a).

Conclusion

These few archaeological insights do not offer confirmation of the hypothesis, but this examination has also failed to impeach it. Along with the other human and animal images, the owls and possible owl-poles call for further interpretation. The possibility of an amalgamation of a mortuary sodality with a medicine-healing sodality was raised earlier in regard to the Midewiwin. If that speculation is correct, then the Ghost Lodge may have had a diffusion pattern of its own, one not necessarily connected with the shamanistic healing organization. It is possible that the owls at Moundville point to a Ghost Lodge relationship that may have been diffused without a connection to a medicine lodge.

The current interpretation of a shift at Moundville from a living community to a necropolis calls for explanations of how that transition was brought about. One of the agencies that could help in explaining that transformation is a sodality focused particularly on the rituals and secrets connected to successful access to and passage on the Path of Souls. One avenue of examination that may prove fruitful has already been pointed out by Erin Phillips (2006, this volume)—to continue to probe the meanings of the design groups in the Hemphill Engraved ceramic corpus for evidence of sodality connections. The presence of such a lodge and its specialized knowledge and tools for dealing with death, whether diffused from another place or indigenous to Moundville, may be a useful hypothesis in understanding the rise of a necropolis.

Acknowledgments

Thanks to Vernon J. Knight Jr., Kevin E. Smith, Vincas P. Steponaitis, and John Blitz, as well as Jon Marcoux and one anonymous reviewer, for their careful reading and detailed responses to an earlier draft of this paper. Many of their suggestions have been incorporated here, to the benefit of this study. I also express gratitude to Chris Peebles for his leadership in deriving social structure from the sifting of dirt. I was not fortunate enough to have been one of his students or workers, but our paths did cross briefly at Moundville, just when a new graduate needs good role models. I remain grateful for the inspiration.

6

The Distribution of Hemphill-Style Artifacts at Moundville

ERIN E. PHILLIPS

This study uses techniques of mortuary analysis to examine the meanings and uses of Hemphill-style pottery, stone palettes, stone pendants, and copper gorgets at Moundville. I suggest that if there is patterned distribution of these items in Moundville burials, they probably mark specific social identities. In an attempt to determine whether such identities are indicated, burials possessing these four artifact genres were compared with one another and with other contemporaneous burials, specifically examining burial location, age and sex of the interred individual, and the other contents of the burials. While previous studies have described Moundville burials (McKenzie 1964) and have discussed social statuses within that population (Peebles 1971, 1974; Peebles and Kus 1977), this study tracks the contexts in which specific artifact genres are found, to investigate their possible association with particular identities.

Several individuals have examined Moundville burials over the years. Burials were intentionally sought out and excavated by Moore in 1905 and 1906, and again by the Alabama Museum of Natural History from 1930 to 1941. Later researchers used the excavation records of these early archaeologists for their studies (McKenzie 1964; Peebles 1971, 1974; Peebles and Kus 1977). Integral to Peebles' work, and that of others at the time, was the Binford–Saxe approach, which suggests that "age, sex, social position, sub-group affiliation, cause of death, and the location of death" (Binford 1971: 18; Saxe 1970) have a determining effect on the characteristics of a burial. Peebles' work was criticized by Parker Pearson (1999), who suggested that, rather than reflecting the deceased, burials more accurately reflected mourners of the dead. While this may be a theoretical possibility, I would argue that if patterning is found with respect to the age, sex, and burial location, then grave inclusions are much more likely to be linked to the identity of the deceased.

After briefly describing the Hemphill style and its genres, I will discuss the mortuary contexts of each genre and evaluate what kind of social identity, if any, each might mark.

The Hemphill Style and Four of Its Genres

The Hemphill style gets its name from the ceramic category Moundville Engraved, *var. Hemphill* (Steponaitis 1983a: 318), from which the style was first defined. Later, Knight and Steponaitis expanded the concept of the Hemphill style beyond *Hemphill* pottery to include representational designs on locally produced stone palettes, stone pendants, and copper gorgets, as well as incised and painted pottery and shell gorgets (Knight and Steponaitis 2011). This study does not include painted pots and shell gorgets, because they are rare; and it does not include incised pots, because they tend to come later in time.

Hemphill-Style Pottery

Pottery bearing Hemphill-style representational art is found in two basic vessel shapes: bottles and bowls, the majority being bottles (figure 6.1). This art was the subject of three important MA theses written by students at the University of Alabama in the mid-1990s. Lacefield's (1995) study was a stylistic analysis using multivariate statistics, in which she offered a detailed examination of the crested bird. Schatte (1997) focused attention on the Winged Serpent theme and created a stylistic seriation of that theme. Gillies (1998) set out to define the Hemphill style more rigorously and compared it with the neighboring Mississippian engraved art styles in pottery. While there are numerous motifs depicted in the Hemphill style, much of the discussion has centered around five themes (figure 6.2), which include about 90 percent of the images produced in the Hemphill style (Knight 2007). These themes are the Winged Serpent, Crested Bird, Raptor, Center Symbols and Bands, and Trophy. Recently, the design characterizing Steponaitis' Moundville Engraved, *var. Cypress* has been subsumed into the Center Symbols and Bands theme (Knight 2007).

Figure 6.1. Hemphill-style bottles (courtesy Alabama Museum of Natural History, photograph numbers 1027 and 1049).

Figure 6.2. Five main themes of the Hemphill style: (*a*) Winged Serpent; (*b*) Crested Bird; (*c*) Raptor; (*d*) Center Symbols and Bands; (*e*) Trophy (after Steponaitis and Knight 2004: figure 6).

Stone Palettes

Moundville palettes (figure 6.3) are made of Upper Pottsville sandstone, a local raw material (Whitney et al. 2002). Most palettes are round, but they can take other shapes as well, including rectangles and ovals. They vary in size from 9 to 35 cm in diameter and from 0.6 to 3 cm in thickness. On the obverse (top) face, most palettes have one or two incised concentric circles along the rim, and a notched or scalloped edge. Palettes without the notches or scallops sometimes have an incised border, which can exhibit complex designs, such as a reverse scallop or a step-and-meander. While several palettes exhibit representational art, typically on the reverse side, this is rather unusual. Most palettes depict no engraved representational art at all, although it has been argued that the form itself is representational (Knight and Steponaitis 2011).

Mississippian stone palettes were recognized at least as early as 1873 in Jones' *Antiquities of the Southeastern Indians* (1873: 373–76). They were dubbed "palettes" by Moore (1907: 392) as they were often found with quantities of red and white paint still on them. Similar palettes have been found at Etowah in Georgia, and individual palettes have been found at sites in Alabama, Arkansas, Louisiana, Mississippi, North Carolina, and Tennessee (Fundaburk and Foreman 1957: plates 93–94; Webb and DeJarnette 1942: 290–91; Weinstein 1984). Steponaitis speculates that both the Etowah and Moundville palettes may have been portable altars that were kept in medicine bundles (Steponaitis and Knight 2004: 174; Steponaitis et al. 2011; Steponaitis, this volume). Possession of such a bundle might indicate membership in a particular social group like the medicine societies of Plains Indians, an example of an earned religious identity. Residue analysis of the Etowah palettes has revealed both mineral and organic substances (Steponaitis et al. 2011). If the stone discs from Moundville are indeed portable altars, then one would expect them to reflect certain earned identities when found in mortuary contexts.

Stone Pendants

Unlike the stone palettes and copper gorgets examined here, tabular stone pendants (figure 6.4) are not a prominent genre of skillfully crafted goods at other major Mississippian sites, although they have been found at other sites in Alabama. The Moundville tabular stone pendants have

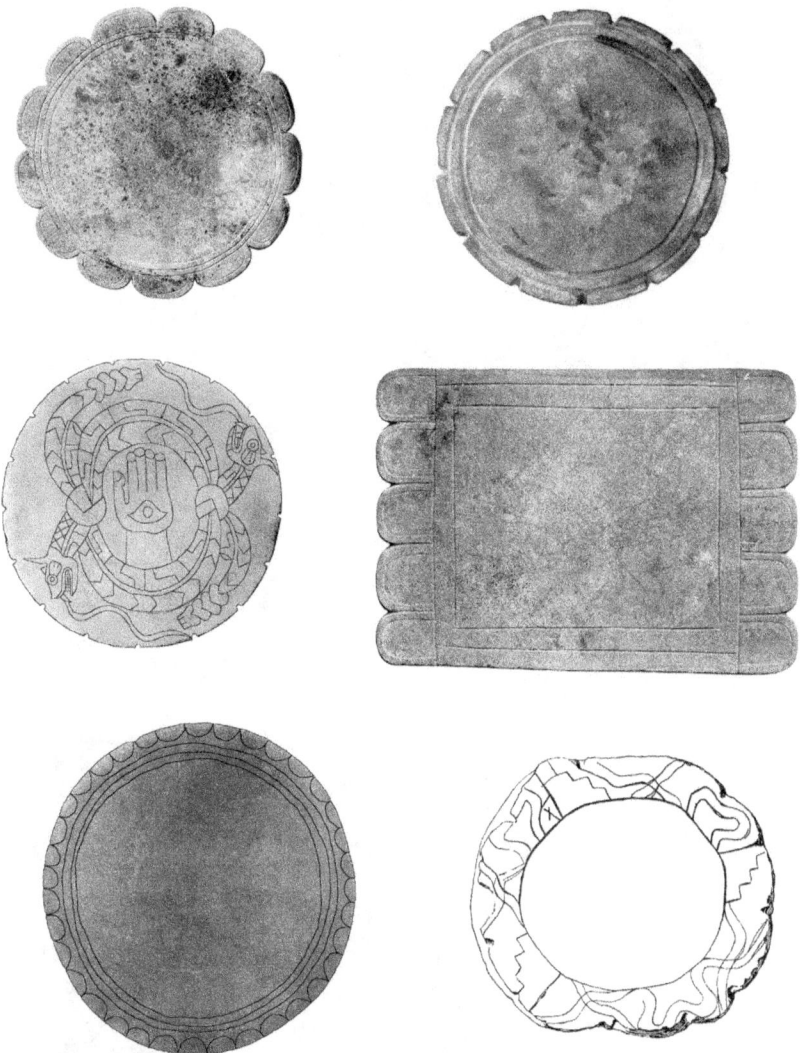

Figure 6.3. Stone palettes (after Moore 1905: figures 7, 19, 66, 103, 110, 1907: figure 88).

been determined to be local products. There is physical evidence of local production of the stone pendants, as they are found at Moundville in various stages of completion (Marcoux 2000: 57, 2007; Steponaitis 1983b; Steponaitis and Knight 2004: 175). The raw materials of many of these locally produced stone pendants are thought to be of local origin, as similar rocks have been found in the area (Steponaitis and Knight 2004: 175).

Figure 6.4. Stone pendants (after Moore 1907: figure 93; Knight and Steponaitis 2011: figures 9.18a, 9.23c; Krebs et al. 1986: 50; Webb and DeJarnette 1942: plate 58.2).

Such materials include red and yellow ferruginous claystone and Upper Pottsville micaceous sandstone. Pendants were also made from nonlocal materials. Two of these materials have yet to be identified, but one is potentially limestone, and the other is an unidentified red metamorphic rock. Additionally, there is a greenstone fragment that is probably the tip of an oblong pendant. Some pendants have the same hand-and-eye motif as Moundville palettes, copper gorgets, and engraved pottery. All are rendered in the local Hemphill style (Knight and Steponaitis 2011). Many of the stone pendants have an oblong shape, some are round, one is in the shape of a head, while others are shaped like a stone axe, and two are mace shaped (figure 6.4). The pendants have perforations for suspension or, in the case of the stone axe pendants, a groove for suspension at the end of the handle. Tabular stone pendants are small in comparison to some of the copper gorgets.

Copper Gorgets

Moundville copper gorgets come in two general shapes, oblong and round (figure 6.5). The oblong copper gorgets are very similar in form to the oblong stone pendants. The round copper gorgets are similar in form to both the stone palettes and the upper field of the oblong stone pendants. Most of the copper gorgets have representational art embossed on them. Some have fenestrations as well, especially at the central rayed circle (sometimes called a scalloped circle, scalp motif, or star) or swirl cross (often called a swastika) (Brain and Phillips 1996; Moore 1905, 1907; Steponaitis and Knight 2004).

Like other Hemphill-style genres, copper gorgets are believed to be a local Moundville product (Marcoux 2000: 59, 2007; Steponaitis and Knight 2004: 176). While copper is not locally found, it was widely traded in the form of raw material as well as finished products (Steponaitis and Knight 2004: 176). Copper gorgets have been found at other sites, including Etowah in Georgia and Spiro in Oklahoma, although they are quite different from these Hemphill-style gorgets (Hamilton et al. 1974: 141; Webb and DeJarnette 1942: 297–98). Other copper objects found at Moundville, such as copper hair ornaments, clearly are imports from elsewhere, sharing similarities to copper artifacts found at other Mississippian mound centers (Steponaitis and Knight 2004: 176).

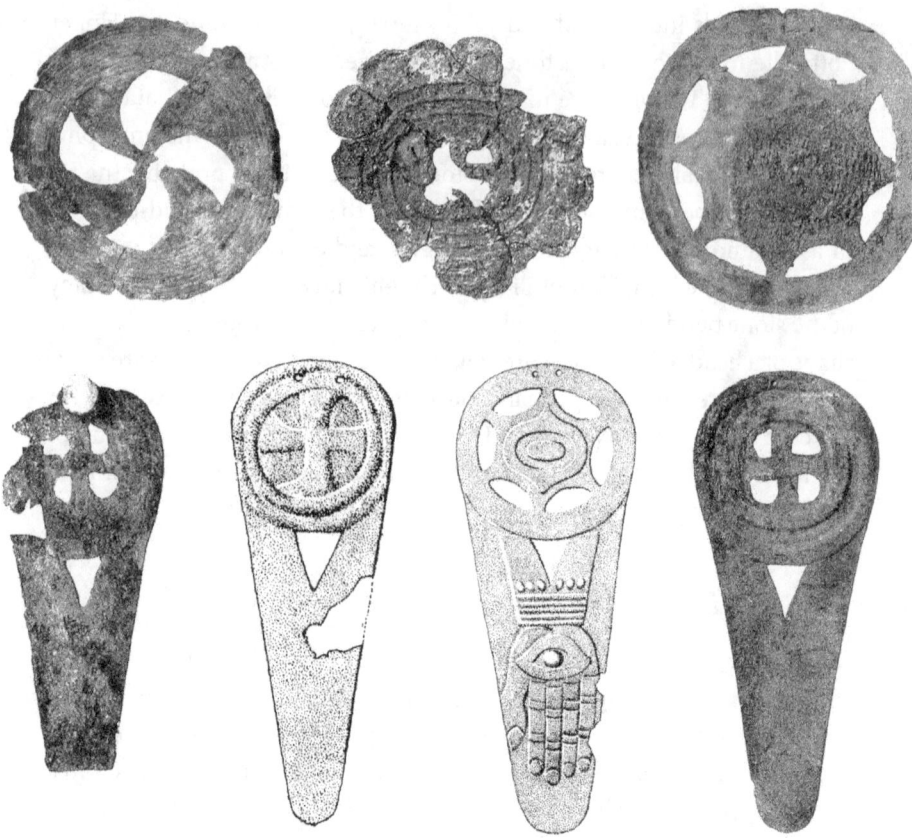

Figure 6.5. Copper gorgets (after Moore 1905: figures 29, 34, 43, 1907: figures 101–4).

Analysis of Moundville Burial Data

Little is known of the meaning and use of Hemphill pottery, stone palettes, tabular stone pendants, and copper gorgets. Except for Moore's attribution of the stone palettes as paint-mixing implements, most other meanings and uses assigned to these four classes of artifacts have been speculations based on ethnographic evidence. If, however, there is patterned distribution of these four classes of artifacts in Moundville burials, then they probably mark specific religious, economic, or kin-based social identities.

Very few of the 3,051 documented human burials excavated at Moundville between 1905 and 1941 possess any of the four artifact forms of inter-

Table 6.1. Frequency of Burials with Hemphill-Style Artifacts

	Moundville II–III Burials[a]		All Burials[b]	
	(n)	(%)	(n)	(%)
Burials with:				
Hemphill-style pottery	95	20.52	97	3.18
Stone palettes	11	2.38	30	0.98
Stone pendants	1	0.22	8	0.26
Copper gorgets	5	1.08	23	0.75

[a]Counts are of burials that have been assigned to the Moundville II–III span (Steponaitis 1989), and that contain artifacts of each genre. Percentages are computed relative to the total number of burials that have been assigned to this span (n = 463).
[b]Counts are of all burials containing artifacts of each genre. Percentages are computed relative to all documented burials at Moundville (n = 3,051).

est in this study. This study includes 97 documented burials with pottery engraved in the Hemphill style, 30 possessing stone palettes, 8 possessing stone pendants, and 23 with copper gorgets. To give a better sense of the rarity of these artifact forms as grave goods, their percentages relative to all dated Moundville II and III phase burials and all 3,051 documented burials from Moundville were calculated (table 6.1). The percentages relative to Moundville II–III burials are inflated, because most of the documented burials at the site remain undated, but many probably relate to the Moundville II and III phases. Only the frequency of burials with Hemphill-style pottery relative to the total number of Moundville II–III burials seems to be substantial, at 20.5 percent, but one might expect this proportion to be large, as such vessels are among the best diagnostics for Moundville II and III. Burials possessing the other three artifact genres are much rarer than the burials with Hemphill pottery. In fact, the number of burials containing any of the other genres is smaller than the number with Hemphill pottery.

Because a person's social identities are often correlated with age or sex, both of these variables were considered here. The age and sex data come from the burial forms created at the time of excavation, the skeletal inventory completed by the Alabama Museum of Natural History for NAGPRA compliance in the mid-1990s (University of Alabama Museums 1996),

Table 6.2. Frequency of Burials with Hemphill-Style Artifacts by Age Group

	Total (n)	Older Adult (n)	Older Adult (%)	Adult (n)	Adult (%)	Adolescent (n)	Adolescent (%)	Child (n)	Child (%)	Infant (n)	Infant (%)
Moundville II–III burials[a]	325	34	10.5	197	60.6	11	3.4	61	18.8	22	6.8
Moundville II–III burials[b] with:											
Hemphill-style pottery	65	4	6.2	50	76.9	—	—	8	12.3	3	4.6
Stone palettes	15	2	13.3	13	86.7	—	—	—	—	—	—
Stone pendants	5	—	—	2	40.0	1	20.0	1	20.0	1	20.0
Copper gorgets	17	—	—	14	82.4	—	—	2	11.8	1	5.9

[a]Counts include burials that have been assigned to the Moundville II–III span (Steponaitis 1989) and whose age has been determined.
[b]Counts include burials that have been assigned to the Moundville II–III span, and burials that are undated but presumed to fall within that span.

Table 6.3. Frequency of Burials with Hemphill-Style Artifacts by Sex

	Total[a] (n)	Male (n)	Male (%)	Female (n)	Female (%)
Moundville II–III burials[a]	77	31	40.3	46	59.7
Moundville II–III burials[b] with:					
Hemphill-style pottery	14	5	35.7	9	64.3
Stone palettes	9	7	77.8	2	22.2
Stone pendants	2	1	50.0	1	50.0
Copper gorgets	4	4	100.0	—	—

[a]Counts include burials that have been assigned to the Moundville II–III span (Steponaitis 1989) and whose sex has been determined.
[b]Counts include burials that have been assigned to the Moundville II–III span, and burials that are undated but presumed to fall within that span.

and a variety of published sources (Moore 1905, 1907; Brain and Phillips 1996).

A key priority was to ensure that all of the burials possessing a certain artifact form were contemporary. This is important because the artifact forms of interest would seem rarer if they were not in use for a certain period of time, and the background sample would be skewed in other ways as well. Also, the same form may have had different meanings or group associations at different points in time. Chronological control came from an unpublished list of burial dates by Steponaitis (1989; also see Steponaitis 1991: table 9.1) based on his ceramic seriation and the associated pottery (Steponaitis 1983a). The vast majority of dated burials for all four genres fell within the Moundville II and III phases. The only exceptions were three burials containing stone palettes, one of which was assigned to Moundville I, and the other two to Moundville I–II. Because of this strong chronological pattern, I assumed that all of the undated burials fell within the Moundville II and III phases as well.

Once chronological control was established, I tabulated the distribution of burials containing each of the Hemphill genres against age (table 6.2), sex (table 6.3), and mound versus nonmound location (table 6.4). When one realizes that Hemphill pottery was often used as a diagnostic for the Moundville II and III phases, one would expect the burials possessing such vessels to be quite similar to the general Moundville II–

Table 6.4. Frequency of Burials with Hemphill-Style Artifacts by Context

	Total (n)	Mound		Off-Mound	
		(n)	(%)	(n)	(%)
Moundville II–III burials[a]	463	13	2.8	450	97.2
Moundville II–III burials[b] with:					
Hemphill-style pottery	97	5	5.2	92	94.8
Stone palettes	30	9	30.0	21	70.0
Stone pendants	8	—	—	8	100.0
Copper gorgets	23	9	39.1	14	60.9

[a]Counts include all burials that have been assigned to the Moundville II–III span (Steponaitis 1989).
[b]Counts include burials that have been assigned to the Moundville II–III span, and burials that are undated but presumed to fall within that span.

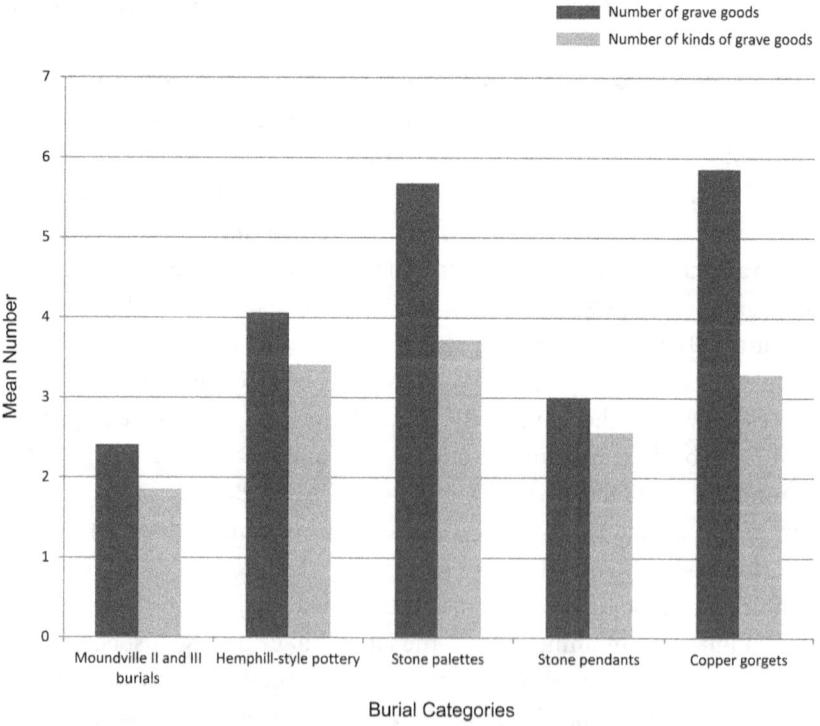

Figure 6.6. Mean richness, all Moundville II–III burials containing datable artifacts compared with those containing Hemphill-style artifacts of each genre.

III burial population in terms of age, sex, location, and richness. While this expectation holds true for some of these dimensions, it does not for others.

I also calculated two measures for the richness of grave goods within a burial: (1) the number of artifacts present, and (2) the number of artifact categories present. The mean values of these measures were then compared for each of the Hemphill artifact categories in relation to the Moundville II–III burial population as a whole (figure 6.6).

To look for spatial patterns, I plotted the distribution of burials containing each Hemphill genre on a map of Moundville (figure 6.7) and also plotted the spatial centroid of each distribution (figure 6.8), the latter calculated as the mean grid coordinates, or "center of gravity," for each genre. The distributions and centroids were compared to those for all Moundville II–III burials. Finally, I considered the degree to which the Hemphill genres are found together in the same burials, and whether they commonly occur with other artifact forms.

The composite result is a view of the kinds of people who were buried with Hemphill-style engraved vessels, stone palettes, tabular stone pendants, and copper gorgets, and their similarities or differences from the general population. The patterns for each artifact genre are now considered in turn.

Hemphill-Style Pottery

Burials possessing Hemphill-style pottery are quite similar to those of the general Moundville II and III burial population in terms of age, sex, and location at Moundville. Because they were used as part of the process of assigning phase dates to the burials, all burials with Moundville Engraved, *var. Hemphill* pottery by definition date to the Moundville II and III phases. Most of those buried with Hemphill-style pottery are adults or older adults, while a few are infants or children (table 6.2). This is not substantially different from the ages represented in the general Moundville II–III burial population. Fourteen of the burials could be sexed, yielding five males and nine females, which is not significantly different from the expected values (table 6.3; $x^2 = 0.120$, $df = 1$, $p > 0.05$). Both ways of calculating richness indicated that burials possessing Hemphill pottery were significantly richer than the general Moundville II and III burial popula-

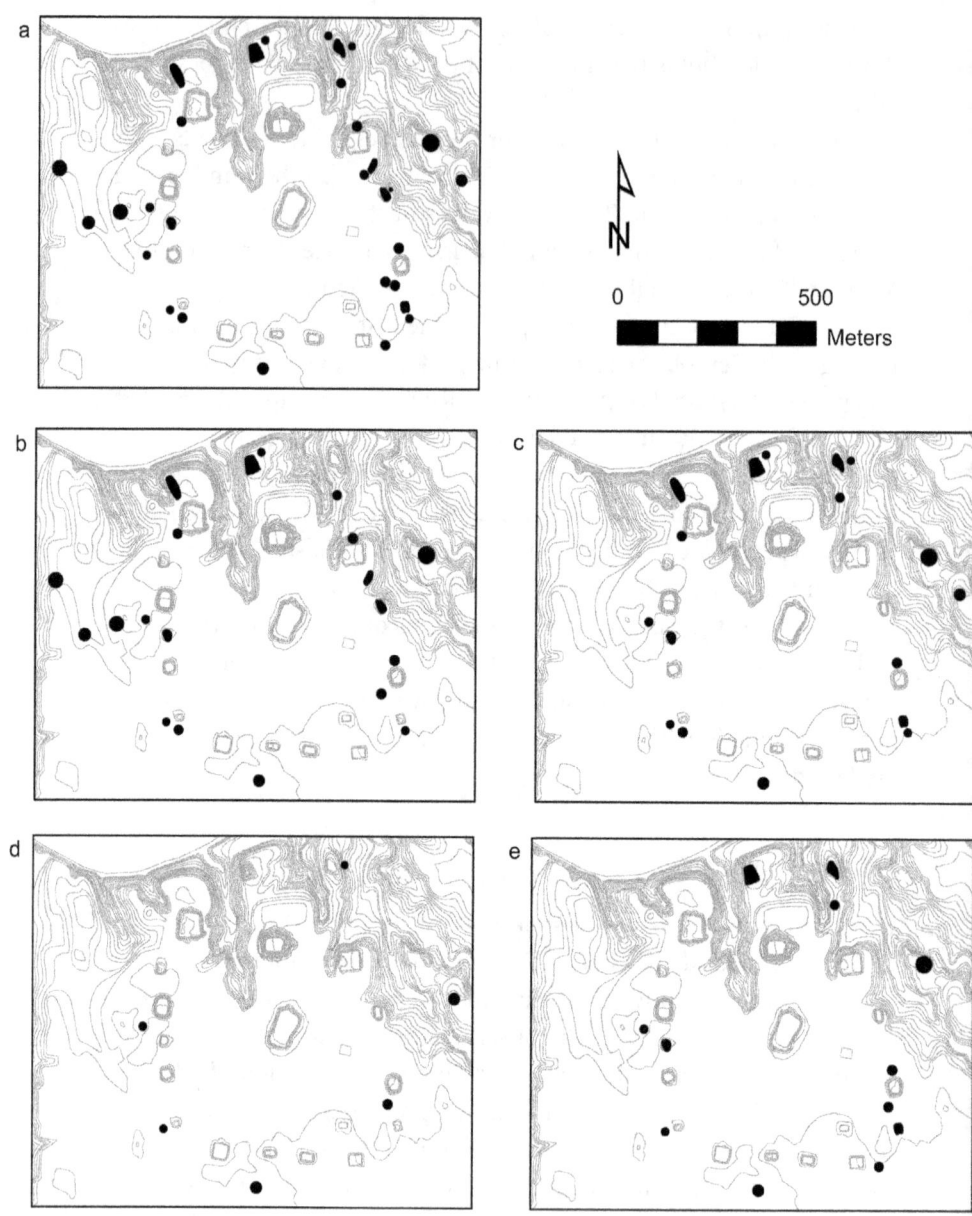

Figure 6.7. Spatial distribution of excavation areas with (*a*) Moundville II–III phase burials, (*b*) burials possessing Hemphill-style pottery, (*c*) burials with stone palettes, (*d*) burials with stone pendants, and (*e*) burials with copper gorgets.

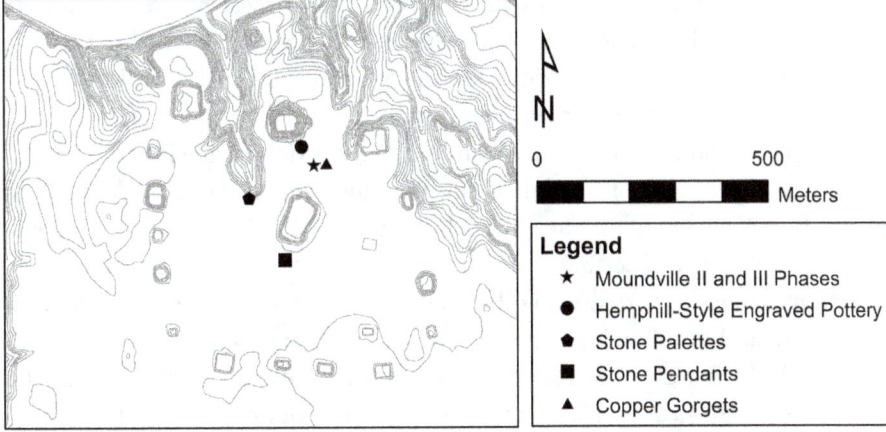

Figure 6.8. Spatial centroids of burials with Hemphill-style artifacts by genre, compared with the centroid of all Moundville II–III burials.

tion (figure 6.6; sign test for number of artifacts: $\xi_1 = 4$, $p < 0.0005$; sign test for number of kinds of artifacts: $\xi_2 = 3$, $p = 0.024$).

Burials with Hemphill-style pottery have locational tendencies quite similar to the Moundville II and III burials as a whole. Both groups occur more often in off-mound locations, and there is no significant difference between them in this regard (table 6.4; $\chi^2 = 1.94$, $df = 1$, $p = 0.16$). Both groups are also distributed throughout the site (figure 6.7), and their centroids are very close (figure 6.8).[1]

The most common artifact forms found in burials with Hemphill-style pottery are, in decreasing order of frequency, bowls, jars, water bottles, shell beads, and copper-clad wooden ear discs. Burials with Hemphill-style pottery are also found with many kinds of objects that are not found with burials possessing stone palettes, stone pendants, and copper gorgets. These include an assortment of effigy forms, such as bird-effigy bowls and human-head rim adornos, mussel shells, and a limestone feline-effigy pipe. Three burials with Hemphill-style vessels also have stone palettes; two burials each contain two palettes, while none of the burials with Hemphill-style pottery also have stone pendants or copper gorgets.

Stone Palettes

Burials with stone palettes differ from other Moundville II and III burials as well as from those with other Hemphill genres. While they occur most often during the Moundville II and III phases, apparently they are not entirely restricted to this period. At least one palette comes from a burial that has been assigned to the Moundville I phase, and two come from Moundville I or II phase burials. For palettes, however, there is a substantial age bias compared to the general Moundville II and III burial population. All of the individuals for which an age could be determined (n = 15) were adults or older adults (table 6.2). Yet it appears that only people above a certain age could possess palettes, whereas people of any age could be buried with other Hemphill genres. Of the nine sexed individuals buried with palettes, seven were male and two were female (table 6.3). Both ways of calculating richness indicated that burials with palettes were significantly richer than the general Moundville II and III burial population (figure 6.6; $\xi_1 = 4, p < .0005; \xi_2 = 3, p = .001$).

While burials with palettes, like their contemporary Moundville II–III burials, have been found most often in off-mound locations, they are found significantly more often in mounds than in other Moundville II and III burials (table 6.4; $x^2 = 81.55, df = 1, p < .0001$). Like Moundville II and III burials in general, burials with palettes are found throughout the Moundville site (figure 6.7), but the centroids indicate different locational tendencies (figure 6.8). Burials with palettes are generally distributed farther south and west than the general burial population; even so, they are still concentrated in the northern half of the site.

It is also interesting to note that burials with Hemphill pottery and those with palettes share the same five most commonly associated artifact forms, although they occur in a different order of frequency: jars, water bottles, copper-clad ear discs, bowls, and beads (generally marine shell, but often unspecified on the burial forms). Four burials have other artifacts bearing Hemphill representational art, three have Hemphill-style pottery, and one has a copper gorget, while none has a stone pendant. In one intriguing case a single palette was found broken and distributed among five nearby burials. Artifact forms that occur in burials with stone palettes, but not the other three Hemphill-style genres, include a bear's tooth, green pigment, a paint bowl with yellow pigment, a greenstone celt, a bird-beak awl, a bird claw, mica, a garfish snout, and a stone drill point. Each of these objects was found only once with stone palettes. The indicators of age, sex, richness, and locational differences show that individuals who possessed palettes were a special segment of the Moundville population.

Stone Pendants

The rarest artifact class bearing Hemphill representational art is the stone pendant. The only dated burial possessing a stone pendant has been assigned to the Moundville III phase, and some of the nonburial examples of these pendants have been found in contexts dating to late Moundville II and Moundville III (e.g., Knight 2004). The eight burials possessing stone pendants reveal no age or sex bias. Approximately half of the sample were adults, and half were younger, with one infant, one child, and one adolescent represented (table 6.2). Only two of the burials with stone pendants could have their sex determined, yielding one male and one female (table 6.3). Unlike the other three artifact classes examined, burials possessing stone pendants are no richer than the general Moundville II and III burial population (figure 6.6; $\xi_1 = 3, p = .375; \xi_2 = 3, p = .625$).

Burials with stone pendants are also different from the norm in that they are never found in mounds (table 6.4), although given the small number of burials with stone pendants and the low percentage of Moundville II and III burials found in mounds, this is not altogether surprising. Despite the fact that none of the burials with stone pendants were found in mounds, there is evidence of their production on mounds (Knight 2004: 309, 311; Marcoux 2000: 57, 2007). Despite the fact that burials with stone pendants are so rare, they are distributed fairly evenly throughout the site, with a slight proclivity toward the south (figures 6.7 and 6.8).

The most common artifact categories found in burials with stone pendants are beads (probably of marine shell) and pottery jars. However, these categories are each found with only two of the eight burials possessing stone pendants. Beads are among the five most common artifact forms for burials with each of the other Hemphill genres, and jars are among the most common for burials with all genres except copper gorgets. Interestingly, the one burial with a stone pendant and a copper gorget is the only instance of a stone pendant with copper of any sort. All of the artifact classes found in burials with stone pendants are found with burials of at least one of the three other genres. While these burials may seem unremarkable in their apparent lack of exclusivity, the rarity of the artifact form itself suggests an exclusive nature.

Copper Gorgets

Burials possessing copper gorgets are different still. All of the copper gorget burials that have been dated clearly come from the Moundville II–III phase range. While there is a range of ages of individuals represented within burials that possess copper gorgets, there is a clear bias toward adults, with a few infants and children present (table 6.2). As with the burials possessing Hemphill-style pottery, this distribution is not substantially different from the general Moundville II and III burial population. All four of the sexed burials possessing copper gorgets were male (table 6.3). Both ways of calculating richness indicated that burials possessing copper gorgets were all significantly richer than the general Moundville II–III burial population (figure 6.6; $\xi_1 = 5, p = .007; \xi_2 = 3, p = .143$).

Like the burials with stone palettes, those with copper gorgets are found significantly more often in mounds than the typical Moundville II and III burial ($x^2 = 110.39, df = 1, p < .0001$) but are most often found in off-mound cemeteries (table 6.4). Burials with copper gorgets are found throughout Moundville (figure 6.7), and their spatial distribution is quite similar to burials with Hemphill-style pottery and that of Moundville II and III burials in general (figure 6.8).

The five most common artifact classes found with burials possessing copper gorgets are, in order of decreasing frequency, shell beads, copper-clad ear discs, copper axes, water bottles, and beads unspecified as to material (but probably marine shell). The only artifact class that appears on this list but not on any of the others is copper axes. In addition to the aforementioned axes, several artifact classes are found in burials with copper gorgets, but never with stone palettes, stone pendants, or Hemphill-style pottery. These include graphite, matting, a copper "dagger," copper-covered wooden beads, a strip of copper, and small arrow points. Like the raw material from which these copper gorgets were made, most of the commonly associated artifacts are imported, except for the pottery water bottles. Burials with copper gorgets thus appear to represent a distinct group of people.

Co-occurrence of Hemphill-Style Genres in Burials

Burials possessing artifact classes bearing Hemphill art form distinct segments of the Moundville burial population. While they have some simi-

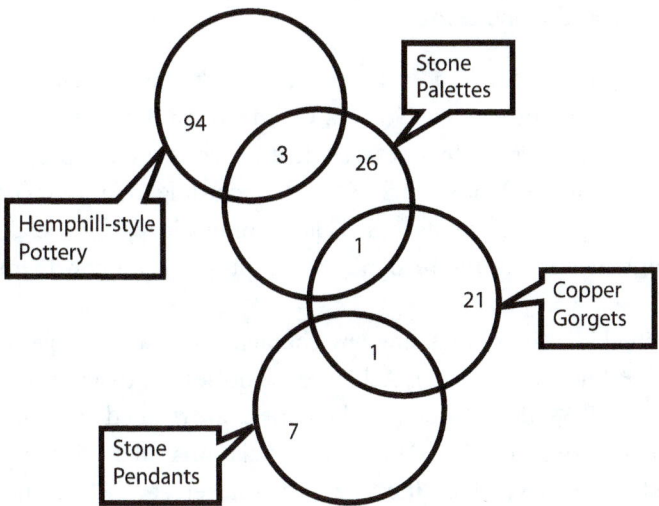

Figure 6.9. Venn diagram showing the rarity of burials with more than one Hemphill genre.

larities, they differ in their distributions. Their subject matter and distributions in terms of age, sex, richness, and location suggest that these artifact forms may mark different socio-religious identities. Assuming that is the case, these identities could overlap, as is shown in figure 6.9. Three of the 97 burials with Hemphill-style engraved vessels also have stone palettes, two of these having two palettes, while none of the burials with Hemphill-style pottery also have stone pendants or copper gorgets. Burials possessing stone palettes on three occasions also possess Hemphill-style pottery and on one occasion also possess a copper gorget. None of the 30 burials possessing stone palettes have a stone pendant. Two burials of the 23 with copper gorgets have other artifacts bearing Hemphill-style representational art, one with a stone palette, and one with a stone pendant. There is only one instance of any of the eight burials with a stone pendant also possessing another one of the artifact classes, that being a copper gorget.

The rarity of burials containing more than one Hemphill genre is striking. Only 12 of 153 burials with Hemphill artifacts contain two genres, and none contains three (figure 6.9). If these objects mark different identities, the identities they represent are not necessarily all elite. Burials possessing Hemphill pottery, stone palettes, and copper gorgets are all significantly richer than Moundville II and III phase burials generally, but burials possessing stone pendants are not.

Discussion and Conclusions

An identity is anything about the self that makes a difference in social relationships (Goodenough 1965: 3). Goodenough uses the term "social persona" as the "composite of several identities selected as appropriate to a given interaction" (Goodenough 1965: 7). According to Binford (1971: 17), the "social persona of the deceased" is "a composite of the social identities maintained in life and recognized as appropriate for consideration at death."

Ascribed identities are defined by characteristics such as age, sex, and kinship (Edmonson 1958: 8). Achieved identities are defined by actions (Edmonson 1958: 18). Associational identities are defined by group membership (Edmonson 1958: 32). Often associational identities cut across ascribed and achieved identities. As Diaz-Andreu et al. (2005) note, one cannot look at any of the dimensions of social identity in a vacuum. For example, sometimes age can affect gender roles, as when an older woman takes on identities that are otherwise exclusively male.

If the totality of a burial reflects a social persona, then aspects of a burial may be indicators of particular social identities. This is not to say that the number of identities held by the individual is equal to the number of dimensions and artifacts possessed by a burial, but rather that they are all clues as to the social persona of the individual interred. As seen by the variety of grave goods found within Moundville burials possessing Hemphill-style pottery, stone palettes, stone pendants, and copper gorgets, it is evident that there are numerous social personae represented within the sample. In the following, I will advance conjectures about the social identity represented by each of the four artifact classes.

Hemphill-style pottery is found with burials that are not significantly different from other Moundville II and III burials in terms of age, sex, and locational distribution. They are, however, significantly richer. The difference in richness and the clearly supernatural imagery depicted on these vessels may well indicate some sort of religious identity, such as a ritual specialist, a priest, or a member of a medicine society (see Lankford, this volume). Because there are no clear sex or locational differences, this identity does not appear to be ascribed. An achieved identity is not clearly indicated either, as there are no significant age differences. If a social identity is represented, it is much more likely to be a religious associational identity—for example, membership in one or more medicine societies whose patron supernaturals are represented in the five main themes engraved on this pottery.

At Moundville stone palettes are found with adults who are primarily male and with grave goods richer than the typical contemporary burial. Burials with stone palettes also have a different spatial distribution within the site than the average Moundville II or III burial, weighted more to the west and south. Based on these data, it appears that stone palettes represent an achieved identity. It may very easily be an achieved identity open only to those within a given ascribed identity, as Linton (1936: 128) suggests is often the case. Because the representational art incised on a few of the palettes has supernatural referents, stone palettes most likely represent some sort of religious identity. They were probably used for ritual purposes, such as manipulating a supernatural entity through the mixing of paints or medicines. Thus, stone palettes probably mark an achieved religious social identity, perhaps drawn from an ascribed pool of candidates.

The individuals who possessed stone pendants run the spectrum of infant through adult in age distribution and include both males and females. These individuals also possess a richness on par with other Moundville II and III burials. While in these respects such burials are virtually indistinguishable from other contemporary burials, stone pendants are quite rare. They have a different spatial distribution within the site than contemporary burials, and they are never found in mounds. It is difficult to tell if these pendants mark a specific identity, because the sample is so small (n = 8). Also, five shapes are represented, each of which could indicate a different social identity. If such were the case, then conflating them as a single category could result in a distribution not very different from the average burial of the time period. Regardless of whether the stone pendants denoted one thing or multiple things, their iconography is clearly supernatural, so if a social identity (or multiple identities) is represented, it is undoubtedly religious. There may also have been counterparts in other media, perhaps including perishable media that have not survived. For example, there is a shell axe pendant that looks similar to the axe-shaped stone pendant, and there are small tabular pottery pendants similar to the circular stone pendants (Knight and Steponaitis 2011; Moore 1907: 398). Also, there may be a connection between the oblong stone pendants and the oblong copper gorgets that are so similar in design. Thus, the social significance of the stone pendants is as of yet less clear than that of the other artifact classes discussed.

Individuals buried with copper gorgets span the range from infant to adult, and all who could be sexed are male. In addition, these individuals are richer than the typical Moundville II or III phase burial, and they have a geographic distribution similar to that of the average burial from the time, except for the fact that they are much more commonly found in mounds. Copper gorgets, like Hemphill pottery, stone palettes, and stone pendants, have supernatural referents in their representational art. Thus, they probably mark a religious social identity held exclusively by males.

In sum, based on the evidence, it appears that stone palettes and copper gorgets mark religious identities, the former achieved and the latter ascribed. Hemphill pottery may mark a religious associational identity that may not be ascribed and is not likely to be achieved. Stone pendants may well mark one or more religious identities as well, but with the limited data at hand, such a designation is conjectural. The four artifact classes associated with Hemphill art thus seem to mark different sorts of socioreligious identities that are neither mutually exclusive nor exclusively elite.

Acknowledgments

This study is an outgrowth of work begun by Chris Peebles in his dissertation research. Not only was his work inspirational, but both his analytical contributions and organization of the Moundville burial data were invaluable. I would like to thank Jim Knight, Vin Steponaitis, and Keith Jacobi for their help during this research endeavor. They have variously given me access to data from previous research, critiqued earlier drafts, and provided encouragement. I also appreciate the comments from my reviewers. Any remaining errors are my own.

Notes

1. As burials with each of the four Hemphill genres have somewhat different distributions, I investigated the notion that burials with each of the five main themes found on Hemphill pottery might have different distributions as well. While there are slight differences, none are substantial.

7

Moundville Palettes—Prestige Goods or Inalienable Possessions?

VINCAS P. STEPONAITIS

Over the years the so-called prestige goods model has been highly influential in the study of middle-range societies. It was initially developed in the 1970s by Frankenstein and Rowlands (1978) and later was adopted by others trying to understand the origins and political economy of middle-range societies. In essence, the model presumes that chiefs acquire and maintain power by gaining control of the production and/or distribution of socially valued objects—that is, prestige goods—which are often elaborately crafted and made of exotic materials. The root of chiefly power, according to this model, lies in giving such objects away in order to attract followers, to cement alliances, or to inflict debt.

This model was applied to the Mississippian world by a variety of scholars (e.g., Peregrine 1991; Trubitt 2000; Wesson 1999), and to Moundville in particular by Welch in his seminal treatise *Moundville's Economy*, which appeared in 1991. During the same year, I published a paper showing that the highest frequency of exotic items in burials coincided with Moundville's emergence as a paramount chiefdom (Steponaitis 1991). Arguably, this finding was consistent with the prestige-goods model, and it led to a program of research that I have pursued ever since. This research involves various attempts, in collaboration with many other scholars, to determine the geological sources of these "prestige goods" and to trace their movements across the ancient American South (Gall and Steponaitis 2001; Steponaitis et al. 1996; Steponaitis and Dockery 2011; Steponaitis et al. 2011; Whitney et al. 2002).

Originally, I assumed that the mechanism of movement was the one posited by the prestige-goods model: gift-giving by chiefs. In recent years, however, I have come to believe that the prestige-goods model may not be the best way to understand this movement. A number of younger scholars have raised questions about this model, based on the quantity of exotica at Moundville and the absence of evidence for extensive production (Marcoux 2007; Wilson 2001). My own doubts stem not only from such evidence, but also from the nature of the objects themselves: the more I examine the functions of these fancy Mississippian artifacts and the contexts in which they are found, the less they look like "prestige goods" at all—at least in the economic sense implied by the Frankenstein and Rowlands model.

To illustrate this point, I will focus on one particular class of objects: the so-called stone palettes. Although these items are widely distributed across the South (Holmes 1883: 277–79, 1906; Webb and DeJarnette 1942: 287–91), the vast majority of palettes, particularly whole palettes, come from only two sites: Moundville and Etowah. Here, I will principally discuss the palettes from Moundville, although I will also harness some evidence from Etowah to help make my case. After providing some basic information about the palettes themselves, I will organize my discussion around three key questions: (1) Where were the palettes made? (2) How were the palettes used? (3) How did they move across the Mississippian world (i.e., what were the mechanisms of this movement, and what does this tell us about the nature of Mississippian societies)?

Description and Context

Moundville palettes are typically the size and shape of a modern dinner plate: most are circular, 15–25 cm in diameter, and about 1 cm thick (figure 7.1). Both smaller and larger examples exist, with diameters as small as 9 cm or as large as 41 cm. A few rectangular examples are known, but these are uncommon. In cross section the palettes are invariably tabular (figure 7.2), undoubtedly because of the parallel planes of cleavage in the sedimentary rock of which they are made.[1]

The top (or obverse) face of these palettes is usually decorated with a scalloped or notched edge and a band of parallel lines along the rim (see figure 7.1). At first glance this design may not seem to have much iconographic significance, but in fact it does. The simplest way to illustrate this point is by means of comparison. Note that the palette design is essentially the same as that found on copper gorgets at Moundville, except that the

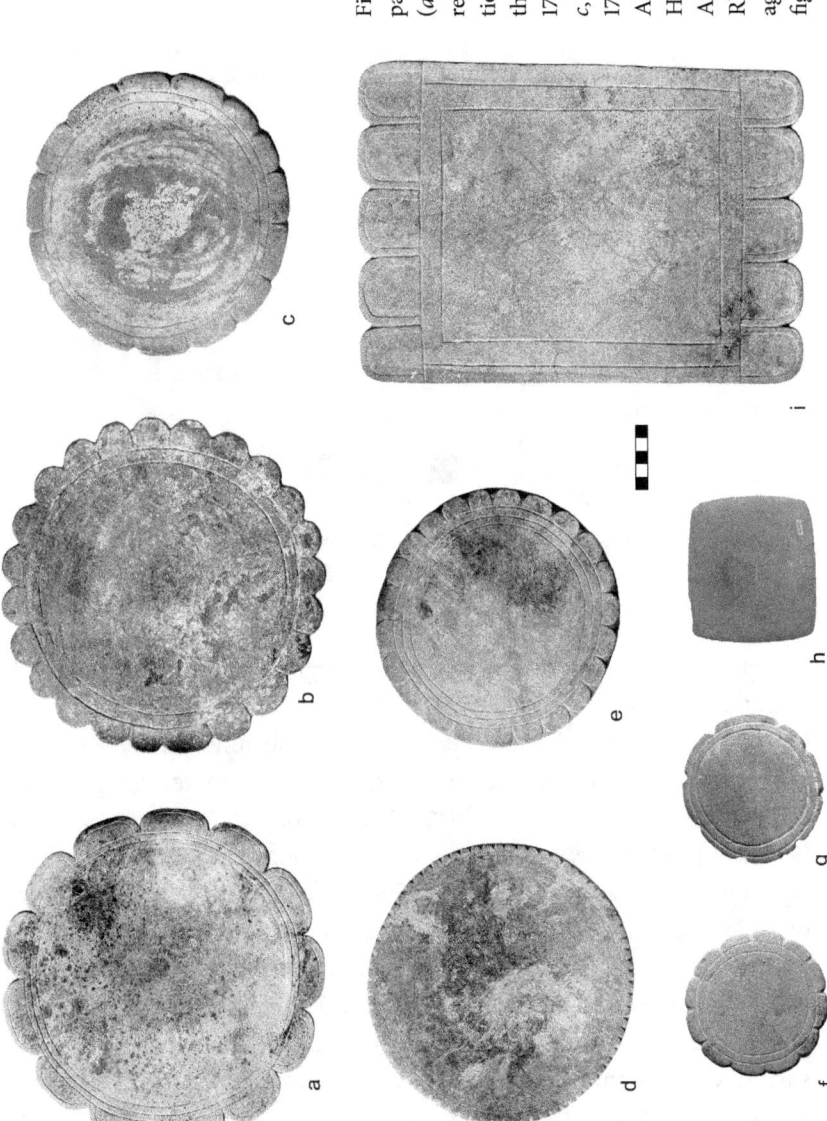

Figure 7.1. Typical stone palettes from Moundville: (*a–g*) circular palettes; (*h–i*) rectangular palettes. (Collections: *a*, National Museum of the American Indian [NMAI], 17/1474; *b*, NMAI, 17/1475; *c*, NMAI, 17/1483; *d*, NMAI, 17/1489; *e*, NMAI, 17/1476; *f*, Alabama Museum of Natural History [AMNH], EE296; *g*, AMNH, SEH12; *h*, AMNH, Rho86; *i*, NMAI, 17/1493. Images: *a–e*, *i*, after Moore 1905: figures 19, 23, 65, 110, 111, 116)

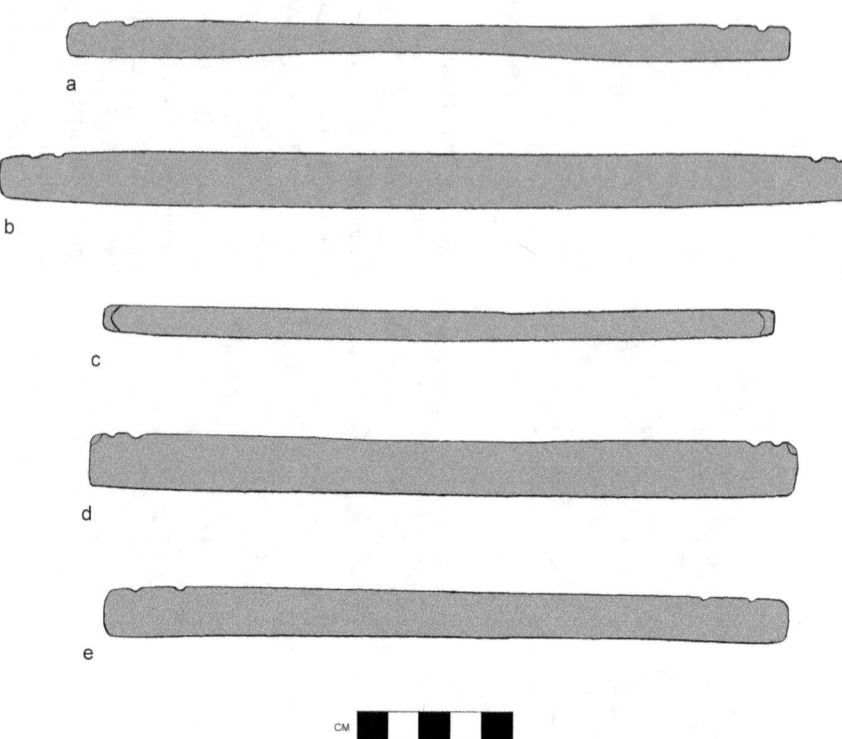

Figure 7.2. Cross sections of typical Moundville palettes. (Collections: *a*, AMNH, WP206; *b*, AMNH, WP125; *c*, AMNH, SM51; *d*, AMNH, SD2; *e*, AMNH, NG14)

gorgets have a cross in the center of the design field, whereas on the palettes this portion of the field is blank (figure 7.3). These representations all express a theme called "centering," whose meaning entails defining a center, or *axis mundi*, a place that is by definition sacred or spiritually powerful (Knight and Steponaitis 2011: 219–26).

A few palettes are also decorated with elaborate representational designs on the reverse face (figure 7.4). Such palettes are rare, and the design on each is unique, which has led to the practice of giving these objects proper names. The so-called Rattlesnake Disk is among the best-known and most-illustrated artifacts from Moundville (Moore 1905: figure 7; Steponaitis and Knight 2004: figure 1). It depicts intertwined serpents surrounding a hand, which thematically is thought to represent a portal to the Path of Souls (Lankford 2007c; Knight and Steponaitis 2011). The Willoughby Disk, just as famous, shows a melange of elements, including

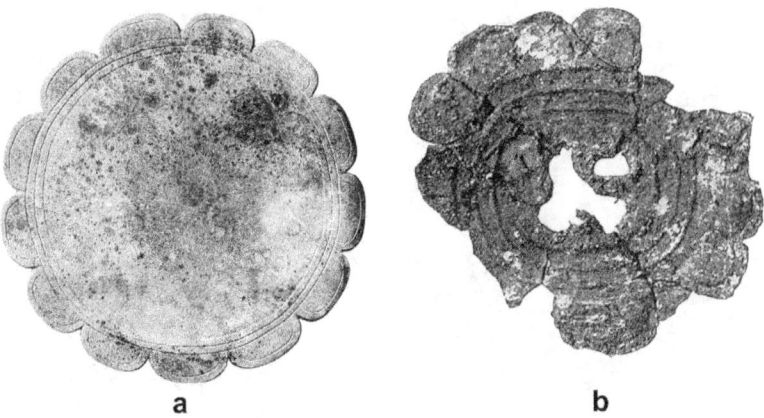

Figure 7.3. The centering theme in stone and copper: (*a*) stone palette; (*b*) copper pendant. Note the similar design structure. Images not to scale. (Collections: *a*, NMAI, 17/1474; *b*, NMAI, 17/3095. Images: *a–b*, after Moore 1905: figures 19, 29)

a supernatural moth, a bilobed arrow, hands, and a central element with bindings and skulls, which Reilly interprets as a sacred bundle (Moore 1905: figures 4–5; Reilly 2007; Steponaitis and Knight 2004: figure 13). Less well known is the Brannon Disk, which has a bilobed arrow in the same off-center position as on the Willoughby Disk (Brannon 1923; Knight and Steponaitis 2011: figure 9.22d). Not surprisingly, the reverse face of these palettes is always the one illustrated or displayed, but if one turns any of these palettes over, on the obverse side one finds the typical notched edge and multilinear band.

When one compares the palettes found in mound versus nonmound contexts, an interesting difference emerges. Palettes from mound contexts tend to be larger, with a mean diameter of 23 cm, as compared to 19 cm for nonmound contexts. The smallest palettes, with diameters in the 9–13-cm range, are found only in nonmound settings. About 20 percent of the palettes in both mound and nonmound settings are undecorated.

At least 52 whole palettes were discovered at Moundville between 1868 and 1941. These were typically found in burial contexts (Moore 1905, 1907; Peebles 1979; Steponaitis 1983b: 132). In most cases the specific position within the burial was not recorded, but where we do have such data, the palettes were usually placed near the head, and less frequently near the feet, torso, or arms.

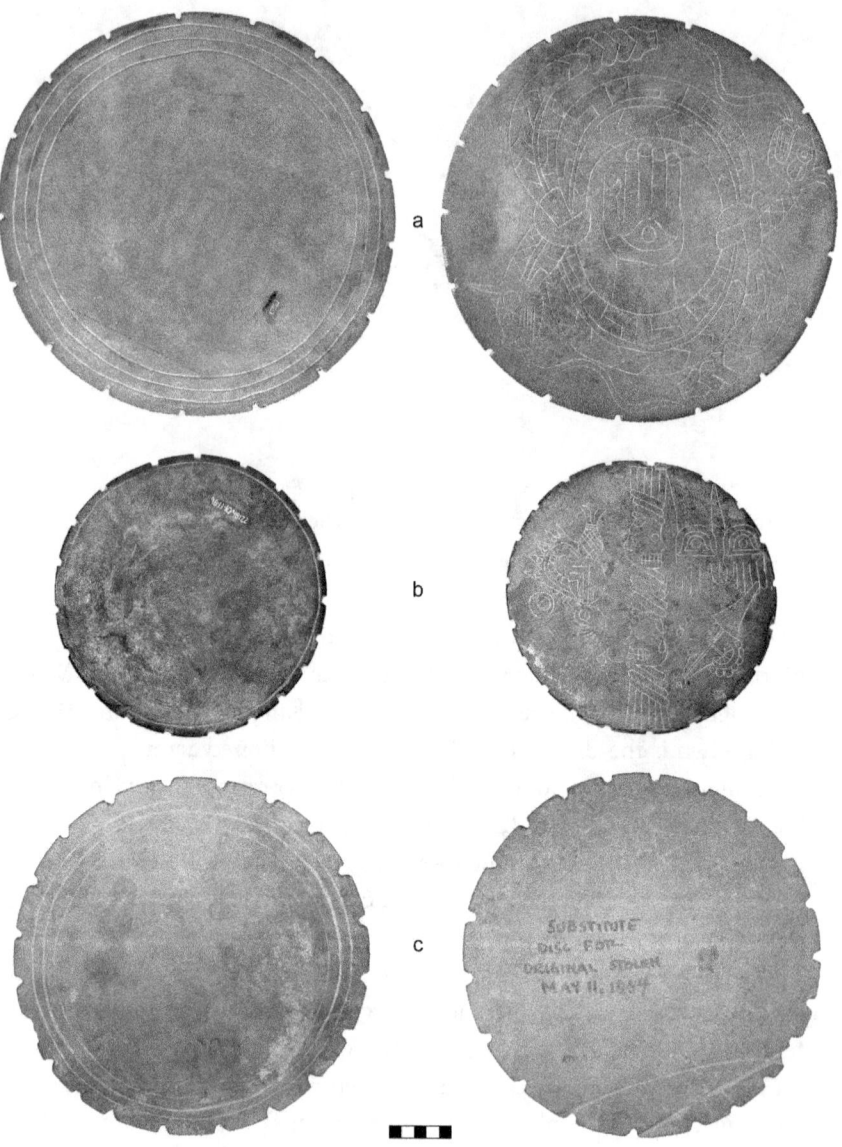

Figure 7.4. Palettes with engraved designs on reverse face: (*a*) Rattlesnake Disk; (*b*) Willoughby Disk; (*c*) Brannon Disk. Both faces of each disk are shown, obverse on the left and reverse on the right. Note that the obverse face on each of these palettes shows the typical lines around the rim. (Photo a obverse courtesy of David H. Dye. Collections: *a*, AMNH, Mi922; *b*, © 2019 President and Fellows of Harvard College, Peabody Museum of Archaeology and Ethnology, PM# 96-11-10/48122; *c*, AMNH, Mi993)

As recent excavations have amply shown, broken palette fragments are also found on the summits and in the flank middens of mounds (Knight 2010: 61–62, 148–49). These are often associated with other elements of what Knight has called the "pigment complex": limonite, galena, glauconite, mica, and other colorful or specular minerals, found either as lumps or in ceramic containers (Knight 2010: 158–59). Clearly, palettes were not only buried with the dead but also actively used on or near mounds, and occasionally were broken and discarded. Whether this breakage was accidental and informal, or deliberate and ritualized—as in a formal "decommissioning"—we simply do not know, but a case can be made for the latter interpretation, at least in some instances. Perhaps the best example of ritual decommissioning was found in a cemetery west of Mound R at Moundville, where fragments of the same broken palette were placed with five different burials (Peebles 1979: 665–66; see also Davis 2010; Phillips, this volume). Most palettes probably date between late Moundville I and early Moundville III, or ca. AD 1200–1450.

Sourcing and Distribution

Moundville's palettes are made of a very distinctive sandstone—gray in color, very fine grained, and micaceous. As early as the 1870s, at least one observer noted the similarities between the rock used to make palettes and that which outcrops at the Fall Line near Tuscaloosa, only 20 km from Moundville (Maxwell 1876: 70). This similarity has since been confirmed by a petrographic study (Whitney et al. 2002). The rock is clearly local in origin, and we have every reason to believe that palettes made from this rock were crafted somewhere in the vicinity of Moundville.

Indeed, excavations at Pride Place (1Tu1), a small residential site dating to the Moundville III phase, have yielded evidence of such crafting (Johnson 1999, 2001; Johnson and Sherard 2000; Sherard 1999; Davis, this volume; Scarry et al., this volume). The site is located north of Moundville, just below the Fall Line, and right next to the sandstone outcrops that served as the source of raw material. Additional evidence of palette crafting has been found in refuse associated with the summits of Mounds E and Q at Moundville (Knight 2004, 2010: 148–49, 221–23). Taking this evidence at face value, one might conclude that palettes were made in both commoner and elite contexts. As Davis (this volume) points out, these contexts might also represent different stages of production, with the initial shaping located near the source, and the final shaping and decorating occurring on the mounds.

Regardless of how their production was organized, the finished palettes made of this distinctive stone have a wide geographical distribution. In addition to being common at Moundville, they have been found at numerous sites in the Lower Mississippi Valley, some 300 km to the west. These sites include some of the most important Mississippian mound sites in the area, including Lake George, Glass, and Anna, as well as smaller mound sites, such as Landrum and Rosedale (Knight and Steponaitis 2011: figures 9.27, 9.28; Weinstein 1984: figure 3; Williams and Brain 1983: figure 7.41a). From the standpoint of both style and raw material, there can be no doubt that these palettes were made in the Moundville region and were transported to the Lower Mississippi Valley.[2]

Evidence of Use

Long ago, Moore pointed out the most obvious evidence for how these objects were used: the presence of white, red, and/or black mineral pigment on the obverse face (Moore 1905: 145–47, 1907: 392). He surmised that these objects were used to prepare the pigments—which is why he called them "palettes." Soon after, Holmes (1906: 105) took this functional argument a step further and suggested, correctly in my view, that these palettes "filled some important sacred or ceremonial office, as in preparing colors for shamanistic use or religious ceremony."

Understanding more specifically how these objects were used requires that we look in detail at their archaeological contexts and surface residues. At Moundville, such interpretations are hampered by two practices that were common when the site was excavated, prior to World War II. First, critical information on the specifics of artifact placement within the burials was often not recorded. And second, the palettes were heavily scrubbed, thereby removing all but the most persistent residues.

To take our argument further, therefore, we must digress a bit and consider the evidence on similar palettes from Etowah. Although they were made of a different raw material, I believe the Etowah palettes were functionally similar to those from Moundville, and the fact that they were excavated in the 1950s gives us a much richer body of evidence to consider (Steponaitis et al. 2011). For present purposes the salient facts on Etowah palettes are as follows:

- The palettes found in burials tend to occur in "kits," consisting of the palette, a large lump of pigment, and a large piece of a heavy, metallic mineral—usually galena (Steponaitis et al. 2011: table 6).
- The elements of these kits tend to be found in the same relative positions, with the pigment and galena resting against the palette's obverse face, and these relative positions remain the same regardless of the kit's orientation, that is, whether the kit was placed in the ground right-side up or upside down (Steponaitis et al. 2011: 91–94).
- Virtually all the palettes found at Etowah have fabric impressions on the reverse face, as though they were wrapped with this fabric. This fabric presumably surrounded everything in the kit. The weave of this fabric is a type often found in ethnographic medicine bundles from the Great Plains (Steponaitis et al. 2011: 94–98).

These observations, taken together, clearly indicate that the Etowah palettes were ritual gear kept in bundles.

The residues on the Etowah palettes also tell an interesting story: they consist of multiple layers of different colorful or shiny minerals—calcite, graphite, hematite, and mica, to name a few—as well as some sort of organic, resinous substance. I suspect these materials were viewed as spiritually potent substances rather than paints, and that the palettes themselves were portable altars on which spiritual medicines were prepared (Steponaitis et al. 2011: 90–91, 98–99).

Returning now to the palettes from Moundville, one also finds evidence, albeit not as consistently, of these items being wrapped. One palette shows very clear impressions of a soft wrapping, which could be either leather or textile, on its reverse face (figure 7.5a). Another has impressions from a (cane?) basket or woven mat visible in the white pigment on its obverse face (figure 7.5b). There was also a burial in Mound C where C. B. Moore observed a stack of three palettes that were "covered with decayed wood," suggesting some sort of decomposed container or covering (Moore 1905: 149–50). Overall, the number of palettes with direct evidence of wrapping is small, but the fact that such evidence occurs at all is significant, especially given that the artifacts have all been heavily scrubbed and that details of the context of discovery were usually not recorded.

One other line of evidence, albeit indirect, bears mention. Palettes found in burials at Moundville often exhibit areas containing circular

Figure 7.5. Palettes exhibiting clear impressions of wrappings or containers: (*a*) circular palette with impressions of soft wrapping on reverse face (obverse face shown in fig. 1c); (*b*) rectangular palette with matting or basketry impressions visible in white pigment. The impressions on palette (*a*) consist of manganese-rich black stains that are probably microbial in origin (see text). These stains may have formed in air pockets between the folds of a wrapping material, perhaps made of a textile or soft leather. (Collections: *a*, NMAI, 17/1483; *b*, AMNH, NE137)

black stains of varying size, typically less than a centimeter in diameter, which appear to be postdepositional in origin (see figures 7.1a, 7.1c, 7.3a, 7.5a). These bear a strong resemblance to the manganese-rich stains that occur on west Mexican ceramic figurines, which are caused by metal-fixing bacterial or fungal colonies in microenvironments created by shaft-and-chamber tombs (Pickering and Cuevas 2003).[3] I strongly suspect, but cannot yet prove, that the stains on Moundville palettes are also biological in origin, a byproduct of objects being buried in an organic wrapping, which provided the nutrients and perhaps air pockets in which these microorganisms could thrive. The fact that some of the wrapping impressions described previously consist entirely of these stains lends credence to this idea (figure 7.5a), although the hypothesis remains to be tested by geochemical and microscopic studies.

As mentioned previously, the pigment residues found on Moundville palettes are mostly white or red in color, and sometimes black. The only chemical analysis ever done on these pigments was commissioned by C. B. Moore in 1905, when his colleague, H. F. Keller, determined that the white substance on one of the palettes was cerrusite, a weathering product of galena (Moore 1905: 145–47). There can be little doubt that the red consists of hematite, but the black remains a mystery. Clearly, much more work needs to be done along these lines.

All in all, it is reasonable to conclude that palettes at Moundville were kept in bundles, like those at Etowah. Unlike at Etowah, however, there is little evidence that these bundles contained anything other than the palettes themselves, or at least anything nonperishable. Lumps of colorful or specular minerals—such as galena, hematite, glauconite, psilomelane (black hematite), and mica—are not uncommon at Moundville, but they tend *not* to occur in the same burials with palettes. Of the 36 palette burials that are reasonably well documented, only seven contained lumps of pigment, and in only five of these cases were the pigments placed near the palette itself. In other words, even though palettes and pigments were clearly used together—as indicated by pigment residues on palette surfaces and their co-occurrence in mound contexts (Knight 2010: 158–59)—they were not consistently placed together in the same graves. This suggests that the palette rituals at Moundville entailed a division of labor in which various elements used in the ritual were contributed by different groups or individuals. Such an interpretation is entirely consistent with the kind of partitive ritual structure that Knight (2010: 348–60) has inferred for Moundville, based on the overall distribution of ritual paraphernalia among the mounds.

Implications

If we accept, at least for the sake of argument, that Moundville palettes were ritual gear kept in sacred bundles, what does this tell us about Moundville and the other Mississippian sites where these objects were found? Let us consider some implications, which are informed by the extensive ethnographic literature on bundles and their use in the Eastern Woodlands and Great Plains (see Hanson 1980; Richert 1969; Sidoff 1977; Zedeño 2008; and references therein).

First and foremost, it becomes implausible to think of these palettes as "prestige goods" in the Frankenstein and Rowlands (1978) sense. Ethnographically, we know that such bundles could never be given away as gifts. Owning a bundle required having the spiritual knowledge to handle the powers it embodied and the ritual paraphernalia it contained. One could acquire a bundle either by holding an office with ritual responsibilities or by apprenticing oneself to someone who held a bundle, acquiring the necessary songs and other knowledge, and eventually gaining the right to make one's own copy of the bundle.[4] These objects were more like what Weiner (1985, 1992) has called "inalienable possessions" than Frankenstein and Rowlands' "prestige goods."

Second, the individuals who used these palettes were "bundle keepers" who had acquired the necessary ritual knowledge and may have served as priests. This is entirely consistent with the finding by Phillips (this volume) that people buried with palettes could be either male or female but were always adults. Ethnographically, bundles varied along a continuum from "corporate" bundles, which were kept by religious or political officials on behalf of a social group, to "personal" bundles, which were kept by individuals for their own use. Elsewhere I have argued that the palette bundles at Etowah were corporate, based on their rarity and restricted contexts in Mound C (Steponaitis et al. 2011: 99). At Moundville, on the other hand, the relative abundance of palettes and their widespread distribution suggests that the bundles were personal. Sites and regions with unusual concentrations of palettes, such as Moundville and its environs, were places with many trained practitioners of the ritual in which the palettes were used. In other words, they were centers for certain kinds of religious practice.

Third, the dispersal of palettes from such centers does not represent trade or the giving of "prestige goods" as gifts, but rather the transmission of ritual knowledge. Ethnographically, the most plausible mechanism for such transmission would have been for those seeking ritual power to come to Moundville and apprentice themselves to the established practitioners. After acquiring the necessary knowledge, the new practitioner could then create a bundle containing a palette and bring it home as a tangible manifestation of this knowledge and the spiritual power it conferred.

In sum, the realization that palettes were parts of sacred bundles requires us to change our notions about the nature of Mississippian centers and how such objects moved across the landscape. In addition to seeing Moundville as a seat of political power, we must now also see it as a center of spiritual power, a place of priestly activity. Along the same lines, neither "trade" nor gift-giving can account for the movement of these objects over hundreds of kilometers. We must instead understand Moundville as a place of pilgrimage, where people came from great distances to acquire the knowledge that its priests and other religious practitioners possessed.

Acknowledgments

I wish to thank the many individuals who helped me with access to the museum collections that are at the heart of this study: Mary Bade, Patricia Capone, Thomas Evans, Viva Fisher, Eugene Futato, Gloria Greis, Susan Haskell, James Krakker, Mary Jane Lenz, Pamela Edwards Lieb, Diana Loren, Patricia Miller-Beech, Jo Miles-Seeley, Patricia Nietfeld, and Bruce Smith. Crucial support for travel to these museums was provided by the Graham Research Fund at the University of North Carolina at Chapel Hill. C. Margaret Scarry and Laurie Steponaitis, Jon Marcoux, and an anonymous reviewer gave useful comments on earlier drafts. But above all I wish to acknowledge, with heartfelt gratitude, my debt to Christopher Peebles, who in 1974 invited me to join him in his Moundville research and thereby started me on a road that I am still traveling today.

Notes

1. In this respect the Moundville palettes differ markedly from those at Etowah, which often have rounded bottoms and depressed centers on top (Steponaitis et al. 2011: 2, figure 2).

2. Another possible Moundville palette was found at the Long Island site in Roane County, Tennessee (Chapman 1982: figure 70). It currently resides at the McClung Museum in Knoxville (catalog number 42/29Re17). This palette is made of gray sandstone, and its decoration is consistent with the Hemphill style (Knight and Steponaitis 2011), but I cannot be certain of its source without examining the stone in more detail.

3. The literature on this staining, which is usually called "rock varnish" or "desert varnish," is considerable (e.g., Aronson and Kingery 1990; Dorn and Oberlander 1981; O'Grady 2004; Taylor-George et al. 1983; and references therein). At Moundville these stains occur most often on palettes and pipes—exactly the kind of ritual gear that was likely to have been bundled.

4. Ethnographic accounts from the Great Plains sometimes refer to the "purchase" of bundles, but this term is misleading. Such transactions were actually more like apprenticeships, in which the owner instructed the recipient in the proper treatment and use of the bundle, and the recipient in turn was expected to compensate the owner with gifts (see Richert 1969; Sidoff 1977).

8

Rural Settlement in the Black Warrior Valley

SCOTT W. HAMMERSTEDT, MINTCY D. MAXHAM,
AND JENNIFER L. MYER

Archaeologists have long been interested in the famous mounds and artifacts found at Moundville in west central Alabama. While we have known the location of most of the mounds within the Black Warrior Valley for much of the past century, comparatively little attention has been paid either to these mounds or to the more numerous nonmound sites within the valley and in the surrounding uplands. However, in the last decade there has been an increase in interest in outlying sites, their distribution on the landscape, and their role in Moundville's political, social, and religious systems. Our purpose in this chapter is to summarize the results of two projects: the University of Alabama's Black Warrior Valley Survey (Hammerstedt 2000, 2001; Hammerstedt and Myer 2001; Myer 2002a, 2002b, 2003) and Maxham's analysis of the Moundville Coal Degasification Field (Maxham 2000, 2004). We discuss the environmental and social conditions that drove settlement location in the Black Warrior Valley during the Late Woodland and Mississippi periods and provide a concrete picture of basic population trends.

History of Research

Until the 1970s, research in the Black Warrior Valley focused largely on Moundville and on the outlying mounds found along a roughly 40-km stretch of the river (figure 8.1). At least 14 mounds are known to exist; nearly all were visited by Clarence B. Moore in the early 1900s (Moore 1905, 1907).[1] Welch (1998) described most of these mounds in detail, and it is not necessary to replow that ground here. However, Moore (1905:

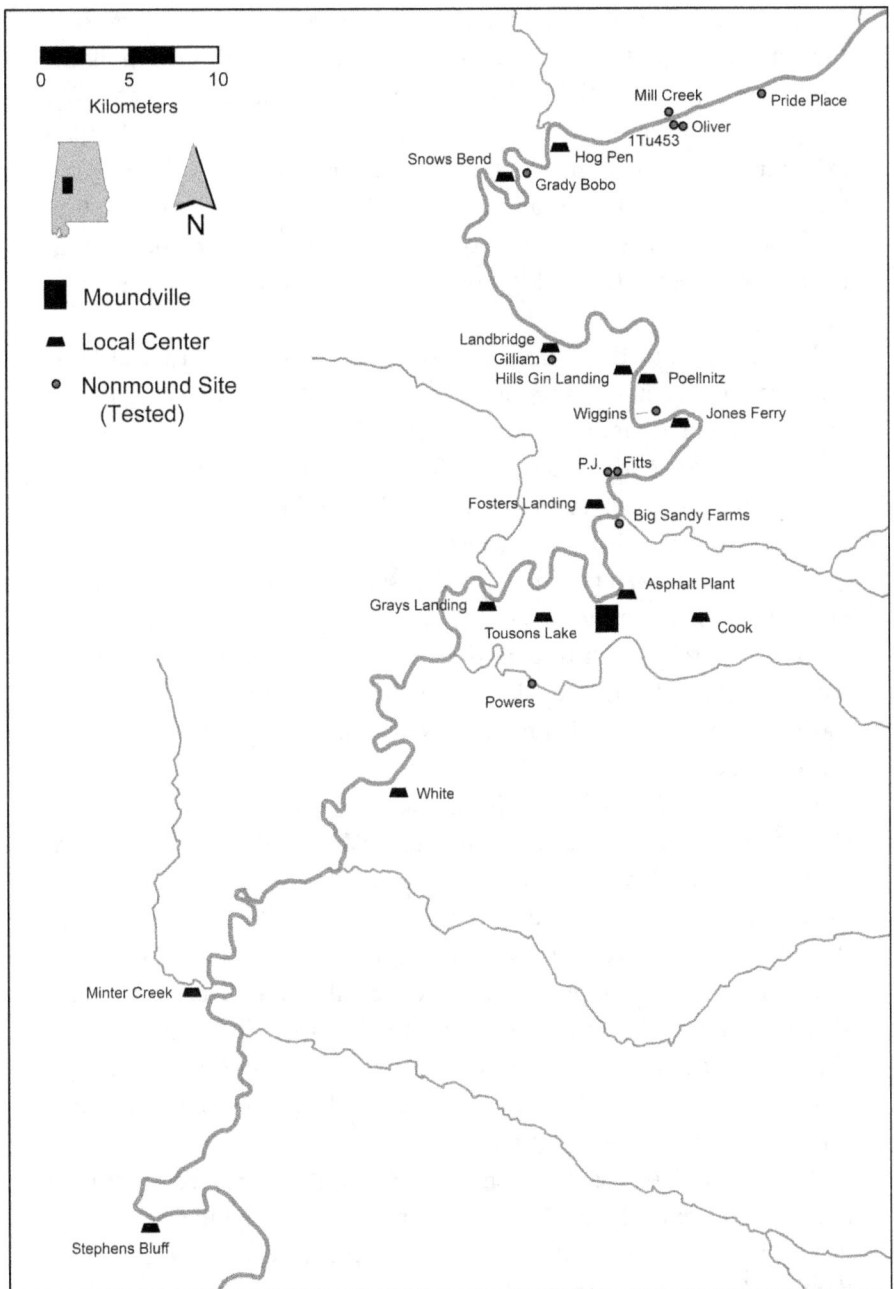

Figure 8.1. Sites in the Black Warrior Valley.

124, 244) described a remnant mound on the bank of the Black Warrior River below the Foster's Ferry Landbridge. As this mound was completely eroded by the river in the intervening years, it was largely forgotten. We do not know when this mound was constructed, because no collections exist, but since all other mounds in the valley are clearly Mississippian, we feel comfortable including it as a Moundville-related site. Myer (2002a) used the locations of known sites on Moore's map to digitize the approximate location of the Landbridge mound, and it is included in the analyses presented here.[2]

Lacking data to the contrary, it was once assumed that all of these mounds were contemporary and that the population was nucleated in towns centered at mounds (Bozeman 1982; Welch 1998). The first efforts to model settlement patterns came from Peebles (1978) and Steponaitis (1978) using data from surveys conducted by Walter B. Jones and David DeJarnette in the 1930s. Peebles recognized three clusters of villages and mound-village pairs and proposed that sites were preferentially located on well-drained and fertile soils. He also argued for a three-tiered settlement hierarchy consisting of major center, minor center, and village-hamlet. Steponaitis agreed with this hierarchy but added a "farmstead" category and suggested that mounds were selectively placed to minimize movement costs.

In 1978 and 1979, the University of Michigan Museum of Anthropology (UMMA) conducted a survey in the Black Warrior Valley, during which known sites were revisited, and controlled surface collections were made. Bozeman (1982), in his analysis of these surface collections, eliminated the village-hamlet category. His artifact-density maps indicated that what were thought to be large villages were actually large, overlapping Late Woodland artifact scatters mixed with smaller, spatially restricted, Mississippian occupations. This caused overestimates of site size. Bozeman's work also showed that the mounds were not all contemporary and were actually occupied at different times.

As Paul Welch (1998: 138) has noted, until the 1970s archaeologists were largely unaware of the existence or abundance of outlying sites, mainly due to the lack of systematic surveys. Nielsen et al. (1973) surveyed portions of Hale and Greene counties south of Moundville and reported the presence of what they termed "camps," but the first systematic survey in the Black Warrior Valley was not conducted until 1976. A University of Alabama field school directed by John Walthall surveyed 6 sq km along

Big Sandy Creek, resulting in the identification of 20 small scatters of shell-tempered pottery that were identified as farmsteads. Similarly, UMMA crews surveyed several plowed fields in 1978 and 1979 and found numerous small scatters of shell-tempered sherds (Bozeman 1982: 216–27; Welch 1998: 138). Cultural resource management projects in the 1980s and 1990s, as well as the research presented here, have identified even more of these sites, nine of which have been tested (figure 8.1).

From this evidence it became clear that there were numerous outlying settlements—which we will simply call nonmound sites or rural settlements rather than "farmsteads," which is a more loaded term, because it implies function. Until the two projects to be discussed here, only the most basic information on the presence and distribution of nonmound sites was known (Welch 1998: 138).

University of Alabama Black Warrior Valley Survey

In 1998 the University of Alabama, under the direction of Vernon J. Knight, Jr., initiated the Black Warrior Valley Survey (BWVS). The goals of the project were to investigate portions of the floodplain in tandem with reanalysis of existing collections from previously known sites. Two transects, each 4.8 km (3 mi) wide, were chosen for intensive survey (figure 8.2). These were oriented east to west, to take advantage of varying topographic conditions within the alluvial floodplain and to provide coverage both near and far from known mounds. The southern boundary of the southern transect followed the Hale-Tuscaloosa county line, intersecting Moundville and the Touson Lake mounds, and also included the Asphalt Plant, Gray's Landing, and Fosters Landing mounds. The other transect was placed 4.8 km (3 mi) north and contained the Hill's Gin Landing, Poellnitz, and Landbridge mounds. The western boundaries of both transects were delineated by the valley wall, and the eastern boundary was delineated by Highway 69 and the Great Southern Railroad.

The first two seasons of the BWVS were largely restricted to surface survey of plowed fields within the floodplain, although limited shovel testing was conducted late in the second season to increase the representativeness of survey coverage by including more marginal areas (Hammerstedt 2000; Hammerstedt and Myer 2001). The third season combined surface collection and shovel testing, and the fourth season focused on test excavations at several sites recorded during seasons 1–3 (Myer 2002a,

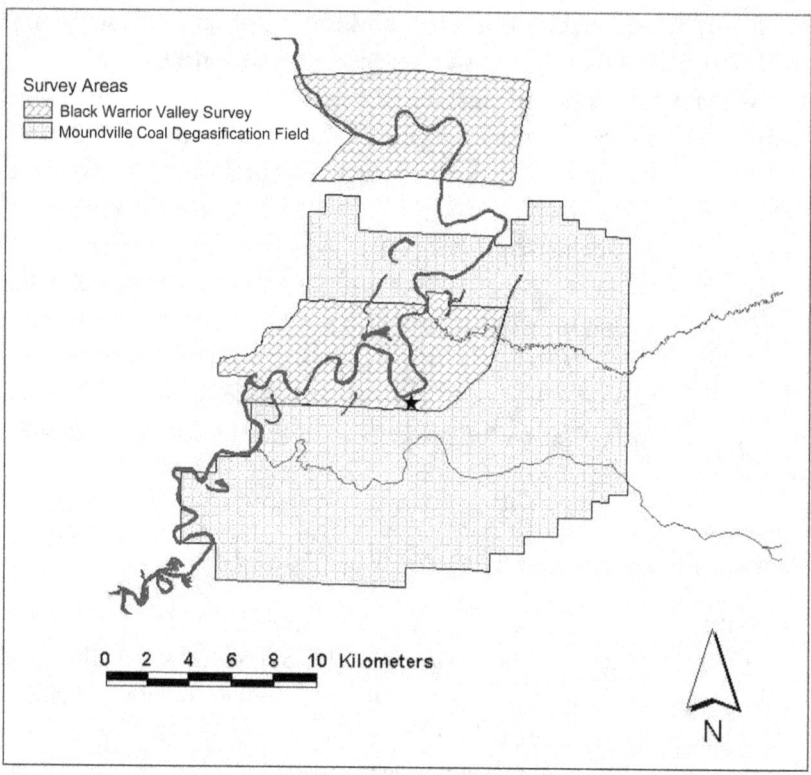

Figure 8.2. Black Warrior Valley Survey (BWVS) transects and Moundville Coal Degasification Field (MCDF). A star shows Moundville's location.

2002b, 2003). The three seasons of survey covered almost 13 sq km, over 100 sites were recorded, and collections from over 100 previously recorded sites were reexamined.

Moundville Coal Degasification Field Project

Maxham's analysis of the Moundville Coal Degasification Field (MCDF) began in the late 1990s. The MCDF covers 265 sq km in both Hale and Tuscaloosa counties, encompasses the heart of the Moundville chiefdom, and is one of 22 coal degasification fields in Alabama. These fields are bounded areas in which wells are drilled to release methane gas from coal seams. Unlike the BWVS, which focused primarily on the floodplain, the MCDF includes sections of both floodplain and uplands (figure 8.2).

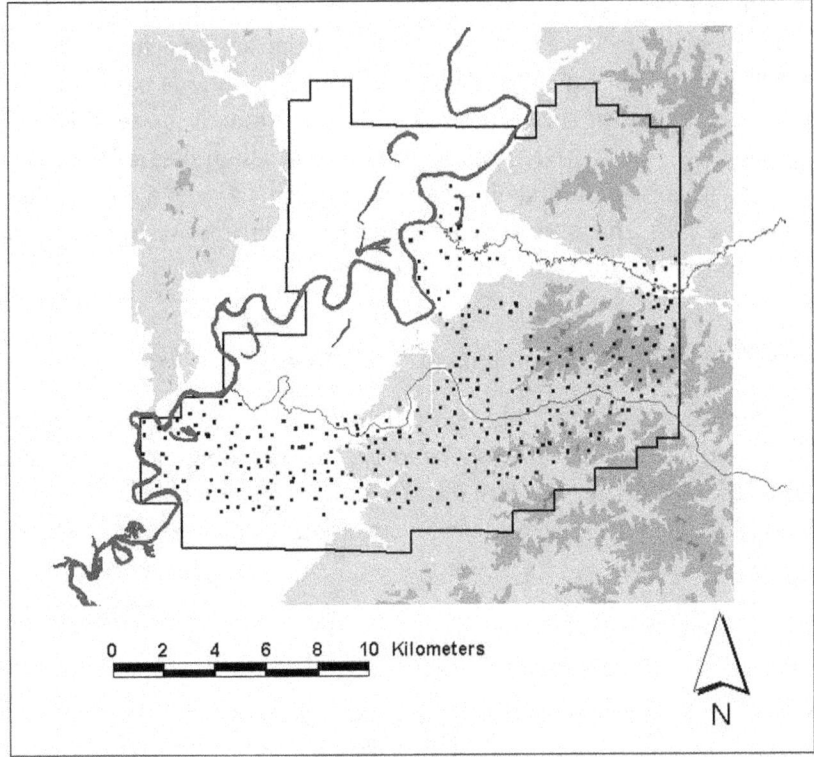

Figure 8.3. Surveyed well pads in the Moundville Coal Degasification Field (MCDF).

Within the MCDF, 357 well pad areas and accompanying access roads totaling nearly 3 sq km have been surveyed for archaeological sites by cultural resource management firms (figure 8.3; Maxham 2004: 31) with a total of 202 sites recorded in the Alabama State Site Files. No new survey work took place during Maxham's analysis of the MCDF, but detailed GIS analysis on both environmental and social variables was conducted. Data generated by the BWVS and Big Sandy survey was included in the MCDF analysis when their physical boundaries overlapped.

Both of these projects, while providing important data, have their flaws. The BWVS has excellent coverage of large portions of the floodplain, but very little coverage of the uplands. The MCDF covers a large area and includes both upland and floodplain settings, but only a fraction of it has been surveyed. Neither includes the entire geographic extent of the Moundville polity. However, by combining these data, we are able to obtain a clearer picture of the native landscape of Moundville. A further problem is the lack of diagnostic artifacts from outlying sites. We can assign sites to the Late Woodland or Mississippi periods based on the presence of grog- or shell-tempered pottery, but more time-sensitive diagnostics are rare. In most cases we are unable to assign sites to individual phases within the Moundville sequence as defined by Knight and Steponaitis (1998). Therefore, until newer data are available, we are restricted to broad comparisons of the Late Woodland and Mississippi periods.

Late Woodland and Mississippian Landscapes

Of interest to us is not only the settlement pattern of the Moundville chiefdom, but also the site distribution of the preceding Late Woodland West Jefferson phase (figures 8.4 and 8.5). Earlier studies suggest a striking similarity in the type of environmental setting preferred by both West

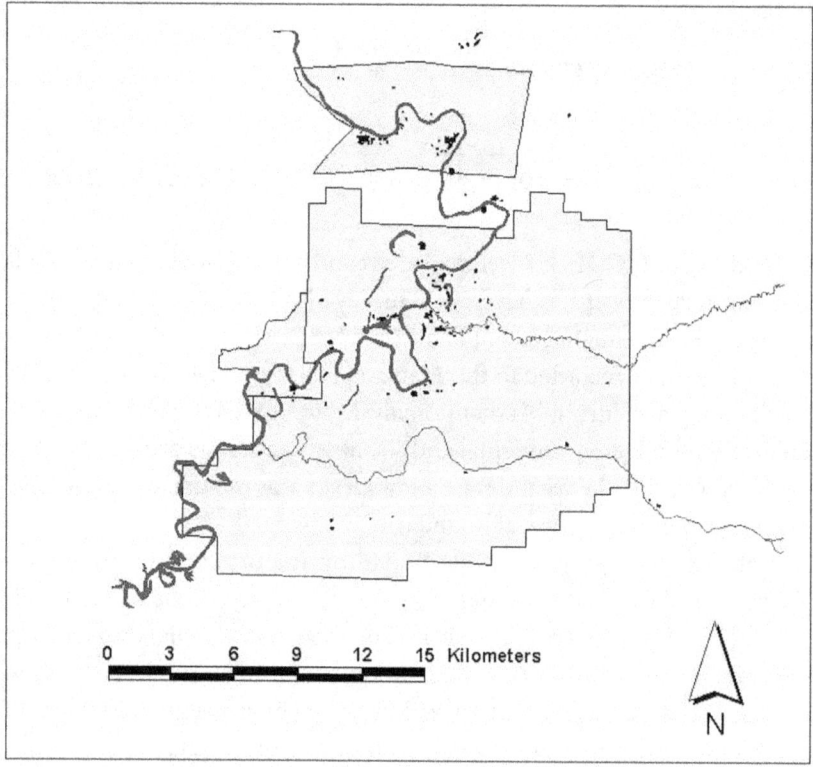

Figure 8.4. Late Woodland period sites in the combined MCDF-BWVS study area.

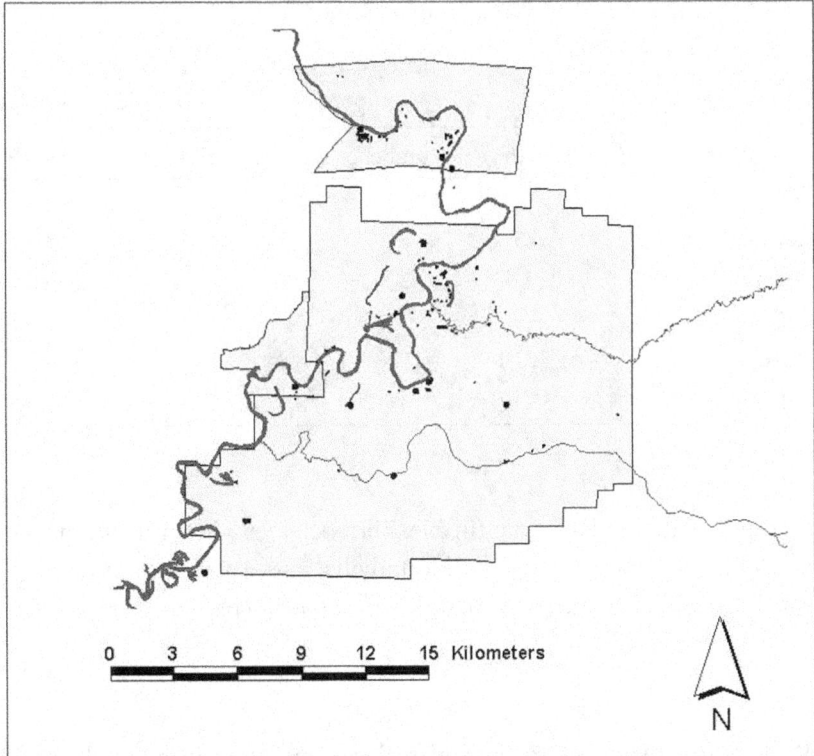

Figure 8.5. Mississippi period sites in the combined MCDF-BWVS study area.

Jefferson and Moundville people (Hammerstedt 2000), but these did not account for upland habitation. To make meaningful statements about the Black Warrior Valley landscape over time, we use the distribution of Late Woodland and Mississippian sites to investigate environmental and social variables and the ways in which these variables affected the choices people made when selecting site locations.

To quantify site densities, we employ a site-density index in which we count the number of sites in the surveyed portion of a given stratum (as defined by one of the variables below), divide this number by the surveyed area in that stratum (in hectares), then multiply by 100 (Maxham 2004: 47).[3] This index is a relative measure that can serve as a proxy for site or population density. In other words, indices can be compared to one another but do not translate directly into population.

The environmental variables we explore are topographic zone, distance to water, and soil type. These are readily available in the Alabama archaeo-

Table 8.1. Nonmound Sites by Topographic Zone

Project: Topographic Zone	Surveyed Area (ha)	Late Woodland Components		Mississippian Nonmound Components	
		Number	Density	Number	Density
MCDF:					
Floodplain	125	6	4.8	4	3.2
Uplands	171.5	2	1.2	1	0.6
BWVS:					
Floodplain	1,322.1	110	8.3	89	6.7
Uplands	55.1	3	5.4	2	3.6

logical site files and are quantifiable. The social variables are distance to single mound sites, distance to Moundville, and distance to other nonmound sites. Each of these variables is now considered in turn.

Topographic Zone

We use only two topographic zones: floodplain and uplands (table 8.1). These are determined by whether a site is more or less than 50 m above sea level. Some 52 percent of the MCDF and 96 percent of the BWVS fall in the floodplain. Over 80 percent of both Late Woodland and Mississippian sites are in the floodplain. However, the indices for upland Late Woodland sites are somewhat higher than we would expect, although this is somewhat inflated by the BWVS results, which recorded three Late Woodland components in only 55 ha surveyed. The indices for the Mississippian components are less than those for the Late Woodland for both surveys, but a higher number of sites are recorded for the floodplain. This could indicate that Mississippian people were drawn to the floodplain in greater numbers, but more upland survey is necessary to confirm this possibility.

Distance to Water

There are three major waterways in the study area: the Black Warrior River, Big Sandy Creek, and Elliotts Creek (figure 8.1). While other water sources, such as oxbows, swamps, and intermittent streams, do ex-

Table 8.2. Sites by Distance to Water

Project: Distance to Major Waterway (m)	Surveyed Area (ha)	Late Woodland Components		Mississippian Non-mound Components	
		Number	Density	Number	Density
MCDF:					
0–400	72.3	5	6.9	5	6.9
400–800	51.8	1	1.9	—	—
800–1200	38.5	—	—	—	—
1200+	133.9	2	1.5	—	—
BWVS:					
0–400	654.9	82	12.5	68	10.4
400–800	443.5	22	5	20	4.5
800–1200	168.9	8	4.7	3	1.8
1200+	119.7	1	0.8	—	—

ist, these three waterways would have served as transportation routes in addition to being important sources of food and water. To assess the importance of these water sources, zones or "buffers" were arbitrarily constructed around each at 400-m intervals using GIS software, and the relative abundance of site within these buffers was examined.

The vast majority, 70 percent, of both Late Woodland and Mississippian sites fall within 400 m of one of these major waterways (table 8.2). The Late Woodland site density indices for this interval are 6.9 for the MCDF and 12.5 for the BWVS, with very similar indices for the Mississippian. This indicates that people's preference for water was nearly the same in both the Late Woodland and Mississippi periods.

Soil Type

There are five general soil series in the study area. Cahaba-Adaton-Ellisville, Smithdale-Luverne-Maubila, and Lucedale-Greenville-Bama are by far the most plentiful. The other two units represent only 5 percent and 1 percent of the soils, respectively. Cahaba-Adaton-Ellisville include diverse floodplain soils with a wide range of drainage characteristics, Smithdale-

Table 8.3. Sites by Soil Type

Project: Generalized Soil Map Unit	Surveyed Area (ha)	Late Woodland Components		Mississippian Components		
		Number	Density	Nonmound Number	Mound Number	Total Density
MCDF:						
Cahaba-Adaton-Ellisville	154.9	8	5.2	4	6	2.6
Bama-Smithdale-Shatta	—	—	—	—	—	—
Smithdale-Luverne-Maubila	81.5	—	—	—	—	—
Cahaba-Leaf-Alamuchee	1.7	—	—	—	—	—
Lucedale-Greenville-Bama	58.5	—	—	1	—	1.7
BWVS:						
Cahaba-Adaton-Ellisville	1,373.9	113	8.2	91	6	6.6
Bama-Smithdale-Shatta	8.5	—	—	—	—	—
Smithdale-Luverne-Maubila	4.7	—	—	—	—	—
Cahaba-Leaf-Alamuchee	—	—	—	—	—	—
Lucedale-Greenville-Bama	—	—	—	—	—	—

Luverne-Maubila are well-drained soils, and Lucedale-Greenville-Bama are well-drained upland soils (Johnson 1981; Maxham 2004).

The majority of Late Woodland sites are found in the Cahaba series soils, with high density indices in both survey areas (table 8.3). Clearly, the West Jefferson inhabitants preferred floodplain soils. The same pattern holds true in the Mississippi period, when nearly all sites, including all mounds, are found in these soils. However, one site in the MCDF is in the Lucedale-Greenville-Bama series, which is a deep, well-drained upland soil. This indicates that not all sites were placed in areas suitable for agriculture, as this soil series is not conducive to farming (Johnson 1981).

Geologic formation was also examined. Within both the MCDF and BWVS survey areas, all Late Woodland and Mississippian sites fall into geologic zones that correspond with alluvial, coastal, and low terrace deposit—in other words, floodplain soils. Most of the surveyed well pads in the MCDF are in upland geologic zones where no sites were found, indicating that sampling bias is not influencing these results (Maxham 2004).

Distance to Single-Mound Sites

As mentioned previously, we believe that social factors also played a role in the Moundville landscape. The combined MCDF and BWVS survey areas include most of the known single mounds. These mounds were constructed during the Mississippi period, so the distribution of nonmound

Table 8.4. Sites by Distance to Mound

Project: Distance to Mound (km)	Surveyed Area (ha)	Late Woodland Components		Mississippian Non-mound Components	
		Number	Density	Number	Density
MCDF:					
0–1	19.2	1	5.2	—	—
1–2	47.7	3	6.3	2	4.2
2–3	56	3	5.4	2	3.6
3–4	50.2	1	2.0	—	—
4–5	51	—	—	1	2.0
5–6	38.5	—	—	—	—
6+	74.4	—	—	—	—
BWVS:					
0–1	333	50	15.0	45	13.5
1–2	589.5	39	6.6	27	4.6
2–3	333.7	23	6.9	16	4.8
3–4	102.2	1	1.0	2	2.0
4–5	27.8	—	—	1	3.6
5–6	0.9	—	—	—	—
6+	—	—	—	—	—

sites with respect to mounds is potentially important. Late Woodland sites, while not contemporary with mound construction, are also examined here. The distribution of Late Woodland sites can indicate whether the areas in which mounds were eventually built had some importance prior to construction.

Buffers were constructed at 1-km intervals around each mound within the study areas. In both the BWVS and MCDF, the majority of Late Woodland sites are within 3 km of a mound (table 8.4). However, the site density for the 0–1-km interval in the BWVS sample is more than double the next-highest density. These results suggest that the areas in which mounds were later constructed were important before the Mississippi period. During the Mississippi period, these results are repeated and more pronounced. Nearly half of all Mississippian sites in the BWVS sample are within 1 km of a mound, and the vast majority are within 3 km. The MCDF data are slightly different and, on the surface, seem to show that people preferred to be some distance from a mound. However, only 19 ha within 1 km of a mound were actually surveyed in the MCDF; we therefore consider the BWVS data to be more reliable.

Distance to Moundville

We now turn to the impact of Moundville on the placement of rural sites. We constructed 2-km buffers around Moundville, since larger intervals mask variation in density indices, and again looked at both Late Woodland and Mississippian components. Within the MCDF, most people in both periods seem to have lived within 2–6 km of Moundville, with a denser population between 4 and 6 km (table 8.5). One surprise is the high density index for Late Woodland within 2 km of Moundville. This could indicate the importance of this area before Moundville was constructed, but more likely is a result of two Late Woodland sites intersecting by chance in a relatively small surveyed area. The latter suggestion is supported by the much lower site density index for the same area in the BWVS data.

The BWVS data extend further from Moundville than the MCDF. During both Late Woodland and Mississippian, there is a spike in site density at 2–6 km and another at 10–14 km. There is a gap at 6–10 km simply because the BWVS transects do not include this area (table 8.5).

Table 8.5. Nonmound Sites by Distance to Moundville

Project: Distance to Moundville (km)	Surveyed area (ha)	Late Woodland Components		Mississippian Nonmound Components	
		Number	Density	Number	Density
MCDF:					
0–2	9.2	2	21.7	—	—
2–4	43.5	1	2.3	1	2.3
4–6	67.7	4	5.9	3	4.4
6–8	81.9	1	1.2	—	—
8+	96.1	—	—	1	1.3
BWVS:					
0–2	177.6	7	3.9	4	2.3
2–4	347.1	24	6.9	20	5.8
4–6	256.4	27	10.5	28	10.9
6–8	35.8	1	2.8	—	—
8–10	—	—	—	—	—
10–12	254.8	36	14.1	28	11
12–14	181.1	13	7.2	9	5
14–16	134.3	5	3.7	2	1.5

Distance to Nonmound Sites

The last social variable is distance between nonmound sites. Four concentric buffers at intervals of 0.25 km were defined around each nonmound site, both Late Woodland and Mississippian. Any site whose buffers do not overlap with another site is more than 2 km from its nearest neighbor.

The vast majority of sites in both the Late Woodland and Mississippian are within 1 km of another site (table 8.6). People appear to have deliberately chosen to live near one another. The nearest neighbor statistics for both periods are almost zero (Late Woodland $R^2 = 4.8 \times 10^{-6}$; Mississippian $R^2 = 4.2 \times 10^{-6}$), indicating a strong tendency toward clustering. Nearly 7 percent of sites, however, are more than 1 km apart. Many of these are considerably larger than average, suggesting that more people

Table 8.6. Sites by Distance to Nearest Nonmound Site

Distance to Nearest Nonmound Site (km)	Late Woodland Components			Mississippian Components		
	MCDF (n)	BWVS (n)	Combined (n)	MCDF (n)	BWVS (n)	Combined (n)
0.0–0.5	72	115	131	67	100	116
0.5–1.0	13	11	18	10	4	11
1.0–1.5	7	3	8	3	1	4
1.5–2.0	1	1	1	1	—	1
2.0+	2	—	2	3	—	3

lived at them. It should be noted, however, that not all these sites are contemporary, and further study will undoubtedly revise this picture.

Summary of Environmental and Social Variables

So, what does this all mean? It is apparent that there was continuity between land-use patterns from Late Woodland through Mississippian, thus confirming earlier observations (Hammerstedt 2000; Steponaitis 1983a: 167). People preferred to live on the floodplain and low terraces of major waterways and on the deepest well-drained soils. Location near a water source was important, although frequently flooded areas were avoided. We expect that further excavations and tighter chronological control at rural settlements, particularly within the Moundville phases, will refine the patterns presented here.

Given the lack of rural sites near Moundville, it seems likely that the outlying mound sites were more central to the daily life of the valley's Mississippian inhabitants than Moundville itself. People may not have traveled to Moundville on a regular basis, if at all. This could be linked to Knight and Steponaitis's (1998) interpretation of Moundville as a vacant ceremonial center in which the majority of the residents of the site moved outward into the valley around AD 1300, leaving only a small population of resident elites.

Clearly during both periods, people chose to live near one another. During the Mississippi period, clusters of sites were often located near mounds (figure 8.6). Being near a mound would have made it easy for people to access political, religious, and social activities and likely would

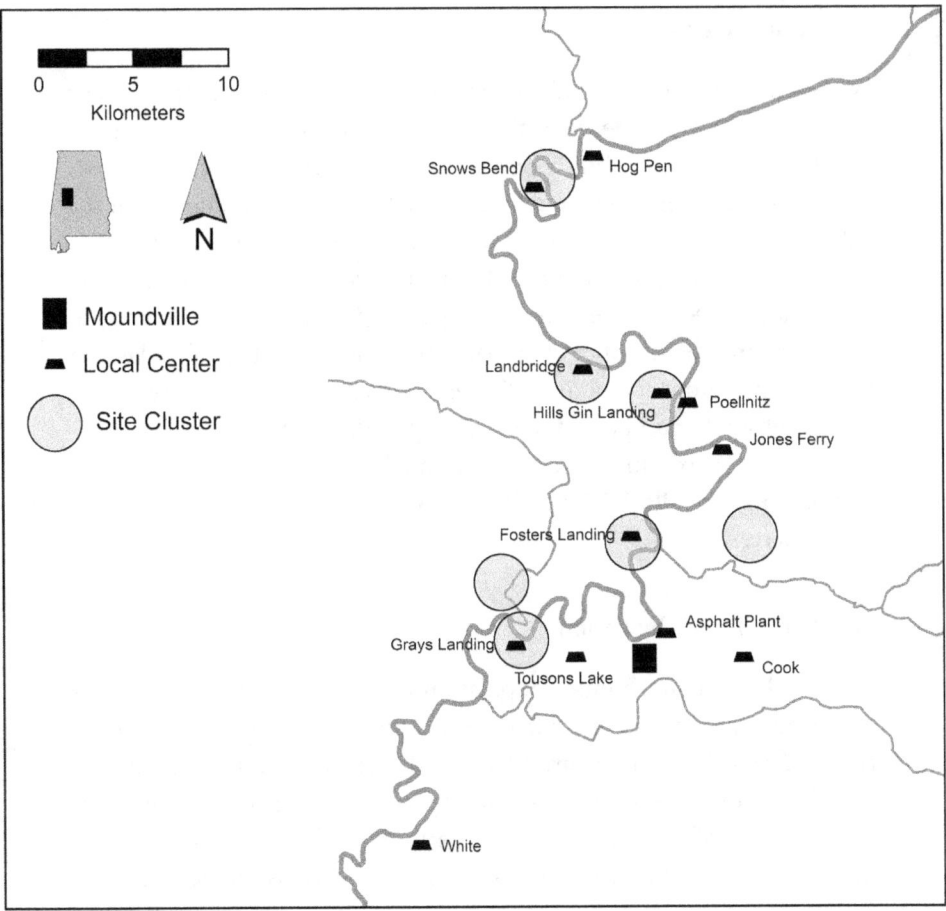

Figure 8.6. Known site clusters.

have provided a sense of community outside one's immediate household. Elsewhere, we have suggested that these clusters represent rural communities, perhaps towns (Hammerstedt 2000; Maxham 2004; Myer 2002a). The continuity of site locations suggests that these communities may have begun in the Late Woodland and continued after the construction of Moundville.

People made many decisions when determining where they were going to live. As we have shown, many factors, both environmental and social, came into play. Practical matters such as access to water and good soil were just as important as social issues, such as proximity to mounds and relatives.

Population Trends

We now turn from the social and environmental characteristics of Black Warrior Valley settlements to the more thorny issue of the number of people who lived there. Early population estimates proposed 3,000 residents of Moundville itself, and between 10,000 and 30,000 people in the entire valley (Peebles 1983: 190; 1987: 9–10). More recent work suggests that the maximum population at Moundville was probably closer to 1,000 (Steponaitis 1998). It is clear that more people lived at Moundville early in its history and that most of the inhabitants moved into the valley later in time (Knight and Steponaitis 1998; Steponaitis 1998), although the data to provide absolute numbers of the valley's population currently do not exist. However, Maxham (2004) has examined relative changes in the rural population of the Black Warrior Valley over time, and we summarize her results here.

Population Trends by Period

The simplest way to estimate population is to count the number of sites by period. Sites were assigned to periods using a straightforward decision rule: sites with at least one grog-tempered sherd were designated as Late Woodland, and sites with at least one shell-tempered sherd as Mississippian. A count of sites dating to each period reveals that 160 sites date to the Late Woodland period, and 135 date to the Mississippi period (table 8.7).

To convert these counts to population trends, one must take into account the lengths of these archaeological periods, as sites were not occupied for the entire duration of each period. The Late Woodland period dates to AD 600–1120, a span of 520 years. The Mississippi period dates to AD 1120–1520, 400 years. If we assume that sites were occupied the same average length of time during the Late Woodland and Mississippi periods, dividing the number of sites by the span of the archaeological period gives us a very rough measure of relative site density. By this estimate, site densities were roughly equivalent during these periods (table 8.7), a conclusion one might intuit by examining the distributions of sites across the valley (see figures 8.4–8.5).

Of course, a major weakness of this simple measure is that it fails to take into account site size. Archaeologists have long asserted that Late

Table 8.7. Distribution of Sites by Survey Area and Period

Study Area	Surveyed Area (ha)	Late Woodland Components		Mississippian Non-mound Components	
		Number	Number per Century	Number	Number per Century
MCDF	296.5	95	18.3	84	21.0
BWVS	1,377.2	130	25.0	105	26.3
Combined		160	30.8	135	33.8

Woodland sites are larger, on average, than Mississippian sites. If site size varies in proportion to population (see Peebles 1978: 408), more people lived at the late Woodland sites. Thus, equal site densities from the Late Woodland and Mississippi periods would not translate to equal populations. Rather, with more people at each site, Late Woodland population would be much larger.

Are Late Woodland sites in fact larger than Mississippian sites? Archaeologists have sometimes made this argument by assertion rather than with numbers, based largely on the observation that surface scatters of grog-tempered pottery in the valley tend to be larger than scatters of shell-tempered pottery (Bozeman 1982). One reason archaeologists have not made quantitative comparisons is that many sites have multiple occupations of potentially varying size, yet for each such case only one size, the site's maximum extent, is officially recorded in the files.[4]

The only way to compare site sizes with currently available data is to exclude all multicomponent sites. Within the study area, 63 sites are Late Woodland only, with a mean size of 0.56 ha, and 41 sites are Mississippian only, with a mean size of 0.32 ha. This provides some quantitative confirmation that Late Woodland sites are generally larger than Mississippian sites (see also Hammerstedt and Myer 2001). However, this conclusion is not as straightforward as we would like, for several reasons. First, as mentioned previously, we cannot tease apart palimpsests of multiple occupations on the same site. And second, grog-tempered sherds preserve better than shell-tempered sherds, thus making comparisons based on surface scatters problematic—an issue to be taken up more fully below.

Thus, period-to-period site counts offer only very limited information about population change in the valley through time. The distribution of sites indicates that the valley was not heavily populated in either the Late Woodland or Mississippi periods (see figures 8.4 and 8.5). Site densities were roughly equal, but Late Woodland population was probably larger, as Late Woodland sites are on average larger than Mississippian sites. To examine population change on a finer chronological scale, we turn now to a second approach, one that examines population on a phase-by-phase basis.

Population Trends by Phase

It is difficult to date sites to relatively short archaeological phases, especially when the number of diagnostics from any one site may be very low. Many nonmound sites are represented by only a handful of plain shell- and grog-tempered sherds. To look at rural population trends by phase, one must combine the pottery assemblages from three surveys and consider population in the valley as a whole, rather than on a site-by-site basis (table 8.8). In this approach one assumes that the overall number of sherds dating to each phase reflects the relative size of the regional population. The goal then becomes to determine what proportion of the

Table 8.8. Sherd Counts from the UMMA, BWVS, and MCDF Assemblages

Category: Type	UMMA	BWVS-MCDF	Combined Assemblage
Shell-tempered:			
Bell Plain	298	140	438
Bell Plain (with beaded rim)	16	12	28
Carthage Incised	39	11	50
Mississippi Plain	9,045	2,084	11,129
Moundville Engraved	38	13	51
Moundville Incised	45	18	63
Grog-tempered:			
Alligator Incised	49	3	52
Baytown Plain	46,675	8,653	55,328
Benson Punctated	0	0	0
Mulberry Creek Cord Marked	299	150	449
Total	56,504	11,084	67,588

combined assemblage was deposited during each phase. That proportion, corrected for differences in phase length, can be used as a proxy for regional population size, at least in a relative sense.

Initially, Maxham tried Kohler and Blinman's (1987) regression method to partition this aggregated assemblage into phases, based on the model assemblages compiled by Steponaitis (1998: table 2.1). This attempt was unsuccessful, largely because the model assemblage for the Moundville II–III phases was inappropriate for the dataset at hand: it was based on material excavated at Moundville, and its most distinctive engraved varieties—elaborately decorated finewares—almost never occur at rural sites (Maxham 2004: 104–18).

A more suitable method for our dataset relies on specific ceramic markers that correspond to discrete units of time. Unlike the regression method, which takes the frequencies of multiple pottery types into account, this method considers only one key marker per phase.

For example, Bell Plain beaded rims are diagnostic markers of post–AD 1350 Mississippian, the late Moundville II and Moundville III phases (LM2–M3). The premise of the diagnostic method is that beaded rims represent a constant proportion of an LM2–M3 assemblage. If one knows this proportion (based on a model assemblage) and also the number of beaded rims in a mixed collection, one can then estimate the percentage of that mixed collection that dates to LM2–M3. In simple mathematical terms, this relationship can be expressed as follows:

$$\frac{D_{model}}{N_{model}} = \frac{D_{mixed}}{N_{mixed}}$$

where D_{model} is the number of beaded rims (diagnostics) in the model assemblage, N_{model} is the total number of late LM2–M3 sherds in the model assemblage, D_{mixed} is the number of beaded rims in mixed assemblage, and N_{mixed} is the total number of LM2–M3 sherds in mixed assemblage. In this equation the number of beaded rims (D_{model}) and the total number of sherds (N_{model}) in the model LM2–M3 assemblage are known. We also know the number of beaded rims in the mixed assemblage (D_{mixed}). The unknown is the number of sherds in the mixed assemblage that date to LM2–M3 (N_{mixed}).

Ideally, one would like to estimate the number of sherds in the study collection that date to each of the phases of interest. To do that, one must

Table 8.9. Sherd Counts for Model Phase Assemblages

Category: Type	Carthage[a]	West Jefferson[b]	MI–Early MII[c]	Late MII–MIII[d]
Shell-tempered:				
Bell Plain	—	—	1,384	1,060
Bell Plain, beaded rim	—	—	2	14[e]
Carthage Incised	—	—	29	68
Mississippi Plain	—	94	2,553	2,572
Moundville Engraved	—	—	113	121
Moundville Incised	—	1	129[e]	39
Grog-tempered:				
Alligator Incised	—	4	—	1
Baytown Plain	90	8,266[e]	18	9
Benson Punctated	—	5	—	—
Mulberry Creek Cord Marked	10[e]	5	1	—
Total	100	8,375	4,229	3,884
D_{model} / N_{model}	0.1000	0.9870	0.0305	0.0036

[a]Model assemblage adapted from Jenkins 2003. See text for discussion.
[b]Model assemblage based on type counts from the West Jefferson type sites (1Je31, 1Je32, and 1Je33); see Jenkins and Nielsen (1974) and Steponaitis (1998:table 2.1).
[c]Model assemblage based on excavated data from Moundville, north of Mound R, 6N2W/AU.1, 6N2W/AU.2, 8N2E/AU.1, and 8N2E/AU.2; see Steponaitis (1983a:94–98, tables 18, 21, A.5, A.6).
[d]Model assemblage based on excavated data from Moundville, north of Mound R, 6N2W/AU.3a, 6N2W/AU.3b, and 8N2E/AU.3; see Steponaitis (1983a:94–98, tables 18, 21, A.5, A.6).
[e]Key marker (D_{model}) used in calculating sherd estimates.

have unique phase markers that are abundant in both the model and mixed assemblages, something that just is not possible. Instead we use the following analytical units, which correspond to relatively abundant and easily identifiable markers: Carthage phase (AD 600–1000), West Jefferson phase (AD 1000–1120), Moundville I–early Moundville II (AD 1120–1330), and late Moundville II–Moundville III (AD 1330–1520). The model assemblages for these units are presented in table 8.9.

The marker for the Carthage phase is the pottery type Mulberry Creek

Cord Marked. Jenkins (2003: 17) states that an ideal Carthage-phase assemblage should contain a maximum of 10–15 percent Mulberry Creek Cord Marked; we assume 10 percent. Our West Jefferson phase marker is Baytown Plain, which constitutes 98.7 percent of the model assemblage. For the Moundville I and early Moundville II phases, the marker is Moundville Incised, which for present purposes also includes sherds originally called Barton Incised, *var. Oliver*, nowadays commonly classified as Moundville Incised, *var. Oliver* (Knight 2010: 34–36). This category comprises 3 percent of the model assemblage. Finally, the late Moundville II–Moundville III assemblage is marked by the presence of beaded rims, an attribute of Bell Plain, *var. Hale* bowls and other forms, which appears on only 0.4 percent of the sherds in the model assemblage but is highly distinctive and reliably present in any reasonably sized sample from this time.

Given these parameters, the method just described estimates the number of sherds from each temporal unit as follows (table 8.9): Carthage phase, 4,490 sherds; West Jefferson phase, 56,058 sherds; Moundville I–early Moundville II phases, 2,065 sherds; and late Moundville II–Moundville III phases, 7,768 sherds. The equation yields individual estimates totaling 70,381 sherds, a reasonably good fit with the actual total of 67,588.

These numbers, of course, do not account for the differential decomposition of shell-tempered pottery. The acidic soils in the Southeast leach shell from shell-tempered pottery and leave it more vulnerable to destruction by plowing than Late Woodland grog-tempered sherds, a problem compounded by a switch from chisel plowing to disking in the 1970s (Hammerstedt 2000: 44; see also Milner 1998: 105). Maxham (2004: 110–12), using published sherd counts from five sites in the Big Sandy Creek/Hull Lake area collected more than 20 years apart (Hammerstedt 2000; Walthall and Coblentz 1977), calculated a decomposition rate for shell-tempered sherds of 4.7 percent per year.

Because grog-tempered sherds are not affected by shell decomposition, the Carthage and West Jefferson phase estimates remain the same. To correct the estimates for the later phases, the decomposition factor can be applied to the shell-tempered types, taking account of when the collections were made and standardizing the counts to the year 1976, when the first modern survey in the Black Warrior Valley was carried out (table 8.10). Not surprisingly, the estimates for the Mississippi period increase substantially: the sherd count for Moundville I–early Moundville II rises to 2,983, and that for late Moundville II–Moundville III almost doubles to 14,704.

Dividing the number of sherds by the span of each temporal unit allows us to calculate annual deposition rates, expressed in units of sherds per year (table 8.10). This rate provides a crude estimate of the relative population size in each interval. It appears that rural population increased dramatically in West Jefferson, then declined dramatically in Moundville I–early Moundville II, and rebounded in late Moundville II–Moundville III, albeit not nearly to the same level as before (figure 8.7).

The attenuated rebound in late Moundville II–Moundville III might well be the result of differential sherd decomposition or biases in our sampling. First, recall that the empirically calculated decomposition rate for shell-tempered sherds since 1976 is 4.7 percent per year. That translates to a loss rate of 90 percent over 50 years! Even if the calculated rate is the result of modern farming practices and the actual rate was much lower before the 1970s, it is easy to see how this factor may have greatly decreased our relative estimates of Mississippian population given the method we used. Second, there are several large single-mound centers located outside the MCDF-BWVS study area. Therefore these mounds and surrounding nonmound sites are not included. If this study were expanded to include these sites, the later population estimates would likely increase.

The results presented here indicate that population was lower during the Carthage phase than the West Jefferson phase. The increase in people

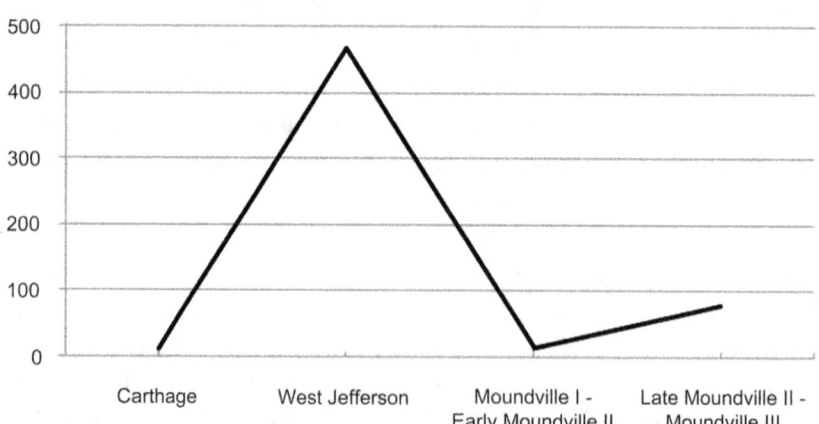

Figure 8.7. Estimated annual sherd deposition rates, corrected for differential sherd preservation.

Table 8.10. Estimated Rates of Sherd Deposition by Temporal Unit

Temporal Unit	Phase Duration (years)	Key Marker (n)	D_{model}/N_{model}	Uncorrected			Corrected[a]		
				Estimated Sherds in Assemblage		Deposition Rate	Estimated Sherds in Assemblage		Deposition Rate
				(n)	(%)	(sherds/yr)	(n)	(%)	(sherds/yr)
Late Moundville II–Moundville III	195	28	0.0036	7,768	11	39.8	14,704	18.8	75.4
Moundville I–early Moundville II	205	63	0.0305	2,065	2.9	10.1	2,983	3.8	14.6
West Jefferson phase	120	55,328	0.9870	56,058	79.6	467.1	56,058	71.7	467.2
Carthage phase	400	449	0.1000	4,490	6.4	11.2	4,490	5.7	11.2
Total				70,381			78,235		

[a]Shell-tempered sherd counts corrected for decomposition. Counts standardized to the year 1976, assuming a decomposition rate of 4.7% per year. See discussion in text.

from Carthage to West Jefferson was probably an in-migration from outside the valley, perhaps from the nearby Tombigbee Valley, where population densities were high (Jenkins and Krause 1986: 78). There was a significant drop in rural population between West Jefferson and Moundville I, but the extent of that decrease is somewhat unclear (Maxham 2004: 126). It is unlikely, however, that the inhabitants of the valley left the area, since the population at Moundville itself drastically increased at this time (Steponaitis 1998). Rather, we suggest that people moved from outlying areas to Moundville.

We wish to stress that our scenario of an in-migration of population differs from that proposed by Jenkins (2003). In our view, people moved to the Black Warrior Valley prior to West Jefferson; West Jefferson and Mississippian people were not distinct, coexisting ethnic groups. This is consistent with the argument that there is continuity in land use from West Jefferson through Mississippian (Hammerstedt 2000; Maxham 2004).

Despite the limitations of the data, we are able to provide a concrete picture of basic population trends in the Black Warrior countryside. During the Carthage phase, the valley was sparsely populated. Population increased during the West Jefferson phase when people moved into the Black Warrior Valley from neighboring drainages. Around AD 1120, people began to move from the countryside to Moundville. Both commoners and elites lived at Moundville, and the construction of the mounds and palisade was undertaken. Around AD 1200, some people left Moundville and built three single mounds north of Moundville. By AD 1300, mound construction was complete, and most commoners left Moundville and moved back into the valley, leaving only the elites in residence (Knight and Steponaitis 1998; Steponaitis 1998). Some people built additional mounds in the valley and lived near them, while others may have left the valley entirely. By the late 1400s, people had abandoned most of these mounds, and the population continued to decline.

Conclusions

As outlined above, it is impossible to relate outlying settlement exactly to the named chronological phases defined for Moundville (Knight and Steponaitis 1998), due to a lack of diagnostics. However, despite the lack of fine chronological control, we are able to highlight some trends.

During the Late Woodland (AD 600–1120), the population of the Black Warrior Valley was low. It seems that people preferred to live in the floodplain, presumably to take advantage of fertile soils. While the data suggest that the uplands were more popular during the Late Woodland than in the Mississippian, further work is necessary to determine the degree to which this is accurate. Maxham (2004) hypothesized that both nucleated villages and single-family sites were present during the West Jefferson phase. While archaeologists have suggested that Late Woodland sites were larger than later Mississippian sites, it is possible that sites that have been described as large West Jefferson villages are actually multiple superimposed small sites (Scarry and Scarry 1997). Excavations of West Jefferson sites are necessary to address this issue.

During the Mississippi period (AD 1120–1520), population in the valley decreased. Presumably, people moved to Moundville to build mounds and the palisade, perhaps under the direction of elites. The population at Moundville was highest during the early phase of the polity's development (Steponaitis 1998). At the same time, mounds were being built in the valley; three were constructed during late Moundville I. It is likely that only a few people, presumably elites, lived at these sites. Other people lived at sites grouped in loose clusters around these mounds. It seems that people preferred to live near one another and did not evenly distribute themselves across the valley, although there was a tendency to live in the floodplain.

During Moundville II, the number of Moundville's inhabitants declined significantly. Knight and Steponaitis (1998) argue that elites and their retainers remained at Moundville and that the rest of the people moved into the valley. Although the rural population did increase at this time, the population of the valley during the entirety of the Moundville sequence remained surprisingly low.

Out of necessity we have treated Mississippian nonmound sites as equivalent, yet excavations show that these sites were not all used for the same purpose, with some serving as residences, and others, such as Grady Bobo, serving as community gathering places (e.g., Maxham 2000, 2004; J. Scarry et al., this volume). It is far too simplistic to refer to all of these sites as "farmsteads." The landscape was much more nuanced.

It is clear that Late Woodland and Mississippian people chose to live in clusters in the same areas: those with deep, well-drained soils on the floodplain. This continuity in land use was a product of both environmental and social factors. Not only was the farmland economically important, but people chose to live on the same land their ancestors had lived on and worked. These site clusters represented communities, probably towns.

The relationships among communities, mound sites, and environmental features constitute landscapes which were shaped by the decisions and actions of the Black Warrior Valley's residents. Overall, the character of the countryside did not change drastically from Late Woodland through Mississippian. This suggests a continuity in land-use even as the Moundville chiefdom consolidated.

The addition of mounds to the landscape was a significant change. During the Mississippi period, people lived in communities near single-mound sites. Interestingly, it appears that mounds came to the people rather than vice versa. People lived in the same areas they had during the West Jefferson phase and the mounds were then built in these locations. This raises several questions. First, did the same people who lived in the surrounding areas build the mounds? Who planned and organized mound building? Clearly, single-mound sites, as well as nonmound sites, are poorly understood and warrant further study as landscapes in the Black Warrior Valley were more complicated than previously thought. These landscapes were not static, but were the results of the decisions and actions of commoners, ordinary people who were the foundation of the countryside.

Acknowledgments

The analyses presented here would not have been possible without the groundbreaking contributions to Moundville archaeology made by Christopher Peebles and his students. We would like to thank Vincas P. Steponaitis and C. Margaret Scarry for their invitation to contribute to this volume. Funding was provided by the Alabama Historical Commission, the Alabama Archaeological Society, the University of Alabama Graduate Council, the Research Laboratories of Archaeology, and the Center for Study of the American South, the last two at University of North Carolina at Chapel Hill.

Notes

1. The Grants Swamp mound (1Tu387 and 1Tu388) is not included in this total, as it is unclear whether it is prehistoric or historic.

2. Since the Landbridge mound no longer exists, no Alabama State Site Files number has been assigned to it.

3. This site density index is slightly different than that used by Myer (2002a). Therefore, the density indices calculated for the BWVS by Myer have been recalculated.

4. In fact, many sites have no officially recorded size. Approximately a third of the sites in the study area have a recorded size of zero. When Maxham digitized sites in ArcView, she traced them exactly as they were drawn on the USGS topographic quadrangles in the Alabama State Site Files. Although we have some doubt as to the accuracy of these drawings, they represent the only size information we have for many sites.

9

Late Prehistoric Social Practice in the Rural Black Warrior River Valley

JOHN F. SCARRY, H. EDWIN JACKSON, AND MINTCY D. MAXHAM

The people of the Moundville polity were a diverse lot. Some appear to have possessed status, wealth, and authority, while others had little of these things. Some lived at Moundville, building their houses around the mounds, while others lived in the rural countryside. Some could act and influence many, while others struggled to shape their own circumstances. The factors constraining their agency varied among individuals and groups within the society, but we would argue that all contributed to the construction of some aspects of Moundville society and that their actions were integral to its ongoing reproduction and transformation.

While people from all sections of Moundville's society contributed to its construction, archaeological investigations in the Black Warrior Valley have historically concentrated on Moundville itself, with less attention paid to smaller mound centers, and even less to the many sites without mounds. Although recent studies (e.g., Davis 2008; Ensor 1993; Hammerstedt 2000, 2001; Johnson 1999; Maxham 2000, 2004; Michals 1998; Myer 2003) have begun to remedy this imbalance, in many respects we still know considerably less about the people who lived away from Moundville than we do about those who lived at the center.

In the Southeast, small Mississippian sites located away from mound centers are often identified as "farmsteads." The people who lived at such sites are thought to be few in number, of relatively low status, and related to one another by ties of descent, marriage, and spatial propinquity. It is often assumed that the activities in which they engaged were predominantly domestic (e.g., food production, food consumption, and the manufacture of everyday tools). This is not, of course, to say that they made no contributions to the broader society. However, their contributions have, in many cases, been seen as the providing of tribute, especially comestibles, and labor for monument construction.

This picture suggests that the people who lived at small rural sites likely had only limited involvement in the consumption of wealth and status goods. It also suggests that their participation in rituals was passive, consisting largely of roles as members of the audience in rituals conducted at mound centers. It suggests that their involvement in the production of wealth and status goods was limited, with the crafters of such goods being either members of the elite or attached to elite households (e.g., Grimes 1987; Pauketat 1997), although we note that there are some exceptions where "status goods" have been found in burials away from larger mound centers.

This picture of rural life now seems to provide an incomplete depiction, especially for aspects of practice other than subsistence. Despite the attention the iconography of Mississippian societies has drawn over the years (Galloway 1989; Lankford et al. 2011; Phillips and Brown 1978; Reilly and Garber 2007; Waring and Holder 1945), we still need to learn more about the ritual practices that served to lend meanings and significance to Mississippian iconography, especially in rural and domestic contexts. The political and economic structure of Mississippian societies has been a focus of attention for decades (Brown 1971; Emerson 1997; Muller 1997; Pauketat 1994; Peebles and Kus 1977; Scarry 1992; Steponaitis 1978; Welch 1991), but we lack a nuanced picture of the social relations and structures of small communities and households in Mississippian societies.

Recent investigations of sites in the Moundville countryside have provided data regarding the activities of the rural populace and have begun to illuminate some of the ways it contributed to the construction of Moundville society. While more limited than we would like, these investigations have allowed us to begin to incorporate the rural populace into our models. They have also hinted at a rich and varied ritual and economic life that went well beyond the mundane activities of agricultural production (Davis 2008, this volume; Marcoux 2007).

Several factors hinder our ability to interpret the evidence from the small, rural sites. First, we have few large-scale excavations, so our samples of material culture and contexts are limited. Second, it is evident that these sites are highly variable in terms of their material assemblages and the activities that produced those assemblages. Finally, much of the evidence garnered from the small sites of the Black Warrior Valley is not

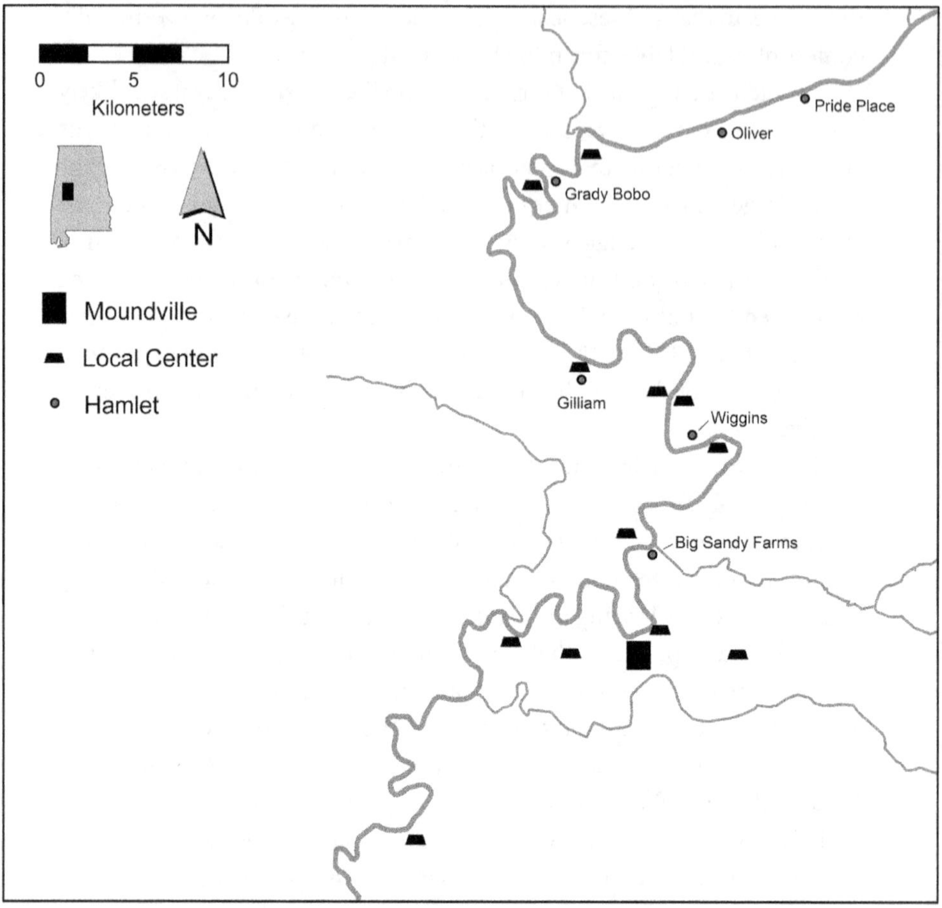

Figure 9.1. The Black Warrior Valley, showing the locations of sites discussed in this chapter.

what the typical notion of a "farmstead" might lead us to expect, so we need a revised model of rural settlement and practice (see Hammerstedt et al., this volume, for a similar argument).

In trying to make sense of the evidence from rural sites, two fundamental issues must be addressed. The first concerns the nature of the activities that took place there. That is, we must ask what kinds of practices could have produced the material culture assemblages and archaeological contexts found at these sites. The second concerns the nature and composition of the social groups who participated in these activities. Who were the people, how did they identify themselves, what were the social ties that linked them to one another, and what were the social ties that linked them to others in the Moundville society? Unfortunately, we cannot completely answer these questions. We can, however, make some suggestions, given the available evidence.

The picture of rural production and ritual that we present here comes largely from limited investigations at three sites: Wiggins (1Tu768), Grady Bobo (1Tu66), and Gilliam (1Tu904) (figure 9.1). In 1995 two of us (JS and MM, along with C. M. Scarry) conducted test excavations at several small sites north of Moundville (Scarry and Scarry 1997). At Wiggins we excavated a shallow, irregularly shaped pit that contained abundant food remains as well as cooking and serving wares and stone tools. At Grady Bobo we discovered a large, shallow, irregularly shaped pit containing possible evidence of craft production and refuse from communal meals. In 1999 and 2000 we conducted additional excavations at Grady Bobo that allowed us to completely excavate the 1995 feature, as well as a number of other features revealed through test excavations and the stripping of the plow zone from approximately 50 percent of the prehistoric occupation. In 2002 Knight and Myer conducted test excavations at Gilliam, a nonmound site located near the center of a cluster of 18 nonmound sites near the Landbridge mound (Myer 2003). They recovered limited evidence from a large, irregularly shaped Moundville-era pit containing materials we believe were linked to ritual practices. In each of these cases, our data come from a single feature. However, while the features vary in content and are not replicated at their respective sites (at least to the best of our knowledge), they do form a pattern, which we discuss below.

Rural Production in the Moundville Polity

We have usually assumed that Moundville's rural populace produced most of the food and material culture they used in the course of their daily lives. This would include such things as domestic cooking and serving wares, stone tools, and houses. While we have no direct evidence of pottery making and only limited evidence of stone-tool manufacture at the sites we investigated, we have no reason to believe that the people who lived at these small sites did not make such things for themselves. And we certainly have no reason to believe that the production of mundane household goods was centralized or under the control of elites living at Moundville. Wilson (2001) has convincingly argued that the production of greenstone tools at Moundville was not centrally controlled. If production was not centrally controlled at Moundville, then probably the same was true at outlying sites such as Grady Bobo.

While the available evidence does not seem to indicate centralized production of the goods used by rural peoples (Barry 2004), it is possible that some rural households produced more of some goods than they themselves needed, and that they provided those goods to other households. In fact, there is limited evidence to suggest that people who lived away from Moundville and the minor mound centers produced goods for others. Ensor has suggested that stone tool production beyond the needs of the household may have taken place at Big Sandy Farms (1993: 183), citing the abundance of ferruginous sandstone and hematite in the assemblage recovered from the site.

Comestibles

We assume that the most important goods produced by Moundville's rural population were foodstuffs. Previous studies indicate that crops, particularly maize, provided the bulk of the diet, and that people consumed wild plants and animals as well. Peebles (1978: 400–408, 411) argued that the distribution of the single-mound centers and their dependent populations was linked to the distribution of arable land in the Black Warrior Valley. This suggested that the distribution of the rural population was a consequence of the importance of agricultural production in the economy. Moundville itself appears to violate this characterization, however. Peebles found that the area of arable land within Moundville's catchment was not as large as his postulated population for the site would suggest (Peebles 1978: 408–9). He argued that this discrepancy was a consequence of the provisioning of agricultural foodstuffs to the population of Moundville from a wider area, a rural hinterland, by the people who lived and farmed in that hinterland.

Evidence from Moundville itself indicates that people at the center consumed maize that was processed elsewhere (Jackson et al., this volume; Scarry 1993b; Scarry and Steponaitis 1997; Welch and Scarry 1995). The Moundville data also suggest that the people eating at Moundville had greater access to preferred cuts of deer than people at small rural sites (Jackson and Scott 1995, 2003; Michals 1998; Welch and Scarry 1995). However, the Moundville data do not tell us how, or by whom, those foods were produced, nor do they tell us how or why those foods were mobilized and brought to Moundville.

One possibility, of course, is that the people at Moundville were members of an elite group who could commandeer the production of individuals beyond their own households. Ethnohistoric accounts describe such mobilization in some Mississippian societies (e.g., the Apalachee; see Hann 1988; Wenhold 1936), and archaeological evidence suggests a similar pattern at Moundville as well (Jackson et al., this volume; Scarry and Steponaitis 1997; Steponaitis 1978).

This is not the only plausible scenario, however. Another possibility is that the foods consumed at Moundville were produced by kin of those who consumed them and that they were mobilized and provisioned through kinship ties (Jackson et al., this volume). That is, the people who ate at Moundville got their food from relatives who lived elsewhere (Knight and Solís 1983; Scarry 1993b). A similar mechanism might have involved provisioning of people at Moundville by others who were members of the same social house (see Knight, this volume). It is also possible that the foods eaten at Moundville were brought to the site by those who consumed them. That is, the food remains at Moundville might reflect the temporary aggregation of people who came there for specific events or occasions. Gatherings of individuals drawn from religious sodalities, kin-based groups, social houses, or towns for political or religious events are possible examples of these models.

We cannot now say with any confidence which of these possibilities played out in the Moundville polity. But we do know that the people who lived in Moundville's countryside produced foods, particularly maize. Furthermore, it seems likely that they produced food supplies beyond those needed for their own households.

Comestibles were not the only products of Moundville's hinterland. People in the rural countryside also made pottery and stone tools. We have generally assumed, however, that rural "commoners" did not produce (or consume) ceramic finewares, elite paraphernalia and costumery, or items bearing elaborate iconography (although finewares have been recovered from smaller sites). It is this assumption about manufacturing that recent investigations have called into question. It now seems likely that people who lived at small rural sites in the Black Warrior Valley produced fine engraved ceramics and elaborate costumery and possibly consumed these items in local rituals.

Ceramic Serving Vessels

The pottery found at Mississippian sites in the Black Warrior Valley is often divided into two broad categories: serving vessels (e.g., bottles, beakers, and bowls) and cooking or storage vessels (jars). The former tend to have fine temper and burnished surfaces, while the latter tend to have coarse temper and surfaces that are smoothed but not burnished. This distinction has also been linked to the social status of the individual or household that possessed the vessel and to meanings of the vessels themselves (Knight 2010: 353–54). Along these lines, Knight suggests that greater quantities of engraved serving wares in an assemblage reflect greater ostentation on the part of the people who contributed to the assemblage. He also notes that engraved serving wares "may have had a broader scope of application in elite contexts" (2010: 354). In this vein, finely tempered, burnished ceramics, particularly vessels decorated by engraving, were seen as likely associated with the social elite. Furthermore, "elite" individuals were assumed to have resided at Moundville or the single-mound centers, rather than at "farmsteads" where commoners lived.

Steponaitis and Wilson (2010) were able to demonstrate that many of these fine engraved vessels, previously thought to have been foreign imports from the trans-Mississippi Caddo region, were in fact locally made, but they could not determine the loci of manufacture within the Moundville system. Investigations at several small sites away from Moundville now suggest that the association of engraved ceramics with high-social-status individuals and elite contexts at mound centers is not always valid. While they do not appear to be abundant, engraved bottles and bowls do appear at some rural sites (Maxham 2004: 104–18).

At the Wiggins site we excavated an irregular shallow pit (figure 9.2) that contained several fragmentary vessels, food remains, and other domestic debris, such as hoe flakes. Among the vessels was one shallow, carinated, engraved bowl with an engraved geometric design (figure 9.3). The remaining vessels included several jars, presumably common domestic cooking pots. At Grady Bobo, we excavated another large shallow pit (figure 9.4) that contained a diverse assemblage of ceramic vessels, food remains, nonfood faunal remains, and other artifacts. The ceramics included an engraved vessel bearing a more complex but similar geometric design (figure 9.5), as well as a bottle and flaring-rim bowl.

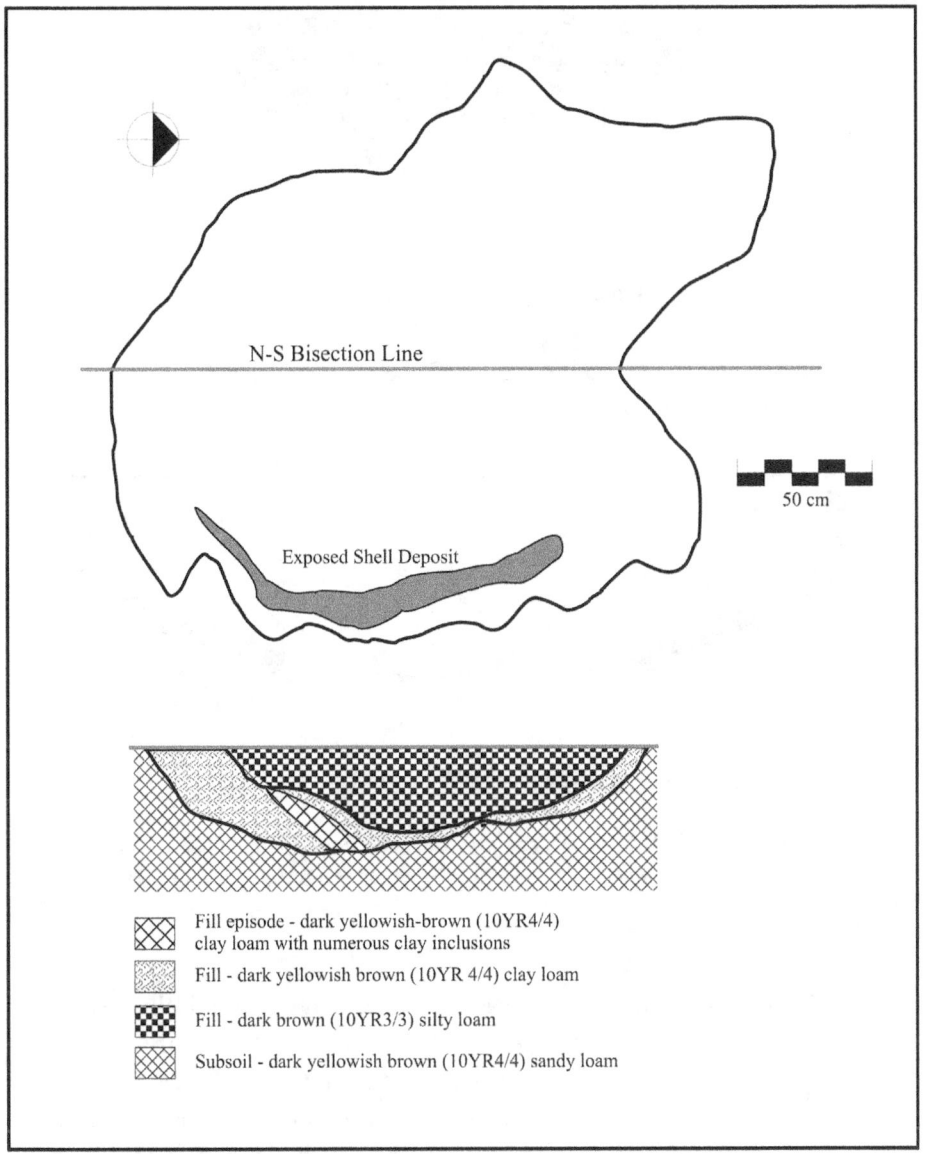

Figure 9.2. Wiggins site, Feature 1, profile and plan.

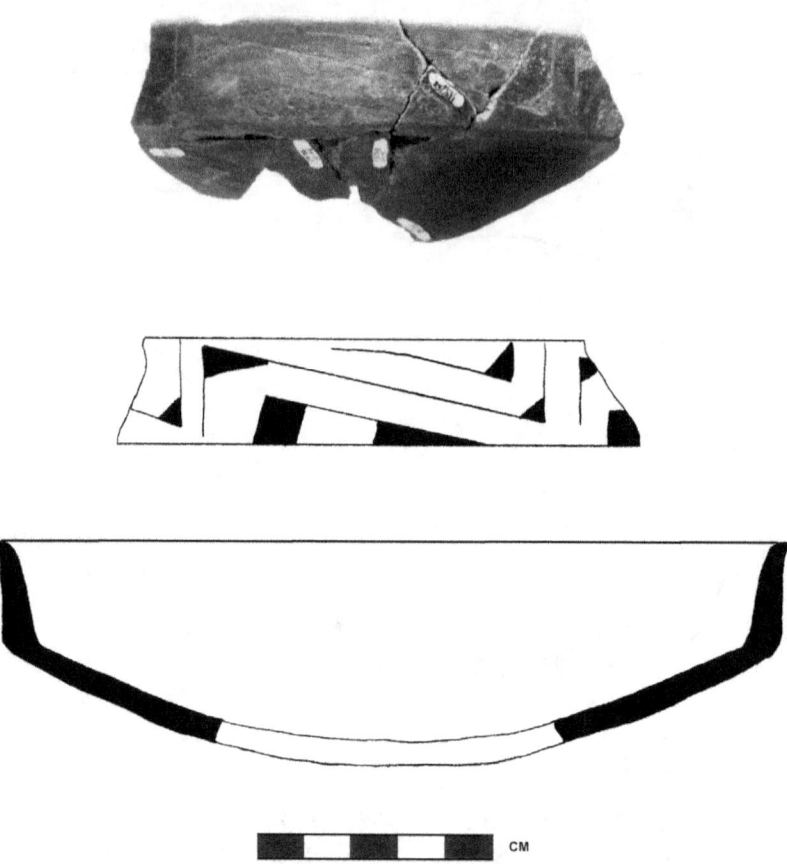

Figure 9.3. Wiggins site, Feature 1, engraved carinated bowl: (*top*) photograph of reconstructed vessel; (*middle*) drawing of design; (*bottom*) reconstructed vessel profile. (Drawings by Vincas P. Steponaitis)

The designs on the engraved vessels from Grady Bobo and Wiggins are variants of the Davis Rectangle, which is found elsewhere in the Mississippian world on both ceramic vessels and engraved shell cups (Phillips and Brown 1978: 150). These vessels reflect a ceramic style that combines a very finely tempered (or temperless) fabric with a design created by a combination of engraving and excision that is widely spread across the southeastern United States and may serve as a horizon marker for early Mississippian manifestations.

The engraved vessels from Wiggins and Grady Bobo are intriguing. On the one hand, their presence at these small rural sites suggests that

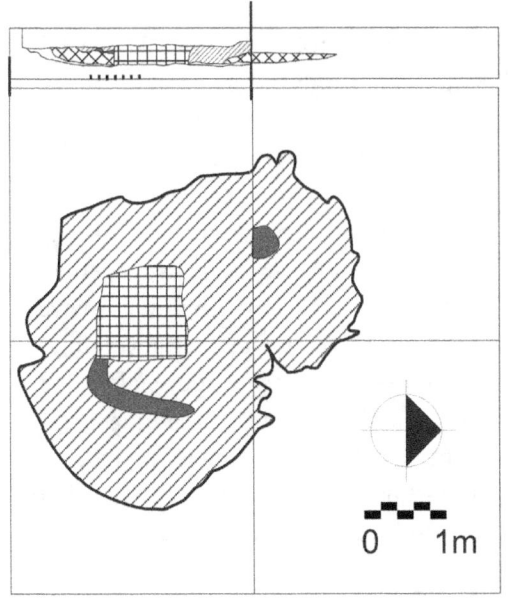
 Dark yellowish-brown clay-loam

 1995 Test Unit

 Dark yellowish-brown clay-loam with moderate yellowish-brown inclusions

 Dark yellowish-brown clay-loam with shell inclusions

Figure 9.4. Grady Bobo site, Feature 10, profile and plan.

Figure 9.5. Grady Bobo site, Feature 10, engraved beaker: (*top*) photograph of reconstructed vessel; (*bottom*) roll-out of engraved design. (Drawing by Vincas P. Steponaitis)

they (and presumably vessels like them) were not strictly associated with elite households or elite social contexts, but rather were components of domestic ceramic assemblages at both Moundville and rural sites, and that they were used by both elites and commoners. On the other hand, the engraving on the vessel from Grady Bobo was extremely well executed, perhaps beyond the skills of an average potter. Such engraved vessels may have been manufactured by a few highly skilled individuals. Together, these inferences suggest the possibility that rural communities may have included individuals who specialized in the making of special ceramics but were not necessarily attached to or members of elite households, that is, that the economy of rural households and communities was more complex than our models suggest. LeBlanc has suggested a similar mechanism for the manufacture of painted, white-slipped bowls among the Mogollon of southwestern New Mexico (Hegmon 2002; LeBlanc 2004; LeBlanc and Ellis 2001).

Feature 4 at the Gilliam site did not contain an abundance of serving wares. Myer reports that only about 4 percent of the sherds from the small assemblage recovered from the pit were from serving vessels, while 96 percent were from utilitarian coarse-ware vessels (Myer 2003: 26). Together with the faunal remains from Feature 4 (see below), this suggests that the pit was not used to dispose of the debris from communal meals, although utilitarian vessels could have been used to cook communal meals. However, the unusual faunal assemblage does suggest that the materials deposited in Feature 4 were not the products of quotidian activities.

Feather Garments and Other Ritual Paraphernalia

Avian remains from Grady Bobo and Gilliam suggest that the people associated with these small rural sites used birds for meaningful purposes as well as for food. Feature 10 at Grady Bobo yielded a large faunal assemblage (n = 9,268), with many bird bones (n = 1,753) recovered by water-screening through nested 6.4-mm and window-screen mesh (table 9.1). Some of these birds—such as turkey, duck, quail, and passenger pigeon—were likely eaten, but the assemblage also included several species that were probably sources of feathers, not food. In particular, we think that the remains of crows and grackles, which occur in substantial numbers compared with other southern sites, were exploited for their black feath-

Table 9.1. Birds from Grady Bobo

Taxon	1995 Test Unit		1999 Fine Screen		1999 6.4-mm Screen		1999 All
	NISP	Weight (g)	NISP	Weight (g)	NISP	Weight (g)	MNI
Unidentified bird	35	12.9	499	9.7	75	5.4	—
Unidentified large bird	54	16.1	83	4.8	493	233.9	—
Unidentified medium bird	1	0.3	—	—	195	31.3	—
Unidentified small bird	54	8.9	19	0.6	8	0.4	—
Ducks, geese, swans (Anatidae)	1	0.1	—	—	—	—	—
Swan (*Olor buccinator*)	—	—	—	—	1	0.8	1
Mallard, black duck (*Anas platyrhynchos, rubripes*)	1	0.3	—	—	3	1.1	1
Medium duck (*Anas* sp.)	—	—	—	—	4	0.7	1
Little blue heron (*Egretta caerulea*)	—	—	—	—	1	1	1
Herons, bitterns (Ardeidae)	—	—	—	—	1	1.1	—
Turkey (*Meleagris gallopavo*)	16	8.2	—	—	45	56.4	2
Quails, partridges (Phasianidae)	—	—	—	—	1	0.3	—
Bobwhite (*Colinus virginianus*)	5	2.8	3	0.3	7	1	2
Screech owl (*Otus asio*)	—	—	—	—	2	0.3	1
Passenger pigeon (*Ectopistes migratorius*)	—	—	—	—	15	2.6	2
Common flicker (*Colaptes auratus*)	1	0.1	—	—	—	—	—
Crows, jays (Corvidae)	1	0.1	—	—	1	0.1	—
American crow (*Corvus brachyrhynchos*)	18	6.1	—	—	66	28.9	7
Blackbirds, orioles, etc. (Icteridae)	—	—	—	—	1	1	1
Grackle (*Quiscalus* sp.)	3	0.1	1	0.1	—	—	—
Songbirds (Passeriformes)	16	1.7	15	0.3	—	—	—
Cardinal (*Cardinalis cardinalis*)	4	0.2	—	—	—	—	—
Robin (*Turdis migratorius*)	1	0.1	—	—	3	0.4	1

Note: MNI is the minimum number of individuals; NISP is the number of identified specimens.

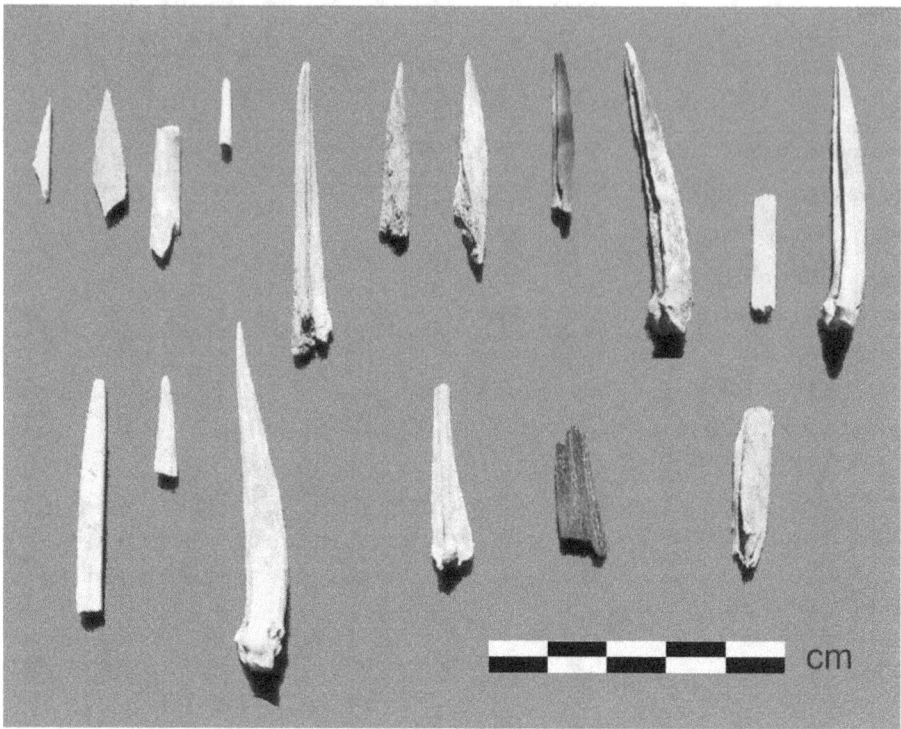

Figure 9.6. Grady Bobo site, Feature 10, bone tools.

ers. The number of crow and grackle specimens collected from the feature at Grady Bobo far exceeds those from sites producing much larger faunal assemblages. Other birds with colorful feathers were also part of the assemblage, including little blue heron, cardinal, oriole or blackbird, flicker, and robin. Two other birds with potentially symbolic value found in the feature were swan and screech owl. Swan feathers played a significant role in rituals at Cahokia (Kelly and Kelly 2007) and were used in rituals and headdresses during the historic period (Swanton 1946: 251). Screech owls played a prominent role in southern Indian views of creation, afterlife, and witchcraft (Hudson 1976: 128).

It is tempting to see the peculiar bird assemblage recovered from Grady Bobo as evidence for meaningful, symbolic practices involving the feathers of those birds. A precedent for our inference that these bird remains represent color symbolism using feathers is provided by the assemblage from mound contexts at Lubbub Creek in west central Alabama, where cardinal, mockingbird, Carolina parakeet, crow, and blue jay were found in association with a merlin, as well as bear and bobcat bones (Jackson and Scott 1995: 113).

The assumption that the people at Grady Bobo were using feathers is given further support by the artifacts recovered from Feature 10. The assemblage included several sharpened and burned bone tools that we have interpreted as needles and awls (figure 9.6). Presumably, these were used in the manufacturing of garments and textiles. Given the number of tools found, this activity was quite important at the time Feature 10 was filled with refuse. Jackson has suggested that one activity that people undertook at Grady Bobo was the production of feathered garments or perhaps other feathered paraphernalia (Jackson 2003b).

If colorful feathered garments, regalia, or artifacts decorated with feathers were made at Grady Bobo, for whom and for what purposes were they made? If the people who lived in the vicinity of Grady Bobo were making feathered goods for members of the Moundville elite, either at Moundville or at the nearby single-mound center (the Hog Pen mound), it would raise the question of the relationship between the makers and the users of the goods, or it might indicate that the makers of these garments were decoupled from the value, status, and meaning of the objects. On the other hand, if the objects were made for local use, by local peoples, it would indicate a significant involvement in ritual practice on the part of "commoners." Regardless, it does seem that members of the rural populace were likely producers of special feathered goods.

The bird assemblage recovered from Gilliam was unlike that from Grady Bobo (Jackson 2003a, 2003b). At this site, one of several small sites about 10 km northwest of Moundville, Myer (2002b, 2003) recovered a small faunal assemblage from a single, irregularly shaped, shell-filled pit, dating from late Moundville I to early Moundville II times. Of this collection of about 500 identified specimens, 29 percent are bird remains (table 9.2). All bird specimens identified below the level of class were collected by 0.64-cm screening. Rather than passerine and other birds possibly bearing colorful feathers, an abundance of raptors marked the Gilliam assemblage (Jackson 2003a). Of the 30 specimens identified more specifically than by class, two-thirds are from hawks, including at least two red-tailed hawks (*Buteo jamaicensis*) and one smaller specimen identifiable only to the genus *Buteo*. Given the importance of raptors in Mississippian iconography, the question naturally arises how the people at Gilliam used the birds and what that use meant. Evidence from Moundville suggests

Table 9.2. Birds from Gilliam

	Fine Screen		6.4 mm Screen	
Taxon	NISP	Weight (g)	NISP	Weight (g)
Unidentified bird	21	0.3	24	3.0
Unidentified large bird	51	3.0	58	21.9
Unidentified medium bird	—	—	15	3.0
Red-tailed hawk (*Buteo jamaicensis*)	—	—	14	16.1
Hawk (*Buteo* sp.)	—	—	5	3.8
Turkey (*Meleagris gallopavo*)	—	—	10	42.5
Passenger pigeon (*Ectopistes migratorius*)	—	—	1	0.3
Songbirds (Passeriformes)	—	—	2	0.2

Note: NISP is the number of identified specimens.

that raptors were included in bundles along with objects like repoussé copper plates. In the mid-1930s, Walter B. Jones recovered a copper plate from the Rhodes site that was associated with raptor talons and that may have been contained in a basket placed near the head of an interred individual (Reilly 2007; V. J. Knight, personal communication). This suggests that the bodies of hawks were potentially potent objects whose power required control (cf. King and Reilly 2011 for a discussion of raptor imagery at Etowah). We might ask, who at Gilliam had the knowledge and power to manipulate such objects? Unfortunately, we cannot yet answer this question.

Another item that appears to have figured prominently in the ritual life at Moundville was the stone palette. Steponaitis (this volume) has suggested that the palettes were not everyday artifacts, but rather portable altars—powerful, and perhaps dangerous, objects whose use required extensive training or special abilities (also see Steponaitis et al. 2011). These palettes were typically made from a fine gray sandstone that outcrops north of Moundville (Whitney et al. 2002). Pride Place (1Tu1), a small site located near these outcrops, has yielded evidence of palette production (Davis 2008, this volume; also see Gage and Stone 1999; Johnson 1999; Sherard 1999).

Rural Ritual Practices

Considerations of ritual practice in the Moundville polity have generally focused on what happened at Moundville and the single-mound centers of the Black Warrior Valley. These studies have concentrated on mounds, elaborately decorated artifacts, and the iconography these artifacts bore (e.g., Knight 2010; Phillips 2012, this volume). Such ritual practices appear to have been situated at the mound centers, particularly Moundville. Presumably, there was little ritual activity at small, rural sites. Recent excavations, however, indicate otherwise, as we discuss in the sections that follow.

Communal Meals

Evidence suggesting that activities including communal, multi-household meals took place at rural sites in the Black Warrior Valley comes from the Wiggins and Grady Bobo sites.[1] The subsistence remains from these two sites are different in several ways from those at other rural sites such as Big Sandy (Ensor 1993).

The feature at the Wiggins site was a large, basin-shaped pit containing abundant refuse, including food remains, lithic debitage, and pottery. The diverse plant food remains included both wild and cultivated plants (Scarry 1997). The animal remains included shellfish, deer, rabbit, squirrel, raccoon, and unidentified large mammal (Holm 1997). The subsistence remains do not include any clearly ritual foods; in fact, all of the food remains from the Wiggins pit are typically found on sites of the Moundville phase. The most striking aspect of this assemblage is the diversity of the subsistence remains included in a single pit.

The ceramics from this feature included both cooking and serving wares (Scarry and Scarry 1997). Several unusually small Moundville Incised jars in the assemblage may have been used for consumption of liquids rather than cooking or storage. The engraved wares discussed previously suggest that the serving and food consumption represented in the refuse was not that of a normal domestic meal.

In addition, the coarse-ware assemblage suggests that the Moundville Incised jars in the assemblage may have been made by several different hands. This interpretation is suggested by differences in the length, angles,

Figure 9.7. Wiggins site, Feature 1, Moundville Incised vessel fragments showing variations in the execution of incised designs.

spacing, and regularity of the incised rays ("eyelashes") extending from the incised arcades (figure 9.7). Characteristics of this sort are often the kinds of habitual practices that characterize individual artisans rather than distinct "types." Gosselain, for instance, has argued that differences of this kind reflect differences in habitual motor patterns among individual potters and are part of the deeply engrained habitus of those individuals (Gosselain 1998, 2000). If this interpretation is correct, it would suggest that the refuse does not derive from a single household. Given this, we suggest that the Wiggins feature contains the remains of a "feast," or at least an event that included members of several different households (Hayden 2001).

Feature 10 at Grady Bobo, which dated to the Moundville I phase, was filled quickly with multiple loads of refuse (Maxham 2004: 172, figure 4–28). The botanical assemblage from this pit included a range of cultivated and wild plant foods, all commonly found in domestic contexts (Jackson et al., this volume; Scarry 1997). The faunal assemblage, however, was quite unusual (Jackson 2003b). Meatier elements were over-represented among the deer bones, suggesting that the assemblage derived from a "special" meal, and these were augmented by other food species, including turkey, passenger pigeon, and a variety of small and medium-sized mammals.

As was the case with the Wiggins assemblage, the diversity of vessels at Grady Bobo suggests that there was more than one household involved. The Grady Bobo assemblage included a flaring-rim bowl with a scalloped rim. Symbolically, this may have conveyed meanings similar to those that Knight and Steponaitis (2011: 219–26) have suggested for the sandstone palettes; that is, it may have served as a ritual centering device.

Mortuary Practice

One area of ritual practice that clearly took place at rural sites was the burial of the dead. While later in the history of the polity, Moundville appears to have been a favored location for the burial of the dead (Knight 2010; Knight and Steponaitis 1998; Phillips 2012: 103), during the early phases most people appear to have been buried away from the center, possibly at smaller, rural sites.

We encountered two burials and one possible burial (in which the bone may have decayed away) in the excavations at Grady Bobo (Maxham 2004: 176–80). Unfortunately, with one exception, there were no chronologically sensitive artifacts found in these features.

Burials at rural sites, like those at Grady Bobo, may reflect a link between meaningful places and the burial of the dead. As Laneri (2007: 5) has argued,

> The actual practice of funerary rituals is a fundamental moment during which the social cohesion of the living community and/or household is reinforced, and the physical remains of this act... stand as a focal point in the social and mnemonic landscape of the society.

The creation of these *loci memoriae* support the society in defining elements of continuity in moments of social and cultural change.

Possible Ritual Paraphernalia

At Grady Bobo there were a large number of bird remains, including crows, songbirds, a swan, an owl, and other taxa that were likely procured for their feathers or symbolic connotation rather than their meat. At Gilliam there were proportionally even more birds than at Grady Bobo. Two-thirds of the identified bird remains were from raptors, but notably two elements from passerine songbirds were also recovered. It seems likely that none of these birds were parts of meals, as none showed evidence of roasting. The passerines may have been sources of brightly colored feathers (as we have suggested was the case at the Grady Bobo site). Raptors and owls, on the other hand, may have had symbolic importance in and of themselves.

Raptors and owls are commonly depicted in Mississippian iconography. In these depictions they may have served as metaphors, alluding to the powers of deities or other supernatural beings (Scarry and Sharp 2010). If this was the case, the procurement and processing of them would have been a symbolically charged practice. We can suggest that the feathers and the bodies of birds may well have been used in rituals.

Conclusions

It seems to us that we can draw several conclusions from these cases. First, at least some rural sites were the loci of production of goods other than everyday tools and quotidian ceramics. Second, at least some rural sites were the loci of rituals that may not have involved members of the social and political elite. Third, the people who lived at rural sites were directly involved in both specialized production and ritual practice in which they could exercise agency as individuals and as groups.

Rural Production

One cannot overestimate the importance of rural peoples in the construction of the Moundville polity. The production of foodstuffs that were consumed at Moundville was crucial to the aggregation of people on both short-term and long-term bases. Without those aggregations, Moundville could not have been constructed, nor could it have served as a place for the construction of identity for the polity or of meaning for the world as the people of the polity came to understand it.

Yet we can now see that rural production was not limited to the satisfaction of local, everyday needs, nor was it limited to meeting the demands of elites for tribute. It also contributed to the meaningful ritual lives of the rural people themselves. Decorated fineware ceramics such as those we recovered from Wiggins and Grady Bobo were undoubtedly meaningful objects to the people who made, possessed, and used them. It seems unlikely they were used for everyday meals, but it also seems unlikely that they were centrally manufactured and distributed to some members of the rural populace by elites residing at mound centers.

Sandstone palettes represent a different situation. It is not clear that they were components of rural material culture rather than objects restricted to a religious elite. Given Steponaitis' (this volume) interpretation of the function and meaning of the palettes, the latter seems more likely. Of course, it is possible that palettes could have been manufactured by people other than the ones who used them (Davis, this volume). Priests might have commissioned them from rural stoneworkers rather than making them themselves. If this were the case, they could appear in rural assemblages even if their uses were tied to elite members of society. Another possibility is that the palettes were linked to religious sodalities rather than elite kin groups. If this were the case, as the ritual paraphernalia of groups that crosscut residence and kinship, the palettes would have been neither a part of generalized rural assemblages nor markers of the sociopolitical elite.

The possible production of feathered garments or paraphernalia at Grady Bobo and the use of raptors at Gilliam are also difficult to interpret. While they suggest an absence of centralized control over these items, the data do not tell us whether the use or the making was by kin groups, social houses, or sodalities. The Grady Bobo data also do not tell us if the goods apparently made from feathers were used at the site by locals or if they were moved to mound centers and used there. We think it possible they were made and used at Grady Bobo, but that cannot be demonstrated given our current data. The presence of raptors in Feature 4 at Gilliam does suggest their use at that site.

Finally, the evidence of rural production suggests that models of centralized control may not be an accurate representation of Moundville's political economy, a conclusion previously reached by Knight (2010), Marcoux (2007), and Wilson (2001). This is not to say that there was no centralized control of the production of some goods, but that Moundville's economy was complex in multiple dimensions. Those dimensions would include some that operated at the level of rural commoners rather than involving social elites. As Davis (2008: 105) has suggested,

> perhaps Moundville's economy never hinged upon the ambitions of an elite minority, and was instead embedded in the ritual and social obligations of every member of society. In such a "ritual economy," it is appeals to sacred authority, not chiefly threats, that sustain surplus production. If this was the case, then making, exchanging, and consuming socially valued goods were practices involved in the reciprocal negotiation of meanings, values, and power among segmented kin groups.

Rural Ritual Practice

While each of our cases is unique, we see reason to link them. First and foremost, none of the features we discuss here appear to contain only accumulated, everyday refuse. Each represents a discrete episode. Second, the contents of the pits, while different from one another, all contain unusual elements, either ceramics, animal remains, or both. At Wiggins and Grady Bobo, we see feasting—special meals marked by abundance and diversity of foods and by participation of more than a single household. At Gilliam and Grady Bobo, we may see the manipulation of meaningful animals for something other than food. Finally, in Feature 10 at Grady Bobo, we see both feasting and the use of birds coupled with the interment of at least one individual and the disposal of tools possibly used in the preparation of feathered garments.

All such practices could have served to integrate and reproduce local social groups. As one of us has argued,

> The Grady Bobo event [Feature 10] was about integration, not differentiation. This event was outside of the elite-commoner hierarchy. People at the Bobo site ate the same foods they did every day and sat around and cooked, sewed, and made tools together. This event was inclusive, not exclusive. The Bobo site event emphasized shared

identity and reinforced ties of kinship and community. (Maxham 2004: 220)

We believe that communal, ritual events were elements of normal practice in the rural communities of the Moundville polity. Such events included feasting, the use of birds and elaborately decorated vessels in ritual, the disposal of food refuse and ceramic vessels in single-episode deposits, and the burial of the dead. Given this view of rural practice,

> the local landscape was composed of more than clusters of undifferentiated farmsteads. We can now imagine a more nuanced landscape, one that included places where people gathered to express solidarity, kinship, and shared beliefs. People had relationships with their neighbors and kin that existed quite apart from the Moundville political hierarchy. (Maxham 2004: 228)

The apparent pervasiveness of ritual practices at rural sites in the Black Warrior Valley has clear implications for our understanding of the Moundville polity. First, and not surprisingly, it argues for the importance of rural social aggregates for both the construction and reproduction of the prehistoric polity and for our understanding of those processes. We will understand neither the structure of the Moundville polity nor its dynamics without a better understanding of the nature of these rural communities and the practices that contributed to their construction and maintenance. Second, we need to focus on the links between the rural communities and Moundville itself. Those links were the structuring foundations for the larger Moundville society, and they undoubtedly shaped the structure of the resident community at Moundville and the activities that took place there.

One obvious element of ritual practice in Moundville's rural countryside was feasting, that is, the shared consumption of food by groups above the level of the household. Our limited data suggest that these feasts did not involve special foods, but they did involve a diverse set of plant and animal foods. This diversity may reflect a "potluck" approach to the provisioning of the feasts, where individuals or households contributed different foods to the event. The diversity of ceramics in the pits at Wiggins and Grady Bobo suggests that participants also provided their own ceramic containers at the event, including both cooking vessels and serving vessels. Most of the vessels appear to have been common components of household assemblages, but some—the engraved vessels from Wiggins and Grady Bobo—may have been special vessels, possibly reserved for ritual or political events.

Rituals involving communal meals would have been important components of the practices that created social ties, evoked sentiments of affinity between rural peoples, and constructed social groups. This would be true for both descent groups and local communities that included individuals from several descent groups.

The evidence from our excavations at the Grady Bobo site suggests continuities in ritual practice between the West Jefferson and Moundville I occupations of the site. First, there is the continuity in location. The same location appears to have been chosen for communal meals (feasting?) in both West Jefferson and Moundville I. There was also continuity in the places chosen for settlement in the two phases. It is not simply that similar landforms and ecological settings were chosen. Within those settings the same specific locations were selected. Second, in both phases, ritual practices involved the provisioning of foods and the vessels used in the preparation and consumption of those foods. This provisioning involved individuals from multiple households, and the rituals were communal (supra-household). The ceramic vessels used in these rituals included both quotidian wares and decorated vessels whose use may have been restricted to special occasions. Finally, the conclusions of the rituals involved the disposal of both food waste and vessels used in the rituals, although the disposal does not appear to have involved the construction of specialized disposal facilities. Finally, those continuities suggest that we might also expect to see continuities in identities, structures, and the broader practices that created them between the Terminal Woodland and the Mississippian.

Beyond these limited and admittedly tentative conclusions, our examination of rural practice in the Black Warrior Valley during the Moundville phase raises several unanswered questions. The first of these questions concern the nature and composition of the rural social groups. Were the groups sets of related individuals (lineages, clan segments, or other unilineal descent groups), were they sodalities (e.g., medicine societies or warrior groups), were they communities (towns) composed of individuals from more than one kin group, or were they some other form of grouping (perhaps something akin to the "house" of Claude Lévi-Strauss)? A second set of questions relates to the social, political, and economic relationships between rural communities and Moundville and the meaningful relationships between the rituals conducted in rural settings and those conducted at Moundville. The available evidence is hardly conclusive, but we will make some suggestions.

First, we suspect the rural communities were composed of individuals and families not necessarily linked to one another by ties of descent or marriage. That is, we think they were comparable to the "towns" or "houses" among historic southern Indians. Rural communities were tied to the land and to particular places on the landscape and were ultimately linked to centers such as Moundville. Within those communities, groups of related people were also tied to field locations and places (especially places of burial and other ritual activities). Rural rituals, be they rites of passage or communal rituals of intensification, would have been important elements in the evocation of sentiments of affinity among the participants, and therefore in the construction of both collective identities and ultimately the groups themselves (following Lincoln 1989).

Second, we feel that the links between rural groups and Moundville were bidirectional. The rural populace did not consist of simple pawns of an elite at Moundville, nor were they mere slavish imitators who were dependent on those elite for inspiration and for the material paraphernalia needed for their own social reproduction. At the same time, Moundville was more than a small rural community writ large. There were structural and material differences between Moundville and the rural communities. The construction of the community at Moundville itself must have involved practices that created identities beyond those of local groups and communities but, at the same time, linked those groups and communities to Moundville. Given this, it seems likely that there would have been communal rituals at Moundville that were both similar to and different from those conducted by the members of local kin groups and the rural communities.

Acknowledgments

First, we wish to acknowledge our intellectual debt to the late Chris Peebles. While Chris focused much of his attention on the paramount center, he was cognizant of the need to examine the entire Moundville polity in order to fully understand the lives of the people and the society they created. His Moundville Project of the late 1970s laid the groundwork for our studies. We also want to thank the landowners and farmers who graciously allowed archaeologists to investigate the sites on their lands. Without their cooperation, there would have been no excavations at Wiggins, Grady Bobo, or Gilliam. Finally, our profound thanks go to our friends and colleagues working in the Black Warrior Valley. In particular, we wish to thank Vin Steponaitis and Margaret Scarry, Jon Marcoux, and an anonymous reviewer for their insightful comments and questions that have made this a better work. The excavations at Wiggins and Grady Bobo were funded through grants from the National Geographic Society and the National Science Foundation. The excavations at Gilliam were funded through a grant from the Alabama Historical Commission.

Notes

1. The faunal remains from Wiggins and the 1995 remains from Grady Bobo were analyzed by Mary Ann Holm (1997). The other faunal remains (from Gilliam and the 2000–2001 excavations at Grady Bobo) were analyzed by Ed Jackson and Susan Scott (Jackson 2003b). The archaeobotanical remains from all of the contexts were analyzed by Margaret Scarry (1997; Jackson et al., this volume). The ceramics from the Wiggins and Grady Bobo sites were analyzed by Mintcy Maxham, while the ceramics from Gilliam were analyzed by Jennifer L. Myer.

10

Domestic and Ritual Meals in the Moundville Chiefdom

H. EDWIN JACKSON, C. MARGARET SCARRY, AND SUSAN SCOTT

Over the past thirty years, archaeologists working in the Black Warrior River Valley have devoted considerable effort to understanding the subsistence and political economy of Moundville and its hinterland. In the course of this research, plant and animal remains have been examined from rural hamlets, single-mound sites, and a variety of contexts at Moundville, including off-mound residential precincts and high-status residences on mounds. Some of these remains pertain to daily foodways, while others document the animals and plants consumed or used in rituals. Our intention is to see how the evidence provided by zooarchaeological and archaeobotanical studies might be integrated into a more holistic view of foodways at different times in Moundville's history and at different places on its cultural landscape. Such integration is challenging. As two distinct archaeological specializations, each with its own taphonomic and interpretative issues, zooarchaeology and archaeobotany contribute evidence of past behavior that is sometimes complementary and at other times divergent. In addition, there is no reason to assume that plants and animals would have had the same significance or meanings when they were used in different cultural contexts.

In spite of recovery efforts, including flotation and fine-screening, designed to obtain both plant and animal remains, there is only partial overlap in our datasets. The plant data are strongest for the early Moundville I through early Moundville II phases (table 10.1; figures 10.1 and 10.2). For these periods we have plant assemblages from four rural hamlets (Big Sandy Farms, Oliver, Grady Bobo, and Wiggins), a single-mound center (Hog Pen), and several distinct areas at Moundville (Northwest Riverbank, North of Mound R, and Mounds E, F, and Q). For the late Mound-

Table 10.1. Plant Assemblages from the Black Warrior Valley, Moundville I–Early Moundville II Phases

Category: Site	Ceramic Phase(s)[a]	Developmental Sequence	Context[b]	Number and Context of Samples	Plant Weight (g)	Wood Weight (g)
Paramount Site:						
Moundville	EMI	Initial centralization	Mound E	1 midden	1.40	1.18
Moundville	EMI	Initial centralization	RB residential	5 pit	262.23	251.07
Moundville	LMI–EMII	Regional consolidation	NR residential	22 midden, 26 pit, 26 floor, 17 lens	447.88	370.36
Moundville	LMI–EMII	Regional consolidation	RB residential	8 midden, 15 pit, 2 floor, 2 lens	275.42	245.78
Moundville	LMI–EMII	Regional consolidation	Mound E	4 pit	10.44	10.16
Moundville	LMI–EMII	Regional consolidation	Mound F	2 midden	4.04	3.89
Moundville	LMI–EMII	Regional consolidation	Mound Q	13 ?	88.31	85.23
Hinterland Single-Mound Site:						
Hog Pen	LMI–EMII	Regional consolidation	Mound	7 midden?	66.14	59.15
Hinterland Hamlet:						
Oliver	EMI	Initial centralization	Farmstead	4 pit	40.85	35.16
Big Sandy Farms	EMI	Initial centralization	Farmstead	12 pit	42.99	31.76
Grady Bobo	LMI–EMII	Regional consolidation	Rural feasting pit	1 pit	378.12	315.10
Wiggins	LMI–EMII	Regional consolidation	Rural feasting pit	1 pit	18.14	15.47

Sources: Knight 2010; Scarry 1986, 1993a, 1993b, 1995, 1997, lab notes; Scarry and Steponaitis 1997; Welch and Scarry 1995.
[a]Key to abbreviations: EMI, early Moundville I phase; LMI, late Moundville I phase; EMII, early Moundville II phase.
[b]Key to abbreviations: RB, Riverbank; NR, North of Mound R.

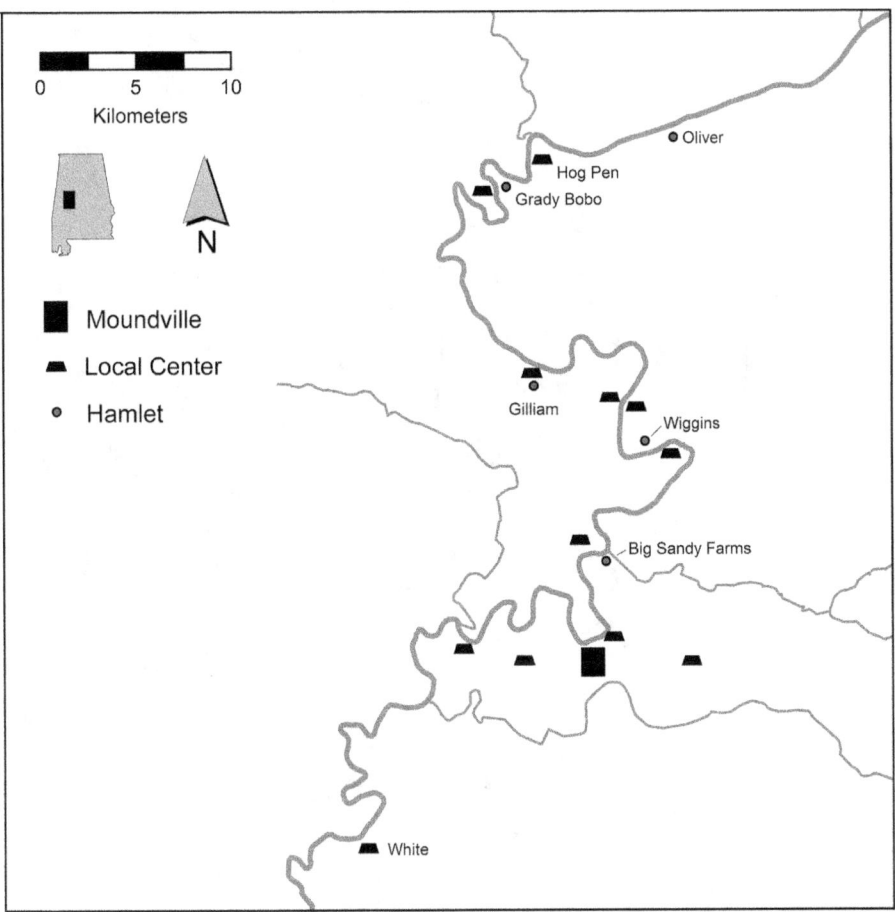

Figure 10.1. The Black Warrior Valley, showing sites with plant and animal assemblages included in this study.

ville II through late Moundville III phases, the plant assemblages are smaller and represent fewer contexts (table 10.2; figures 10.1 and 10.2). For these periods, we have plant data from only one hinterland single-mound site (White) and from several areas at Moundville (North of Mound R, West of Mound R, Mounds E, F, G, Q, and R). Hence, the plant data give us a good window on geographic and social patterns during the period of Moundville's initial centralization and regional consolidation but a much more restricted view of periods when the paramountcy was entrenched and later collapsed and was reorganized. Faunal assemblages from the Black Warrior Valley also have an uneven distribution in time and space, and in some cases come from decidedly nonrepresentative contexts in-

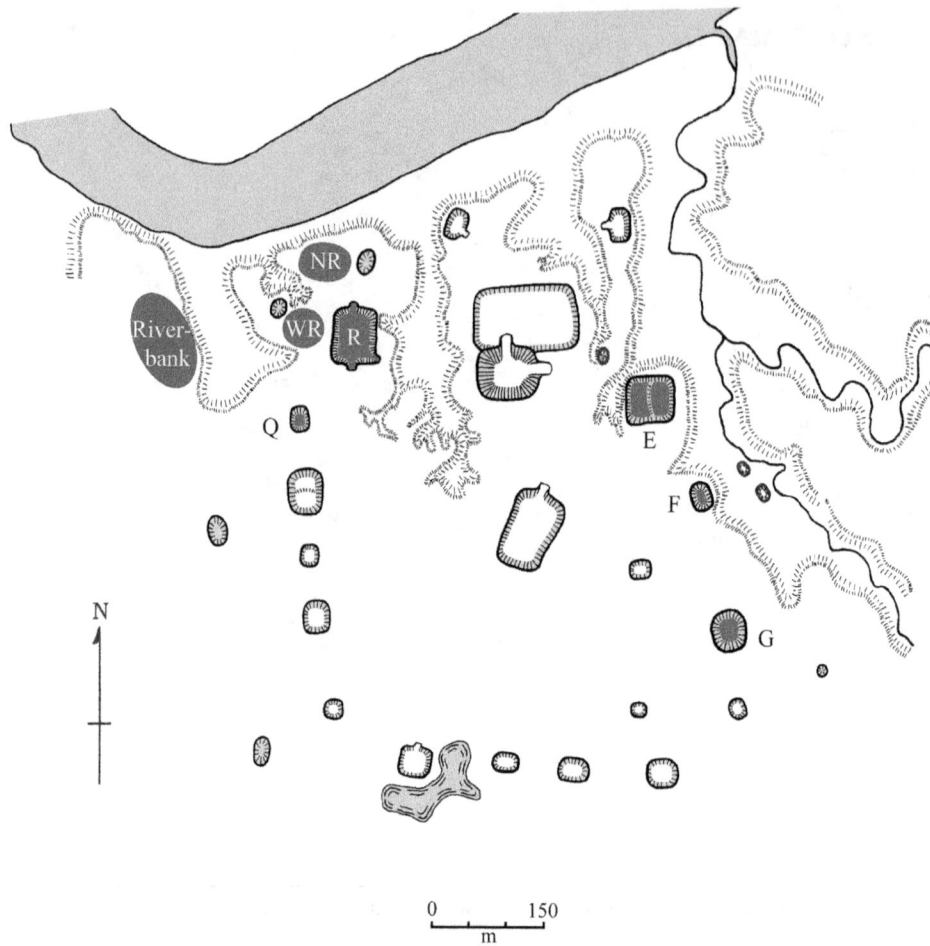

Figure 10.2. The Moundville site, showing localities with plant and animal assemblages included in this study.

cluding elite refuse and debris from special events (table 10.3). Bone samples from late Moundville I phase contexts come from the area north of Mound R at Moundville and two rural hamlets (Grady Bobo, Wiggins). Fauna representing the Moundville II and III phases include large samples from Mounds Q and G, and significantly smaller samples from Mounds R, E, and F at Moundville, as well as from one single-mound site (White) and one hamlet (Gilliam). Despite the differential representation in the plant and animal datasets, our combined samples offer the possibility of

Table 10.2. Plant Assemblages from the Black Warrior Valley, Late Moundville II–Moundville III Phases

Category: Site	Ceramic Phase(s)[a]	Developmental Sequence	Context[b]	Number and Context of Samples	Plant Weight (g)	Wood Weight (g)
Paramount Site:						
Moundville	LMII–EMIII	Paramountcy entrenched	NR residential	1 midden, 1 floor	4.55	4.08
Moundville	LMII–EMIII	Paramountcy entrenched	WR residential	8 midden	9.70	7.14
Moundville	LMII–EMIII	Paramountcy entrenched	Mound E	1 midden, 2 pit	4.73	4.54
Moundville	LMII–EMIII	Paramountcy entrenched	Mound F	2 midden	2.47	2.25
Moundville	LMII–EMIII	Paramountcy entrenched	Mound G	5 ?	36.71	35.96
Moundville	LMII–EMIII	Paramountcy entrenched	Mound Q	2 ?	137.05	127.97
Moundville	LMII–EMIII	Paramountcy entrenched	Mound R	3 midden	10.77	10.33
Moundville	LMIII	Collapse and reorganization	Mound E	1 midden, 2 pit	29.42	27.60
Moundville	LMIII	Collapse and reorganization	NR residential	3 midden	11.14	9.56
Moundville	LMIII	Collapse and reorganization	Mound R	1 ?	0.68	0.65
Hinterland Single-Mound Site:						
White	LMIII	Collapse and reorganization	Residential	3 midden, 4 floor	41.40	21.44

Sources: Knight 2010; Scarry 2003b, lab notes; Welch 1991.
[a]Key to abbreviations: LMII, late Moundville II phase; EMIII, early Moundville III phase; LMIII, late Moundville III phase.
[b]Key to abbreviations: NR, North of Mound R; WR, West of Mound R.

Table 10.3. Faunal Assemblages from the Black Warrior Valley, Moundville I–Moundville III Phases

Category: Site	Ceramic Phase(s)[a]	Developmental Sequence	Context[b]	NISP	Weight (g)
Paramount Site:					
Moundville	LMI–EMII	Regional consolidation	NR residential	—[c]	—[c]
Moundville	MII–EMIII	Paramountcy entrenched	Mound F	477	927.3
Moundville	MII–MIII	Paramountcy entrenched	Mound G	3,119	7,008
Moundville	MI and MIII	Paramountcy entrenched	Mound Q	9,628	17,648
Moundville	MII–MIII	Paramountcy entrenched	Mound R	26	14.4
Moundville	LMIII(?)	Collapse and reorganization	Mound E	506	749.7
Hinterland Single-Mound Site:					
White	LMIII	Collapse and reorganization	Residential	5,326	2,595
Hinterland Hamlet:					
Oliver	EMI	Regional consolidation	Midden	67	—[c]
Wiggins	LMI	Regional consolidation	Refuse pit	83	73
Grady Bobo	LMI–EMII	Regional consolidation	Rural feasting pit	7,069	4,043
Gilliam	MII	Collapse and reorganization	Pit	546	558

Sources: Knight 2010; Jackson 2003, lab notes; Jackson and Scott 2003, 2010; Maxham 2004; Michals 1981, 1992; Scarry and Scarry 1997. NISP refers to the number of identified specimens.
[a]Key to abbreviations: EMI, early Moundville I phase; LMI, late Moundville I phase; EMII, early Moundville II phase; MII, Moundville II phase; LMIII, late Moundville III phase; MIII, Moundville III phase.
[b]Key to abbreviations: NR, North of Mound R.
[c]Not reported.

monitoring processing, transport, and consumption patterns in different contexts at different points in time. We believe these patterns fit well with and perhaps may help refine our notions of historical trends within the Moundville cultural landscape.[1]

Background

We begin with a synopsis of Moundville's history to frame our discussions of foodways. For this, we employ Knight and Steponaitis's (1998) developmental scheme for the Moundville polity, adjusting the dates to fit with the chronology laid out in chapter 1. Knight and Steponaitis' history uses traditional ceramic phases and radiocarbon dates to place deposits in time but focuses attention on changes in demographic, political, and economic organization spanning Moundville's five-century reign in the Black Warrior Valley.

During the century prior to the first construction of houses and mounds at Moundville (West Jefferson phase, AD 1020–1120), there is evidence for increased production of food and material goods from several sites in the valley. At this time people lived in small villages located on arable soils, where they practiced a mixed foraging and farming economy. People gathered large quantities of hickory nuts and acorns, as well as a variety of wild fruits, such as blackberry/raspberry, elderberry, grape, maypops, persimmon, and plum/cherry (Scarry 1986, 1993a). People also raised maize and small quantities of the indigenous crops chenopod, maygrass, little barley, sunflower, sumpweed, and squash. Quantitative comparison of samples from early and late West Jefferson refuse-filled pits indicates that over time people grew and consumed significantly more maize (Scarry 1986, 1993a; Scarry and Steponaitis 1997). Evidence for production of shell ornaments (Pope 1989) may point to efforts by town or clan leaders to amass followers (Knight and Steponaitis 1998: 13), an effort that may also have spurred the intensification of food production (Scarry 1993c).

Early in the twelfth century (early Moundville I, AD 1120–1225), some people from the valley moved to a new community on a high terrace overlooking the Black Warrior River. There they built two mounds and established hamlets dispersed across the terrace. When they moved, people adopted new architectural styles for their houses and began to make a variety of new vessel forms using shell to temper their pottery. Knight and Steponaitis (1998: 13) suggest that local leaders used mound-building rituals and distribution of exotic goods to consolidate and solidify their authority. These activities seem to mark the initial centralization efforts that led to Moundville's paramountcy. Elsewhere in the valley, people also adopted new architectural and ceramic styles, but they continued to live in the same locations their ancestors had dwelt (Hammerstedt et al., this volume; Hammerstedt and Myer 2001; Maxham 2004; Myer 2002a). At Moundville and the hinterland communities, people also hunted, gathered, and grew the same suite of resources their ancestors had consumed. The evidence suggests, however, that they increased their reliance on maize (Scarry 1986, 1993a; Scarry and Steponaitis 1997).

In the following century (late Moundville I–early Moundville II, AD 1200–1300), the leaders at Moundville consolidated their power over a regional polity that stretched some 40 km below the Fall Line at Tuscaloosa. Concurrently, people reorganized themselves on the landscape; some remained in rural hamlets, but many more moved to Moundville, where they settled in discrete neighborhood clusters, built an elaborate mound-and-plaza complex, and erected a palisade (Knight and Steponaitis 1998; Maxham 2004; Scarry 1995; Steponaitis 1998; Wilson 2008). Population estimates for this phase of the site's history range from 1,000 to 3,000 people. During this period, people who remained in the countryside also constructed mounds at three towns (Jones Ferry, Poellnitz, and Hog Pen) where they had lived for generations (Bozeman 1982; Welch 1998). Although there are indications for this period that food moved from hinterland communities to Moundville (Scarry and Steponaitis 1997; Welch and Scarry 1995; see below), the foods consumed changed little. Bone chemistry data suggest maize contributed about 40 percent of people's diets (Schoeninger and Schurr 1998).

In the fourteenth century (late Moundville II–early Moundville III, AD 1300–1450), people once again reorganized their settlements, and presumably their social and political relations as well. Most people moved back to hinterland communities, leaving a few elite at Moundville who continued to reside on and around the mounds (Knight 1998). Other areas of the site were transformed into cemeteries spatially and presumably socially tied to former residential neighborhoods (Steponaitis 1998; Wilson 2008, 2010), rendering much of Moundville a necropolis. When people moved back to the countryside, mound construction at hinterland towns increased. There are seven or eight single-mound centers that date to this period; several replaced earlier centers, while others were newly established (Bozeman 1982; Welch 1998). Daily meals continued to feature the traditional range of plant and animal foods, although bone-chemistry data suggest that maize increased to as much as 65 percent of people's diets (Schoeninger and Schurr 1998). We also have evidence from mound-top activities for provisioning of venison, and for consumption or manipulation of animals that were not a part of the normal diet (see below).

In the fifteenth century (late Moundville III–Moundville IV, AD 1450–1650), the elite at Moundville seem to have lost their hold over the polity, and most activity there ceased. Several single-mound communities, however, continued to thrive. Indeed, the local leaders at sites such as Snows Bend and White seem to have taken on more power as villages and cemeteries were built alongside the mounds (Knight and Steponaitis 1998; Welch 1998). We have limited subsistence evidence for this period, but what there is suggests that while people continued to use the same foods, they may have grown less maize and relied more on hunted and gathered products (Schoeninger and Schurr 1998; see below).

Provisioning Moundville's Residents

We begin our rethinking of foodways at Moundville and its hinterlands by assessing changing economic integration. Specifically, we consider the timing and extent to which the people living at Moundville were provisioned from hinterland sites. Moundville was built on a high, fertile terrace where the east bank of the Black Warrior River cuts close to the Fall Line Hills. People living at Moundville undoubtedly commanded access to the large swaths of arable bottomland soils that surround the terrace on three sides. From the estimated yields of soils within 2-km catchments around Moundville-era sites in the valley, however, Peebles (1978: 400–410) pointed out that people probably could not have grown sufficient maize in fields around Moundville to support its population. The demand for meat also likely exceeded what could be met by hunting in nearby fields and forests. At the time Peebles was writing, it was presumed that Moundville was a large community throughout its history. Given our current understanding of population trends at Moundville, Peebles' observation seems most applicable to the centuries spanning Moundville's initial centralization and, especially, its regional consolidation.

Provisioning Nuts and Maize

The archaeobotanical data cannot tell us the extent of forests and fields or how much nut mast and maize Moundville residents harvested. It is possible, however, to consider whether processed plant foods were transported from nut groves, outfields, or hinterland sites to Moundville. Some years ago, Scarry and Steponaitis (1997) suggested that people living at rural hamlets were provisioning the elite residents of Moundville with maize and nut products during the polity's initial centralization and consolidation. They based their argument on comparisons of the relative abundances of edible plant parts (maize kernels) to processing debris (maize cupules and nutshells) in flotation samples from early and late Moundville I assemblages from two rural hamlets (Big Sandy Farms and Oliver) and an elite residential deposit (North of Mound R) at Moundville. Welch and Scarry (1995) incorporated additional flotation data from the nonelite residential deposits on the Northwest Riverbank at Moundville and from mound-top activities at the hinterland Hog Pen mound. They used similar comparisons of nutshells and maize remains to discuss status-related variations in foodways.

We now have additional plant assemblages, recovered by flotation, from the early centuries of the Moundville polity from two rural sites (Grady Bobo and Wiggins) and from elite mound-top activities (Mounds E, F, and Q) at Moundville (table 10.1). Inclusion of these new assemblages affirms and strengthens patterns seen in earlier analyses. To the extent that we can determine given variable assemblage sizes, people consumed essentially the same range of plant foods at hamlets, single-mound centers and Moundville (tables 10.4 and 10.5).[2] People ate maize, acorns, and hickory nuts as their dietary staples and supplemented these with a diverse set of indigenous cultigens, fruits, and greens. There are, however, significant differences among assemblages in the abundance of processing debris and edible products from the staples.

Nutmeats are scarce in all Moundville-era assemblages, but hickory and acorn shells are ubiquitous, and in some contexts abundant. The boxplots in figure 10.3 compare the relative abundance of the two types of nutshell in deposits from early Moundville I through early Moundville II at hamlets, Hog Pen mound, and Moundville. The data plotted are natural logs of standardized counts to adjust for differences in sample size.[3] The notches on the boxplots indicate a 95 percent confidence interval; if the

Table 10.4. Plants Identified at Sites in the Black Warrior Valley, Moundville I–Moundville III Phases

Category: Common Name	Taxon	EMI–EMII Moundville	EMI–EMII Hog Pen	EMI–EMII Hamlets	LMII–LMIII Moundville	LMII–LMIII White
Cultigens:						
Corn cob	*Zea mays*	+				+
Corn cupule	*Zea mays*	+	+	+	+	+
Corn kernel	*Zea mays*	+	+	+	+	+
Bean	*Phaseolus vulgaris*	+		+	+	
Tobacco	*Nicotiana* sp.				+	
Squash/gourd	*Cucurbita* sp.	+				
Cucurbit rind	*Cucurbita* sp.	+		+	+	
Amaranth	*Amaranthus* sp.	+	+		+	+
Chenopod	*Chenopodium berlandieri*	+	+	+	+	
Cheno/am	*Chenopodium/Amaranthus*	+	+	+	+	+
Knotweed	*Polygonum erectum*	+			+	+
Little barley	*Hordeum pusillum*	+	+	+		
Maygrass	*Phalaris caroliniana*	+	+	+	+	+
Sumpweed	*Iva annua*					
Sumpweed/sunflower	*Iva/Helianthus*	+				
Sunflower	*Helianthus annuus*	+	+	+	+	
Nuts:						
Acorn	*Quercus* sp.	+	+	+	+	+
Acorn meat	*Quercus* sp.	+		+	+	+
Chestnut	*Castanea dentata*	+				
Beech	*Fagus americana*	+	+			
Hazelnut	*Corylus* sp.	+				
Hickory	*Carya* sp.	+	+	+	+	+
Walnut	*Juglans nigra*	+		+		
Pecan	*Carya illinoinensis*	+				
Fruits:						
Blackberry/raspberry	*Rubus* sp.	+		+		
Elderberry	*Sambucus* sp.	+				
Grape	*Vitis* sp.	+	+	+		+
Grape fruit	*Vitis* sp.				+	
Hackberry	*Celtis* sp.					+
Maypop	*Passiflora incarnata*	+	+	+	+	+
Persimmon	*Diospyros virginiana*	+	+	+	+	+

(continued)

Table 10.4—Continued

Category: Common Name	Taxon	EMI-EMII Moundville	Hog Pen	Hamlets	LMII-LMIII Moundville	White
Plum/cherry	*Prunus* sp.	+			+	
Sumac	*Rhus* sp.	+				+
Miscellaneous:						
Wild bean	*Strophosteles* sp.	+			+	
Peavine/vetch	*Vicia* sp.	+	+	+	+	
Bean family	Fabaceae	+	+		+	
Bearsfoot	*Smallanthus uvedalius*		+			
Carpetweed	*Mollugo verticilliata*	+	+		+	
Cleaver	*Galium* sp.	+	+		+	+
Evening primrose	*Oenothera* sp.	+				
Holly	*Ilex* sp.	+				+
Hornbeam	*Carpinus* sp.	+			+	
Morninglory	*Ipomoea/Convolvulus*	+	+		+	
Nightshade	*Solanum* sp.	+	+	+	+	
Pokeweed	*Phytolacca americana*	+	+	+		+
Purslane	*Portulaca oleracea*	+	+			+
Smartweed	*Polygonum* sp.	+	+			
Verbena	*Verbena* sp.	+		+		
Water privet cf.	*Forestiera angustifolia*				+	
Wild rice	*Zizania aquatica*	+			+	
Wood sorrel	*Oxalis* sp.		+			+
Yaupon	*Ilex vomitoria*	+				
Yellow stargrass	*Hypoxis* sp.	+			+	
Composite family	Compositae	+				+
Grass family	Poaceae	+	+	+	+	+
Mallow family	Malvaceae	+	+	+		
Pink family	Caryophyllaceae				+	
Sedge family	Cyperaceae	+	+	+	+	
Spurge family	Euphorbiaceae	+	+	+	+	

Key to abbreviations: EMI, early Moundville I phase; EMII, early Moundville II phase; LMII, late Moundville II phase; LMIII, late Moundville III phase.

Table 10.5. Standardized Counts of Plants, Moundville I–Early Moundville II Phases

Category: Common Name	Moundville RB EMI	RB LMI-EMII	NR LMI-EMII	E EMI	E LMI-EMII	F LMI-EMII	Q LMI-EMII	Hog Pen LMI-EMII	Oliver EMI	Big Sandy EMI	Grady Bobo LMI-EMII	Wiggins LMI-EMII
Cultigens:												
Corn cob	—	—	0.004	—	—	—	—	—	—	—	—	—
Corn cupule	1.514	3.148	3.597	5.000	0.958	0.248	3.023	5.292	7.662	8.630	3.465	7.993
Corn kernel	4.870	2.814	4.729	1.429	0.766	1.238	1.042	6.894	3.452	3.954	5.527	3.638
Bean	—	—	0.083	—	—	—	0.057	—	—	0.558	—	—
Tobacco	—	—	—	—	—	—	—	—	—	—	—	—
Squash/gourd	—	—	0.002	—	—	—	0.023	—	—	—	—	—
Cucurbit rind	—	—	—	—	—	—	0.034	—	—	0.442	0.021	—
Amaranth	—	0.004	0.047	—	—	—	0.057	0.197	—	—	—	—
Chenopod	0.919	0.109	0.578	2.143	—	—	0.396	0.272	0.220	—	0.019	0.221
Cheno/am	0.145	0.004	—	0.714	0.287	—	0.091	0.060	—	—	0.016	0.055
Knotweed	—	0.011	0.040	—	—	—	0.011	—	—	—	—	—
Little barley	—	0.004	0.004	—	—	—	0.045	0.575	—	—	0.003	0.662
Maygrass	0.126	0.018	0.375	2.143	1.245	—	0.159	0.106	0.465	0.023	0.106	0.606
Sumpweed	—	—	—	—	—	—	—	—	—	—	—	—
Sumpweed/sunflower	0.004	—	—	—	—	—	—	—	—	—	—	—
Sunflower	—	—	0.007	—	—	—	—	0.015	0.024	—	0.011	—
Nuts:												
Acorn	0.305	2.091	5.571	2.143	0.192	0.248	0.204	4.430	21.983	10.630	12.594	35.612
Acorn meat	0.004	0.051	0.074	1.429	—	0.743	0.011	—	0.049	0.442	0.164	0.606

(*continued*)

Table 10.5—Continued

	Moundville											
	RB		NR	E		F	Q	Hog Pen	Oliver	Big Sandy	Grady Bobo	Wiggins
Category: Common Name	EMI	LMI-EMII	LMI-EMII	EMI	LMI-EMII	LMI-EMII	LMI-EMII	LMI-EMII	EMI	EMI	LMI-EMII	LMI-EMII
Chestnut	—	—	0.002	—	—	—	—	—	—	—	—	—
Beech	—	0.036	0.007	—	—	—	0.011	0.045	—	—	—	—
Hazelnut	—	—	0.004	—	—	—	—	—	—	—	—	—
Hickory	1.205	4.204	1.420	15.000	0.766	1.980	0.668	1.950	4.211	15.655	10.732	1.654
Walnut	—	—	0.002	—	—	—	—	—	—	0.535	—	—
Pecan	0.042	—	—	—	—	—	—	—	—	—	—	—
Fruits:												
Blackberry/raspberry	—	—	0.013	—	—	—	—	—	—	—	0.005	0.055
Elderberry	—	—	0.033	—	—	—	—	—	—	—	—	—
Grape	0.004	0.062	0.013	—	—	—	—	0.197	—	—	0.005	—
Grape fruit	—	—	—	—	—	—	—	—	—	—	—	—
Hackberry	—	—	—	—	—	—	—	—	—	—	—	—
Maypop	—	0.007	0.027	—	—	—	0.023	0.166	0.049	0.023	0.217	0.110
Persimmon	0.217	0.436	1.286	0.714	0.192	—	0.294	0.060	0.563	0.582	0.066	—
Plum/cherry	—	—	0.004	—	—	—	0.034	—	—	—	—	—
Sumac	—	—	0.004	—	—	—	—	—	—	—	—	—
Miscellaneous:												
Wild bean	—	—	0.004	—	—	—	—	—	—	—	—	—
Peavine/vetch	0.015	—	—	0.714	—	—	—	0.121	—	—	0.362	1.599
Bean family	—	0.007	0.038	—	—	—	—	0.091	—	—	—	—
Bearsfoot	—	—	—	—	—	—	—	0.030	—	—	—	—

Carpetweed	0.088	0.171	0.016	—	—	0.034	0.227	—	—	—	—
Cleaver	—	—	0.011	—	—	—	0.151	—	—	—	—
Evening primrose	—	—	0.007	—	—	—	—	—	—	—	—
Holly	—	0.015	0.002	—	—	—	—	—	—	—	—
Hornbeam	—	—	—	—	0.096	—	—	—	—	—	—
Morninglory	0.004	—	0.047	—	—	0.023	0.166	—	—	—	—
Nightshade	—	0.004	0.036	—	—	0.011	0.015	—	0.023	0.016	0.055
Pokeweed	0.423	0.443	0.002	—	—	—	0.091	—	—	0.011	—
Purslane	—	0.410	0.007	—	—	0.113	0.197	—	—	—	—
Smartweed	0.015	—	—	—	—	—	0.136	—	—	—	—
Verbena	—	—	—	—	—	0.011	—	—	—	0.042	—
Water privet cf.	—	—	—	—	—	—	—	—	—	—	—
Wild rice	—	—	0.065	—	—	—	—	—	—	—	—
Wood sorrel	—	—	—	—	—	—	0.015	—	—	—	—
Yaupon	—	—	0.004	—	—	—	—	—	—	—	—
Yellow Stargrass	—	0.062	0.002	—	0.096	0.011	—	—	—	—	—
Composite family	—	0.004	0.013	—	—	—	—	—	—	—	—
Grass family	14.434	0.621	0.165	0.714	0.383	0.181	0.151	—	0.070	0.013	—
Mallow family	—	0.004	0.011	—	—	0.034	0.045	—	—	—	0.165
Pink family	—	—	—	—	—	0.011	—	—	—	—	—
Sedge family	0.175	—	0.020	—	—	—	0.091	—	—	—	0.110
Spurge family	—	0.004	0.013	—	—	0.011	0.015	—	—	0.005	—

Key to abbreviations: RB, Riverbank; NR, North of Mound R; E, Mound E; F, Mound F; Q, Mound Q; EMI, early Moundville I phase; LMI, late Moundville I phase; EMII, early Moundville II phase.

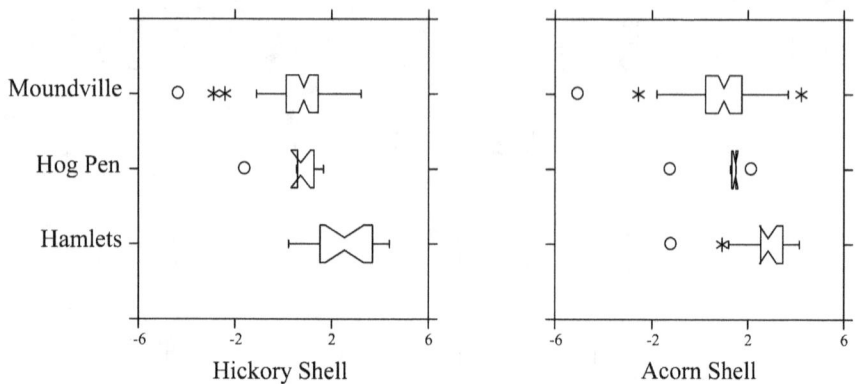

Figure 10.3. Abundance of hickory and acorn shell from Moundville I contexts at hamlets, Hog Pen mound, and Moundville. Abundance is calculated as log (count/plant weight).

notches do not overlap, the differences between the median values for the assemblages are statistically significant. For both hickory and acorn, quantities of nutshell are significantly higher at the hamlets. In contrast, quantities of nutshell are comparable in the assemblages from Hog Pen mound and Moundville. There are several possible explanations for this pattern. The simplest is that hamlet households were processing and consuming more acorns and hickory than were used in mound-top activities at Hog Pen or in the residences and on the mounds at Moundville. Acorn is primarily a source of carbohydrates (McCarthy and Matthews 1984); maize may have been the preferred source of starch for meals at hinterland mounds and at the paramount center. Hickory, a good source of fat and protein (McCarthy and Matthews 1984), was generally used by Indians as a source of oil (Gardner 1997; Scarry 2003a; Swanton 1946). Perhaps animal oils such as bear grease were more readily available or preferred for meals and rituals at single-mound centers and at Moundville. Keeping in mind that we have only nut processing debris, it is also possible that nuts were being processed at hamlets or collection sites in nut groves, and that hickory oil or knudgie balls (Fritz et al. 2001) and parched acorn meats or meal were transported to the center. (Note that knudgie balls contain small bits of hickory shell among the pressed meats, but the bulk of the nutshell is discarded when the balls are made.)

Whether or not hamlet residents ate more hickory and acorn or provisioned nut products to center residents, the distribution of nutshells may be an indirect clue to land use around Moundville. There are many species of hickories and oaks in the region; some favoring bottomlands and terraces, others found on drier upland soils (Scarry 1986). If people cleared extensive areas of the bottomlands and terraces around Moundville for fields, they may have eliminated nearby nut groves, thereby reducing nuts available for consumption or increasing the incentive to transport processed nut products from hinterland communities or nut collection camps.

For maize, the primary agricultural staple, we can examine the distribution of kernels to monitor cooking and consumption and use the distribution of cupules to monitor processing. Both kernels and cupules are ubiquitous in the assemblages, but they vary in abundance among the communities dating to the polity's centralization and consolidation. The boxplots in figure 10.4 compare standardized counts of kernels and cupules, as well as ratios of kernels to cupules at hamlets, Hog Pen mound, and Moundville. Quantities of kernels are comparable among the communities, suggesting equivalent levels of activities (cooking and eating) that result in losses of edible grains. Quantities of cupules are lower at Hog Pen mound and Moundville than they are at hamlets, though the notches on the boxes overlap, indicating that the differences are not significant at the 95 percent confidence level. When ratios of kernels to cupules are calculated, however, the differences are significant; Hog Pen mound and Moundville have higher ratios of kernel to cupule than do the hamlets (see also table 10.6). These results suggest that people at the various communities were eating but not shelling comparable amounts of maize. Put another way, some of the maize at Hog Pen mound and Moundville was arriving in the form of kernels already separated from the cobs. This fits with what we know about storage at Moundville (Barrier 2011; Scarry 1995; Wilson 2008); there are no large storage pits associated with the houses at Moundville, and there is scant evidence for aboveground storage structures. The primary storage method seems to have been in very large ceramic jars, which would be more appropriate for storing shelled grain than for far bulkier ears of maize. Whether the grain was provisioned from hamlets to residents at the centers or shelled in outfields before being transported is an open question.

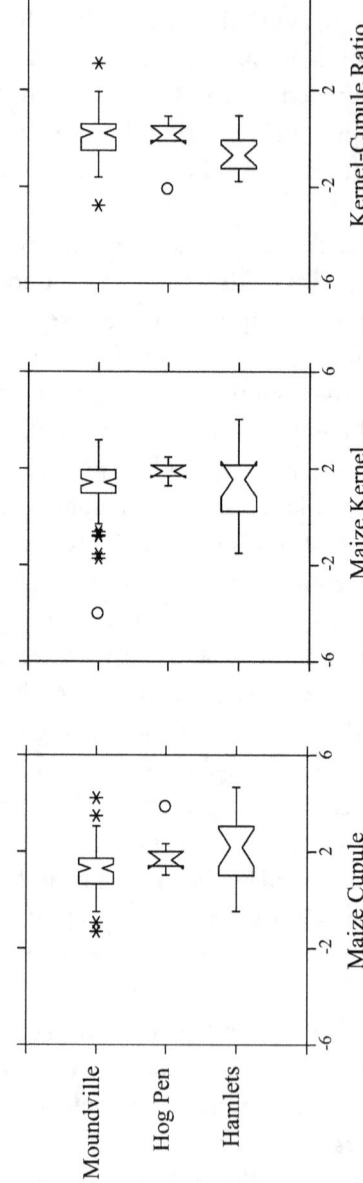

Figure 10.4. Abundance of maize cupules and kernels, and the kernel-to-cupule ratio from Moundville I contexts at hamlets, Hog Pen mound, and Moundville. Abundance is calculated as log (count/plant weight); the ratio as log (count/count).

Table 10.6. Ratios of Maize Kernels to Cupules

Category: Site	Ceramic Phases	Developmental Sequence	Context	Kernels (n)	Cupules (n)	Kernel-to-Cupule Ratio
Paramount Site:						
Moundville	EMI	Initial centralization	RB residential	1,277	397	3.21
Moundville	EMI	Initial centralization	Mound E	2	7	.28
Moundville	LMI–EMII	Regional consolidation	RB residential	775	867	.89
Moundville	LMI–EMII	Regional consolidation	NR residential	2,118	1,615	1.31
Moundville	LMI–EMII	Regional consolidation	Mound E	8	10	.80
Moundville	LMI–EMII	Regional consolidation	Mound F	5	1	5.00
Moundville	LMI–EMII	Regional consolidation	Mound Q	92	267	.34
Moundville	LMII–EMIII	Paramountcy entrenched	NR residential	5	36	.14
Moundville	LMII–EMIII	Paramountcy entrenched	WR residential	27	115	.23
Moundville	LMII–EMIII	Paramountcy entrenched	Mound E	2	4	.50
Moundville	LMII–EMIII	Paramountcy entrenched	Mound F	7	3	2.33
Moundville	LMII–EMIII	Paramountcy entrenched	Mound G	22	65	.34
Moundville	LMII–EMIII	Paramountcy entrenched	Mound Q	156	582	.27
Moundville	LMII–EMIII	Paramountcy entrenched	Mound R	5	67	.07
Moundville	LMIII	Collapse and reorganization	NR residential	26	72	.36
Moundville	LMIII	Collapse and reorganization	Mound E	73	84	.87
Moundville	LMIII	Collapse and reorganization	Mound R	—	3	—

(continued)

Table 10.6—*Continued*

Category: Site	Ceramic Phases	Developmental Sequence	Context	Kernels (n)	Cupules (n)	Kernel-to-Cupule Ratio
Hinterland Single-Mound Site:						
Hog Pen	LMI–EMII	Regional consolidation	Mound	456	350	1.30
White	LMIII	Collapse and reorganization	Residential	146	343	.42
Hinterland Hamlet:						
Oliver	EMI	Initial centralization	Farmstead	141	313	.45
Big Sandy Farms	EMI	Initial centralization	Farmstead	170	371	.46
Grady Bobo	LMI–EMII	Regional consolidation	Rural feasting pit	2,090	1,310	1.60
Wiggins	LMI–EMII	Regional consolidation	Rural feasting pit	66	145	.46

Key to abbreviations: EMI, early Moundville I; LMI, late Moundville I; EMII, early Moundville II; LMII, late Moundville II; EMIII, early Moundville III; LMIII, late Moundville III; RB, Riverbank; NR, North of Mound R; WR, West of Mound R.

Looking only at Moundville, when we examine the distribution of maize kernels and cupules from distinct areas at the site, we see the picture is more complex than simple provisioning of shelled maize and nut products to the elite residing at the center. The boxplots in figure 10.5 compare the abundance of maize remains in off-mound nonelite and elite residential deposits to those from mound-top activities. Quantities of cupules are comparable in the various assemblages, but there are significantly fewer kernels in the assemblages from the mounds, resulting in kernel-to-cupule ratios that are significantly lower (see also table 10.6).

We still think that shelled maize was flowing from hinterland sites (or possibly outfields) to Moundville. The strongest data are all from contexts dating to the peak of residential population and mound-building activities. It seems likely that fields around Moundville were indeed insufficient to support the people living there. But it was not solely the elite who were receiving processed maize. Given the evidence for discrete neighborhoods and complementary but segmentary organization of elites (Knight 2010, this volume; Wilson 2008, 2010), the flow of food from the hinterlands to Moundville probably moved more along kinship or lineage paths rather than into or through chiefly hands. Economic integration during this intensified phase of mound construction appears to us to have been between hinterland farmers and their kinfolk living in neighborhoods at Moundville, as well as their leaders residing atop the newly constructed mounds. Relief from at least a portion of subsistence responsibilities would have enabled the people living at Moundville to devote more of their energies to mound building and other ritual efforts.

Assuming that shelled maize was being moved from hinterland sites or outfields to Moundville, the comparatively low ratios of kernels to cupules in deposits created by mound-top activities seem anomalous (figure 10.5, table 10.6). It seems unlikely that mound-top residents were shelling maize and sending or consuming it off-mound. Of course, the low kernel-to-cupule ratios may be a result of sample bias, as we have few plant samples dating to early Moundville I through early Moundville II from mound contexts. Nonetheless, we can suggest several explanations other than small sample size for the pattern. It may be that the elite living on the mounds were provisioned with ears of maize rather than shelled kernels. If so, the transport costs would be higher due to the greater bulk that would have to be moved, but the grain would have a longer shelf life, as maize in the husk is more resistant to mold and insects (Smyth 1990). Al-

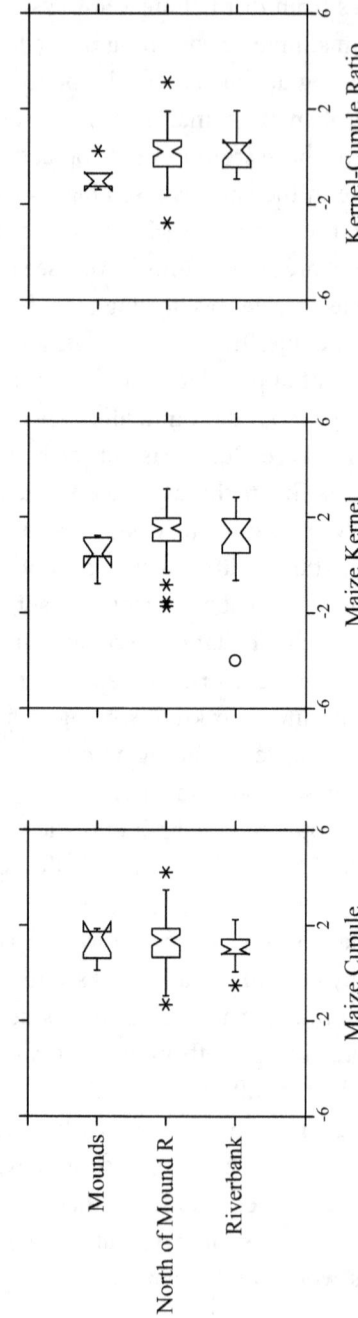

Figure 10.5. Abundance of maize cupules and kernels, and the kernel-to-cupule ratio from Moundville I contexts on the Riverbank, North of Mound R, and the mounds at Moundville. Abundance is calculated as log (count/plant weight); the ratio as log (count/count).

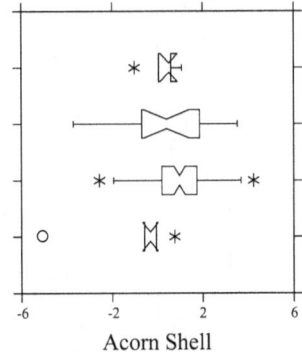

Figure 10.6. Abundance of hickory and acorn shell from Moundville through time. Abundance is calculated as log (count/plant weight).

ternatively, mound-top ritual meals may have given symbolic importance to maize prepared and consumed in ways that resulted in loss of fewer kernels; for example, maize may have been roasted and consumed on the cob more often than it was pounded into flour or made into hominy.

We have fewer and smaller plant assemblages for sites and activities that postdate the out-migration of people from Moundville (tables 10.2, 10.7). Nonetheless, the samples that we have from Moundville allow us to consider patterns in the use of plant staples at a time when few but the elite remained in residence at the center. The boxplots in figure 10.6 compare the relative abundance of nut processing debris in Moundville deposits through time. After the period of initial centralization, quantities of hickory and acorn nutshells are more or less constant. Either nut consumption remained low or nut groves had not reestablished themselves in the bottomlands and terraces near Moundville, resulting in continued provisioning (or at least off-site processing) of nuts.

Later assemblages from Moundville do show changes in the proportions of maize kernels and cupules. The boxplots in figure 10.7 show significantly more cupules in deposits dating to late Moundville III. There are also fewer kernels in later deposits, but the differences are not significant. The ratios of kernels to cupules, however, are significantly lower than in earlier periods at Moundville. Indeed, the ratios are more comparable to those from earlier hamlets than they are to earlier assemblages at the paramount center (table 10.6). We should note, that while the boxplots in figure 10.7 include mound-top assemblages, similar patterns are seen

Table 10.7. Standardized Counts of Plants, Late Moundville II–Moundville III Phases

Category: Common Name	Moundville										
	E		F	G	Q	R		NR		WR	White
	LMII-EMIII	LMIII	LMII-EMIII	LMII-EMIII	LMII-EMIII	LMII-EMIII	LMIII	LMII-EMIII	LMIII	LMII-EMIII	LMIII
Cultigens:											
Corn cob	—	—	—	—	—	—	—	—	—	—	0.024
Corn cupule	0.958	2.855	1.215	1.771	4.247	6.221	4.412	7.912	6.463	11.771	8.285
Corn kernel	0.766	2.481	2.834	0.599	1.138	0.464	—	1.099	2.334	2.764	3.527
Bean	—	—	—	—	0.015	—	—	—	0.090	—	—
Tobacco	—	—	—	—	0.007	—	—	—	—	—	—
Squash/gourd	—	—	—	—	—	—	—	—	—	—	—
Cucurbit rind	—	0.034	—	—	—	—	—	—	—	—	—
Amaranth	—	—	0.405	—	—	—	—	—	—	—	0.024
Chenopod	—	—	0.810	0.354	0.022	0.093	—	0.440	0.180	0.102	—
Cheno/am	0.287	0.068	0.405	0.054	0.117	—	—	—	—	—	0.024
Knotweed	—	—	—	—	0.007	—	—	—	—	0.102	0.072
Little barley	—	—	—	—	—	—	—	—	—	—	—
Maygrass	1.245	—	1.215	0.708	0.088	—	—	—	—	0.102	0.169
Sumpweed	—	—	—	—	—	—	—	—	—	—	—
Sumpweed/sunflower	—	—	—	—	—	—	—	—	—	—	—
Sunflower	—	—	0.405	—	—	—	—	—	—	—	—
Nuts:											
Acorn	0.192	0.272	1.215	0.027	0.131	0.371	—	1.319	0.898	7.677	26.111
Acorn meat	—	—	0.810	0.054	0.073	—	—	—	—	—	2.971

Chestnut	—	—	—	—	—	—	—	—	—	—
Beech	—	—	—	—	—	—	—	—	—	—
Hazelnut	—	—	—	—	—	—	—	—	—	—
Hickory	0.766	1.020	1.619	0.436	1.364	1.486	—	0.659	1.077	7.165	21.643
Walnut	—	—	—	—	—	—	—	—	—	—
Pecan	—	—	—	—	—	—	—	—	—	—
Fruits:										
Blackberry/raspberry	—	—	—	—	—	—	—	—	—	—
Elderberry	—	—	—	—	—	—	—	—	—	—
Grape	—	—	—	—	0.007	—	—	—	—	0.048
Grape fruit	—	—	—	—	—	—	—	—	—	—
Hackberry	—	—	—	—	—	—	—	—	—	0.048
Maypop	—	—	0.405	0.027	—	—	—	—	0.269	—	0.145
Persimmon	0.192	0.136	0.405	0.082	0.336	0.093	—	1.978	—	2.149	3.720
Plum/cherry	—	—	—	—	—	—	—	—	0.090	—	—
Sumac	—	—	—	—	—	—	—	—	—	—	0.024
Miscellaneous:										
Wild bean	—	—	—	—	0.007	—	—	—	—	—
Peavine/vetch	—	—	0.405	—	—	—	—	—	—	—
Bean family	—	—	—	—	—	0.093	—	—	—	—
Bearsfoot	—	—	—	—	—	—	—	—	—	—
Carpetweed	—	—	—	0.027	—	—	—	—	—	—
Cleaver	—	—	—	—	0.015	—	—	—	—	—	0.024
Evening primrose	—	—	—	—	—	—	—	—	—	—
Holly	—	—	—	—	—	—	—	—	—	—	0.121

(*continued*)

Table 10.7—Continued

	Moundville										
	E	E	F	G	Q	R	R	NR	NR	WR	White
Category: Common Name	LMII-EMIII	LMIII	LMII-EMIII	LMII-EMIII	LMII-EMIII	LMII-EMIII	LMIII	LMII-EMIII	LMIII	LMIII-EMIII	LMIII
Hornbeam	0.096	—	—	—	—	—	—	—	—	—	—
Morninglory	—	—	—	—	0.015	—	—	—	—	—	—
Nightshade	—	—	—	0.054	0.007	—	—	—	—	—	—
Pokeweed	—	—	—	—	—	—	—	—	—	—	0.097
Purslane	—	—	—	—	—	—	—	—	—	—	0.024
Smartweed	—	—	—	—	—	—	—	—	—	—	—
Verbena	—	—	—	—	—	—	—	—	—	—	—
Water privet cf.	—	—	—	—	0.007	—	—	—	—	—	—
Wild rice	—	—	—	0.027	—	—	—	—	—	—	—
Wood sorrel	—	—	—	—	—	—	—	0.220	—	—	0.048
Yaupon	—	—	—	—	—	—	—	—	—	—	—
Yellow	0.096	—	—	—	0.007	—	—	—	—	0.102	—
Stargrass											
Composite family	—	—	—	—	—	—	—	—	—	—	0.024
Grass family	0.383	0.170	—	0.082	0.058	—	—	0.220	0.090	—	3.043
Mallow family	—	—	—	—	—	—	—	—	—	—	—
Pink family	—	—	0.405	—	—	—	—	—	—	—	—
Sedge family	—	—	—	—	0.007	—	—	—	—	—	—
Spurge family	—	—	0.405	—	—	—	—	—	—	—	—

Key to abbreviations: E, Mound E; F, Mound F; G, Mound G; Q, Mound Q; R, Mound R; NR, North of Mound R; WR, West of Mound R; LMII, late Moundville II; EMIII, early Moundville III; LMIII, late Moundville III.

when the mound assemblages are excluded. The changes in the proportions of maize remains suggest that provisioning of maize kernels from hinterland sites or outfields drops off by late Moundville II/early Moundville III. This makes sense. With the out-migration of most people from Moundville, the small residential population would need less maize, which could come from nearby fields. With transport costs no longer an issue, maize from infields could be shelled on site or stored in the husk to extend its shelf life.

The only plant assemblage we have from a hinterland site that postdates the out-migration from Moundville comes from residential deposits at White, a single-mound center that dates to late Moundville III (Welch 1991). The boxplots in figures 10.8 and 10.9 compare quantities of nutshells and maize remains from White to contemporary remains from Moundville. There are significantly more hickory and acorn nutshells in White's residential deposits; the boxes do not even overlap with those from Moundville. The quantities of nutshell at White are more similar to those from Moundville I hamlets than they are to deposits from any period at Moundville. The maize remains show a different pattern from the nutshells. Quantities of cupules are comparable to those in late deposits at Moundville, while kernels appear to be somewhat more abundant. The ratios of kernels to cupules reflect this difference; they are higher, although not significantly so at White than at Moundville (see also table 10.6). The White occupation dates to the period of the polity's collapse and reorganization. It is also located at the southern extreme of the polity where the land becomes much swampier. We think the differences seen in the White assemblage result in part from changes in economic structure as local communities reasserted their authority and in part from the particulars of the site's environmental setting. We suggest that White's residents gathered nuts for their own use and returned home to process them. In contrast, some of the maize they consumed seems to have been shelled at outfields or provisioned from nearby hamlets with ties to the community. If we are correct, it is worth noting that relatively less shelled maize entered the White community than the earlier residential districts at Moundville.

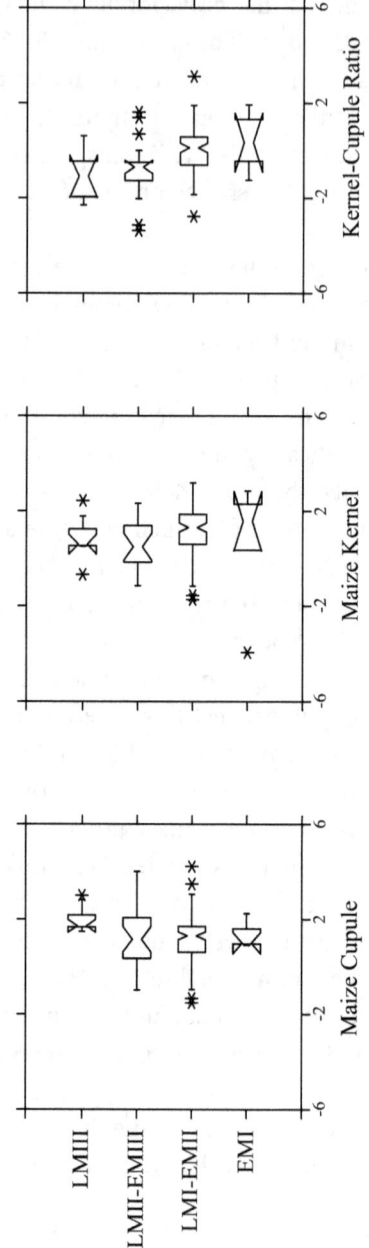

Figure 10.7. Abundance of maize cupules and kernels, and the kernel-to-cupule ratio from Moundville through time. Abundance is calculated as log (count/plant weight); the ratio as log (count/count).

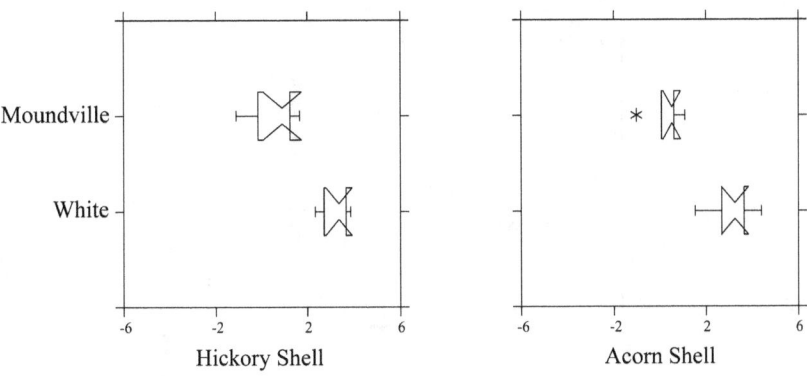

Figure 10.8. Abundance of hickory and acorn shell from late Moundville III contexts at Moundville and White. Abundance is calculated as log (count/plant weight).

Provisioning Meat

As Moundville shifted from a bustling community in the midst of a ceremonial precinct under construction to a ceremonial precinct inhabited only by the elite, there was less provisioning of plant foods by outlying communities. In contrast, hinterland communities supplying meat to the elite appears to be a persistent zooarchaeological pattern, at least to the limits of available evidence. Analyzed faunal samples come from Moundville I contexts North of Mound R (Michals 1981, 1992), from Moundville II and Moundville III contexts from Mound Q, and Moundville II/III contexts from Mound G (Jackson and Scott 2003, 2010). Michals's analysis of fauna from late Moundville I contexts North of Mound R suggests transport of prebutchered portions of venison, most often shoulders, to elite residents. Anatomical representation of deer remains from later flank deposits on Mounds Q and G suggests that after the out-migration of most of Moundville's population, the elite continued to be supplied with deer butchered elsewhere (Jackson and Scott 2003). There is, however, enough bone representing primary butchering to suggest that at least occasionally whole carcasses were brought to the mounds for processing, more often to Mound Q than Mound G. Looking specifically at Mound Q, where deposits can be sorted by phase, there is a minor increase in large mammal (deer and unidentified large mammal) by weight relative to

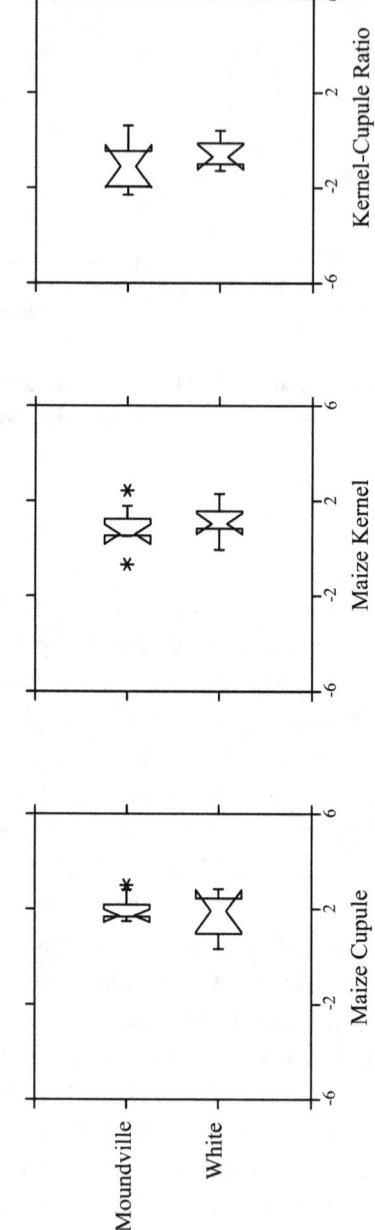

Figure 10.9. Abundance of maize cupules and kernels, and the kernel-to-cupule ratio from late Moundville III contexts at Moundville and White. Abundance is calculated as log (count/plant weight); the ratio as log (count/count).

other taxonomic categories during Moundville III (table 10.8), which may mark a change in provisioning, resulting in a greater emphasis on deer.

If we compare deer-element representation between the Moundville II and III mound deposits, some subtle differences point to the nature of this change. First, it is clear that the Moundville II and the Moundville III samples are quite similar. Using percent of expected minimum number of elements (MNE), both samples are dominated by high-value cuts, especially forequarters, but medium-value anatomical portions are present, as are small amounts of primary butchering remains (skull, mandible, toes) (figure 10.10). A closer look reveals that, overall, low-utility elements decline during Moundville III, perhaps indicating an increase in field butchery due to increased transport costs. While we assume that provisioning during Moundville I would also have been the responsibility of outlying communities, the subsequent dispersal of Moundville's population back to the countryside would likely have increased pressure on deer populations in the valley. As a result, hunters may have had to range farther than previously. If we step back and look at temporal trends in the valley as a whole, chronologically ordered assemblages show a decline in the proportion of large mammal (figure 10.11), which further attests to possible increasing pressure on deer populations over time. The single-mound White site runs counter to this trend, suggesting reorganization of provisioning to supply local centers. This reorganization may have affected the Moundville elite during the Moundville III phase (at least those residing on Mound Q) in several ways; they may have consumed more medium-utility anatomical portions, in particular meat attached to thoracic and lumbar vertebrae, and they may have received and consumed less meat from high-utility portions. Nonetheless, a high-utility element (distal humerus) served as the basis for calculating percent MNE for the Moundville III sample. The perceived reduction in the high-utility deer elements based on percent MNE could equally likely be a product of greater bone processing in the later phase, moving greater numbers of deer elements to the unidentified-large-mammal category as a consequence of greater fragmentation. If unidentified-large-mammal material is factored in (which can be accomplished only in a general way by examining bone weight), the combined contribution of fore- and hindquarters may in fact be greater in the Moundville III sample (figure 10.12).

Table 10.8. Fauna from Mound Q at Moundville, Moundville II–Moundville III Phases

Category: Common Name	Taxon	Moundville II			Moundville III		
		NISP	Weight (g)	MNI	NISP	Weight (g)	MNI
Mammals:							
Opossum	*Didelphis virginiana*	3	1.5	1	5	4.5	1
Eastern cottontail	*Sylvilagus floridanus*	14	8.2	1	7	3.7	1
Swamp rabbit	*Sylvilagus aquaticus*	3	4.1	1	1	0.4	1
Rabbit sp.	*Sylvilagus* sp.	7	3.4		1	0.1	
Mouse	*Peromyscus* sp.	5	0.2	1			
Rat	Cricetidae	1	0.1	1			
Eastern gray squirrel	*Sciurus carolinensis*	41	16.5	3	51	11.8	4
Eastern fox squirrel	*Sciurus niger*	35	22.7	3	5	3	1
Squirrel sp.	*Sciurus* sp.	8	1.9		2	0.3	
Beaver	*Castor canadensis*	5	20	1	4	7.5	1
Raccoon	*Procyon lotor*	2	2.4	2	1	0.3	1
Mink	*Mustela vison*	7	1.3	1	2	0.6	1
Black bear	*Ursus americanus*	2	25.2	1			
Domestic dog	*Canis familiaris*	2	4.3	1			
Unid. medium carnivore	Carnivora	1	0.1				
White-tailed deer	*Odocoileus virginianus*	409	4,592.1	8	420	3,350.3	10
Very large mammal		1	3.6		2	8.4	
Large mammal		1,803	2,101.1		2,225	1,906.4	
Medium mammal		12	9.9		7	3.5	
Small mammal		47	14.1		38	9	
Unid. mammal		1	0.6		1	0.4	
Subtotal		2,409	6,833.3	25	2,772	5,310.2	22
Birds:							
Canada goose	*Branta canadensis*				1	0.9	1
Wood duck	*Aix sponsa*	2	0.9	1			
Medium duck	Anatidae	1	0.7		1	0.3	1
Red-tailed hawk	*Buteo jamaicensis*	2	0.9	1	2	1.1	1

(continued)

		Moundville II			Moundville III		
Category: Common Name	Taxon	NISP	Weight (g)	MNI	NISP	Weight (g)	MNI
Hawk	*Buteo* sp.	1	0.3	1			
Turkey	*Meleagris gallopavo*	109	334.6	5	61	119	3
Crow	*Corvus brachyrhynchos*	1	0.7	1	1	0.3	1
Passenger pigeon	*Ectopistes migratorius*	8	1.5	1	3	0.7	1
Unid. large bird		603	284.1		347	143.8	
Unid. medium bird		19	4.6		16	4.9	
Unid. small bird		1	0.7		3	0.5	
Unid. bird		3	0.3		23	4.3	
Subtotal		750	629.3	10	458	275.8	8
Reptiles:							
Snapping turtle	*Chelydra serpentina*				4	3.3	1
Painted turtle/ Florida cooter	*Chrysemys picta/ Pseudemys floridana*	1	3.3	1	5	9.7	1
Box turtle	*Terrapene carolina*	21	33.8	2	22	14.3	1
Musk turtle	*Sternotherus* sp.	2	1.4	1	1	0.7	1
Mud/musk turtle	Kinosternidae	2	0.9		3	0.4	
Soft-shelled turtle	Trionychidae	3	5.8	1	12	21.3	1
Unid. turtle	Testudines	57	17.4		67	27.1	
Coachwhip/racer	*Coluber/ Masticophus*				1	0.1	1
Viper	Viperidae	2	0.8	1	1	0.4	1
Subtotal		88	63.4	6	116	77.3	7
Amphibians:							
Frog/toad	*Rana/Bufo* sp.	1	0.1	1			
Pisces:							
Bowfin	*Amia calva*	5	5	3	1	0.2	1
Alligator gar	*Atractosteus spatula*				1	0.7	1
Short-nosed gar	*Lepisosteus platostomus*				1	0.4	1
Gar	Lepisosteidae	4	1.7	3	1	0.2	1
Smallmouth buffalo	*Ictiobus bubalus*	8	6.7	2	1	0.3	1

(continued)

Table 10.8—Continued

Category: Common Name	Taxon	Moundville II			Moundville III		
		NISP	Weight (g)	MNI	NISP	Weight (g)	MNI
River redhorse	*Moxostoma carinatum*				1	0.2	1
Blacktail redhorse	*Moxostoma poecilurum*	1	0.2	1			
Redhorse sp.	*Moxostoma* sp.	5	3.8		1	0.5	1
Sucker	Catostomidae	41	11	8	1	0.4	
Flathead catfish	*Pylodictis olivaris*	1	0.3	1			
Blue catfish	*Ictalurus furcatus*	3	1.3	1			
Channel catfish	*Ictalurus punctatus*	2	1.4	2	3	1.3	1
Blue/channel catfish	*I. furcatus/ punctatus*	12	5.2		1	0.2	1
Catfish	Ictaluridae	5	0.9	1	3	0.9	1
Largemouth bass	*Micropterus salmoides*				1	0.2	1
Bass	*Micropterus* sp.	1	0.3	1			
Bass/crappie	*Micropterus/ Pomoxis*				1	.3	1
Centrarchids	Centrarchidae	3	0.5	2			
Freshwater drum	*Aplodinotus grunniens*	30	26.7	8	22	11.6	5
Perciformes		5	2.1	2			
Unid. fish	Pisces	161	31.4		28	4	
Subtotal		287	98.5	35	67	21.4	17
Total identified specimens		3,535	7,624.6	77	6,759	11,348	54
Indeterminate specimens		214	30.4		573	54	
Grand total		3,749	7,655.0		7,332	11,402	

Key to abbreviations: NISP, number of identified specimens; MNI, minimum number of individuals; unid., unidentified.

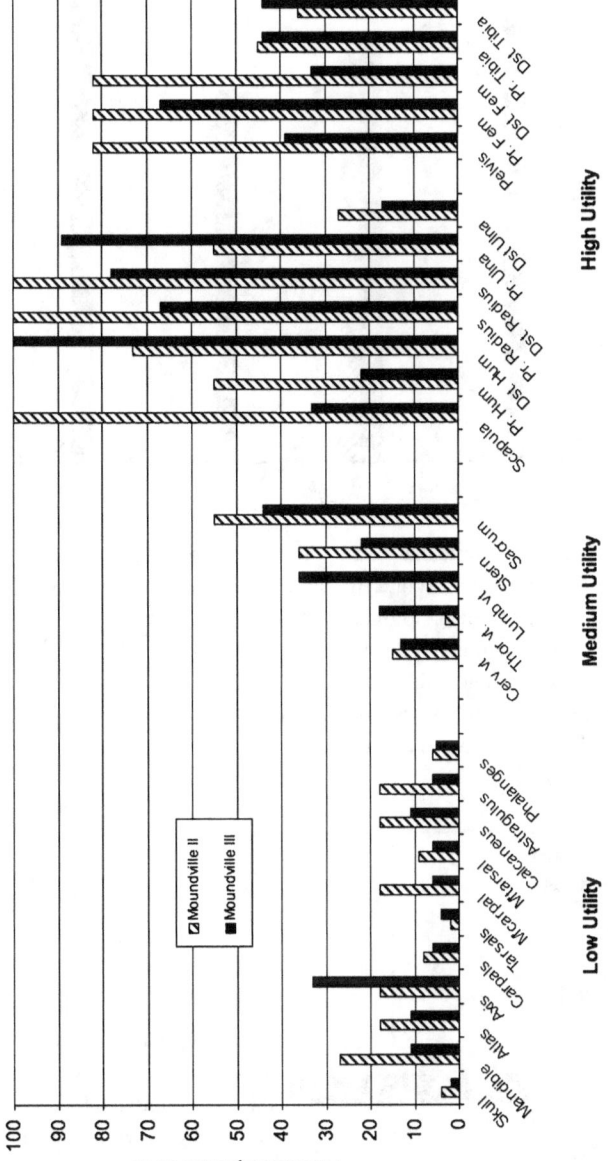

Figure 10.10. Abundance of anatomical units for deer from Moundville II and III assemblages in Mound Q at Moundville. Abundance is calculated as the percent of expected minimum number of elements (MNE) for a modern deer.

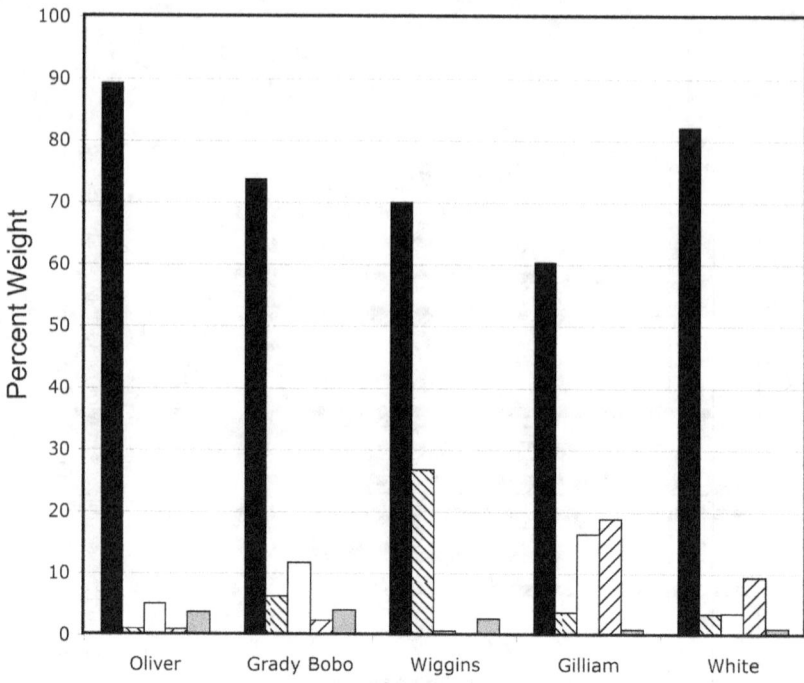

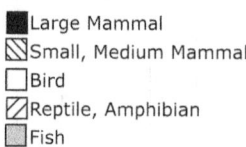

Figure 10.11. Abundance of major faunal taxa at Oliver, Grady Bobo, Wiggins, Gilliam, and White. The sites are ordered chronologically from left to right, showing a gradual decrease in large mammals during the time of Moundville's prominence, followed by an increase after Moundville's decline. Abundance is calculated as a percentage (by weight) of the faunal assemblage.

■ Large Mammal
◩ Small, Medium Mammal
☐ Bird
▨ Reptile, Amphibian
▨ Fish

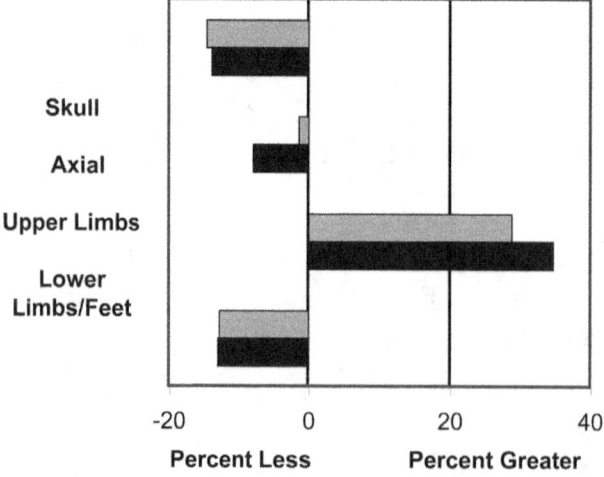

Figure 10.12. Abundance of anatomical units for large mammals from Moundville II and Moundville III contexts in Mound Q at Moundville. Abundance is calculated as a percentage difference (by weight) relative to a modern deer.

Altogether, the faunal evidence suggests that throughout Moundville's history venison was provisioned from the hinterlands. Nonetheless, over time there are indications of changes in hunting and butchering patterns, including an increased frequency in field butchering as a consequence of changed residential patterns and a more extensive use of carcasses (wider range of cuts consumed and a higher degree of bone processing) by mound residents. These differences are subtle rather than drastic and subject to the vagaries of sampling. If real, however, then the slightly increased contribution of large mammal to the Moundville III assemblage is an expectable outcome of increased transport costs due to longer-range hunting. Speth and Scott (1989), in examining the tethering effect of agricultural production and more sedentary settlements, have argued that over time the distances traveled for hunting will increase as a consequence of reduced local game. As distance increases, they predict, procurement activities will focus on the larger packages of meat provided by larger game (in this case deer) as a means of increasing the efficiencies of transporting meat back to the settlement. The dispersal of the Moundville polity population away from the capital would effectively have increased transportation costs, particularly if every rural settlement was also supplying itself with game.

Even if venison was brought to Moundville from outlying communities, the same need not have been true of small game. We know that, regardless of source, small mammals were brought to Mound Q as complete carcasses. Such animals could have been either provisioned or hunted locally, in which case long-distance transport would not have been a factor. We have no way archaeologically to gauge the relative contributions of small game from these alternative sources. However, if our expectation regarding the strategies of distant hunters is correct, it would imply that most, if not all, of the small game included in the mound samples was procured nearby. Whether the elites themselves, as opposed to their kin or followers, hunted these animals is difficult to say.

The only faunal assemblage dating to late Moundville times other than those from Moundville's mounds comes from residential deposits at the White site (Welch 1991). As noted earlier, this single-mound center rose to local prominence as the sway of Moundville was diminishing. Unfortunately, the zooarchaeological data are reported in a coarse fashion, only as weights for broad taxonomic categories (large mammal, small mammal, bird, turtle, other reptiles, amphibians, and fish). In addition, weights by

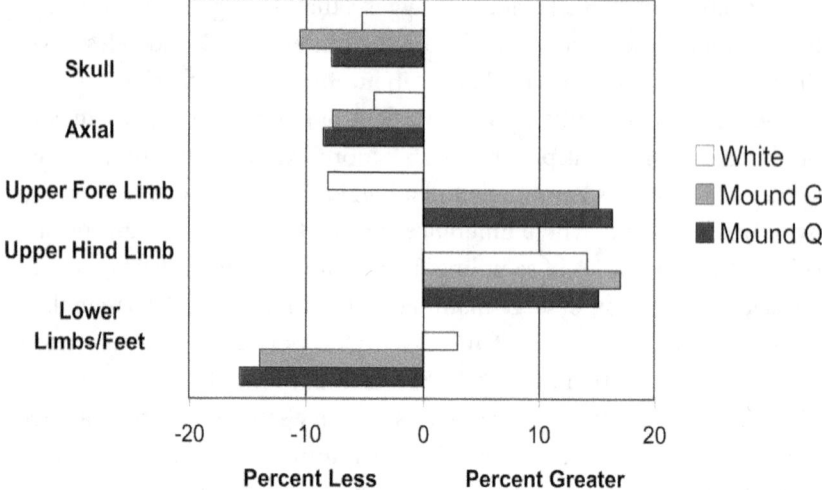

Figure 10.13. Abundance of anatomical units for deer from White and Mounds G and Q at Moundville. Abundance is calculated as a percentage difference (by weight) relative to a modern deer.

anatomical portion are reported for the large-mammal component of the assemblage. A comparison of large-mammal element representation at White to the assemblages from Mounds Q and G offers a hint of the effects of procurement reorganization near the end of Moundville's reign. The proportionate representation of large mammals in the White assemblage approaches that from Moundville's Mounds Q and G. In contrast to Q and G, where high-utility meat cuts are more often represented by elements of the forelimbs, the White assemblage is somewhat impoverished in regard to forelimbs but has greater than expectable hind limb representation (figure 10.13).

Moundville's Changing Landscape

Our discussion of provisioning assumes that when Moundville's population was at its highest, there were extensive fields on the terrace and bottomlands around Moundville. As we noted earlier, the plant data do not speak directly to the sizes of fields or, for that matter, the absolute quantities of maize grown. The faunal samples from Mound Q are sufficiently large, however, to offer hints about changes in the landscape. Small mammals are particularly useful for judging land clearance or forest regrowth, since they are not likely to have been targets of longer-distance forays. In previous analyses of Mississippian assemblages (Scott 1983), we have used ratios of gray squirrels to fox squirrels, and swamp rabbits to cottontails, to assess the impact of clearing land for agriculture on the structure of animal populations. Gray squirrels and swamp rabbits are more characteristic of woodland habitats, while cottontails and fox squirrels prefer open or edge settings. Assuming that capturing small mammals was opportunistic or a function of latent technology, that is, traps or snares, the small animals represented in an assemblage should reflect general abundances of local species at any point in time. In the Mound Q assemblage, the ratio of fox squirrel to gray squirrel declines from 0.85 in Moundville II to 0.09 in Moundville III. Similarly, swamp rabbits increase slightly in the Moundville III samples. The shift could represent a decrease in the amount of cultivated land surrounding Moundville. As the majority of people moved back to the hinterlands, the amount of cultivated land needed to support the mound-residing elite would not have been as extensive as previously needed to support the larger community. These faunal indicators of forest regrowth are consistent with botanical data suggesting a decrease in provisioning of shelled maize. The extent of local fields required to provide for the needs of the remaining resident elite would be much smaller than that needed to feed Moundville's earlier bustling population.

Meals of Mound Residents

Despite some shifts revealed in temporally sequent deposits, it is abundantly clear that consumption and other uses of animals by the elite who resided atop Moundville's mounds were distinctive, yielding faunal assemblages that are different from more mundane contexts. Knight's (2010) excavations in mound summit and flank deposits produced debris from elite meals from Mounds E, F, G, Q, and R, with the largest faunal assemblages coming from Mounds G and Q and dating to late Moundville II and Moundville III (Jackson and Scott 2003, 2010). The bones represent refuse from mainly private elite meals, punctuated by ritual meals that involved special animals and perhaps the use of specific animal products in other, presumably ritual, ways. Taken together, the Mound G and Q samples differ from what might be expected from faunal refuse generated by commoner families. When compared to each other, the Mound G and Q samples exhibit nuanced differences that suggest something about the variability in animal use among different social groups constituting the elite stratum of society. These differences seem to correspond with variability in other aspects of the material record of mound-summit residents (Knight 2004, 2010, this volume).

Ample amounts of venison are represented in the Mound G and Q faunal samples, although there are indications of differences in how the venison was obtained. Provisioning is apparent in element distribution, though for both samples some deer were delivered as whole carcasses rather than as prebutchered units. Differences between the mound assemblages include a somewhat broader representation in cuts of meat on Mound Q and less evidence that bones were processed for marrow by the residents of Mound G. The samples also set themselves apart from other contemporary samples in the variety and character of animals represented. This variety is particularly evident in the mammals and birds. From Mound Q, mammalian species that occur along with the expectable rabbits, squirrels, beavers, and raccoons are bobcat, cougar, bear, gray fox, and mink. Notably these are all carnivores, and bobcat, bear, and cougar might reasonably fall into the category of dangerous animals (Jackson and Scott 1995). Mink, a relatively rare small carnivore, might represent a diminutive example of this same theme. Before dismissing this suggestion out of hand, it is worth noting that recent mound excavations by Jackson at another Mississippian center, Winterville Mounds in the Mississippi Delta, produced a mink skull. The skull was cut vertically just behind the second premolar, but leaving the palate intact to serve as a tab for insertion. The bones from the various carnivores could be byproducts of ritual consumption, or they could be debris from the use of carnivore skins to produce craft items, an apparent proclivity of the Mound Q elites (Knight 2004, 2010). Production of ritual or elite paraphernalia from skins or feathers has been given less attention than that of the more obvious durable goods such as shell gorgets and copper plates, but we would expect parts of costumes, sacred bundles, or other necessary ritual goods for display or exchange to have been made from plant and animal products. Birds also were used as sources of restricted foods, raw material, and symbolic referents to cosmology and power. Relatively unusual birds from Mound Q include passenger pigeon and hawks (table 10.9). Passenger pigeon became more available to Indians in the South after about AD 1000 as the range of this species expanded. There is evidence from sites across the South that pigeons are more likely to be present or to occur in

Table 10.9. Unusual Animals from Mounds G and Q at Moundville

Common Name	Taxon	Mound Q NISP (n)	Mound Q NISP (%)	Mound G NISP (n)	Mound G NISP (%)
Mink	*Mustela vison*	9	0.09	—	—
Skunk	*Mephitis mephitis*	1	0.01	1	0.03
Bobcat	*Lynx rufus*	1	0.01	—	—
Cougar	*Felis concolor*	1	0.01	—	—
Black bear	*Ursus americanus*	2	0.02	2	0.06
Gray fox	*Urocyon cinereoargenteus*	—	—	1	0.03
Domestic dog	*Canis familiaris*	2	0.02	2	0.06
Dog	Canidae	1	0.01	2	0.06
Cow/bison (cf/bison?)	*Bos/Bison* sp.	—	—	3	0.10
White ibis	*Eudocimis alba*	1	0.01	—	—
Canada goose	*Branta canadensis*	2	0.02	6	0.19
Wood duck	*Aix sponsa*	2	0.02	—	—
Redhead	*Aythya americana*	1	0.01	—	—
Greater scaup	*Aythya marilla*	1	0.01	—	—
Sandhill crane	*Grus canadensis*	—	—	1	0.03
Red-tailed hawk	*Buteo jamaicensis*	4	0.04	—	—
Red-tailed hawk	*Buteo* cf. *jamaicensis*	—	—	1	0.03
Hawk	*Buteo* sp.	1	0.01	—	—
Peregrine falcon	*Falco peregrinus*	—	—	2	0.06
Crow	*Corvus brachyrhynchos*	3	0.03	—	—
Passenger pigeon	*Ectopistes migratorius*	12	0.12	1	0.03
Shark	Carcharhinidae	—	—	1	0.03

Note: Quarter-inch samples (Jackson and Scott 2010: table 8.2). NISP refers to the number of identified specimens.

greater numbers in elite or ritual deposits than in other contexts (Jackson 2005).

The much smaller sample from Mound G has an even greater representation of unusual animals, including striped skunk, bear, gray fox, bison, passenger pigeon, sandhill crane, red-tailed hawk, peregrine falcon, and shark. This list requires some consideration of why we classify these animals as "unusual." Some were present on the local landscape but in low densities; some were present only seasonally or infrequently; and others were clearly not local at all. The local species would have been much less likely to be encountered by hunters than animals such as deer or turkey, so their presence implies a significance beyond a use as simple, everyday foods. And animals that were not local would have had social or symbolic value as commodities from a distant place (*sensu* Helms 1993). Indeed, the Mound G assemblage is conspicuous in the variety of bird taxa represented. Concentrations of bird bones, and particularly raptor bones, occur elsewhere in the Mississippian world in the context of intense ritual such as Mound 34 at Cahokia (Kelly 2010). To recapitulate, we believe that the range and variety of unusual animals present in the two mound assemblages were consumed or otherwise used in rituals that were conducted by and served to reinforce the status of mound-residing elites. The similarities between the Mounds G and Q assemblages—including their high diversity, ample venison, and a suite of taxa not normally encountered in Mississippian food refuse—should not mask the subtle but significant contrasts that point to varied access to prestige networks, possible differences in activities by which they participated in such networks, as well as to the association of the Mound G and Q residents with distinctive ritual realms.

While faunal assemblages from elite contexts include a diverse set of carnivores and birds that we interpret to have special ritual significance or to in some way mark the social position of their consumers, the botanical assemblages from North of Mound R and atop the mounds suggest that only a few specific plants were reserved for elite dining or ritual use. Allowing for differences in sample sizes, the plant assemblages from across the site and in the hinterlands seem to contain a similar range of everyday foods (tables 10.5 and 10.7). The notable exception is that wild rice occurs only in the elite deposits from North of Mound R, where it is present in 45 samples, and in one sample from Mound G. While most people associate wild rice with the upper Midwest, the plant also grows in brackish and freshwater marshes throughout the South (Chase 1971). Its edible seeds, however, are rare in archaeological deposits; in addition to Moundville, small quantities of wild rice have been identified from Archaic and Cherokee deposits in Tennessee (Chapman and Shea 1981), from the early Late Woodland Graveline Mound in Mississippi (Peles and Scarry 201), and from a mound at the Mississippian Bottle Creek site in the Mobile Delta (Scarry 2003b). We suspect that consumption of wild rice in the South was restricted to ritual or elite meals.

The plant assemblages from the mounds at Moundville differ from nonmound assemblages, including the elite deposits North of Mound R, in several other ways. Maize accounts for a greater proportion of all plant food remains and the ratio of kernels to cupules is lower than in deposits from nonmound residential deposits (see above). The predominance of maize in summit and flank deposits may indicate that mound-top meals emphasized this food over other plant staples. The low ratios of kernels to cupules suggest either that maize was served and consumed on the cob or that it was shelled when meals were prepared atop the mounds. Perhaps the emphasis on maize and the special handling it received signified the importance of "mother corn" in ritual meals. While this suggestion may be a stretch, we are on firmer ground suggesting mound-top rituals involved smoking tobacco and imbibing Black Drink. Despite diligent flotation, the only tobacco seed thus far identified from Moundville-era sites in the Black Warrior Valley comes from Mound Q. Indirect evidence for the use of Black Drink also comes from Mound Q, which produced an unfired clay humanoid figurine with impressions of yaupon leaves, the primary constituent used in brewing the Black Drink.

Ritual Integration in Outlying Communities

Mound summits at Moundville were not the only locations where members of Moundville society participated in rituals. As Maxham (2000, 2004) cogently argued, rural ritual life served to promote kin and social cohesion both within and among communities. We have evidence for ritual meals or feasts at Hog Pen, a hinterland mound center, and several rural hamlets that lack mounds (Grady Bobo, Wiggins, and Gilliam).

A rich midden on the flank of the Hog Pen mound provided evidence about plant foods consumed at a late Moundville I single-mound center. As on the mounds at Moundville, the assemblage contains a varied assortment of plant foods, but maize does not seem to dominate the assemblage to the same degree. Acorn and perhaps other foods were also featured. Moreover, relatively high ratios of kernels to cupules suggest that some maize served on the Hog Pen mound was shelled (and perhaps cooked) elsewhere (see figure 10.4). It makes us wonder whether ritual meals at hinterland centers were more communal potluck than largesse from the elite. Either way, maize seems to have been consumed differently on Hog Pen mound than on contemporary mounds at Moundville (see above).

Ritual meals were not confined to mound-tops, nor were they always staged by the elite. Good evidence of rural ritual that is reflected in animal remains was recovered from the Grady Bobo site (Maxham 2000, 2004; Scarry et al., this volume). Here we note that a large shallow pit at Grady Bobo produced another unusual faunal assemblage. A sample of just over 7,000 specimens was analyzed. Mammals in the sample are what we would expect to find in rural deposits: deer, squirrels, rabbits, and raccoons. It is the unique variety and quantity of birds that suggest other-than-normal refuse. Along with the expectable—turkey, ducks, geese, and quail—are the unusual, including a swan, a little blue heron, a screech owl, a flicker, a cardinal, a grackle, a passenger pigeon, and 85 crow elements representing at least eight individuals. Crows were not regular components of Indian diets. To put the number of crow elements into perspective, from Toqua in Tennessee an assemblage of 76,000 specimens included just two crow elements (Bogan 1980), and from Lubbub Creek on the Tombigbee an assemblage of more than 20,000 bones included only one crow specimen associated with a ritual structure below the site's mound (Scott 1983). Besides the unusual assemblage of birds, utilized fish dorsal spines suggest production of some sort of craft item presumably involving feathers was among the activities that produced the refuse in the pit at Grady Bobo. There is a growing appreciation that birds were a central feature of Mississippian ritual, related to world renewal, fertility, and kin-group sanctification (e.g., Kelly and Kelly 2007). Birds represented the Above World and also served as representatives of other important resources. Their use extended far beyond nutritional contributions and even ritual consumption to components of regalia and medicine bundles and even temple adornment (e.g., Power 2004: 64). The assemblage of birds from the Grady Bobo pit is as clear an example of ritual effort as a zooarchaeological sample could depict (see also Scarry et al., this volume).

While the animal assemblage at Grady Bobo speaks of a dramatic mustering of unique resources, the composition of the plant assemblage for the most part mirrors what is found at other small hinterland sites (see table 10.5). The amount of plant refuse associated with the pit is large, but so is the sample (table 10.1); standardized counts of nuts, indigenous crops, and fruits are in line with those from more mundane contexts (table 10.5). The ratio of maize kernels to cupules, however, is quite high (table 10.6).[4] The kernel-to-cupule ratio is more comparable to those from contemporary off-mound residential deposits at Moundville and mound-top deposits at Hog Pen mound than it is to those from rural hamlets (table 10.6). As on the Hog Pen mound, it appears that shelled maize was featured in the cooking activities that created the debris. Looking at the combined animal and plant assemblage at Grady Bobo, it seems that everyday plant foods fed the hungry, while symbolic aspects of the rituals were strongly marked by the animals processed for the event.

We have plants, but only scant animal data, from another isolated feature that may contain feasting debris at the Wiggins site, which dates to late Moundville I times (Scarry et al., this volume). Nothing in the plant assemblage (table 10.5) distinguishes it from refuse in household deposits at other hamlets. Animals represented in the small (NISP = 83) sample included deer and large mammal, rabbit, dog, raccoon, unidentified bird, freshwater drum, and catfish (Holm 1997). If the feature does contain debris from feasting, it reinforces our sense that rural rituals were not strongly marked by the kinds of plant foods that were consumed—although we cannot speak to the recipes that were used to prepare those foods.

A final site to mention is the Moundville II Gilliam site excavated by Jim Knight and Jennifer Myer (Myer 2003). Here a single shell-filled pit produced a small sample of 600 bones, which, like the pit at Grady Bobo, is dominated by birds—nearly a third of the identified specimens (Scarry et al., this volume). Along with turkey these included bones of at least three hawks, a passenger pigeon, and an unidentified songbird. Once again, we are struck by the ritual nature of this unfortunately isolated deposit at a rural site, but it underscores Maxham's (2000, 2004) contention that rural ceremonialism was integral to the broader ritual concerns that seem to have fueled the Moundville chiefdom. Unfortunately, we have no plant data for this pit.

Final Thoughts

The multiple dimensions—plant versus animal, urban versus rural, everyday versus special, and early versus late—of the subsistence data that have accumulated for the Moundville chiefdom are best understood in the context of the more nuanced picture of Moundville's history as a site and as the center of an evolving polity, as well as in the new ways of considering its social, economic, and ritual integration. While we are far from a comprehensive picture of Moundville-era subsistence in the Black Warrior Valley, a number of conclusions can be reached.

First, changes in the demands for subsistence resources resulted from the changed demography of the center as it shifted from a large residential community to a necropolis. Higher demands to provide for not only the elite, but also those who labored in the construction of mounds, resulted in structured provisioning efforts early in Moundville's history. Once the center was vacated by all but the nobility, some effort to provide for the elite certainly persisted, but as landscapes changed and the levels of demand diminished, agricultural production and meat procurement took on a more local scope.

Second, social factors structured the composition of faunal and botanical assemblages. Refuse in mound-related deposits reflects elite prerogatives as well as elite responsibilities played out in everyday meals and special rituals. This is best demonstrated by the distinctive foods that are not present in other contexts. But ritual was not the exclusive right of Moundville-dwelling elite, as the evidence from the countryside now indicates. Rural communities were bound together in their own ritual schedules, and these too are marked by the unusual nature of their faunal refuse.

A third and final conclusion to be drawn is that plants and animals played different roles in social and ritual symbolism. Thus, while faunal assemblages included particular animals that had ritual significance or reflected the social position of their consumers, plant remains most often varied in quantities rather than composition. Domestic and wild plant foods were essentially the same throughout the Moundville polity, varying mainly according to local circumstances, i.e., resource availability at particular times and places. The one possible exception is the restriction of wild rice, tobacco, and yaupon to elite residential and mound-top contexts at Moundville. In contrast, animals appear to have very specific uses in very particular circumstances. Plants and animals were complementary, not only in their nutritional contributions, but also in the roles they played in the everyday and not-so-everyday lives of the Moundville people.

Acknowledgments

Christopher S. Peebles provided fieldwork and analytical opportunities that set all three of us on the research trajectories we have followed for the last three decades. Scarry's dissertation project was a part of Chris's University of Michigan Moundville Archaeological Project in 1978–79

(National Science Foundation BNS 7807139 and BNS 8007130). Jackson's introduction to Mississippian archaeology was while serving as a crew chief for Chris at the Lubbub Creek Site (U.S. Army Corps of Engineers). Scott's first major zooarchaeological analysis was the fauna produced by that same excavation. We appreciate Chris's collaboration, mentorship, and friendship over the years. In addition subsequent excavation of the Northwest Riverbank area (U.S. Army Corps of Engineers), Jim Knight's mound excavations at Moundville (National Science Foundation SBR 9220568 and 9727709), Scarry and Scarry's 1999–2000 work at rural sites (National Science Foundation SBR 9818082) and a variety of CRM projects managed by the University of Alabama's Office of Archaeological Research provided important animal and plant assemblages described in this chapter. We wish to acknowledge the collegiality, lively debates, and genuine support of all Black Warrior Valley students and professionals with whom we have worked over the years.

Notes

1. State numbers for the sites used in this study are as follows: Big Sandy Farms, 1Tu552; Gilliam, 1Tu904; Grady Bobo, 1Tu66; Hog Pen, 1Tu56; Moundville, 1Tu500; Oliver, 1Tu459; White, 1Ha8; Wiggins, 1Tu768.

2. All plant data used in these analyses were recovered using flotation systems in which the heavy fractions were caught on 1.6-mm ($1/16$-in) screen, and light fractions were captured on cloth. Minimum sample size was 10 liters, but in many cases the entire contents of a feature were floated, giving volumes significantly larger than 10 liters. Standardized counts presented in tables 10.5 are calculated as the taxon count divided by the total plant weight in grams for the samples assigned to each spatial-temporal division (see Scarry 1986 for discussion of the reasons for standardizing by plant weight).

3. In the boxplots the standardized counts are taxon count divided by plant weight calculated for each sample rather than for aggregated samples.

4. Because the Grady Bobo assemblage comes from a single pit, we cannot use boxplots to compare it to other nonmound sites.

11

Crafting Moundville Palettes

JERA R. DAVIS

Palettes are some of the largest and most beautiful stone artifacts found at sites in the Moundville polity of west central Alabama and so have attracted a good deal of attention (figure 11.1). We know a lot about them as a result. They are typically thin, circular objects averaging about 25 cm in diameter, often with notched or scalloped edges and incised lines about the rim; less frequently they are rectangular in shape. A few are so elegant that they have acquired names like the Willoughby Disk and the Rattlesnake Disk (Alabama's state artifact); these bear elaborate representational engravings on the reverse face in the local Hemphill style (Steponaitis and Knight 2004; Knight and Steponaitis 2011).

We also know how they were used: organic and mineral residues smudge the reverse faces of many palettes where paints or medicines were prepared (Moore 1905: 146–47), so archaeologists have suggested that these objects featured in ritual settings in which human bodies were either painted or tattooed, the latter achieved with fish spines sometimes found in related archaeological contexts (Knight 2010: 153, 299; cf. Jackson et al., this volume), or in which sacred objects were anointed with pigments (Steponaitis et al. 2011). Steponaitis (this volume) argues that palettes were included in sacred bundles, because some show signs of having been wrapped in fabric or placed in baskets, and examples from Etowah show unequivocal evidence of being wrapped with grinding stones and lumps of mineral pigment (Steponaitis et al. 2011).

We also know that palettes were made somewhere near Moundville. Several lines of evidence support this. The vast majority have been found at Moundville despite their recovery from sites up to 300 km away (Lafferty 1994; Steponaitis, this volume), they were embellished in the local style (Steponaitis and Knight 2004; Knight and Steponaitis 2011), and archaeologists have confirmed petrographically that the distinctive gray mi-

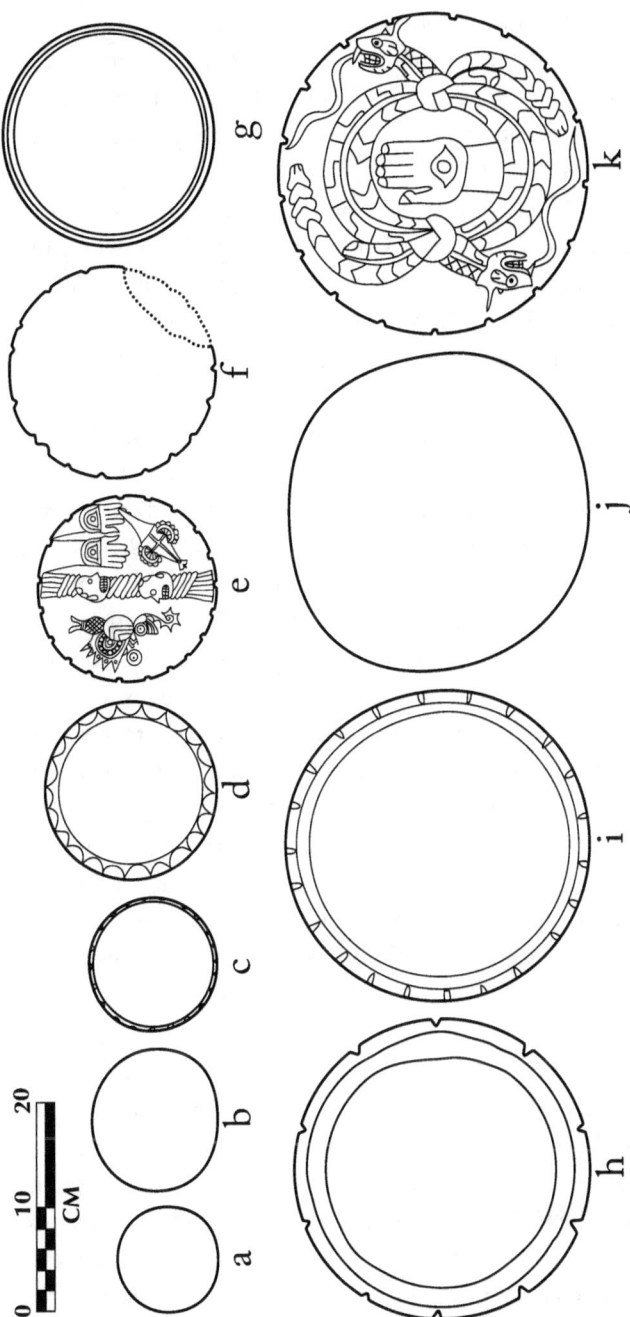

Figure 11.1. Stone palettes from the Black Warrior Valley: (*a–b, d–k*) Moundville; (*c*) Pride Place. Palettes (*e*) and (*k*) are commonly called the Willoughby Disk and the Rattlesnake Disk, respectively; the elaborate engraving shown on these two objects appears on the reverse face. (Collections: *a*, Alabama Museum of Natural History [AMNH], A939.2.73; *b*, AMNH, A936.1.100; *c*, AMNH; *d*, AMNH, A930.4.83 [SEH15]; *e*, Peabody Museum of Archaeology and Ethnology, 48122; *f*, AMNH, A930.7.26; *g*, AMNH, A930.1.68; *h*, AMNH, A930.5.23; *i*, AMNH, A936.1.101; *j*, AMNH, A930.1.121; *k*, AMNH, A941.4.549)

caceous sandstone of which they were made derives from local outcrops of the Pottsville geological formation (Whitney et al. 2002). But defining the nuances of Moundville's economy demands that we go beyond the scale of local versus nonlocal and explore specific places on the landscape for evidence of palette production. As it stands, palettes are thought to have been made exclusively at the local center under the auspices of a paramount chief (Marcoux 2007; Welch 1991), a conclusion influenced more by Moundville archaeology's historic role in political-economic discussions than by available archaeological data from sites in the Black Warrior Valley. Should off-mound and rural commoner contexts yield such evidence, we would have to reevaluate our understanding of the role of palettes in Moundville's economy.

In this study, experimental sandstone crafting and mass analysis of sandstone debitage provide evidence of palette production that has thus far gone unrecognized in Moundville literature. Important similarities are noted between the experimental assemblage and that of the Pride Place site, an outlying hamlet. Based on these similarities, I argue that palettes and other sandstone items were made at Pride Place. This conclusion has important implications for the organization of palette production and use in the Moundville polity. Noting distinctions in the degrees to which palettes were highly crafted, and recognizing that, in general, palettes are found in contexts that map onto their supposed worth, I propose that palettes were perceived in terms of a gradation of value that reflects the different ranks of the Moundville cult or sodality that used them in rituals. Low-level members were not uncommon and could have lived in Moundville's hinterland, but those who had risen to the uppermost ranks conducted rituals involving palettes on mound tops at the local center.

Pride Place

The Pride Place site (1Tu1) has received some scrutiny as a place where palettes might have been made (Davis 2008; Jacobi 1999; Sherard 1999). It is a Moundville III phase (AD 1400–1550) hamlet located about 23 km north of the Moundville site, situated atop a natural rise on a first terrace overlooking the falls of the Black Warrior River (Johnson 2001). The Mississippian component consists of a palimpsest of two domestic structures, numerous associated pits, a broad sheet midden, a tiny, special-purpose flexed-pole construction, and no fewer than nine burials (figure 11.2). The

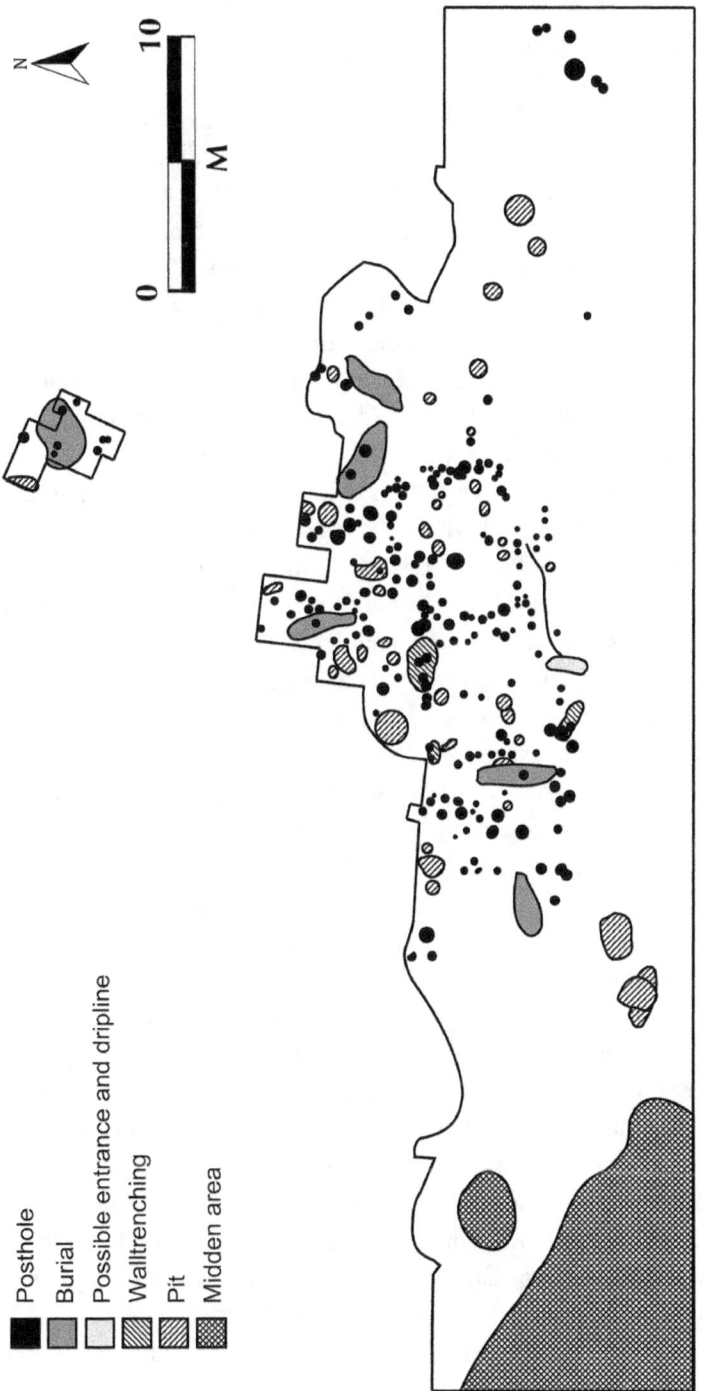

Figure 11.2. Map of excavations at Pride Place.

domestic structures likely represent a single household that built and then rebuilt its dwelling. If so, the Mississippian occupation of Pride Place was short-lived, perhaps under 25 years.

Importantly, the Pottsville formation outcrops only 200 m east of Pride Place across a drainage cut by Marr's Spring Creek. Sandstone from this source was used in numerous and sometimes unusual ways by the site's Mississippian occupants. For example, substantial slabs of it were crammed into postholes associated with the special-purpose structure. It also featured prominently in Pride Place mortuary ritual. One woman was placed in a sandstone-lined pit in the "stone box" fashion more typical of contemporaneous northern Alabama and Tennessee populations. The grave of a man over 50 years old, an individual Mississippians would have respected as an elder, was marked with a sandstone "headstone," a memorial of sorts. Another grave is that of a young man lying prone with a small jar at his feet and his head resting as if pillowed on a notched sandstone palette (Jacobi 1999). This last item may highlight a crafting component, evidenced by ample sandstone debris in various states, mostly in the form of thousands of unground, angular fragments.

In fact, few archaeologists would challenge the assertion that Pottsville sandstone was put to use in crafting activities at Pride Place. The problem is determining exactly what was crafted at this small outlying site. A glance at the inventory of whole and fragmentary sandstone craft items recovered in excavations there suggests a number of candidates: pendants, celts, palettes, and small disks (henceforth called diskettes). It is possible that all of these items were crafted at Pride Place, but the focus here is on palettes, because of their ritual importance and role in Moundville's political economy.

Abundant sandstone debris, a fragment of a scalloped palette, a couple of sawed pieces, ground and polished pieces of fine gray sandstone, and lapidary tools such as grinding slabs and hand-held abraders attest to the possibility that palettes were made at Pride Place (table 11.1). This modest assemblage contrasts with that recovered from Mound E at Moundville, where palettes are also thought to have been made. Ferruginous sandstone saws found in that context were apparently first employed to groove and snap palettes into shape and then to apply rim embellishments such as notches, scallops, and incised concentric lines (Knight 2010: 222–23). If palettes were made at Pride Place, their crafting did not involve the use of saws in this way, for relatively few saws have been found there.

Table 11.1. Ground-Stone Debris, Tools, and Craft Items from Pride Place and Moundville

Category	Pride Place	Moundville[a]	
		Mound E	Mound Q
Sawed and/or snapped sandstone	2	2	—
Hammerstone	15	4	4
Grinding slab[b]	1	1	2
Abrader[c]	9	18[d]	9[e]
Saw	5	48	21
Palette	2[f]	12	17[g]
Stone diskette	30	6	9

[a]Counts from Mounds E and Q after Knight (2010).
[b]Blocks of stone described as large and with at least one flattened surface.
[c]Including grooved abraders and smaller chunks of stone described as "mullers" or as having one or more faces heavily ground.
[d]Including 16 grooved abraders, one whetstone, and one muller.
[e]Including six grooved abraders, one whetstone, and two mullers.
[f]Including one whole and one fragment.
[g]Representing 12 different palettes.

Review of the debitage suggests an alternate method.[1] Instead of snapping palettes into shape along sawed grooves, crafters may have used hammerstones to reduce the tabular raw material chip by chip into approximate shapes. This could explain the amount of raw debris. The rough edges of the resulting preform would then have been smoothed with handheld abraders and large sandstone grinding slabs to produce an undecorated palette blank.[2] Saws were almost certainly involved in the final step, the application of rim decorations, but this was not likely a very intensive part of the process. And yet, if palettes were made in this way, the primary evidence, abundant raw debitage, must be rather ambiguous. For instance, the sheer quantity of diskettes, if crafted on site, could account for much of it. A principal goal of this study, therefore, is to define signatures of palette production not previously recognized, so that the activities involved in creating assemblages like that at Pride Place can be better parsed.

An Experimentally Based Evaluation

Here I adopt an experimental approach to generate new insights into the Pride Place sandstone assemblage. Experimental archaeology has been called an inescapable element of interpretation (Reynolds 1999). Advocates are quick to distinguish it from practicing traditional skills for their own sake or "experiencing" the past by way of historical reenactment. Though the latter activities may be personally beneficial, they do not advance knowledge. Experiments, on the other hand, are held to scientific standards. They are hypothesis-driven and must therefore be replicable, replicated, and statistically assessable. Good experiment does not admit the variables of human motivation: time, effort, emotion. These are meaningless in the context of experiment because they are notions defined differently in different cultural settings. My experiment abided by these standards. It falls under the "simulation experiment" category as described by Reynolds (1999: 160); that is, it seeks to provide "a paradigm which can be compared with actual data and, if correlation is found, can elucidate the physical processes involved in creating the data."

The only types of material involved in my experiments were those available to the Mississippian residents of Pride Place. With the exception of tabular ferruginous sandstone, which is ubiquitous in west central Alabama, all experimental materials (fine gray sandstone, quartz cobbles for hammerstones, and sandstone for grinding slabs) were collected from Marr's Spring Creek. This locale was the logical choice for two reasons. First, fine gray sandstone collected from the creek is petrographically similar to that which was used to make Moundville palettes (Whitney et al. 2002). Second, the outer surfaces of many of the fine gray sandstone artifacts recovered from Pride Place appear waterworn, evidence that prehistoric crafters gathered from nearby shallows. Thus, to the extent that it was possible, I ensured that my raw material had been subjected to the same chemical and mechanical conditions as that used by Pride Place crafters.

Two items were replicated: a notched palette like the burial item found at Pride Place, and a sandstone diskette approximately 3 cm in diameter (see Knight 2010: 61–64 for a description of objects of the latter type, which he calls "small disks"). I replicated each multiple times to capture a range of debitage variance. I could have crafted a palette as well as multiple diskettes from each more-or-less tabular piece of raw material but chose not to do so, in order to keep the debitage associated with each separate for later analysis.

Both types of experiments followed at least the first two steps outlined above: initial hammerstone shaping and then grinding on a sandstone slab to smooth rough edges and surfaces. Not surprisingly, palette crafting was a bit more involved. A quartz microdrill drawn out on a string from a central point provided draft lines that aided in creating a circular form. Once shape had been satisfactorily established, palettes were notched with a ferruginous sandstone saw. The tools and debris, including that which resulted from rejuvenating worn tools, were bagged separately by stage and held for morphological comparison to Pride Place artifacts. I purposely did not record exactly how long it took to accomplish each step, because I do not feel that this is a very useful variable to consider when examining the crafting of ritual objects. Moreover, I hardly consider my skill on a par with that of ancient crafters who had been exposed to stone working their entire lives. That being said, in the following section I do provide some coarse time estimates to convey the relative ease with which simple palettes are made.

All debitage resulting from initial reduction was sifted en masse through a series of four nested screens with effective, circular openings of 5.1, 2.5, 1.3, and 0.6 cm (2, 1, 0.5, and 0.25 in, respectively). The same was done for Pride Place fine gray sandstone debitage from Mississippian domestic features (sheet midden, pits, and postholes containing shell-tempered pottery) excavated in 1998 by the University of Alabama's Office of Archaeological Research. Counts and weights in each resulting category were tallied. The assemblages are compared below. Although this so-called aggregate or mass analysis was pioneered by Newcomer (1971) and Ahler (1972, 1989) to analyze debitage assemblages of cryptocrystalline stone (e.g., cherts and flints that fracture more predictably than fine gray sandstone), I believe it can be applied to any study that seeks to identify quantitatively whether an assemblage evidences the production of small or large items, for it is generally accepted that the size of debitage is directly related to the size of the objective piece (Andrefsky 2001). I felt that this was an appropriate method because palettes and diskettes are essentially disks of different sizes.

In the following section, the process of making palettes and diskettes is described in hindsight of my multiple attempts at both. Data generated experimentally are then compared to those recovered from the Pride

Place site. Qualitative and quantitative similarities and differences between the two datasets are specified and discussed.

Results

The method gleaned from the Pride Place lithic assemblage was simple and effective. Every attempt ended in success, though the quality of the finished products did improve as I became experienced with the material. In total, I made three palettes and eight diskettes. These experiments not only granted numerous new insights into the artifacts recovered from Pride Place but also highlighted some previously undocumented lines of sandstone knapping and grinding evidence. Here I review the crafting process in more detail and discuss the types of materials that are diagnostic of each stage. These are organized in table 11.2 and discussed below so as to provide a baseline for any future study of sandstone and palette crafting.

Each palette began as a somewhat tabular piece of fine gray sandstone that was reduced with a quartzite hammerstone to an approximate circle in less than half an hour (figure 11.3). Hammerstones involved in this process showed minimal signs of wear even after extensive use. Rough diskette preforms were crafted by a two-step process: initial reduction of a large piece of raw material to produce usable flakes, followed by reduction of the flakes deemed to be of suitable size (figure 11.4). In every case, exploiting the material's planar fracture pattern in thinning and shaping reduced the amount of grinding required in the subsequent stage of manufacture. As a word of caution, this planar fracture pattern has the potential to confuse analysts inexperienced with fine gray sandstone, who might misidentify its naturally flat surfaces as ground ones.

In two main ways, debitage created in the first stage holds great interpretive potential. First, hammerstone reduction of fine gray sandstone produces a distinctive type of trapezoidal debitage marked by a crude sort of bulb of percussion that fans out from an impact dimple (figure 11.5a, b). Because fine gray sandstone is not as homogeneous and predictable as, say, chert, this distinctive debitage is not produced each time hammerstone meets material. Still, a preponderance of trapezoidal debitage was noted in all of the experimental assemblages and in the archaeological assemblage, a strong sign that hammerstones featured heavily in sandstone

Table 11.2. Archaeological Correlates of Sandstone and Palette Crafting

Quality of Evidence	Sandstone Crafting		Palette Crafting	
	Direct	Indirect	Direct	Indirect
Strong	Abundant sandstone debitage		Unground palette preforms and production failures[a]	
	Trapezoidal debitage with impact dimples		Sawed and sawed and snapped sandstone	
	Ground blade-like debitage[a]	Ferruginous sandstone saws	Numerous large unworked flakes of sandstone	Large unworked sandstone tablets
Moderate	Ground sandstone	Grinding slabs and handheld abraders	Undecorated or partially decorated palettes[a]	
		Polished ferruginous sandstone flakes[a]		
		Hammerstones	Circular incisions (draft lines)[a]	Grinding slabs with flat, expansive grinding zones
Weak			Palette fragments	

[a]Not noted in Pride Place assemblage.

crafting at Pride Place. Moreover, several heavily used hammerstones have been recovered in excavations at Pride Place.

Second, size-grade data obtained through aggregate analysis of initial reduction debris can parse crafting activities to a certain extent. Here it supports the conclusion that large sandstone items, presumably palettes, were made at Pride Place (table 11.3). All three efforts at palette crafting produced numerous flakes of every size grade, including, importantly, the largest one. Not one of the eight diskette craft experiments yielded

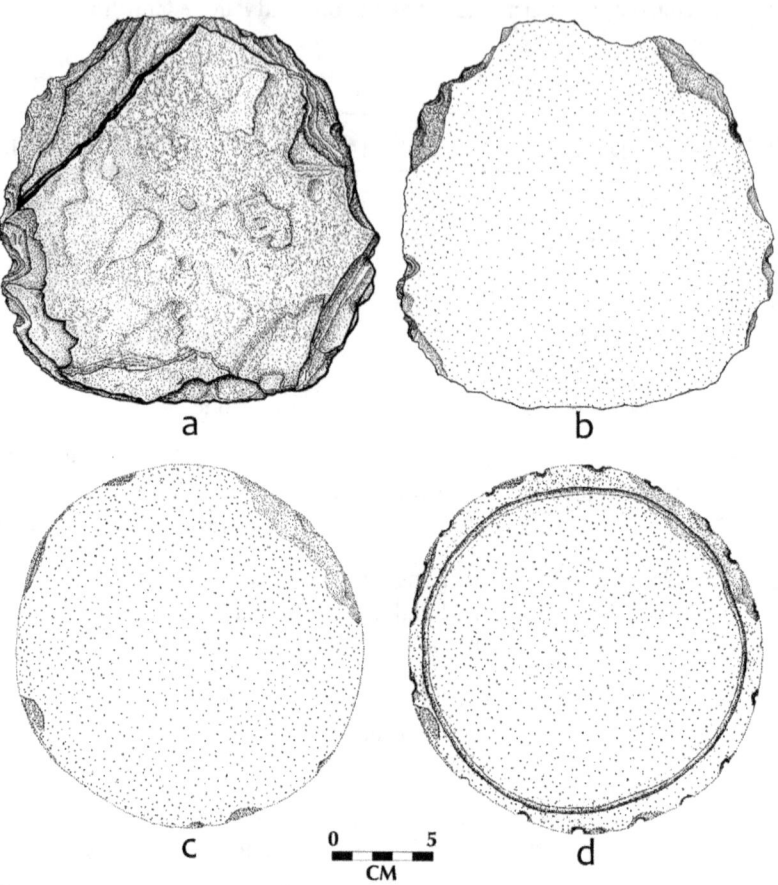

Figure 11.3. Stages of experimental palette production: (*a*) preform; (*b*) preform with ground faces; (*c*) undecorated palette; (*d*) notched and incised palette. (Illustration by Shawn P. Lambert)

flakes in the largest grade, and two of those efforts did not produce flakes in the second-largest grade. At the top of the size-grade scale, sandstone debitage recovered from Pride Place compares favorably with that created in the palette experiments. However, in all size-grade categories except the largest, Pride Place yielded greater percentages than did the palette experiments. I believe this indicates that smaller items, particularly diskettes, were crafted alongside palettes at Pride Place. This would have affected final percentages in two ways: by increasing the amount of smaller debitage and decreasing the amount of larger debitage as appropriately sized scraps were converted into useful items.

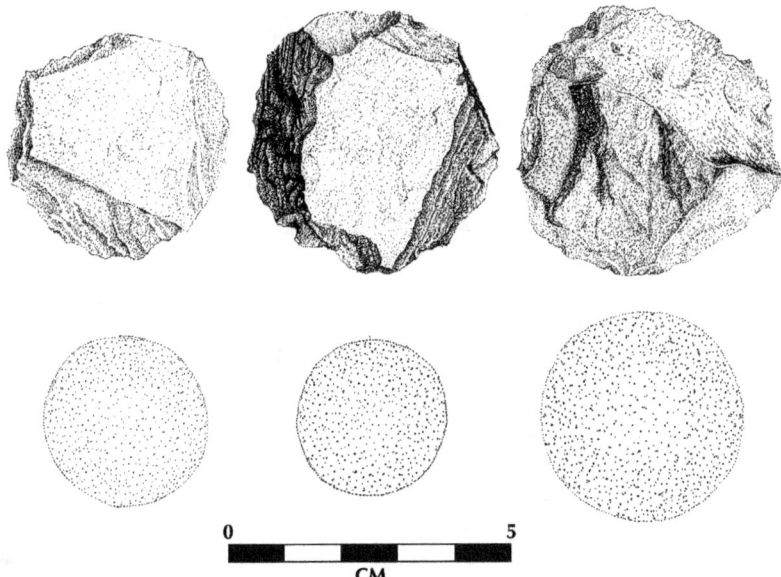

Figure 11.4. A sample of the experimentally produced diskette preforms (*top*) and finished diskettes (*bottom*). (Drawing by Shawn P. Lambert)

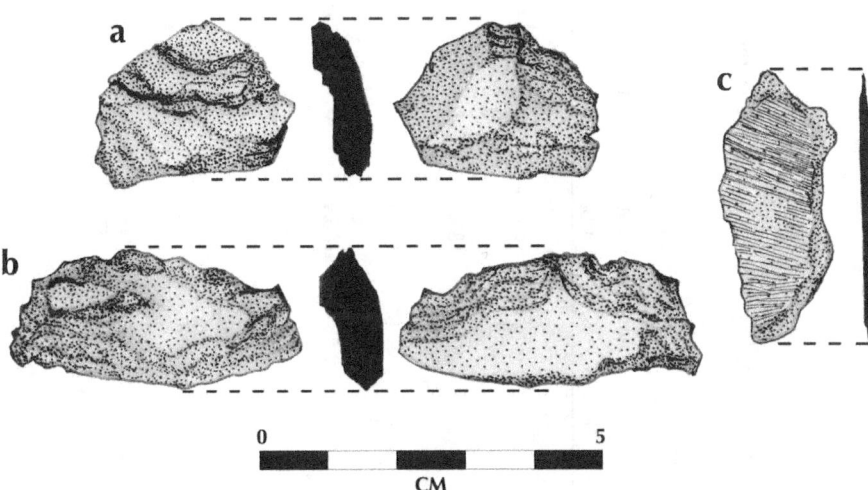

Figure 11.5. Replicated debitage: (*a–b*) representative pieces of trapezoidal debitage, showing both faces and cross section; (*c*) an example of the ground bladelike fragments that sometimes result from grinding palette faces, face and cross section. Note the impact dimples and associated steplike lumps of material on the trapezoidal debitage.

Table 11.3. Size-Grade Data of Experimental and Archaeological Sandstone Debitage Assemblages

	>2 in			1–2 in			0.5–1 in			0.25–0.5 in		
	Count (n)	Weight (g)	Mean Weight (g)	Count (n)	Weight (g)	Mean Weight (g)	Count (n)	Weight (g)	Mean Weight (g)	Count (n)	Weight (g)	Mean Weight (g)
Palettes:												
Attempt 1	7	1,389.7	198.53	13	214.9	16.53	57	131.2	2.3	156	51.9	0.33
Attempt 2	5	925.6	185.12	33	565.4	17.33	91	260.2	2.86	245	93.5	0.38
Attempt 3	4	572.5	143.13	14	371.9	26.56	51	154.3	3.03	127	47.3	0.37
Total	16	2,887.8	180.49	60	1,151.2	19.19	199	545.7	2.74	528	192.7	0.37
Diskettes:												
Attendant refuse[a]	—	—	—	5	169.3	33.86	8	39	4.88	12	3.5	0.29
Attempt 1	—	—	—	1	17	17	8	23.8	2.98	27	12.4	0.46
Attempt 2	—	—	—	1	10.3	10.3	5	12.3	2.46	12	3.6	0.3
Attempt 3	—	—	—	2	64.6	32.3	4	6	1.5	19	6.6	0.35

Attempt 4	—	—	—	—	—	—	9	28.8	3.2	26	11.2	0.43
Attempt 5	—	—	—	2	31.7	15.85	3	10.9	3.63	8	1.8	0.23
Attempt 6	—	—	—	1	18.1	18.1	5	27.7	5.54	9	3.2	0.36
Attempt 7	—	—	—	—	—	—	8	30.4	3.8	8	2.3	0.29
Attempt 8	—	—	—	1	16.8	16.8	4	11.3	2.83	23	12.7	0.55
Total	—	—	—	13	327.8	25.22	54	190.2	3.52	144	57.3	0.4
Pride Place sample	15	2,427	161.8	54	631.2	11.69	166	382.8	2.31	586	255.8	0.44

[a] Refuse resulting from producing flakes for diskette blanks.

Very little archaeologically recoverable debris was produced in the subsequent steps. The grinding can be subdivided into two parts: abrading faces to thin and polish, followed by abrading rough edges into shape. Both parts resulted in a profusion of stone dust. In most cases, abrading a palette face produced a few very thin blade-like fragments ground on one side (figure 11.5c). Striations running across the width of these fragments indicate that each was removed in the same way. These are flakes loosened in the percussion stage that remained attached until tugged repeatedly through abrasion with the grain of the stone. Because they are very fragile objects that would not likely survive anything but the mildest of postdepositional stresses, it is not surprising that none were noted in the archaeological sample.

A slab upon which palettes have been ground looks different from one used to grind diskettes and other small objects. Grinding broad palette faces tends to effect expansive flat zones on slabs, whereas grinding the faces of smaller objects such as diskettes more often results in depressions (Adams 2002). Of course, this is not to say that all slabs with flat grinding surfaces were used in palette production. Other activities or even different grinding techniques could account for the development of either wear pattern. It bears mentioning, however, that a substantial, flat-surfaced grinding slab was recovered from Pride Place.

Decorating palettes resulted in practically no archaeologically recoverable debris. In each case I used two parallel edges of a piece of tabular ferruginous sandstone to incise 20 notches around the border of the palette blanks. As a result, the working edges of the saws were rapidly polished and had to be knapped after almost every notch to restore their abrasiveness. As a very crude guide, applying 20 simple notches exhausts approximately one saw. Scalloping or incising multiple concentric lines would likely exhaust many more. Note that 21 saws were recovered from Moundville's Mound Q and 48 from Mound E, contexts where palettes are thought to have been decorated in this way (Knight 2004, 2010: 149). Five saws have been found at Pride Place.

Although previous researchers, myself included, have focused on the ground-stone debris from Pride Place (Davis 2008; Sherard 1999), I now believe that quantitative and qualitative aspects of sandstone shatter best denote palette production there. The sample of Pride Place sandstone artifacts analyzed for this study accounts for only 7.1 percent of the total weight of fine-gray-sandstone debitage recovered in the 1998 excavations

(3,697 of 51,950 g). It matches that produced experimentally in some significant ways. Much of it exhibits the telltale signs of percussion, trapezoidal debitage with impact dimples. Size-range data point to the production of both large and small sandstone items. These large items are presumed to be palettes, because they were the only common class of large objects made of fine gray sandstone in the Moundville polity, and because other artifacts at Pride Place are associated with palette production. Evidence that these important ritual objects were crafted at a modest site on the very edge of the polity demands a rethinking of the social and ritual dimensions of Moundville's economy.

Discussion

At the outset of the experiments described here, I possessed little stoneworking skill and a rudimentary knowledge of the material I had determined to work. I conclude, therefore, that making a basic Moundville palette requires no more than the right stone, patience, and an eye for symmetry. The raw material is locally available, especially in the vicinity of the Pride Place site, and most people innately possess the other two necessities. In other words, if palette production or ownership was in some way restricted to certain individuals, culture—not skill or the availability of raw materials—was the chief determining factor.

Two ways in which palettes could have been restricted to only some members of society have been suggested. First, it has been proposed that fine gray micaceous sandstone was controlled by aggrandizing elites. Much of it had been found in "elite" contexts, and palettes often featured as grave goods in elaborate Moundville burials (Peebles and Kus 1977). However, insights gained by coupling ethnohistoric references, examinations of use wear and wrapping impressions on the artifacts themselves, and reference to the archaeological contexts from which they have been recovered have effected a shift in our understanding of these objects. Steponaitis (this volume), an early supporter of palettes as possible elite goods (Steponaitis 1992), argues that palettes were instead inalienable possessions included with other objects in sacred bundles not unlike those described ethnohistorically (also see Steponaitis et al. 2011). He goes on to speculate that people who used palettes had attained the knowledge necessary to serve as bundle keepers. Moundville, then, where the bulk of palettes have been discovered, is argued as a nexus of ritual knowledge that once transmitted from senior practitioner to apprentice mandated the creation of a new bundle. In other words, palettes may be seen as a sort of sumptuary item—first earned, then made.

A paint-smeared sandstone palette found in the grave of a young man at Pride Place may thus attest to his status as a bundle keeper. Evidence that he performed the palette ritual on site is in the form of numerous artifacts associated with the so-called pigment complex (Knight 2004, 2010: 67–69): pigment-quality rock, pigment-yielding rock, and diskettes bearing pigment residues.[3] Membership in the cult or sodality that used palettes was apparently not limited to elites residing at the Moundville site but was open to individuals living even at the outskirts of the polity. Archaeologists may therefore expect to find evidence of palette production and use at other sites in Moundville's hinterlands.

However, it cannot be assumed that those who used palettes also made them. In considering another Pride Place burial, that of a man over 50 years old whose grave was unusually memorialized with a "headstone," one is reminded of ethnohistoric accounts that tell of old men and "beloved superannuated women" (Adair 1775: 161), nonpractitioners who nonetheless possessed the right to make sacred objects. Mooney (1900: 237) learned many Cherokee stories from such a person, an octogenarian named Itagû'nahi, but better known as John Ax: "Although not a professional priest or doctor, he was recognized, before age had dulled his faculties, as an authority upon all relating to tribal custom, and was an expert in the making of rattles, wands, and other ceremonial paraphernalia." Among the Cheyenne, such accomplished craftspeople worked closely with councils of principal men and medicine makers that periodically commissioned pipes from them for spiritually gifted individuals (Grinnell 1962: 136). Finished pieces were critiqued by council members who knew how pipes should be made, and they often suggested changes in form or adornment. Once their concerns had all been addressed, these items were bestowed upon initiates in ceremonies organized specifically for that purpose, rather public affairs performed in front of ritual specialists and laypeople alike. In such open settings, skill, not social rank, is typically the primary criterion for the production of sacred objects (Spielmann 1998).

In more hierarchical societies where control over the materialization of ideology underwrites certain claims to power (DeMarrais et al. 1996; Earle 1997), religious orders might have sought to limit participation by crafting ritual objects themselves (Brandt 1980; Spielmann 1998). The variously composed sacred bundles that they manipulated were bound up, both figuratively and literally, in clan, cult, and society charter, fundamental to the continued well-being of their associated groups. Much was asked of aspiring ritual practitioners and of those initiates who aimed to augment their position, but the acquisition of esoteric knowledge was a powerful incentive. Oftentimes, these individuals sought membership and promotion in larger orders, such as the widespread Midé Society described by Lankford (this volume), who supplies some tantalizing clues that such a sodality of shamans may have existed even at prehistoric Moundville. The Midé Society, says Lankford, was composed of four or eight ranks. Members accrued power and knowledge with advancement, but this demanded so great an outlay of wealth for required feasts and other ceremonies that most members never rose above the first or second degree.

Current archaeological data from Moundville period sites cannot conclusively address exactly who made palettes—artisan-priests, skilled laypeople, or some other category of individuals—but if "the evaluation of objects can serve as metaphors for the evaluation of people" (Lesure 1999: 28), then I believe that finished palettes do say something about the status of the people who owned them (see Phillips, this volume). Palettes vary in formality (see figure 11.1). Many, like the example from Pride Place, are quite simple, decorated with notches and/or concentric incisions. Meanwhile, the Rattlesnake Disk, the Willoughby Disk, and other palettes bordered in embellished scallops or engraved with representational art evidence a higher degree of workmanship executed entirely in the latter stages of production. These simple and elaborate "types" bracket a range of formality. It may be that these differences map on to levels of achievement or competency within the organization that used palettes, such that further advancement permitted use of more elaborate items. From this perspective, the rarity of highly crafted palettes reflects the restricted number of practitioners who had risen to the uppermost echelons. At the same time, access to initiate-level knowledge may not have been too far out of reach of the bulk of the population.

A new bundle might have been made not only when an individual was initiated into this order, but also when he or she achieved a new rank within it, their older palette intentionally broken as a way of deactivating its power. On the other hand, the used palette may not have been discarded, but rather thinned, polished, engraved with esoteric designs, or otherwise enhanced. Thus, some of the finer known examples of Moundville palettes might have begun as aesthetically plain items. If so, they were not the only southeastern objects to have undergone such a process. Historically described shell bead necklaces, for example, took on increasingly inalienable qualities as they were detailed by successive owners (Swanton 1931b). If palette production was in fact organized in this way, one would expect to find evidence of early-stage manufacture in relatively mundane contexts, and evidence of late-stage detailing in more restricted or sacred contexts. With this in mind, consider that Pride Place yielded abundant evidence of heavy hammerstone reduction and extensive grinding and only ephemeral signs that finer work ever took place. Contrastingly, Moundville's Mounds Q and E yielded a good number of precision lapidary tools, but no rough sandstone debris (Knight 2010: 148–49).

Objects have complex social lives by virtue of the human relationships that they maintain (Appadurai 1986). Because ritual crosscuts so many aspects of society, objects crafted for it were especially rich repositories of human experience. Palette production may be seen as a multilayered process that unfolded tangibly on the artifacts themselves and intangibly in the minds of the people who used and beheld them. Though individual palettes surely acquired histories of their own, both mundane and mythical, fundamental to how they were perceived, newly made pieces had not yet been circulated, used, or curated enough to accrue individual histories. In other words, it was in the production stage that their meanings were most uniform. That being said, the spiritual qualities of palettes may have derived in part from their crafters, who were likely associated with a supernatural or magical aspect of their own (Helms 1993: 53), a source of symbolic capital drawn upon in status-seeking efforts. Future research on Moundville-related sites will provide greater detail on these individuals, their social connections, and their craft.

Conclusions

This study examined the sandstone assemblage of a nonmound hinterland site, Pride Place (1Tu1), in light of insights gained through multiple palette- and diskette-crafting experiments. All debitage from these experiments was size graded, as was a sample of sandstone debitage recovered from secure Mississippian contexts at Pride Place. The resulting data were compared, and it was concluded that large sandstone items, presumably palettes, were made alongside smaller items there. This study also provided a practical model that I hope will aid archaeologists in recognizing the signs of palette production, so that as more archaeological data are recovered from contexts up and down the Black Warrior Valley, our vision of how the production and use of these important items were organized will sharpen.

I offered two possibilities regarding the organization of palette production. First, palettes might have been commissioned by ritual practitioners from skilled crafters in an arrangement consistent with that of many other middle-range societies where esoteric knowledge does not play as crucial a role in status competition as it does in more complex societies (Spielmann 1998). Conversely, ritual practitioners might have made their own palettes to intensify the aura surrounding such sacred mysteries and, in turn, reinforce their social distinction. In either case, palette crafting would likely have served as a solid basis for social mobility.

Lastly, recognizing that palettes were symbolically entangled objects graded in value, and remembering that such objects may serve as metaphors for people (Lesure 1999; Thomas 1991), I suggested above that low-level members of the cult or sodality that used palettes were not uncommon, but perhaps those who had risen to the uppermost ranks conducted palette-related rituals on mound tops at the local center. As practitioners rose in rank, they assumed increasingly elaborate ritual gear, including finer palettes. The palettes, like their owners, may have been upgraded rather than made anew, a craft process carried out in increasingly sacred locations—from lowly hamlets in Moundville's hinterlands to mound tops at the local center.

Acknowledgments

This research is dedicated to Christopher Peebles, whose life and work continue to inspire a younger generation of southeastern archaeologists. I gratefully acknowledge the comments and criticisms of John Blitz, V. James Knight, Jon Marcoux, F. Kent Reilly III, Marvin Smith, Vincas Steponaitis, and an anonymous reviewer, which greatly improved this research. I am thankful also for the support of my partner, Elizabeth, who still does not think I am crazy even after I spent several days chipping and grinding rocks. Artifacts from the Pride Place site (1Tu1) are housed at the David L. DeJarnette Archaeological Research Center, Mound State Monument, Moundville, Alabama, and the experimental assemblages are in possession of the author. Of course, any sins of commission or omission also reside with me.

Notes

1. Nearly all Moundville palettes were made of fine gray micaceous sandstone. Rare specimens of other materials were probably made by methods different than those outlined here. The Willoughby Disk, for example, was made of a fine siltstone of a sort that may outcrop around modern Lake Tuscaloosa. This material lends itself poorly to hammerstone reduction and would likely have had to have been grooved and snapped in a manner suggested by Knight (2010: 221).

2. The method outlined here has been proposed by Knight (2010) for the production of small sandstone diskettes. It has also been postulated for the production of engraved slate plaques by Neolithic Iberians (Lillios 2008). Yet it has not been suggested for Moundville palette production until now.

3. These diskettes might have been intentionally painted or used pestle-like to grind paints on a palette. Diskettes exhibiting possible pigment residue have also been found in mound contexts in association with palettes at the Moundville site (Knight 2010).

12

Moundville as a Ceremonial Ground

C. MARGARET SCARRY AND VINCAS P. STEPONAITIS

When talking about sites and settlement patterns, archaeologists often use terms such as "community," "village," "farmstead," "capital," "ceremonial center," "settlement hierarchy," and so on. These generic categories work for many purposes, but we seldom examine how such units relate to ethnographic structures in specific cultural contexts. Our failure to look beyond conventional archaeological meanings may lead us to overlook social arrangements that shaped the settlement patterns we seek to understand. Moundville, which dominated the Black Warrior Valley of west central Alabama from ca. AD 1100 to 1500, is a case in point.

The Moundville polity had a large mound-and-plaza complex, several single-mound sites, and numerous small, rural settlements. We and our colleagues have commonly used the conventional terms to describe Moundville and its hinterland communities. For example, Moundville has been called a mound-and-plaza complex (Scarry 1998: 64), a palisaded town (Knight and Steponaitis 1998: 15), a ceremonial center (Knight 2010: 60; Peebles and Kus 1977: 435), a political and ceremonial center (Wilson 2008: 1), a paramount center (Welch 1991: 33; Welch and Scarry 1995: 399), and a regional center (Steponaitis 1983a: 168). These terms have their uses, but they tell us little about how Moundville society was organized. Here we take a different perspective. We look at Moundville from the standpoint of social units that come from the ethnography and ethnohistory of native peoples of the American South. Specifically we ask, "Was Moundville a town?" Not whether it was a town in the generic, archaeological sense, but rather in the local, ethnographic sense. In thinking about this question, we have come to realize that the conventional meanings of some terms we have used to describe Moundville do not fit comfortably with ethnographic data. Examining these meanings more closely provides new insights about Moundville that root it more firmly in history and ethnography.

Although southern Indian societies spoke different languages and differed in their degree of political centralization, they were organized in broadly similar ways (Brightman and Wallace 2004; Galloway and Kidwell 2004; Hudson 1976: 184–257; Swanton 1946: 629–41, 654–61; Walker 2004). Notably, they shared two complementary structural elements with distinct social roles, namely towns and clans. The "town"—a social unit that was called *talwa* in Creek (Knight 1994: 375; Swanton 1946: 92) and *okla* in Choctaw (Galloway and Kidwell 2004: 500)—was the basic building block of Indian polities. It was generally seen, by Indians and Europeans alike, as a named corporate entity, marked by a defined area of settlement. At first glance, the answer to our question may seem obvious. Of course, Moundville was a town; what else could it have been? But when we look more closely, we find that the answer is not at all obvious.

To make our case, we address four issues. First, what were the characteristics of southern Indian towns and clans? To answer this question, we draw on descriptions from colonial-era tribes to discuss common structural elements. Where possible, we focus on records for Muskogean groups such as the Creek, Choctaw, and Chickasaw. Not coincidentally, these were the tribes that in colonial times surrounded the area where the Moundville polity was located. Second, does the archaeological evidence from the Black Warrior Valley suggest that Moundville exhibits the characteristics of a town? To anticipate our answer, we believe that Moundville was something fundamentally different. Third, if Moundville was not a town, then what was it? We argue that Moundville was not a town in the social sense, but rather bore more resemblance to ceremonial grounds where clan identities took precedence over town affiliations. Fourth, what are the implications of our view of Moundville not only for understanding Moundville but for the Mississippian world in general? We apply our ethnographic understandings of towns and clans to a consideration of how the people in the Black Warrior Valley reworked these basic structures to organize their communities and write their social arrangements on the landscape.

Indian Community Structures in the American South

Southern Indian towns were more than places where people lived; they were social and political entities with which people identified (Brightman and Wallace 2004; Galloway and Kidwell 2004; Hudson 1976: 184–257; Swanton 1946: 629–41; Walker 2004). They ranged in population from a few dozen to several hundred people (Urban and Jackson 2004: 703). Whatever their size, most towns had a central precinct with square grounds, ball fields, and public buildings—council houses, earthlodges, or temples—sometimes on mounds, sometimes not (Brightman and Wallace 2004: 478; Urban and Jackson 2004: 703; Walker 2004: 377–78). Households from matrilocal extended families comprising mothers, daughters, and their families tended to live near one another, but otherwise there was no set pattern to household location (Galloway and Kidwell 2004: 504; Urban and Jackson 2004: 704; Walker 2004: 378). Towns were led by town chiefs and war chiefs who varied in influence and were generally advised by councils of elders (Brightman and Wallace 2004: 486; Swanton 1931b: 90–91, 1946: 629–41). Although their power varied over time and space, such chiefs oversaw their towns' governance and diplomatic relations with other towns.

People saw themselves as members of named towns that persisted over many generations (Brightman and Wallace 2004: 479; May 2004: 410; Walker 2004: 383). We emphasize that towns were social units not intrinsically tied to specific locations. Town affiliations were part of social identities in much the way that church membership is today. At any given time, towns had a presence on the landscape in the form of houses, gardens, and public buildings. But when circumstances warranted, towns could and did move while retaining their names and identities. The essence of a town was not its physical location, but rather the ties among people who considered themselves a community.

But what did a town look like? To answer this question, we draw on ethnohistoric descriptions. Some sixteenth-century towns, like those in the Central Mississippi Valley described in the De Soto narratives, were nucleated and fortified (Clayton et al. 1993: 1: 117, 2: 391). Other sixteenth-century towns (for example, among the Apalachee) and many eighteenth-century towns had households that were widely dispersed around central precincts (Clayton et al. 1993: 1: 71, 2: 197; Ewen and Hann 1998: 140; Foster 2007; Galloway and Kidwell 2004: 499; Swanton 1931b: 76, 1946:

629–41; Walker 2004: 383). Whether dispersed or nucleated, towns were spatially discrete units that often clustered with other such units to form polities. These polities were separated from each other by large buffer zones, a pattern well illustrated by the work of Hally and his colleagues in northern Georgia (Hally 1993; Hally, ed. 1994). It can also be seen in the distribution of Mississippian societies across the South, where clusters of sites are separated by apparently empty territory (see, for example, Scarry 1999: figures 5.1, 5.4, 5.5), as well as in the accounts of the De Soto entrada, which traveled through significant unpopulated areas between polities (Clayton et al. 1993). Sometimes, one town within a polity was the first among equals, a capital. But even when this capital was a paramount center—as in the case of Little Egypt or the King site in the Coosa polity (Hally 1994, 2008; Hudson et al. 1985) or Anhaica in Apalachee (Ewen and Hann 1998: 140)—it was still a town. It may have had a few more, or larger, public buildings or mounds, but the town itself was not fundamentally different from its neighbors in size or layout.

Of course, towns were not the only source of communal ties and social identities. By birth, people were members of exogamous, matrilineal clans, which formed networks connecting members of towns within a tribe or polity to one another (Knight 1990: 5–6; Swanton 1946: 654–65; Urban and Jackson 2004: 697). Clan membership was filiative; an individual belonged to his or her mother's clan, and there was no assumption that all clan members shared a common ancestress. Although local matriline segments often formed residential or landholding units—sometimes called corporate subclans or house groups (see Knight, this volume)—the clans themselves were neither residential nor corporate.[1] Rather, clan members were spread across multiple towns, and within any given town they lived intermingled with members of other clans (Knight 1990: 5–6; Swanton 1931b: 77). Clans defined acceptable marriage partners and codified relations among members, including obligations of hospitality and support in settling disputes (Knight 1990: 5–6; Spoehr 1941; Urban and Jackson 2004: 697). Clans were said to have characteristic personalities, lifeways, and demeanors (Knight 1990: 8). More importantly, clans had distinct but reciprocal roles in rituals and ceremonies. They were led by elders and priests, who held complementary sacred knowledge and, presumably, ritual gear. Within a clan, members were not ascriptively ranked, but the clans themselves were usually divided into two groups for ritual purposes. One division was generally held to be superior to the other, and within a division the clans often formed graded ranks (Swanton 1946: 654–65).

Clans were associations of people that came together for special purposes. Unlike towns, which were daily materialized in houses and public structures, clans normally had only ephemeral, situational physical presences—usually at ceremonial occasions or when people gathered from multiple communities. Thus, for example, many towns maintained square grounds or townhouses, where, during ceremonies, people sat together by clan (Brightman and Wallace 2004: 486; Swanton 1931a, 1931b: 77; Urban and Jackson 2004: 706; Walker 2004: 378, 382). Likewise at larger ceremonial grounds, when people from multiple towns gathered, they arrayed themselves by clan and clan rank around a central space (Knight 1998: 54–55; Speck 1907). The variations on this general pattern were numerous, and the relevant groups were not always clans—as among the Yuchi, where men's sodalities played a similar role (J. B. Jackson 2004: 417, 420). Even so, the dominant theme is clear: it was principally in ceremonial and multi-town gatherings that people arranged themselves according to larger, crosscutting social units, and among southern Indians these units were usually clans or their local manifestations—the corporate subclans or "house groups."

It should be noted that this pattern is not confined to the South but also occurred quite commonly in the Great Plains. There, priests and other celebrants typically arranged themselves in ceremonial lodges by clan (e.g., Bailey 1995: 55–60), and large tribal gatherings took the form of "camp circles" in which individual households positioned themselves according to their clan or band (e.g., Dorsey 1897; Fletcher and La Flesche 1911: 140–42; Nabokov 1989: 158–63)

Moundville's Settlement and Demographic History

We turn now to archaeological evidence to consider whether Moundville was a town in the ethnographic sense, and if not, what it was. The Moundville polity developed within a 40-km stretch of the Black Warrior Valley just south of present-day Tuscaloosa, Alabama (see figure 1.2). Over the last three decades, there has been considerable work at Moundville, as well as survey and testing at outlying sites (e.g., Astin 1996; Barrier 2007; Blitz 2007; Bozeman 1982; Gage 2000; Hammerstedt 2001; Hammerstedt and Myer 2001; Knight 2010; Lacquement 2009; Maxham 2004; Myer

2002a, 2002b; Ryba 1997; Scarry 1995; Steponaitis 1998; Thompson 2011; Wilson 2008). When combined, these sources make it possible to chart settlement and demographic changes over time.

In the West Jefferson phase, AD 1000 to 1120, people lived in small (0.2–0.5 ha) villages located on the fertile bottomland soils of the valley (Welch 1990: 211). There were no mounds, but clusters of sites were separated by vacant areas (Hammerstedt 2001; Hammerstedt and Myer 2001; Hammerstedt et al., this volume; Maxham 2004; Myer 2002a, 2002b). These clusters may have been early towns. There is little evidence for occupation at Moundville itself in this period. Sometime around AD 1100, two mounds and a presumably small but unknown number of widely dispersed houses were built at Moundville (Blitz 2007, this volume; Knight and Steponaitis 1998; Scarry 1995, 1998; Steponaitis 1992). This early settlement at Moundville also looks like a town in the ethnographic sense.

Around AD 1200 Moundville underwent a rapid spate of reorganization and building, from which it emerged as a densely populated monumental center. People decommissioned the existing mounds (Blitz, this volume). They then constructed an elaborate mound-and-plaza complex and surrounded it with a bastioned palisade (Knight and Steponaitis 1998; Scarry 1995, 1998; Steponaitis 1998). To achieve their desired layout, they dismantled at least one mound and leveled the terrace by filling in ravine heads before erecting new mounds (Blitz 2007, this volume; Lacquement 2009; Knight 2010). The end result was a clearly planned community of some 30 mounds around an open plaza (Knight 2010: 2). The arrangement is bilaterally symmetrical and composed of pairs of substructural and burial mounds, which get smaller as one moves from north to south around the plaza (Knight 1998; Peebles 1971, 1983). Clusters of closely spaced residential buildings are associated with the mound pairs (Wilson 2008, this volume). This new arrangement does *not* resemble a typical native town of the American South. While much of the valley's population resided in the dense neighborhoods at Moundville, some people remained in the countryside (Hammerstedt et al., this volume; Maxham 2004; Steponaitis 1998). There they lived in clusters of farmsteads on land that had been occupied by their ancestors (Bozeman 1982; Hammerstedt et al., this volume). Sometime during this period, people built single mounds at the Jones Ferry, Poellnitz, and Hog Pen sites, all of which are located within these hinterland clusters (Bozeman 1982; Welch 1998).

About AD 1300 there was another demographic shift. Moundville itself became home to a few high elite, who we presume were ritual specialists (Knight 2004, 2010: 348–66; Steponaitis, this volume). The residential neighborhoods were vacated, however, and the bustling community was transformed to a necropolis where people from throughout the valley buried their dead (Steponaitis 1998). Most people dispersed back to hinterland communities, where population rebounded in long-occupied areas, and activities continued at outlying mound centers (Hammerstedt et al., this volume; Maxham 2004; Steponaitis 1998). It is worth noting, however, that when the population "returned" to the countryside, several new single-mound sites were built—often across the river from earlier single-mound sites that were no longer used (Bozeman 1982; Welch 1998). In all, there were seven active single-mound sites during this period (Bozeman 1982; Welch 1998).

In the fifteenth century, Moundville was gradually abandoned as a ritual center. In contrast, all seven hinterland centers continued to thrive, and an eighth was built. The single-mound centers not only persisted but also took on new functions as people ceased carrying their dead to Moundville and created new local cemeteries (Steponaitis 1998; Welch 1998).

Moundville as a Ceremonial Ground

For our argument there are two important things to note about the settlement and demographic sequence in the Black Warrior Valley. First, the hinterland hamlet clusters have remarkable stability from West Jefferson times onward. Specific household and field locations undoubtedly shifted, but people built mounds near where they had always lived, and communities endured for over 500 years. While they were unusually spatially stable, these mound-hamlet clusters look very much like the dispersed towns described in ethnohistoric sources (figure 12.1; also see figure 8.6). Second, the thirteenth-century transformation of Moundville adds a new type of settlement to the landscape of towns scattered up and down the valley. Moundville has the appearance of a ceremonial ground, albeit a permanent one, that brought together people from many towns. So, in this sense, it was not a town but an entirely different kind of community.

We suggest that the thirteenth-century reconfiguration of Moundville was conceived not as a town, but as a "tribal" ceremonial ground that brought together people from many towns. In some respects our inter-

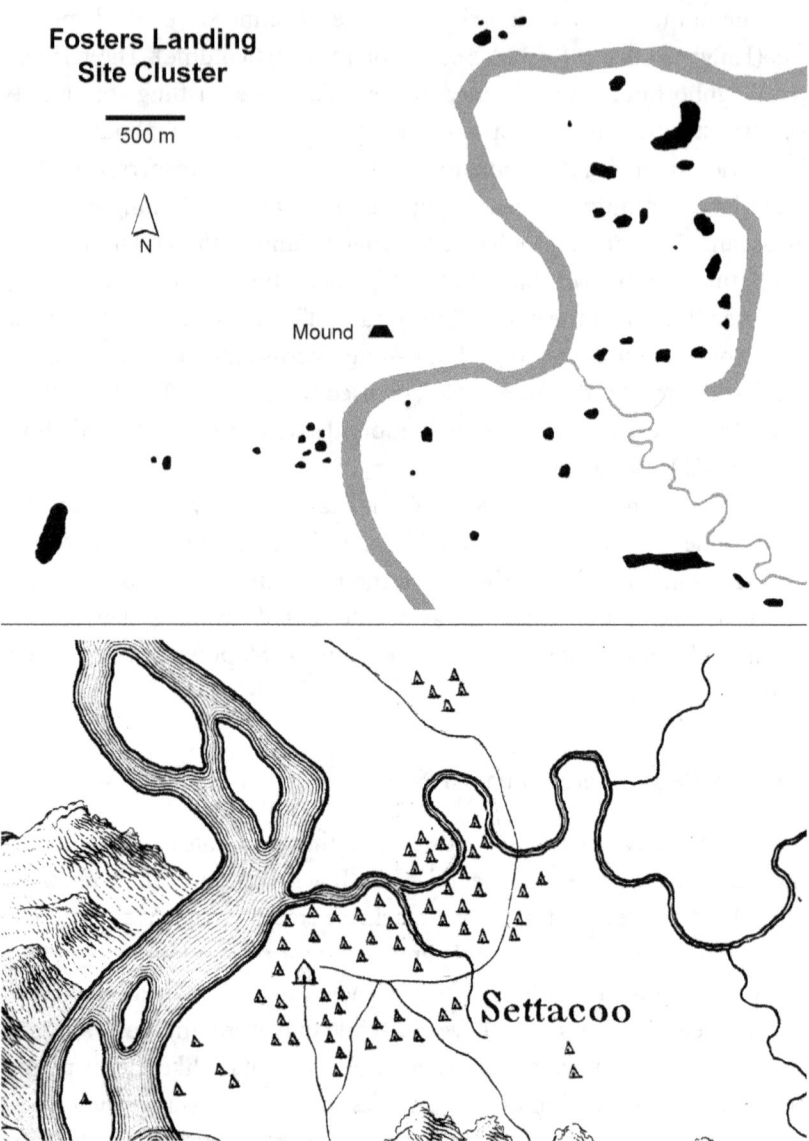

Figure 12.1. Comparison of a Mississippian site cluster in the Black Warrior Valley with an eighteenth-century Indian town: (*top*) the Fosters Landing site cluster on the Black Warrior River north of Moundville, with sites shown in black; (*bottom*) the Overhill Cherokee town of Citico on the Little Tennessee River, as mapped by Henry Timberlake in 1762. Both views are shown at approximately the same scale. The same settlement pattern, hamlets loosely dispersed around a town center, is seen in both. (The map on top is redrawn from Myer 2002a: Figure 33; on the bottom is a detail from "A draught of the Cherokee Country on the west side of the Twenty Four Mountains, commonly called Over the Hills" [Timberlake 1765: frontispiece].)

pretation is not new. More than a decade ago, Knight (1998), building on earlier observations by Peebles (1971, 1983), pointed out that Moundville was laid out much like a "camp square." Knight called attention to Speck's (1907: 53) map of a nineteenth-century Chickasaw camp square in which "subclans were arranged by rank around a rectilinear space, divided bilaterally according to the well-known dual organization and centered on a council fire" (Knight 1998: 54). Knight used this map to make an elegant analogy arguing that the mound pairs at Moundville were associated with ranked corporate groups and that the monumental construction wrote the social position and presumably power relations in "tangible, inviolable, immovable, [and] sacred" form (Knight 1998: 54).

In making this argument, Knight emphasized that Moundville was a "diagrammatic ceremonial center," a settlement in which "the layout of public architecture or monuments calls deliberate attention to key social and cosmological distinctions, in a maplike manner" (Knight 1998: 45). We fully agree with his conclusion and regard it as a key insight in our current understanding of Moundville. But here we are taking his analogy one step further: Moundville was like the Chickasaw camp square not only in its layout, but also in its basic purpose as a place where people from many towns gathered for political and religious activities. In such a setting it is not surprising that clans—which crosscut towns—were the dominant organizational theme. We argue that Moundville was fundamentally the same as a ceremonial camp square, except larger and more permanent.

Not only was Moundville built to a plan that materialized clan relationships, but also there are other clues that the difference between Moundville and other communities in the Black Warrior Valley was fundamental and qualitative. The scale of its monumental architecture—in both the size and the number of its mounds—was an order of magnitude larger than that of any town. The concentration of burials at Moundville, together with the absence of cemeteries in the countryside until after Moundville's decline, suggests that for centuries Moundville was a place of burial for *all* the towns in the Black Warrior Valley. As the chapters in this volume by Davis, Jackson et al., Hammerstedt et al., and J. Scarry et al. show, people at hinterland communities participated in rituals, engaged in feasting and crafting, and had varying access to sumptuary goods made from local and nonlocal materials. But the scale and diversity of crafting and ritual at Moundville dwarfs that seen elsewhere in the valley. Notably, pipes, palettes, pigments, and other items that we believe were ritual gear associated with priestly activities are prominent and widespread at Moundville (Knight 2004, 2010: 348–66; Phillips, this volume; Steponaitis, this volume). This is exactly what we would expect at a ceremonial ground. Finally, as Knight (2010) has demonstrated, the so-called temple or structural mounds at Moundville all show evidence of residential activities, crafting, elite meals, and ritual dining. But the buildings atop the mounds and the crafting activities that took place within these buildings varied remarkably from mound to mound. This pattern is consistent with the complementary ritual roles of clans.

In sum, Moundville was not simply a "first among equals" town, as were historic-era polity capitals. Rather, it was a ceremonial ground that incorporated and integrated people from many towns. Its monumental landscape emphasized clan organization and priestly activities—quite possibly those of clan priests and elders.

Turning outward from the Black Warrior Valley, Williams (2007) presents a similar archaeological case from the Oconee Valley of Georgia, where he argues that the Joe Bell site was used only for periodic gatherings to celebrate the busk. Nor was this pattern confined to the South. Much farther afield, we find a parallel example in DeBoer and Blitz's (1991) discussion of Chachi ceremonial centers in Ecuador, which were used periodically for public events in which people from multiple communities gathered and arranged themselves by social group. These sites differ from Moundville mainly in that they had episodic, rather than permanent, occupations.[2]

Implications and Speculations

We close with some thoughts about the implications of seeing Moundville as a ceremonial ground for understanding the region's history. Recall that colonial-era Indian communities of the American South had both secular and ritual leaders. While their specific duties varied, town chiefs and war chiefs were responsible for the smooth running of the town and for diplomacy with other towns. Clan priests and elders oversaw relations among clan members, who were spread across multiple towns. Clan priests also were responsible for the protection of sacred paraphernalia and for the perpetuation and performance of the clan's ritual responsibilities. We believe these offices have very deep roots in southern Indian communities but that the relative power of town chiefs and clan priests varied over time and space, depending on historical circumstances. In our view, the reconfiguration of Moundville represented a shift in the balance of power between secular town officials and clan ritual specialists. That is, clan priests may have succeeded in making permanent the "ceremonial ground" in which they played dominant ritual and political roles, thereby enhancing their power in relation to the town chiefs.

Here we find Gearing's (1962: 13–29) discussion of "structural poses" among the eighteenth-century Cherokee informative. Gearing (1962: 15) defined a structural pose as "the way a simple human society sees itself to be appropriately organized at a particular moment for a particular purpose." He argued that the Cherokee had multiple ways of organizing themselves, including affiliation by household, clan, village council, and war grade. Individuals held multiple roles such that their varied positions and identities came into play depending on the social arrangements appropriate for the context and activity in which they were engaged. These structural poses were situational and fluid, and they shifted power, leadership, and affiliation among individuals and groups. Gearing further claimed that, in the late eighteenth century, war chiefs gained ascendency in a specific colonial context that enabled them to "fix" the structural pose for war and created a path to permanent power within the community.

Returning to the Black Warrior Valley, we see Moundville arising from a social base that had at least two (and probably more) structural poses: towns and ceremonial gatherings. The West Jefferson and early Moundville I settlements, including the initial two-mound community at Moundville, were towns. We presume either that town chiefs dominated the political scene, or that the power of town chiefs and clan priests was more or less balanced. During the Moundville I phase, something—we leave consideration of the catalyst for a future paper—created a situation that led large numbers of people from the valley's towns to relocate to the terrace at Moundville. The unprecedented size and nucleation of population required mechanisms to integrate people, many of whom were strangers to one another. Byers (2013: 649–700) has suggested that many Mississippian mound centers, including Moundville, were heterarchical and that mounds were maintained by nonresident, religious sodalities; but Knight (this volume) has presented a compelling argument that this model does not work for Moundville. Rather, we suggest that the structural pose of a ceremonial gathering provided a model for organizing people from disparate towns into a residential community at Moundville. Perhaps inadvertently, it also created a situation that gave clan priests a path to fix and expand their power at the expense of town chiefs.

Our model fits with Knight's (2004, 2010) documentation of diverse, but presumably complementary, activities and rituals on mound summits at Moundville. It is also consistent with Wilson's interpretation that each clan-based residential unit at Moundville "included multiple subclan residential groups" (Wilson, this volume). Our view also helps make sense of the decommissioning of Mound X and the apparent deliberate acts of forgetting that preceded the layout of the mound-and-plaza complex (Blitz, this volume). The demolition of Mound X erased the social arrangements for which it stood, replacing a town's local claim to the ground on which Moundville was built with an assertion of a regional ceremonial ground where clan priests held sway. The ritual and political hold of the clans and priests lasted for several generations, but eventually conditions changed, people moved away from Moundville, and the balance of power shifted with a resurgence of town authorities.

If Moundville took form through the ascendency of clan priests over town chiefs, this requires a broader reconsideration of the settlement pattern and political organization within the Black Warrior Valley. Following a neo-evolutionary model of chiefly societies, we and others have previously interpreted Moundville as a "paramount center," which was home to a hereditary chief and other elites. The single-mound sites were depicted as subsidiary centers whose lesser chiefs, drawn from cadet lineages, answered to the paramount chief while simultaneously ruling over people within their districts (Peebles 1978; Steponaitis 1978; Welch 1991; Welch and Scarry 1995). Here, we offer an alternative scheme that fits better with the ethnography of Indian communities in the South. In our view, the single-mound centers were continuations of towns that had their roots in earlier Woodland communities. During the ascendency of the clan priests at Moundville, towns in the countryside dwindled in population, and town chiefs' political power waned but did not altogether disappear. The shifting locations of mound centers within a town's district through time may have resulted from a change in the lineage from which the town chief was drawn (Bozeman 1982; Welch 1998; cf. Hally 1996). Alternatively, the construction of new mounds at the towns may have been an early sign of the resurgence of town chiefs' authority and the weakening of the clan priests' sway. In sum, rather than the settlement pattern reflecting a hierarchy with nested levels of decision making and power, our model gives a heterarchical spin (although different from that of Byers [2013]) with dual competing but complementary forms of leadership at play in the emergence, entrenchment, and disintegration of the Moundville polity.

Our interpretation of Moundville as a ceremonial ground also has implications for the broader Mississippian world. Polities with single mounds are often interpreted as simple chiefdoms, while those with two tiers of mound centers are considered paramount chiefdoms. We suggest the situation is even more complex. There may well be two kinds of Mississippian mound centers, some based in towns, such as Little Egypt (Hally 1994) in the Coosa polity, and others constructed as multi-town ceremonial grounds, such as Moundville and perhaps Cahokia, the St. Louis Mound Group (Fowler 1989; Pauketat 1994), Winterville (Brain 1989; Moore 1908), and Town Creek (Boudreaux 2007). If so, then the ways in which polities were organized and by which leadership was deployed and legitimated may have been profoundly different.

Acknowledgments

We owe an immense debt to Chris Peebles, who catalyzed our interest in Moundville, invited us to become part of his University of Michigan Moundville Archaeological Project for our dissertation research, and set us on a path that has led to over 30 years of collaboration and friendship. Throughout our association with Moundville research, John Blitz, Jim Knight, Paul Welch, Ed Jackson, and many others have been our valued friends and colleagues. We value their open sharing of data and ideas and the lively debates we have had over the years. Kirk Perry's recollections of social gatherings in the Chickasaw communities and Brad Lieb's knowledge of Chickasaw ethnohistory were very helpful in refining the ideas presented in this chapter, as were the suggestions of Jon Marcoux, Brett Riggs, and an anonymous reviewer. Finally, we wish to acknowledge our life partners, John Scarry and Laurie Steponaitis, who have been part of our Moundville team from the outset and, over the years, have offered unbounded practical, intellectual, and emotional support.

Notes

1. Knight correctly points out that the "clans" found among southern Indians do not fit a classic definition of such units in the anthropological literature, because they are neither corporate nor based on descent from a common ancestor (Knight 1990, this volume). We accept his point but still prefer to use the term. The word "clan" in so ingrained in southern Indian ethnography, and among Indians themselves, that substituting another in this context would create confusion, more so than deviating from the textbook definition. Or, to put the matter differently, we see no harm in following local precedent, so long as the differences between the varying usages of the term are understood.

2. Chachi oral traditions hold that at least one of their ceremonial centers, Pueblo Viejo, was a permanent settlement during the early colonial period (DeBoer and Blitz 1991: 55–57). Thus, in this period it may well have been more like Moundville.

References

Adair, James
1775   *The History of the American Indians; Particularly Those Nations Adjoining the Mississippi, East and West Florida, Georgia, South and North Carolina, and Virginia*. Edward and Charles Dilley Printers, London.

Adams, Jenny L.
2002   *Ground Stone Analysis: A Technological Approach*. University of Utah Press, Salt Lake City.

Ahler, Stanley A.
1972   Mass Analysis of Flaking Debris. *Abstracts of the 30th Annual Plains Anthropological Conference*. Lincoln, Nebraska.
1989   Mass Analysis of Flaking Debris: Studying the Forest Rather than the Tree. In *Alternative Approaches to Lithic Analysis*, edited by Donald Henry and George Odell, pp. 85–118. Archeological Papers 1. American Anthropological Association, Washington, D.C.

Alcock, Susan E.
2002   *Archaeologies of the Greek Past: Landscape, Monuments, and Memories*. Cambridge University Press, Cambridge.

Alt, Susan M.
2002   Identities, Traditions, and Diversity in Cahokia's Uplands. *Midcontinental Journal of Archaeology* 27: 217–36.

Anderson, David G.
1994   *The Savannah River Chiefdoms: Political Change in the Late Prehistoric Southeast*. University of Alabama Press, Tuscaloosa.

Andrefsky, William, Jr.
2001   Emerging Directions in Debitage Analysis. In *Lithic Debitage: Context, Form, Meaning*, edited by William Andrefsky, Jr., pp. 1–14. University of Utah Press, Salt Lake City.

Angel, Michael
2002   *Preserving the Sacred: Historical Perspectives on the Ojibwa Midewiwin*. University of Manitoba Press, Winnipeg.

Appadurai, Arjun
1986   Introduction: Commodities and the Politics of Value. In *The Social Life of Things: Commodities in Cultural Perspective*, edited by Arjun Appadurai, pp. 3–63. Cambridge University Press, Cambridge.

Appadurai, Arjun (editor)
1986 *The Social Life of Things: Commodities in Cultural Perspective.* Cambridge University Press, Cambridge.

Aronson, Meredith, and W. David Kingery
1990 Patination of Ceramic Objects, Modern and Prehistoric: A Case from West Mexico. *Materials Research Society Symposium Proceedings* 185: 571–89.

Ashmore, Wendy
2002 "Decisions and Dispositions": Socializing Spatial Archaeology. *American Anthropologist* 104: 1172–83.

Astin, Robyn
1996 Mound M: Chronology and Function at Moundville. Master's thesis, Department of Anthropology, University of Alabama, Tuscaloosa.

Bailey, Garrick A.
1995 *The Osage and the Invisible World: From the Works of Francis La Flesche.* University of Oklahoma Press, Norman.

Balter, Michael
1993 New Look at Neolithic Sites Reveals Complex Societies. *Science* 262: 179–80.

Barrier, Casey R.
2007 Surplus Storage at Early Moundville: The Distribution of Oversize Jars at Mound W and Other Off-Mound Locations. Master's thesis, Department of Anthropology, University of Alabama, Tuscaloosa.
2011 Storage and Relative Surplus at the Mississippian Site of Moundville. *Journal of Anthropological Archaeology* 30(2): 206–19.

Barry, Steven Edward
2004 Lithic Raw Material and Chipped Stone Tools: A Comparison of Two Sites in the Moundville Chiefdom. Master's thesis, Department of Anthropology, University of Alabama, Tuscaloosa.

Bearak, Barry
2001 Over World Protest, Taliban Are Destroying Ancient Buddhas. *New York Times* 4 March. New York.

Beck, Robin A., Jr.
2003 Consolidation and Hierarchy: Chiefdom Variability in the Mississippian Southeast. *American Antiquity* 68: 641–61.

Beck, Robin A., Jr., Douglas J. Bolender, James A. Brown, and Timothy K. Earle
2007 Eventful Archaeology: The Place of Space in Structural Transformation. *Current Anthropology* 48(6): 833–60.

Benton-Banai, Edward
1988 *The Mishomis Book: Voice of the Ojibway.* Indian Country Communications, Hayward, Wisconsin.

Binford, Lewis R.
1971 Mortuary Practices: Their Study and Their Potential. In *Approaches to the Social Dimensions of Mortuary Practices*, edited by James A. Brown, pp. 6–29. Memoirs 25. Society for American Archaeology, Washington, D.C.

Blessing, Fred K., Jr.
1977   *The Ojibway Indians Observed: Papers of Fred K. Blessing Jr., on the Ojibway Indians*. Occasional Publications in Minnesota Anthropology 1. Minnesota Archaeological Society, St. Paul.

Blitz, John H.
1993   Big Pots for Big Shots: Feasting and Storage in a Mississippian Community. *American Antiquity* 58: 80–96.
1999   Mississippian Chiefdoms and the Fission-Fusion Process. *American Antiquity* 64: 577–92.
2007   Test Excavations at Mound X, Moundville (1Tu500), 2004. Early Moundville Archaeological Project. Report on file, Office of Archaeological Research, Moundville Archaeological Park, Alabama.
2008   *Moundville*. University of Alabama Press, Tuscaloosa.

Blitz, John H., and Patrick Livingood
2004   Sociopolitical Implications of Mississippian Mound Volume. *American Antiquity* 69: 291–301.

Blitz, John H., and Karl G. Lorenz
2006   *The Chattahoochee Chiefdoms*. University of Alabama Press, Tuscaloosa.

Bogan, Arthur E.
1980   *A Comparison of Late Prehistoric Dallas and Overhill Cherokee Subsistence Strategies in the Little Tennessee River Valley*. PhD dissertation, Department of Anthropology, University of Tennessee, Knoxville.

Boudreaux, Edmond A.
2007   *The Archaeology of Town Creek*. University of Alabama Press, Tuscaloosa.

Bourdieu, Pierre
1977   *Outline of a Theory of Practice*. Translated by Richard Nice. Cambridge University Press, Cambridge.

Bozeman, Tandy K.
1982   *Moundville Phase Communities in the Black Warrior River Valley, Alabama*. PhD dissertation, Department of Anthropology, University of California, Santa Barbara.

Bradley, Richard
1998   *The Significance of Monuments: On the Shaping of Human Experience in Neolithic and Bronze Age Europe*. Routledge, London.

Brain, Jeffrey P.
1989   *Winterville: Late Prehistoric Culture Contact in the Lower Mississippi Valley*. Archaeological Report 23. Mississippi Department of Archives and History, Jackson.

Brain, Jeffrey P., and Philip Phillips
1996   *Shell Gorgets: Styles of the Late Prehistoric and Protohistoric Southeast*. Peabody Museum Press, Cambridge, Massachusetts.

Brandt, Elizabeth A.
1980   On Secrecy and the Control of Ritual Knowledge. In *Secrecy: A Cross-Cultural*

Perspective, edited by Stanton K. Tefft, pp. 123–46. Human Sciences Press, New York.

Brannon, Peter A.
1923   The Moundville Group. *Arrow Points* 7(6): 105–8, 111, 115, 118.

Brightman, Robert A., and Pamela S. Wallace
2004   Chickasaw. In *Southeast*, edited by Raymond Fogelson, pp. 478–95. Handbook of North American Indians, Vol. 14, William C. Sturtevant, general editor, Smithsonian Institution Press, Washington, D.C.

Bronk Ramsey, Christopher
1995   Radiocarbon Calibration and Analysis of Stratigraphy: The OxCal Program. *Radiocarbon* 37(2): 425–30.
2009   Bayesian Analysis of Radiocarbon Dates. *Radiocarbon* 51(1): 337–60.

Brown, James A.
1971   The Dimensions of Status in the Burials at Spiro. In *Approaches to the Social Dimensions of Mortuary Practices*, edited by James A. Brown, pp. 92–112. Memoirs 25. Society for American Archaeology, Washington, D.C.
2001   Human Figures and the Southeastern Ancestor Shrine. In *Fleeting Identities: Perishable Material Culture in Archaeological Research*, edited by Penelope B. Drooker, pp. 76–93. Occasional Paper 28. Center for Archaeological Investigations, Southern Illinois University, Carbondale.
2007   The Social House in Southeastern Archaeology. In *The Durable House: House Society Models in Archaeology*, edited by Robin Beck, pp. 227–47. Occasional Paper 35. Center for Archaeological Investigations, Southern Illinois University, Carbondale.

Brumbaugh, Lee
1995   Quest for Survival: The Native American Ghost-Pursuit Tradition ("Orpheus") and the Origins of the Ghost Dance. In *Folklore Interpreted: Essays in Honor of Alan Dundes*, edited by Regina Benedix and Rosemary Lévy Zumwalt, pp. 182–98. Garland, New York.

Brumfiel, Elizabeth
1992   Distinguished Lecture in Archaeology: Breaking and Entering the Ecosystem: Gender, Class, and Faction Steal the Show. *American Anthropologist* 94(3): 551–67.

Bushnell, David I., Jr.
1927   *Drawings by A. DeBatz in Louisiana, 1732–1735*. Smithsonian Miscellaneous Collections 80(5). Smithsonian Institution, Washington, D.C.

Byers, A. Martin
2006   *Cahokia: A World Renewal Cult Heterarchy*. University Press of Florida, Gainesville.
2013   *From Cahokia to Larson to Moundville: Death, World Renewal, and the Sacred in the Mississippian Social World of the Late Prehistoric Eastern Woodlands*. Newfound Press, Knoxville, Tennessee.

Case, D. Troy, and Christopher Carr
2008   *The Scioto Hopewell and Their Neighbors: Bioarchaeological Documentation and Understanding.* Springer, New York.

Chapman, Jefferson
1982   *The American Indian in Tennessee: An Archaeological Perspective.* Occasional Paper 3. Frank H. McClung Museum, Knoxville, Tennessee.

Chapman, Jefferson, and Andrea Brewer Shea
1981   The Archaeobotanical Record: Early Archaic Period to Contact in the Lower Little Tennessee River Valley. *Tennessee Anthropologist* 6: 61–84.

Chase, Agnes
1971   *Manual of the Grasses of the United States.* 2nd ed. Dover, New York.

Childe, V. Gordon
1956   *Society and Knowledge.* Harper and Brothers, New York.

Clayton, Lawrence A., Vernon J. Knight, Jr., and Edward C. Moore (editors)
1993   *The De Soto Chronicles: The Expedition of Hernando de Soto to North America in 1539–1543.* 2 vols. University of Alabama Press, Tuscaloosa.

Colwell-Chanthaphonh, Chip, and T. J. Ferguson
2006   Rethinking Abandonment in Archaeological Contexts. *SAA Archaeological Record* 6(1): 37–41.

Comaroff, John L.
1978   Rules and Rulers: Political Processes in a Tswana Chiefdom. *Man* 13: 1–20.

Connerton, Paul
1989   *How Societies Remember.* Cambridge University Press, Cambridge.
2008   Seven Types of Forgetting. *Memory Studies* 1(1): 59–71.

Cottier, John W.
1970   The Alabama River Phase: A Brief Description of a Late Phase in the Prehistory of South-Central Alabama. In *Archaeological Salvage Investigations in the Miller's Ferry Lock and Dam Reservoir.* Report to the National Park Service, Report on file, Office of Archaeological Research, Moundville Archaeological Park, Alabama.

Cox, Stephen D. (editor)
1985   *Art and Artisans of Prehistoric Middle Tennessee: The Gates P. Thruston Collection of Vanderbilt University Held in Trust by the Tennessee State Museum.* Tennessee State Museum, Nashville.

Crane, H. Richard, and James B. Griffin
1963   University of Michigan Radiocarbon Dates VIII. *Radiocarbon* 5: 228–53.

Curren, Caleb
1984   *The Protohistoric Period in Central Alabama.* Alabama Tombigbee Regional Commission, Camden, Alabama.

Davis, Jeremy R.
2008   Crafting in the Countryside: A Comparison of Three Late Prehistoric Nonmound Sites in the Black Warrior River Valley. Master's thesis, Department of Anthropology, University of Alabama, Tuscaloosa.

2010 Mississippian Art as Process. Paper presented at the 67th Annual Meeting of the Southeastern Archaeological Conference, Lexington, Kentucky.

DeBoer, Warren R., and John H. Blitz
1991 Ceremonial Centers of the Chachi. *Expeditions* 33(1): 53–62.

DeJarnette, David L., and Steve B. Wimberly
1941 *The Bessemer Site: Excavation of Three Mounds and Surrounding Village Areas near Bessemer, Alabama*. Geological Survey of Alabama, Museum Paper 17, University, Alabama.

Deleary, Nicholas
1990 Midewiwin: An Aboriginal Spiritual Institution. Symbols of Continuity: A Native Studies Culture-Based Perspective. Master's thesis, Carleton University, Ottawa, Ontario.

DeMarrais, Elizabeth, Luis Jaime Castillo, and Timothy K. Earle
1996 Ideology, Materialization, and Power Strategies. *Current Anthropology* 37(1): 15–31.

Densmore, Frances
1928 *Uses of Plants by the Chippewa Indians*. Bureau of American Ethnology, Annual Report 44. Government Printing Office, Washington, D.C.
1932 *Menominee Music*. Bureau of American Ethnology, Bulletin 101. Government Printing Office, Washington, D.C.

DePratter, Chester B.
1983 *Late Prehistoric and Early Historic Chiefdoms in the Southeastern United States*. PhD dissertation, Department of Anthropology, University of Georgia, Athens.

Dewdney, Selwyn
1975 *The Sacred Scrolls of the Southern Ojibway*. University of Toronto for the Glenbow-Alberta Institute, Toronto.

Díaz-Andreu, Margarita, Sam Lucy, Staša Babić, and David N. Edwards (editors)
2005 *The Archaeology of Identity: Approaches to Gender, Age, Ethnicity, Status and Religion*. Routledge, New York.

Diehl, Richard
2004 *The Olmecs: America's First Civilization*. Thames and Hudson, London.

Dorn, Ronald I., and Theodore M. Oberlander
1981 Microbial Origin of Desert Varnish. *Science* 213: 1245–47.

Dorsey, James Owen
1897 Siouan Sociology. *Bureau of American Ethnology, Annual Report 15*, pp. 205–44. Government Printing Office, Washington, D.C.

Durkheim, Emile
1995 *The Elementary Forms of Religious Life*. Translated by Joseph Swain. Reprinted. The Free Press, New York. Originally published 1915, George Allen and Unwin, London.

Earle, Timothy
1997 *How Chiefs Come to Power: The Political Economy in Prehistory*. Stanford University Press, Palo Alto, California.

Edmonson, Munro S.
1958   *Status Terminology and the Social Structure of North American Indians*. University of Washington, Seattle.

Emerson, Thomas E.
1997   *Cahokia and the Archaeology of Power*. University of Alabama Press, Tuscaloosa.

Ensor, H. Blaine
1993   *Big Sandy Farms: A Prehistoric Agricultural Community near Moundville, Black Warrior River Floodplain, Tuscaloosa County, Alabama*. Report of Investigations 68. Division of Archaeology, Alabama Museum of Natural History, University of Alabama, Tuscaloosa.

Ewen, Charles R., and John H. Hann
1998   *Hernando de Soto among the Apalachee: The Archaeology of the First Winter Encampment*. University of Florida Press, Gainesville.

Flenley, John, and Paul G. Bahn
1992   *The Enigma of Easter Island: Island on the Edge*. Oxford University Press, New York.

Fletcher, Alice C., and Francis La Flesche
1911   *The Omaha Tribe*. Bureau of American Ethnology, Annual Report 27. Government Printing Office, Washington, D.C.

Fortes, Meyer
1953   The Structure of Unilineal Descent Groups. *American Anthropologist* 55: 17–41.

Fortune, Reo F.
1932   *Omaha Secret Societies*. Columbia University Contributions to Anthropology 14. Columbia University Press, New York.

Foster, H. Thomas II
2007   *Archaeology of the Lower Muskogee Creek Indians, 1715–1836*. University of Alabama Press, Tuscaloosa.

Fowler, Melvin L.
1989   *The Cahokia Atlas: A Historical Atlas of Cahokia Archaeology*. Studies in Illinois Archaeology 6. Illinois Historic Preservation Agency, Springfield.

Frankenstein, Susan, and Michael J. Rowlands
1978   The Internal Structure and Regional Context of Early Iron Age Society in Southwestern Germany. *University of London Institute of Archaeology Bulletin* 15: 73–112.

Fried, Morton H.
1967   *The Evolution of Political Society: An Essay in Political Anthropology*. Random House, New York.

Friedman, Jonathan
1998   *System, Structure, and Contradiction: The Evolution of "Asiatic" Social Formations*. 2nd ed. AltaMira Press, Walnut Creek, California.

Fritz, Gayle J., Virginia Drywater Whitekiller, and James W. McIntosh
2001   Ethnobotany of Ku-nu-che: Cherokee Hickory Nut Soup. *Journal of Ethnobiology* 21(2): 1–27.

Fundaburk, Emma Lila, and Mary Douglass Fundaburk Foreman
1957 Sun Circles and Human Hands: The Southeastern Indians Art and Industries. Emma Lila Fundaburk, Luverne, Alabama.

Gage, Matthew D.
2000 Ground-Penetrating Radar and Core Sampling at the Moundville Site. Master's thesis, Department of Anthropology, University of Alabama, Tuscaloosa.

Gage, Matthew D., and V. Stephen Jones
2001 Remote Sensing and Core Drilling of Five Mounds at the Moundville Site. Submitted to the Alabama Historical Commission. Report on file, Office of Archaeological Research, Moundville Archaeological Park, Alabama.

Gage, Matthew D., and Lindsay S. Stone
1999 Artifact Distribution at Pride Place (1Tu1). Paper presented at the 56th Annual Meeting of the Southeastern Archaeological Conference, Pensacola, Florida.

Gall, Daniel G., and Vincas P. Steponaitis
2001 Composition and Provenance of Greenstone Artifacts from Moundville. *Southeastern Archaeology* 20(2): 99–117.

Galloway, Patricia K. (editor)
1989 *The Southeastern Ceremonial Complex: Artifacts and Analysis.* University of Nebraska Press, Lincoln.

Galloway, Patricia K., and Clara Sue Kidwell
2004 Choctaw in the East. In *Southeast*, edited by Raymond Fogelson, pp. 499–519. Handbook of North American Indians, Vol. 14, William C. Sturtevant, general editor, Smithsonian Institution Press, Washington, D.C.

Gardner, Paul S.
1997 The Ecological Structure and Behavioral Implications of Mast Exploitation Strategies. In *Plants, People, and Landscapes*, edited by Kristen Gremillion, pp. 161–78. University of Alabama Press, Tuscaloosa.

Gearing, Frederick O.
1962 *Priests and Warriors: Social Structures for Cherokee Politics in the 18th Century.* Memoir 93. American Anthropological Association.

Giddens, Anthony
1984 *The Constitution of Society: Outline of the Theory of Structuration.* University of California Press, Berkeley.

Gillies, Judith Love
1998 A Preliminary Study of Moundville Hemphill Representational Engraved Art Style. Master's thesis, Department of Anthropology, University of Alabama.

Goldstein, Lynne
1980 *Mississippian Mortuary Practices: A Case Study of Two Cemeteries in the Lower Illinois Valley.* Scientific Papers 4. Archaeology Program, Northwestern University, Evanston, Illinois.

Goodenough, Ward H.
1965 Rethinking "Status" and "Role": Toward a General Model of the Cultural Organization of Social Relationships. In *The Relevance of Models for Social Anthro-*

pology, edited by Michael Banton, pp. 1–24. A.S.A. Monographs 1. Tavistock, London.

Gosselain, Olivier P.
1998 Social and Technical Identity in a Clay Crystal Ball. In *The Archaeology of Social Boundaries*, edited by Miriam T. Stark, pp. 78–106. Smithsonian Institution Press, Washington, D.C.
2000 Materializing Identities: An African Perspective. *Journal of Archaeological Method and Theory* 7: 187–216.

Grim, John A.
1983 *The Shaman: Patterns of Siberian and Ojibway Healing*. University of Oklahoma Press, Norman.

Grimes, Kimberly M.
1987 Mica Production as Evidence of Craft Specialization at the Mulberry Mound Site. Paper presented at the 44th Annual Meeting of the Southeastern Archaeological Conference, Charleston, South Carolina.

Grinnell, George Bird
1962 *The Cheyenne Indians: Their History and Ways of Life*, Vol. II. Cooper Square, New York.

Halbwachs, Maurice
1992 *On Collective Memory*. Translated by Lewis Coser, University of Chicago Press, Chicago. Originally published 1941 and 1952, Presses Universitaires de France, Paris.

Hall, Robert L.
2006 Exploring the Mississippian Big Bang at Cahokia. In *A Pre-Columbian World: Searching for a Unitary Vision of Ancient America*, edited by Jeffrey Quilter and Mary Miller, pp. 187–229. Dumbarton Oaks Research Library and Collection, Washington, D.C.
2007 Review of Cahokia: A World Renewal Cult Heterarchy, by A. Martin Byers. *Wisconsin Archaeologist* 88: 101–5.

Hally, David J.
1993 The Territorial Size of Mississippian Chiefdoms. In *Archaeology of Eastern North America: Papers in Honor of Stephen Williams*, edited by James Stoltman, pp. 143–68. Mississippi Department of Archives and History, Jackson.
1994 The Chiefdom of Coosa. In *The Forgotten Centuries: Indians and Europeans in the American South, 1521–1704*, edited by Charles M. Hudson and Carmen Chaves Tesser, pp. 227–53. University of Georgia Press, Athens.
1996 Platform-Mound Construction and the Instability of Mississippian Chiefdoms. In *Political Structure and Change in the Prehistoric Southeastern United States*, edited by John F. Scarry, pp. 92–127. University Press of Florida, Gainesville.
2008 *King: The Social Archaeology of a Late Mississippian Town in Northwestern Georgia*. University of Alabama Press, Tuscaloosa.

Hally, David J. (editor)
1994 *Ocmulgee Archaeology, 1936–1986*. University of Georgia Press, Athens.

Hamilton, Henry W., Jean T. Hamilton, and Eleanor F. Chapman
1974   *Spiro Mound Copper*. Memoir 11. Missouri Archaeological Society, Columbia.
Hammerstedt, Scott W.
2000   Characteristics of Late Woodland and Mississippian Settlements in the Black Warrior Valley, Alabama. Master's thesis, Department of Anthropology, University of Alabama, Tuscaloosa.
2001   Late Woodland and Mississippian Settlement of the Black Warrior Valley: A Preliminary Assessment. *Journal of Alabama Archaeology* 47: 1–45.
Hammerstedt, Scott W., and Jennifer L. Myer
2001   *Characteristics of Mississippian Settlement in the Black Warrior Valley, Alabama: Final Report of Season II of the Black Warrior Valley Survey*. Report submitted to the Alabama Historical Commission, project no. PT99-SP131. Department of Anthropology, University of Alabama, Tuscaloosa.
Hann, John H.
1988   *Apalachee: The Land between the Rivers*. Ripley P. Bullen Monographs in Anthropology and History 7. University Presses of Florida, Gainesville.
Hanson, Jeffrey R.
1980   Structure and Complexity of Medicine Bundle Systems of Selected Plains Indian Tribes. *Plains Anthropologist* 25(89): 199–216.
Harkin, Michael E. (editor)
2007   *Reassessing Revitalization Movements: Perspectives from North America and the Pacific Islands*. University of Nebraska Press, Lincoln.
Harrison, Julia D.
1982   The Midewiwin: The Retention of an Ideology. Master's thesis, Department of Anthropology, University of Calgary, Alberta.
Hatch, James W.
1976   *Status in Death: Principles of Ranking in Dallas Culture Mortuary Remains*. PhD dissertation, Department of Anthropology, Pennsylvania State University, State College.
Hathcock, Roy
1988   *Ancient Indian Pottery of the Mississippi River Valley*. 2nd ed. Walsworth, Marceline, Missouri.
Hayden, Brian W.
2001   Fabulous Feasts: A Prolegomenon to the Importance of Feasting. In *Feasts: Archaeological and Ethnographic Perspectives on Food, Politics, and Power*, edited by Michael Dietler and Brian W. Hayden, pp. 23–64. Smithsonian Institution Press, Washington, D.C.
Hegmon, Michelle
2002   Recent Issues in the Archaeology of the Mimbres Region of the North American Southwest. *Journal of Archaeological Research* 10(4): 307–57.
Helms, Mary
1993   *Craft and the Kingly Ideal: Art, Trade, and Power*. University of Texas Press, Austin.
Hickerson, Harold
1962   Notes on the Post-Contact Origin of the Midewiwin. *Ethnohistory* 9(4): 404–23.

1963 The Sociohistorical Significance of Two Chippewa Ceremonials. *American Anthropologist* 65(1): 67–85.

Hobsbawm, Eric, and Terence Ranger (editors)
1983 *The Invention of Tradition*. Cambridge University Press, Cambridge.

Hoffman, Walter James
1891 The Midē'wiwin or "Grand Medicine Society" of the Ojibway. *Bureau of American Ethnology, Annual Report 7*, pp. 143–300. Government Printing Office, Washington, D.C.
1896 *Menomini Indians*. Bureau of American Ethnology, Annual Report 14, Part 1. Government Printing Office, Washington, D.C.

Holm, Mary A.
1997 Zooarchaeological Remains from Moundville I Phase Features at 1Tu66 and 1Tu768. In *West Jefferson Community Organization in the Black Warrior Valley, Alabama*, by C. Margaret Scarry and John F. Scarry. Report prepared for the National Geographic Society in fulfillment of Grant 5278-94. Manuscript on file, Research Laboratories of Archaeology, University of North Carolina, Chapel Hill.

Holmes, William Henry
1883 Art in Shell of the Ancient Americans. *Bureau of American Ethnology, Annual Report 2*, pp. 181–305. U.S. Government Printing Office, Washington, D.C.
1906 Certain Notched or Scalloped Stone Tablets of the Mound Builders. *American Anthropologist* 8: 101–8.

Howard, James H.
1977 *The Plains-Ojibwa or Bungi: Hunters and Warriors of the Northern Prairie, with Special Reference to the Turtle Mountain Band*. J&L Reprint, Lincoln, Nebraska. Originally published 1965, Anthropological Papers, W. H. Over Museum, University of South Dakota, Vermillion.

Hudson, Charles M.
1976 *The Southeastern Indians*. University of Tennessee Press, Knoxville.

Hudson, Charles M., Marvin T. Smith, David J. Hally, Richard Polhemus, and Chester DePratter
1985 Coosa: A Chiefdom in the Sixteenth-Century Southeastern United States. *American Antiquity* 50: 723–37.

Hultkrantz, Åke
1957 *The North American Indian Orpheus Tradition: A Contribution to Comparative Religion*. Monograph Series, Publication 2. Ethnographical Museum of Sweden, Stockholm.

Jackson, H. Edwin
2003a Appendix B: Faunal Remains from the Gilliam Site (1Tu904). In *Archaeological Testing at Three Non-mound Mississippian Sites in the Black Warrior Valley, Alabama: Final Report of Season IV of the Black Warrior Valley Survey*. Report submitted to the Alabama Historical Commission, project number: PT02-SP226, by Jennifer L. Myer, pp. 37–46. Department of Anthropology, University of Alabama, Tuscaloosa.

2003b Faunal Remains from Two Mississippian Farmsteads in the Black Warrior Valley, Alabama. Paper presented at the 60th Annual Meeting of the Southeastern Archaeological Conference, Charlotte, North Carolina.
2005 Darkening the Skies: A Zooarcheological Accounting of Passenger Pigeons in the Prehistoric Southeast. In *Engaged Anthropology: Essays in Honor of Richard I. Ford*, edited by Michelle Hegmon and B. Sunday Eiselt, pp. 174–99. Anthropological Papers 94. Museum of Anthropology, University of Michigan, Ann Arbor.

Jackson, H. Edwin, and Susan L. Scott
1995 The Faunal Record of the Southeastern Elite: The Implications of Economy, Social Relations, and Ideology. *Southeastern Archaeology* 14: 103–19.
2003 Patterns of Elite Faunal Utilization at Moundville, Alabama. *American Antiquity* 68: 552–72.
2010 Zooarchaeology of the Moundville Elite. In *Mound Excavations at Moundville: Architecture, Elites, and Social Order*, by Vernon James Knight, Jr., pp. 326–47. University of Alabama Press, Tuscaloosa.

Jackson, Jason Baird
2004 Yuchi. In *Southeast*, edited by Raymond Fogelson, pp. 415–28. Handbook of North American Indians, Vol. 14, William C. Sturtevant, general editor. Smithsonian Institution Press, Washington, D.C.

Jackson, Paul D.
2004 Coexistence of the West Jefferson and Moundville I Phases. *Journal of Alabama Archaeology* 50(1): 1–17.

Jacobi, Keith
1999 Rock of Ages: Sandstone, a Mortuary Legacy. Manuscript on file, Department of Anthropology, University of Alabama, Tuscaloosa.

Jenkins, Ned J.
1978 Terminal Woodland–Mississippian Interaction in Northern Alabama: The West Jefferson Phase. In *David L. DeJarnette: A Southeastern Archaeological Conference Tribute*, edited by Drexel A. Peterson, Jr., pp. 21–27. Southeastern Archaeological Conference, Special Publication 5.
2003 The Terminal Woodland/Mississippian Transition in West and Central Alabama. *Journal of Alabama Archaeology* 49(1–2): 1–62.

Jenkins, Ned J., and Richard A. Krause
1986 *The Tombigbee Watershed in Southeastern Prehistory*. University of Alabama Press, Tuscaloosa.

Jenkins, Ned J., and Jerry J. Nielsen
1974 *Archaeological Salvage Investigations at the West Jefferson Steam Plant Site, Jefferson County, Alabama*. Report to the Alabama Power Company. Report on file, Office of Archaeological Research, Moundville Archaeological Park, Alabama.

Johnson, Hunter B.
1999 Archaeological Investigations at Pride Place (1Tu1) and Its Role in the Mound-

ville Economy. Paper presented at the 56th Annual Meeting of the Southeastern Archaeological Conference, Pensacola, Florida.

2001 Archaeological Excavation at Pride Place (1Tu1) and Its Position in the Moundville Chiefdom. Paper presented at the 66th Annual Meeting of the Society for American Archaeology, New Orleans.

Johnson, Hunter B., and Jeff L. Sherard

2000 Domestic Sandstone Artifact Production. In *Archaeology at Pride Place (1Tu1): Its Position in the Moundville Chiefdom*, edited by Hunter B. Johnson, chapter 6. Manuscript on file, Office of Archaeological Research, Moundville Archaeological Park, Alabama.

Johnson, Kenneth W.

1981 *Soil Survey of Tuscaloosa County, Alabama*. United States Department of Agriculture, Soil Conservation Service and Forest Service, Washington, D.C.

Johnson, Pamela Anne

2005 The Occupational History of Mound "W" at Moundville, Alabama. Master's thesis, Department of Anthropology, University of Alabama, Tuscaloosa.

Johnston, Basil

1976 *Ojibwa Heritage*. Columbia University Press, New York.

1982 *Ojibwa Ceremonies*. McClelland and Stewart, Toronto.

Jones, Charles C., Jr.

1873 *Antiquities of the Southern Indians, Particularly of the Georgia Tribes*. D. Appleton, New York. Reprinted 1999, with an introduction by Frank T. Schnell, Jr. University of Alabama Press, Tuscaloosa.

Jones, Walter B., and David L. DeJarnette

1936 *Moundville Culture and Burial Museum*. Alabama Museum of Natural History, Museum Paper 13. University.

Joyce, Rosemary A.

2003 Concrete Memories: Fragments of the Past in the Classic Maya Present (A.D. 500–1000). In *Archaeologies of Memory*, edited by Ruth M. Van Dyke and Susan Alcock, pp. 104–25. Blackwell, Malden, Massachusetts.

2004 Unintended Consequences? Monumentality as a Novel Experience in Formative Mesoamerica. *Journal of Archaeological Method and Theory* 11(1): 5–29.

Keesing, Felix M.

1939 *The Menominee Indians of Wisconsin, a Study of Three Centuries of Cultural Contact and Change*. Memoirs of the American Philosophical Society 10. American Philosophical Society, Philadelphia.

Kelly, John E.

2006 The Ritualization of Cahokia: The Structure and Organization of Early Cahokia Cults. In *Leadership and Polity in Mississippian Society*, edited by Brian M. Butler and Paul D. Welch, pp. 236–63. Occasional Paper 33. Center for Archaeological Investigations, Southern Illinois University, Carbondale.

Kelly, Lucretia S.

2010 A Bird's Eye View of Ritual at the Cahokia Site. In *Anthropological Approaches to Zooarchaeology: Complexity, Colonialism, and Animal Transformations*, edited by Douglas Campana, Pamela Crabtree, Susan D. deFrance, Justin Lev-Tov, and A. M. Choyke, pp. 1–11. Oxbow Books, Oxford, England.

Kelly, Lucretia S., and John E. Kelly
2007 Swans in the American Bottom during the Emergent Mississippian and Mississippian. *Illinois Archaeology* 15–16: 112–41.

Keyes, Greg
1994 Myth and Social History in the Early Southeast: In *Perspectives on the Southeast: Linguistics, Archaeology, and Ethnohistory*, edited by Patricia B. Kwachka, pp. 106–15. Proceedings of the Southern Anthropological Society 27. University of Georgia Press, Athens.

Kigoshi, Kunihiko, Hiroko Aizawa, and Nobuko Suzuki
1969 Gakushuin Natural Radiocarbon Measurements VII. *Radiocarbon* 11(2): 295–326.

King, Adam
2001 Long-Term Histories of Mississippian Centers: The Developmental Sequence of Etowah and Its Comparison to Moundville and Cahokia. *Southeastern Archaeology* 20: 1–17.
2003 *Etowah: The Political History of a Chiefdom Capital*. University of Alabama Press, Tuscaloosa.
2007 Mound C and the Southeastern Ceremonial Complex in the History of the Etowah Site. In *Southeastern Ceremonial Complex: Chronology, Content, Context*, edited by Adam King, pp. 107–33. University of Alabama Press, Tuscaloosa.

King, Adam, and F. Kent Reilly III
2011 Raptor Imagery at Etowah: The Raptor Is the Path to Power. In *Visualizing the Sacred: Cosmic Visions, Regionalism, and the Art of the Mississippian World*, edited by George E. Lankford III, F. Kent Reilly III, and James F. Garber, pp. 313–20. University of Texas Press, Austin.

King, David
1997 *The Commissar Vanishes: The Falsification of Photographs and Art in Stalinist Russia*. Metropolitan Books, New York.

Kinietz, W. Vernon
1940 *The Indians of the Western Great Lakes, 1615–1760*. Occasional Contributions 10. Museum of Anthropology, University of Michigan, Ann Arbor. Reprinted 1965, 1972. University of Michigan Press, Ann Arbor.

Kirchhoff, Paul
1959 The Principles of Clanship in Human Society. In *Readings in Anthropology: Vol. 2. Cultural Anthropology*, edited by Morton H. Fried, pp. 259–70. Thomas Y. Crowell, New York.

Knapp, A. Bernard, and Wendy Ashmore
1999 Archaeological Landscapes: Constructed, Conceptualized, Ideational. In *Archaeologies of Landscape*, edited by Wendy Ashmore and A. Bernard Knapp, pp. 1–30. Blackwell, Malden, Massachusetts.

Knight, Vernon J., Jr.
1982   Document and Literature Review. In *Phase I Archaeological Reconnaissance of the Oliver Lock and Dam Project Area, Tuscaloosa, Alabama*, edited by Lawrence S. Alexander, pp. 27–102. Report of Investigations 33. Office of Archaeological Research, Moundville Archaeological Park, Alabama.
1986   The Institutional Organization of Mississippian Religion. *American Antiquity* 51: 675–87.
1989a   Symbolism of Mississippian Mounds. In *Powhatan's Mantle: Indians in the Colonial Southeast*, edited by Peter H. Wood, Gregory A. Waselkov, and M. Thomas Hatley, pp. 279–91. University of Nebraska Press, Lincoln.
1989b   Certain Aboriginal Mounds at Moundville: 1937 Excavations in Mounds H, I, J, K, and L. Paper presented at the 46th Annual Meeting of the Southeastern Archaeological Conference, Tampa, Florida.
1990   Social Organization and the Evolution of Hierarchy in Southeastern Chiefdoms. *Journal of Anthropological Research* 46(1): 1–23.
1994   The Formation of the Creeks. In *The Forgotten Centuries: Indians and Europeans in the American South, 1521–1704*, edited by Charles M. Hudson and Carmen Chaves Tesser, pp. 373–92. University of Georgia Press, Athens.
1998   Moundville as a Diagrammatic Ceremonial Center. In *Archaeology of the Moundville Chiefdom*, edited by Vernon J. Knight, Jr. and Vincas P. Steponaitis, pp. 44–62. Smithsonian Institution Press, Washington, D.C.
2004   Characterizing Elite Midden Deposits at Moundville. *American Antiquity* 69(2): 304–21.
2006   Farewell to the Southeastern Ceremonial Complex. *Southeastern Archaeology* 25(1): 1–5.
2007   An Assessment of Moundville Engraved "Cult" Designs from Potsherds. In *Southeastern Ceremonial Complex: Chronology, Content, Context*, edited by Adam King, pp. 151–64. University of Alabama Press, Tuscaloosa.
2009   Discovery and Excavation of the Moundville Earth Lodge. *Bulletin of the Alabama Museum of Natural History* 27: 20–28.
2010   *Mound Excavations at Moundville: Architecture, Elites, and Social Order*. University of Alabama Press, Tuscaloosa.
Knight, Vernon J., Jr., Lyle W. Konigsberg, and Susan R. Frankenberg
1999   A Gibbs Sampler Approach to the Dating of Phases in the Moundville Sequence. Manuscript on file, Office of Archaeological Research, Moundville Archaeological Park, Alabama.
Knight, Vernon J., Jr., and Carlos Solís
1983   The Farmstead Papers II: Mississippian Farmsteads and Their Economic Significance in the Southeast. Paper presented at the 16th Annual Meeting of the Alabama Academy of Sciences, Tuscaloosa, Alabama.
Knight, Vernon J., Jr., and Vincas P. Steponaitis
1998   A New History of Moundville. In *Archaeology of the Moundville Chiefdom*, edited by Vernon J. Knight, Jr. and Vincas P. Steponaitis, pp. 1–25. Smithsonian Institution Press, Washington, D.C.

2007   Preface to the New Edition. In *Archaeology of the Moundville Chiefdom*, edited by Vernon J. Knight, Jr. and Vincas P. Steponaitis, pp. xix–xxi. 2nd ed. University of Alabama Press, Tuscaloosa. Originally published 1998, Smithsonian Institution Press, Washington, D.C.

2011   A Redefinition of the Hemphill Style in Mississippian Art. In *Visualizing the Sacred: Cosmic Visions, Regionalism, and the Art of the Mississippian World*, edited by George E. Lankford, F. Kent Reilly III, and James F. Garber, pp. 201–39. University of Texas Press, Austin.

Knight, Vernon J., Jr., and Vincas P. Steponaitis (editors)
1998   *Archaeology of the Moundville Chiefdom*. Smithsonian Institution Press, Washington, D.C. Reprinted 2007 with a new preface, University of Alabama Press, Tuscaloosa.

Kohler, Timothy A., and Eric Blinman
1987   Solving Mixture Problems in Archaeology: Analysis of Ceramic Materials for Dating and Demographic Reconstruction. *Journal of Anthropological Archaeology* 6: 1–28.

Kowalewski, Stephen A.
2006   Coalescent Societies. In *Light on the Path: The Anthropology and History of the Southeastern Indians*, edited by Thomas J. Pluckhahn and Robbie Ethridge, pp. 94–122. University of Alabama Press, Tuscaloosa.

Krebs, W. Philip, Eugene Futato, Polly Futato, and Vernon J. Knight, Jr.
1986   *Ten Thousand Years of Alabama Prehistory: A Pictorial Resume*. Bulletin 8. Alabama State Museum of Natural History, Tuscaloosa.

Kundera, Milan
1999   *The Book of Laughter and Forgetting*. HarperCollins, New York.

Lacefield, Hyla L.
1995   A Preliminary Study of Moundville Engraved Pottery. Master's thesis, Department of Anthropology, University of Alabama.

Lacquement, Cameron H.
2007   Typology, Chronology, and Technological Changes of Mississippian Architecture in West-Central Alabama. In *Architectural Variability in the Southeast*, edited by Cameron H. Lacquement, pp. 49–72. University of Alabama Press, Tuscaloosa.

2009   *Landscape Modification at Moundville: An Energetics Assessment of a Mississippian Polity*. PhD dissertation, Department of Anthropology, University of Alabama, Tuscaloosa.

Lafferty, Robert H.
1994   Prehistoric Exchange in the Lower Mississippi Valley. In *Prehistoric Exchange Systems in North America*, edited by Timothy G. Baugh and Jonathon E. Ericson, pp. 177–213. Plenum Press, New York.

Landes, Ruth
1968   *Ojibwa Religion and the Midewiwin*. University of Wisconsin Press, Madison.

Laneri, Nicola
2007   An Archaeology of Funerary Rituals. In *Performing Death: Social Analyses of*

Funerary Traditions in the Ancient Near East and Mediterranean, edited by Nicola Laneri, pp. 1-13. Oriental Institute Seminars 3. Oriental Institute, University of Chicago, Chicago.

Lankford, George E.
2004   World on a String: Some Cosmological Components of the Southeastern Ceremonial Complex. In *Hero, Hawk, and Open Hand: American Indian Art of the Ancient Midwest and South*, edited by Richard F. Townsend and Robert V. Sharp, pp. 206-17. Art Institute of Chicago and Yale University Press, New Haven, Connecticut.
2007a   *Reachable Stars: Patterns in the Ethnoastronomy of Eastern North America*. University of Alabama Press, Tuscaloosa.
2007b   The Great Serpent in Eastern North America. In *Ancient Objects and Sacred Realms: Interpretations of Mississippian Iconography*, edited by F. Kent Reilly III and James Garber, pp. 107-35. University of Texas Press, Austin.
2007c   "The Path of Souls": Some Death Imagery in the Southeastern Ceremonial Complex. In *Ancient Objects and Sacred Realms: Interpretations of Mississippian Iconography*, edited by F. Kent Reilly III and James Garber, pp. 174-212. University of Texas Press, Austin.
2011a   The Raptor on the Path. In *Visualizing the Sacred: Cosmic Visions, Regionalism, and the Art of the Mississippian World*, edited by George E. Lankford, F. Kent Reilly III, and James F. Garber, pp. 240-50. University of Texas Press, Austin.
2011b   The Swirl-Cross and the Center. In *Visualizing the Sacred: Cosmic Visions, Regionalism, and the Art of the Mississippian World*, edited by George E. Lankford, F. Kent Reilly III, and James F. Garber, pp. 251-75. University of Texas Press, Austin.

Lankford, George E., F. Kent Reilly III, and James F. Garber (editors)
2011   *Visualizing the Sacred: Cosmic Visions, Regionalism, and the Art of the Mississippian World*. University of Texas Press, Austin.

Latour, Bruno
1992   Where Are the Missing Masses? Sociology of a Few Mundane Artefacts. In *Shaping Technology, Building Society: Studies in Sociotechnical Change*, edited by Wieber Bijker and John Law, pp. 225-58. MIT Press, Cambridge.

Law, John
1991   Power, Discretion, and Strategy. In *A Sociology of Monsters: Essays on Power, Technology and Domination*, edited by John Law, pp. 103-31. Routledge, London.

Leach, Edmund R.
1954   *Political Systems of Highland Burma*. Beacon Press, Boston.

LeBlanc, Steven A.
2004   *Painted by a Distant Hand: Mimbres Pottery of the American Southwest*. Peabody Museum Press, Cambridge.

LeBlanc, Steven A., and Margaret M. Ellis
2001   The Individual Artist in Mimbres Culture: Painted Bowl Production and Spe-

cialization. Paper presented at the 66th Annual Meeting of the Society for American Archaeology, New Orleans.

Le Page du Pratz, Antoine-Simon
1758   *Histoire de la Louisiane.* 3 vols. De Bure (et al.), Paris.

Lesure, Richard
1999   On the Genesis of Value in Early Hierarchical Societies. In *Material Symbols: Culture and Economy in Prehistory*, edited by John E. Robb, pp. 23–55. Occasional Paper 26. Center for Archaeological Investigations, Southern Illinois University, Carbondale.

Lévi-Strauss, Claude
1982   *The Way of the Masks.* Translated by Sylvia Modelski. University of Washington Press, Seattle.

Lillios, Katina T.
2008   *Heraldry for the Dead: Memory, Identity, and the Engraved Stone Plaques of Neolithic Iberia.* University of Texas Press, Austin.

Lincoln, Bruce
1989   *Discourse and the Construction of Society.* Oxford University Press, New York.

Linton, Ralph
1936   *The Study of Man: An Introduction.* Appleton-Century-Crofts, New York.

Little, Keith J., and Caleb Curren
1995   The Moundville IV Phase on the Black Warrior River. *Journal of Alabama Archaeology* 41(1): 55–77.

Lowenthal, David
1985   *The Past Is a Foreign Country.* Cambridge University Press, Cambridge.

Marcoux, Jon B.
2000   Display Goods Production and Circulation in the Moundville Chiefdom: A Mississippian Dilemma. Master's thesis, Department of Anthropology, University of Alabama, Tuscaloosa.
2007   On Reconsidering Display Goods Production and Circulation in the Moundville Chiefdom. *Southeastern Archaeology* 26(2): 232–45.

Markin, Julie G.
1997   Elite Stoneworking and the Function of Mounds at Moundville. *Mississippi Archaeology* 32: 117–35.

Mauss, Marcel
2000   *The Gift: The Form and Reason of Exchange in Archaic Societies.* Translated by W. Hall. W. W. Norton, New York. Originally published in 1925 in *L'Année Sociologique.*

Maxham, Mintcy D.
2000   Rural Communities in the Black Warrior Valley, Alabama: The Role of Commoners in the Creation of the Moundville I Landscape. *American Antiquity* 65: 337–54.
2004   Native Constructions of Landscapes in the Black Warrior Valley, Alabama, AD 1020–1520. PhD dissertation, Department of Anthropology, University of North Carolina, Chapel Hill.

Maxwell, Thomas
1876   *Tuskaloosa, the Origin of Its Name, Its History, Etc.* A paper read before the Alabama Historical Society. Printed at the office of the Tuskaloosa Gazette, Tuscaloosa, Alabama.

May, Stephanie A.
2004   Alabama and Koasati. In *Southeast*, edited by Raymond Fogelson, pp. 407–14. Handbook of North American Indians, Vol. 14, William C. Sturtevant, general editor, Smithsonian Institution Press, Washington, D.C.

McAnany, Patricia
1995   *Living with the Ancestors: Kinship and Kingship in Ancient Maya Society.* University of Texas Press, Austin.

McCarthy, Marie A., and Ruth H. Matthews
1984   *Composition of Foods: Nut and Seed Products.* Agriculture Handbook 8–12. U.S. Department of Agriculture, Washington, D.C.

McKenzie, Douglas H.
1964   *The Moundville Phase and Its Position in Southeastern Prehistory.* PhD dissertation, Department of Anthropology, Harvard University, Cambridge.

Meskell, Lynn
2003   Memory's Materiality: Ancestral Presence, Commemorative Practice and Disjunctive Locales. In *Archaeologies of Memory*, edited by Ruth Van Dyke and Susan Alcock, pp. 34–55. Blackwell, Malden, Massachusetts.

Michals, Lauren M.
1981   The Exploitation of Fauna during the Moundville I Phase at Moundville. *Southeastern Archaeological Conference Bulletin* 24: 91–93.
1992   The Nature of Faunal Exploitation during the Moundville Phase. Paper presented at the 57th Annual Meeting of the Society for American Archaeology, Pittsburgh, Pennsylvania.
1998   The Oliver Site and Early Moundville I Phase Economic Organization. In *Archaeology of the Moundville Chiefdom*, edited by Vernon J. Knight, Jr. and Vincas P. Steponaitis, pp. 209–29. Smithsonian Institution Press, Washington, D.C.

Michelson, Truman
1921   *The Owl Sacred Pack of the Fox Indians.* Bureau of American Ethnology, Bulletin 71. Government Printing Office, Washington, D.C.

Miller, Maury E., III
1992   Owl Effigies in Bone, Clay, and Stone in Tennessee. *Central States Archaeological Journal* 39(3): 126–27.

Milner, George R.
1998   *The Cahokia Chiefdom: The Archaeology of a Mississippian Society.* Smithsonian Institution Press, Washington, D.C.

Mirarchi, Matthew J.
2009   Beneath an Earthen Countenance: The Architecture and Artifacts of the Moundville Earth Lodge Complex. Master's thesis, Department of Anthropology, University of North Carolina, Chapel Hill.

Mooney, James
1900 Myths of the Cherokee. Bureau of American Ethnology, Annual Report 19. Government Printing Office, Washington, D.C.

Moore, Clarence B.
1905 Certain Aboriginal Remains of the Black Warrior River. *Journal of the Academy of Natural Sciences of Philadelphia* 13: 125–244.
1907 Moundville Revisited. *Journal of the Academy of Natural Sciences of Philadelphia* 13: 337–405.
1908 Certain Mounds of Arkansas and of Mississippi. *Journal of the Academy of Natural Sciences of Philadelphia* 13: 479–605.

Moore, Michael C., and Kevin E. Smith
2009 *Archaeological Expeditions of the Peabody Museum in Middle Tennesssee, 1877–1884*. Research Series 16. Division of Archaeology, Tennessee Department of Environment and Conservation, Nashville.

Muller, Jon D.
1997 *Mississippian Political Economy*. Plenum Press, New York.

Myer, Jennifer L.
2002a Among the Fields: Mississippian Settlement Patterns in the Black Warrior Valley, Alabama. Master's thesis, Department of Anthropology, University of Alabama, Tuscaloosa.
2002b *Characteristics of Mississippian Settlement in the Black Warrior Valley, Alabama: Final Report of Season III of the Black Warrior Valley Survey*. Report submitted to the Alabama Historical Commission, project no. PT00-SP180. Department of Anthropology, University of Alabama, Tuscaloosa.
2003 *Archaeological Testing at Three Non-Mound Mississippian Sites in the Black Warrior Valley, Alabama: Final Report of Season IV of the Black Warrior Valley Survey*. Report Submitted to the Alabama Historical Commission, project no. PT02-SP226. Department of Anthropology, University of Alabama, Tuscaloosa.

Nabokov, Peter
1989 *Native American Architecture*. Oxford University Press, New York.

Newcomer, Mark H.
1971 Some Quantitative Experiments in Hand-Axe Manufacture. *World Archaeology* 3: 85–94.

Nielsen, Jerry J., John W. O'Hear, and Charles W. Moorehead
1973 *An Archaeological Survey of Hale and Greene Counties, Alabama*. Report submitted to the Alabama Historical Commission by the University of Alabama Museums, Tuscaloosa.

Ogilvie, Robert Maxwell
1971 Introduction. In *Livy: The Early History of Rome, Books I–V of The History of Rome from Its Foundation*, translated by Aubrey de Selincourt, pp. 7–29. Penguin Books, Harmondsworth, Middlesex, England.

O'Grady, Caitlin R.
2004 Morphological and Chemical Analyses of Manganese Dioxide Accretions on Mexican Ceramics. In *Materials Issues in Art and Archaeology VII*, edited by

Pamela B. Vandiver, Jennifer L. Mass, and Alison Murray, 183–92. Materials Research Society Proceedings 852.

O'Hear, John W.
1975 Site 1Je32: Community Organization in the West Jefferson Phase. Master's thesis, Department of Anthropology, University of Alabama, Tuscaloosa.

Olick, Jeffrey K., and Joyce Robbins
1998 Social Memory Studies: From "Collective Memory" to the Historical Sociology of Mnemonic Practices. *Annual Review of Sociology* 24: 105–40.

Parker Pearson, Michael
1999 *The Archaeology of Death and Burial.* Texas A&M University Press, College Station.

Pauketat, Timothy R.
1993 *Temples for Cahokia's Lords: Preston Holder's 1955–1956 Excavations at Kunnemann Mound.* Memoirs 26. Museum of Anthropology, University of Michigan, Ann Arbor.
1994 *The Ascent of Chiefs: Cahokia and Mississippian Politics in Native North America.* University of Alabama Press, Tuscaloosa.
1997 Specialization, Political Symbols and the Crafty Elite of Cahokia. *Southeastern Archaeology* 16(1): 1–15.
2004 *Ancient Cahokia and the Mississippians.* Cambridge University Press, Cambridge.
2007 *Chiefdoms and Other Archaeological Delusions.* Altamira Press, Lanham, Maryland.

Pauketat, Timothy R., and Susan M. Alt
2003 Mounds, Memory, and Contested Mississippian History. In *Archaeologies of Memory*, edited by Ruth Van Dyke and Susan E. Alcock, pp. 151–79. Blackwell, Malden, Massachusetts.

Pauketat, Timothy, Lucretia Kelly, Gayle J. Fritz, Neal H. Lopinot, Scott Elias, and Eve Hargrove
2002 The Residues of Feasting and Public Ritual at Early Cahokia. *American Antiquity* 67: 257–80.

Payne, Claudine
2002 Architectural Reflections of Power and Authority in Mississippian Towns. In *The Dynamics of Power*, edited by Maria O'Donovan, pp. 188–213. Occasional Paper 30. Center for Archaeological Investigations, Southern Illinois University, Carbondale.

Pease, Theodore Calvin, and Raymond C. Werner (eds.)
1934 *The French Foundations, 1680–1692.* French Series, vol. 1. Collections of the Illinois State Historical Library, vol. 23. Illinois State Historical Library, Springfield.

Peebles, Christopher S.
1971 Moundville and Surrounding Sites: Some Structural Considerations of Mortuary Practices II. In *Approaches to the Social Dimensions of Mortuary Practices*,

edited by James A. Brown, pp. 68–91. Memoirs 25. Society for American Archaeology, Washington, D.C.
1974 *Moundville: The Organization of a Prehistoric Community and Culture.* PhD dissertation, Department of Anthropology, University of California, Santa Barbara.
1978 Determinants of Settlement Size and Location in the Moundville Phase. In *Mississippian Settlement Patterns*, edited by Bruce D. Smith, pp. 369–416. Academic Press, New York.
1979 *Excavations at Moundville: 1905–1951.* Microfiche. University Microfilms, Ann Arbor, Michigan.
1983 Moundville: Late Prehistoric Sociopolitical Organization in the Southeastern United States. In *The Development of Political Organization in Native North America*, edited by Elisabeth Tooker, pp. 183–98. American Ethnological Society, Philadelphia, Pennsylvania.
1987 The Rise and Fall of the Mississippian in Western Alabama: The Moundville and Summerville Phases, A.D. 1000–1600. *Mississippi Archaeology* 22: 1–31.

Peebles, Christopher S., and Susan M. Kus
1977 Some Archaeological Correlates of Ranked Societies. *American Antiquity* 42: 421–48.

Peles, Ashley A., and C. Margaret Scarry
2013 Plant Remains. In *Graveline: A Late Woodland Platform Mound on the Mississippi Gulf Coast*, edited by John Blitz and Lauren Downs, pp. 129–48. Report submitted to the Mississippi Department of Archives and History, Jackson.

Peregrine, Peter
1991 Some Political Aspects of Craft Specialization. *World Archaeology* 23(1): 1–11.

Phillips, Erin E.
2006 Social Status as Seen through the Distribution of Paint Palettes, Stone Pendants, and Copper Gorgets in Moundville Burials. Master's thesis, Department of Anthropology, University of Alabama, Tuscaloosa.
2012 *Social Contexts of Production and Use of Pottery Engraved in the Hemphill Style at Moundville.* PhD dissertation, Department of Anthropology, University of Alabama, Tuscaloosa.

Phillips, Philip, and James A. Brown
1978 *Pre-Columbian Shell Engravings from the Craig Mound at Spiro, Oklahoma, Part 1.* Peabody Museum Press, Cambridge.

Pickering, Robert B., and Ephraim Cuevas
2003 The Ancient Ceramics of West Mexico. *American Scientist* 91: 242–49.

Pope, Melody K.
1989 Microtools from the Black Warrior Valley: Technology, Use, and Context. Master's thesis, Department of Anthropology, State University of New York, Binghamton.

Power, Susan C.
2004 *Early Art of the Southeastern Indians: Feathered Serpents and Winged Beings.* University of Georgia Press, Athens.

Redford, Donald B.
1984   *Akhenaten, the Heretic King.* Princeton University Press, Princeton, New Jersey.

Rees, Mark A.
2001   *Mississippian Political Culture: Contrasting Historical Trajectories in Southeastern North America.* PhD dissertation, Department of Anthropology, University of Oklahoma, Norman.

Reeves, Nicholas
2001   *Akhenaten: Egypt's False Prophet.* Thames and Hudson, London.

Reilly, F. Kent III
2007   By Their Vestments Ye Shall Know Them: Ritual Regalia and Cult-Bearers in Mississippian Art. Paper presented at the 64th Annual Meeting of the Southeastern Archaeological Conference, Knoxville, Tennessee.

Reilly, F. Kent III, and James F. Garber (editors)
2007   *Ancient Objects and Sacred Realms: Interpretations of Mississippian Iconography.* University of Texas Press, Austin.

Reynolds, Peter J.
1999   The Nature of Experiment in Archaeology. In *Experiment and Design: Archaeological Studies in Honour of John Coles*, edited by Anthony F. Harding, pp. 156–62. Oxbow Books, Oxford, England.

Richert, Bernhard E., Jr.
1969   Plains Indian Medicine Bundles. Master's thesis, Department of Anthropology, University of Texas at Austin.

Ryba, Elizabeth A.
1997   Summit Architecture on Mound E at Moundville. Master's thesis, Department of Anthropology, University of Alabama, Tuscaloosa.

Sahlins, Marshall D.
1958   *Social Stratification in Polynesia.* University of Washington Press, Seattle.

Saxe, Arthur
1970   *Social Dimensions of Mortuary Practices.* PhD dissertation. Department of Anthropology, University of Michigan, Ann Arbor.

Scarry, C. Margaret
1986   *Change in Plant Procurement and Production during the Emergence of the Moundville Chiefdom.* PhD dissertation, Department of Anthropology, University of Michigan, Ann Arbor.
1993a   Agricultural Risk and the Development of the Moundville Chiefdom. In *Foraging and Farming in the Eastern Woodlands*, edited by C. Margaret Scarry, pp. 157–81. University Press of Florida, Gainesville.
1993b   Plant Remains from the Big Sandy Farms Site (1Tu552), Tuscaloosa County, Alabama. In *Big Sandy Farms: A Prehistoric Agricultural Community near Moundville, Black Warrior River Floodplain, Tuscaloosa County, Alabama*, edited by H. Blaine Ensor, pp. 205–33. Report of Investigations 68. Division of Archaeology, Alabama Museum of Natural History, University of Alabama, Tuscaloosa.
1993c   Variability in Mississippian Crop Production Strategies. In *Foraging and Farm-

ing in the Eastern Woodlands, edited by C. Margaret Scarry, pp. 78–90. University Press of Florida, Gainesville.

1995 Excavations on the Northwest Riverbank at Moundville: Investigations of a Moundville I Residential Area. Report of Investigations 72. Office of Archaeological Services, University of Alabama Museums, Tuscaloosa.

1997 Archaeobotanical Remains from Sites 1Tu66, 1Tu570, and 1Tu768. In *West Jefferson Community Organization in the Black Warrior Valley, Alabama*, by C. Margaret Scarry and John F. Scarry. Report prepared for the National Geographic Society in fulfillment of Grant 5278-94. Manuscript on file, Research Laboratories of Archaeology, University of North Carolina, Chapel Hill.

1998 Domestic Life on the Northwest Riverbank at Moundville. In *Archaeology of the Moundville Chiefdom*, edited by Vernon J. Knight, Jr., and Vincas P. Steponaitis, pp. 63–101. Smithsonian Institution Press, Washington, D.C.

2003a Patterns of Wild Plant Utilization in the Prehistoric Eastern Woodlands. In *People and Plants in Ancient Eastern North America*, edited by Paul Minnis, pp. 50–104. Smithsonian Institution Press, Washington, D.C.

2003b The Use of Plants in Mound-Related Activities at Bottle Creek and Moundville. In *Bottle Creek*, edited by Ian Brown, pp. 114–29. University of Alabama Press, Tuscaloosa.

Scarry, C. Margaret, and John F. Scarry

1997 *West Jefferson Community Organization in the Black Warrior Valley, Alabama*. Report prepared for the National Geographic Society in fulfillment of Grant 5278-94. Research Laboratories of Archaeology, University of North Carolina, Chapel Hill.

Scarry, C. Margaret, and Vincas P. Steponaitis

1997 Between Farmstead and Center: The Natural and Social Landscape of Moundville. In *Plants, People, and Landscapes*, edited by Kristen Gremillion, pp. 107–22. University of Alabama Press, Tuscaloosa.

Scarry, John F.

1992 Political Offices and Political Structure: Ethnohistoric and Archeological Perspectives on the Native Lords of Apalachee. In *Lords of the Southeast: Social Inequality and the Native Elites of Southeastern North America*, edited by Alex W. Barker and Timothy R. Pauketat, pp. 163–83. Archeological Papers 3. American Anthropological Association, Washington, D.C.

1999 How Great Were the Southeastern Polities? In *Great Towns and Regional Polities in the Prehistoric American Southwest and Southeast*, edited by Jill Neitzel, pp. 59–74. University of New Mexico Press, Albuquerque.

Scarry, John F., and Robert V. Sharp

2010 Living Metaphors: Natural Images in Mississippian Iconography. Paper presented at the 67th Annual Meeting of the Southeastern Archaeological Conference, Lexington, Kentucky.

Schatte, Kevin E.

1997 Stylistic Analysis of the Winged Serpent Theme at Moundville. Master's thesis, Department of Anthropology, University of Alabama, Tuscaloosa.

Schlesier, Karl
1990   Rethinking the Midewiwin and the Plains Ceremonial Called the Sun Dance. *Plains Anthropologist* 35: 1–27.

Schnell, Frank T., Vernon J. Knight, Jr., and Gail S. Schnell
1981   *Cemochechobee: Archaeology of a Mississippian Ceremonial Center on the Chattahoochee River*. University Press of Florida, Gainesville.

Schoeninger, Margaret J., and Mark R. Schurr
1998   Human Subsistence at Moundville: The Stable-Isotope Data. In *Archaeology of the Moundville Chiefdom*, edited by Vernon J. Knight, Jr. and Vincas P. Steponaitis, pp. 120–32. Smithsonian Institution Press, Washington, D.C.

Scott, Susan L.
1983   Analysis, Synthesis, and Interpretation of Faunal Remains from the Lubbub Creek Archaeological Locality. In *Studies of Material Remains from the Lubbub Creek Archaeological Locality*, edited by Christopher Peebles, pp. 272–379. Report on file, U.S. Army Corps of Engineers, Mobile, Alabama.

Service, Elman R.
1962   *Primitive Social Organization: An Evolutionary Perspective*. Random House, New York.

Sheldon, Craig T.
1974   *The Mississippian–Historic Transition in Central Alabama*. PhD dissertation, Department of Anthropology, University of Oregon, Eugene.

Sherard, Jeff L.
1999   Pride Place: A Sandstone Workshop. Paper presented at the 56th Annual Meeting of the Southeastern Archaeological Conference, Pensacola, Florida.

Sidoff, Phillip G.
1977   An Ethnohistorical Investigation of the Medicine Bundle Complex among Selected Tribes of the Great Plains. *The Wisconsin Archeologist* 58(3): 173–204.

Smith, Kevin E., and James V. Miller
2009   *Speaking with the Ancestors: Mississippian Stone Statuary of the Tennessee–Cumberland Region*. University of Alabama Press, Tuscaloosa.

Smyth, Michael P.
1990   Maize Storage among the Puuc Maya: The Development of an Archaeological Method. *Ancient Mesoamerica* 1: 51–70.

Snow, David
2001   Collective Identity and Expressive Forms. Center for the Study of Democracy, University of California, Irvine. Electronic document, http://escholarship.org/uc/item/2zn1t7bj.

Speck, Frank G.
1907   Notes on Chickasaw Ethnology and Folk-Lore. *Journal of American Folklore* 20: 50–58.

Speth, John D., and Susan L. Scott
1989   Horticulture and Large-Mammal Hunting: The Role of Resource Depletion and the Constraints on Time and Labor. In *Farmers as Hunters: The Implications of*

Sedentism, edited by Susan Kent, pp. 71–79. Cambridge University Press, Cambridge.

Spielmann, Katherine A.

1998   Ritual Craft Specialists in Middle-Range Societies. In *Craft and Social Identity*, edited by Cathy Lynne Costin and Rita P. Wright, pp. 153–59. Archeological Papers 8. American Anthropological Association, Washington, D.C.

2002   Feasting, Craft Specialization, and the Ritual Mode of Production in Small-Scale Societies. *American Anthropologist* 104: 195–207.

Spoehr, Alexander

1941   *Camp, Clan, and Kin among the Cow Creek Seminole of Florida*. Anthropological Series 33(1). Field Museum of Natural History, Chicago.

Steponaitis, Vincas P.

1978   Location Theory and Complex Chiefdoms: A Mississippian Example. In *Mississippian Settlement Patterns*, edited by Bruce D. Smith, pp. 417–53. Academic Press, New York.

1980   Some Preliminary Chronological and Technological Notes on Moundville Pottery. *Southeastern Archaeological Conference Bulletin* 22: 46–51.

1983a   *Ceramics, Chronology, and Community Patterns: An Archaeological Study at Moundville*. Academic Press, New York.

1983b   The Smithsonian Institution's Investigations at Moundville in 1869 and 1882. *Midcontinental Journal of Archaeology* 8(1): 127–60.

1989   Chronological Position of Moundville Gravelots. Manuscript on file, Department of Anthropology, University of Alabama.

1991   Contrasting Patterns of Mississippian Development. In *Chiefdoms: Power, Economy, and Ideology*, edited by Timothy K. Earle, pp. 193–228. Cambridge University Press, New York.

1992   Excavations at 1Tu50, an Early Mississippian Center near Moundville. *Southeastern Archaeology* 11(1): 1–13.

1998   Population Trends at Moundville. In *Archaeology of the Moundville Chiefdom*, edited by Vernon J. Knight, Jr. and Vincas P. Steponaitis, pp. 26–43. Smithsonian Institution Press, Washington, D.C.

Steponaitis, Vincas P., M. James Blackman, and Hector Neff

1996   Large-Scale Patterns in the Chemical Composition of Mississippian Pottery. *American Antiquity* 61(3): 555–72.

Steponaitis, Vincas P., R. P. Stephen Davis, and H. Trawick Ward

2009   Field Evaluation of Two Subsurface Augering Methods at Moundville. *Southeastern Archaeology* 28(2): 259–67.

Steponaitis, Vincas P., and David T. Dockery III

2011   Mississippian Effigy Pipes and the Glendon Limestone. *American Antiquity* 76(2): 345–54.

Steponaitis, Vincas P., and Vernon J. Knight, Jr.

2004   Moundville Art in Historical and Social Context. In *Hero, Hawk, and Open Hand: American Indian Art of the Ancient Midwest and South*, edited by Richard

F. Townsend and Robert V. Sharp, pp. 166–81. Art Institute of Chicago and Yale University Press, New Haven, Connecticut.

Steponaitis, Vincas P., Samuel E. Swanson, George Wheeler, and Penelope B. Drooker
2011 The Provenance and Use of Etowah Palettes. *American Antiquity* 76(1): 81–106.

Steponaitis, Vincas P., and Gregory D. Wilson
2010 Early Engraved Wares at Moundville. Paper presented at the 75th Annual Meeting of the Society for American Archaeology, St. Louis, Missouri.

Stout, Charles, and R. Barry Lewis
1998 Mississippian Towns in Kentucky. In *Mississippian Towns and Sacred Spaces: Searching for an Architectural Grammar*, edited by R. Barry Lewis and Charles Stout, pp. 151–78. University of Alabama Press, Tuscaloosa.

Swan, Caleb
1855 Position and State of Manners and Arts in the Creek, or Muscogee Nation in 1791. In *Information Respecting the History, Condition and Prospects of the Indian Tribes of the United States*, Vol. 5, by Henry Rowe Schoolcraft, pp. 251–83. J. B. Lippincott, Philadelphia.

Swanton, John R.
1911 *Indian Tribes of the Lower Mississippi Valley and Adjacent Coast of the Gulf of Mexico*. Bureau of American Ethnology, Bulletin 43. Government Printing Office, Washington, D.C.
1922 *Early History of the Creek Indians and Their Neighbors*. Bureau of American Ethnology, Bulletin 73. Government Printing Office, Washington, D.C.
1928a Social Organization and Social Usages of the Indians of the Creek Confederacy. *Bureau of American Ethnology, Annual Report 42*, pp. 23–472. Government Printing Office, Washington, D.C.
1928b Social and Religious Beliefs and Usages of the Chickasaw Indians. *Bureau of American Ethnology, Annual Report 44*, pp. 169–273. Government Printing Office, Washington, D.C.
1931a Modern Square Grounds of the Creek Indians. *Smithsonian Miscellaneous Collections* 85(8). Smithsonian Institution, Washington, D.C.
1931b *Source Material for the Social and Ceremonial Life of the Choctaw Indians*. Bureau of American Ethnology Bulletin 103. Government Printing Office, Washington, D.C.
1946 *The Indians of the Southeastern United States*. Bureau of American Ethnology, Bulletin 137. Government Printing Office, Washington, D.C.

Taft, Kristi E.
1996 Functionally Relevant Classes of Pottery at Moundville. Master's thesis, Department of Anthropology, University of Alabama, Tuscaloosa.

Taylor-George, Susan, Fred Palmer, James T. Staley, David J. Borns, Brian Curtiss, and John B. Adams
1983 Fungi and Bacteria Involved in Desert Varnish Formation. *Microbial Ecology* 9: 227–45.

Thomas, Nicholas
1991   *Entangled Objects: Exchange, Material Culture, and Colonialism in the Pacific.* Harvard University Press, Cambridge.

Thompson, Claire E.
2011   *Ritual and Power: Examining the Economy of Moundville's Residential Population.* PhD dissertation, Department of Anthropology, University of Alabama, Tuscaloosa.

Thompson, Claire E., and John H. Blitz
2009   Craft Production in Residential Areas at Moundville. Paper presented at the 74th Annual Meeting of the Society for American Archaeology, Atlanta, Georgia.

Thwaites, Reuben G. (editor)
1896–1901 *The Jesuit Relations and Allied Documents.* 73 vols. Burrows Brothers, Cleveland.

Timberlake, Henry
1765   *The Memoirs of Lieut. Henry Timberlake (Who Accompanied the Three Cherokee Indians to England in the Year 1762).* J. Ridley, London.

Trubitt, Mary Beth
2000   Mound Building and Prestige Goods Exchange: Changing Strategies in the Cahokia Chiefdom. *American Antiquity* 65(4): 669–90.

Turner, Victor W.
1957   *Schism and Continuity in an African Society: A Study of Ndembu Village Life.* Manchester University Press, Manchester, England.

University of Alabama Museums
1996   University of Alabama NAGPRA Inventory. 3 vols. Manuscript on file, Alabama Museum of Natural History, University of Alabama, Tuscaloosa.

Urban, Greg, and Jason Baird Jackson
2004   Social Organization. In *Southeast*, edited by Raymond Fogelson, pp. 697–706. Handbook of North American Indians, Vol. 14, William C. Sturtevant, general editor, Smithsonian Institution Press, Washington, D.C.

Van Dyke, Ruth M., and Susan E. Alcock
2003   Archaeologies of Memory: An Introduction. In *Archaeologies of Memory*, edited by Susan E. Alcock and Ruth M. Van Dyke, pp. 1–13. Blackwell, Malden, Massachusetts.

Vecsey, Christopher
1984   Midewiwin Myths of Origin. In *Papers of the Fifteenth Algonquian Conference*, edited by William Cowan. Carleton University Press, Ottawa.

Vogel, Joseph O., and Jean Allan
1985   Mississippian Fortifications at Moundville. *Archaeology* 38(5): 62–63.

Walker, Willard B.
2004   Creek Confederacy before Removal. In *Southeast*, edited by Raymond Fogelson, pp. 373–92. Handbook of North American Indians, Vol. 14, William C. Sturtevant, general editor, Smithsonian Institution Press, Washington, D.C.

Walthall, John A., and Ben I. Coblentz
1977   An Archaeological Survey of the Big Sandy Bottoms in the Black Warrior Valley. Manuscript on file, Office of Archaeological Research, Moundville Archaeological Park, Alabama.

Walthall, John A., and Stephen Wimberly
1978   Mississippian Chronology in the Black Warrior Valley: Radiocarbon Dates from Bessemer and Moundville. *Journal of Alabama Archaeology* 24(2): 118–24.

Waring, Antonio J., Jr., and Preston Holder
1945   A Prehistoric Ceremonial Complex in the Southeastern United States. *American Anthropologist* 47(1): 1–34.

Warren, William W.
1984   *History of the Ojibway People*. Written ca. 1852. Minnesota Historical Society Press, St. Paul.

Webb, William S., and David L. DeJarnette
1942   *An Archaeological Survey of Pickwick Basin in the Adjacent Portions of the States of Alabama, Mississippi and Tennessee*. Bureau of American Ethnology Bulletin 129. U.S. Government Printing Office, Washington, D.C.

Weeks, William Rex, Jr.
2009   *Antiquity of the Midewiwin: An Examination of Early Documents, Origin Stories, Archaeological Remains, and Rock Paintings from the Northern Woodlands of North America*. PhD dissertation, Department of Anthropology, Arizona State University, Tempe.

Weiner, Annette B.
1985   Inalienable Wealth. *American Ethnologist* 12(2): 210–27.
1992   *Inalienable Possessions: The Paradox of Keeping-While-Giving*. University of California Press, Berkeley.

Weinstein, Richard A.
1984   The Rosedale and Shellhill Discs: "Southern Cult" Evidence from Southeastern Louisiana. *Louisiana Archaeology* 11: 65–88.

Welch, Paul D.
1986   *Models of Chiefdom Economy: Prehistoric Moundville as a Case Study*. PhD dissertation, Department of Anthropology, University of Michigan, Ann Arbor.
1990   Mississippian Emergence in West Central Alabama. In *Mississippian Emergence*, edited by Bruce Smith, pp. 197–225. Smithsonian Institution Press, Washington.
1991   *Moundville's Economy*. University of Alabama Press, Tuscaloosa.
1996   Control over Goods and the Political Stability of the Moundville Chiefdom. In *Political Structure and Change in the Prehistoric Southeastern United States*, edited by John F. Scarry, pp. 69–91. University Press of Florida, Gainesville.
1998   Outlying Sites within the Moundville Chiefdom. In *Archaeology of the Moundville Chiefdom*, edited by Vernon J. Knight, Jr. and Vincas P. Steponaitis, pp. 133–66. Smithsonian Institution Press, Washington, D.C.

Welch, Paul D., and C. Margaret Scarry
1995   Status-Related Variation in Foodways in the Moundville Chiefdom. *American Antiquity* 60: 397–419.

Wenhold, Lucy L.
1936 A 17th Century Letter of Gabriel Diaz Vara Calderón, Bishop of Cuba, Describing the Indians and Indian Missions of Florida. Smithsonian Miscellaneous Collections 95(16). Government Printing Office, Washington, D.C.

Wesler, Kit W.
2006 Platforms as Chiefs: Comparing Mound Sequences in Western Kentucky. In *Leadership and Polity in Mississippian Society*, edited by Brian M. Butler and Paul D. Welch, pp. 142–55. Occasional Paper 33. Center for Archaeological Investigations, Southern Illinois University, Carbondale.

Wesson, Cameron B.
1999 Chiefly Power and Food Storage in Southeastern North America. *World Archaeology* 31(1): 145–64.

Whitney, Cynthia, Vincas P. Steponaitis, and John W. Rogers
2002 A Petrographic Study of Moundville Palettes. *Southeastern Archaeology* 21(2): 227–34.

Whitridge, Peter
2004 Landscapes, Houses, Bodies, Things: "Place" and the Archaeology of Inuit Imaginaries. *Journal of Archaeological Method and Theory* 11: 213–50.

Widmer, Randolph J.
1994 The Structure of Southeastern Chiefdoms. In *The Forgotten Centuries: Indians and Europeans in the American South, 1521–1704*, edited by Charles M. Hudson and Carmen Chaves Tesser, pp. 125–55. University of Georgia Press, Athens.

Williams, Mark
1995 Chiefly Compounds. In *Mississippian Communities and Households*, edited by J. Daniel Rogers and Bruce D. Smith, pp. 124–34. University of Alabama Press, Tuscaloosa.
2007 Busk Sites of the Oconee Valley. Paper presented at the 64th Annual Meeting of the Southeastern Archaeological Conference, Knoxville, Tennessee.

Williams, Stephen, and Jeffrey P. Brain
1983 *Excavations at the Lake George Site, Yazoo County, Mississippi, 1958–1960*. Papers 74. Peabody Museum of Archaeology and Ethnology, Harvard University, Cambridge.

Wilson, Eddie W.
1950 The Owl and the American Indian. *Journal of American Folklore* 63: 336–44.

Wilson, Gregory D.
2001 Crafting Control and the Control of Crafts: Rethinking the Moundville Greenstone Industry. *Southeastern Archaeology* 20(2): 118–28.
2008 *The Archaeology of Everyday Life at Early Moundville*. University of Alabama Press, Tuscaloosa.
2010 Community, Identity, and Social Memory at Moundville. *American Antiquity* 75(1): 3–18.

Wilson, Gregory D., Jon B. Marcoux, and Brad Koldehoff
2006 Square Pegs in Round Holes: Organizational Diversity between Early Moundville and Cahokia. In *Leadership and Polity in Mississippian Society*, edited by

Brian M. Butler and Paul D. Welch. Occasional Paper 33. Center for Archaeological Investigations, Southern Illinois University, Carbondale.

Wilson, Gregory D., Vincas P. Steponaitis, and Keith Jacobi
2010   Social and Spatial Dimensions of Moundville Mortuary Practices. In *Mississippian Mortuary Practices: Beyond Hierarchy and the Representationist Perspective*, edited by Lynne P. Sullivan and Robert C. Mainfort, Jr., pp. 74–89. University Press of Florida, Gainesville.

Wright, Henry T.
1977   Recent Research on the Origin of the State. *Annual Review of Anthropology* 6: 379–97.

Yaeger, Jason, and Marcello A. Canuto
2000   Introducing an Archaeology of Communities. In The *Archaeology of Communities: A New World Perspective*, edited by Marcello A. Canuto and Jason Yaeger, pp. 1–15. Routledge, New York.

Young, Bilone W., and Melvin L. Fowler
2000   *Cahokia: The Great Native American Metropolis*. University of Illinois Press, Urbana.

Zedeño, Maria Nieves
2008   Bundled Worlds: The Roles and Interactions of Complex Objects from the North American Plains. *Journal of Archaeological Method and Theory* 15: 362–78.

Contributors

John H. Blitz (PhD, City University of New York, 1991) is professor of anthropology at the University of Alabama. He has done extensive work on the Mississippian cultures of Alabama and Georgia. His books include *Moundville*; *The Chattahoochee Chiefdoms*; and *Ancient Chiefdoms of the Tombigbee*.

Jera R. Davis (PhD, University of Alabama, 2014) is instructor of anthropology and cultural resource investigator at the University of Alabama. Her dissertation examined the role of plaza construction in the formation of the Moundville polity, and her research interests include crafting, identity, and iconography.

Scott W. Hammerstedt (PhD, Pennsylvania State University, 2005) is a member of the research faculty at the Oklahoma Archaeological Survey, University of Oklahoma. His research interests include the political economy and settlement patterns of Mississippian people.

H. Edwin Jackson (PhD, University of Michigan, 1986) is professor of anthropology at the University of Southern Mississippi and a specialist in zooarchaeology, the study of how ancient people used animals. He has published numerous articles on Mississippian, Woodland, and Archaic economies and settlement patterns in the American South.

Vernon James Knight Jr. (PhD, University of Florida, 1981), is professor emeritus of anthropology at the University of Alabama and a preeminent authority on Moundville and the archaeology of Alabama. His books include *Mound Excavations at Moundville*; *The Search for Mabila*; and *Archaeology of the Moundville Chiefdom* (with V. P. Steponaitis).

George E. Lankford (PhD, Indiana University, 1975) is professor emeritus of folklore at Lyon College. He has published extensively on Mississippian iconography and the traditional lore of southern Indians. His books include *Looking for Lost Lore*; *Reachable Stars*; and *Native American Legends*.

Mintcy D. Maxham (PhD, University of North Carolina at Chapel Hill, 2004) studied archaeology at the University of North Carolina at Chapel Hill and subsequently earned a DVM at North Carolina State University. Her archaeological research focused on Moundville's hinterland. She is currently a practicing veterinarian.

Jennifer L. Myer (MA, University of Alabama, 2002) completed one of first systematic surveys of Mississippian sites in Moundville's hinterland. She now teaches at a nationally ranked public high school in Miami, Florida.

Erin E. Phillips (PhD, University of Alabama, 2012) is an archaeologist with Coastal Environments, Inc. Her current research focuses on Mississippian iconography, particularly at Moundville.

John F. Scarry (PhD, Case Western Reserve University, 1984) is lecturer in anthropology at the University of North Carolina at Chapel Hill. He has published numerous articles on the Mississippian cultures of Florida and Alabama and is editor of *Political Structure and Change in the Prehistoric Southeastern United States*.

C. Margaret Scarry (PhD, University of Michigan, 1986) is professor of anthropology, chair of curriculum in archaeology, and director of the Research Laboratories of Archaeology at the University of North Carolina at Chapel Hill. She is an authority on the precolonial and colonial use of plants in the American South and has published extensively on Moundville and related areas. Her publications include *Foraging and Farming in the Eastern Woodlands* and *Case Studies in Environmental Archaeology* (with E. J. Reitz and S. J. Scudder).

Susan Scott is research associate in anthropology at the University of Southern Mississippi. She has published extensively on the zooarchaeology of the southeastern and southwestern United States.

Vincas P. Steponaitis (PhD, University of Michigan, 1980) is distinguished professor of anthropology and archaeology and secretary of the faculty at the University of North Carolina at Chapel Hill. His research deals with Mississippian political economy and iconography, with an emphasis on Moundville and the Lower Mississippi Valley. His books include *Ceramics, Chronology, and Community Patterns at Moundville* and *Archaeology of the Moundville Chiefdom* (with V. J. Knight).

Gregory D. Wilson (PhD, University of North Carolina at Chapel Hill, 2005) is associate professor of anthropology at the University of California at Santa Barbara. He has published on the Mississippian cultures of Alabama and Illinois, including a recent book entitled *The Archaeology of Everyday Life at Early Moundville*.

Index

Page numbers in *italics* refer to illustrations and tables.

Above World, 84, 230; birds as representatives of, 229
Abraders, 238, *239*
Acorn (*Quercus* sp.), 196, *202*, 202–3, 209, *209*, 213, *215*
Afghanistan, 60
Age group, as variable, 107–8, *108*
Alabama Museum of Natural History, 99–100, 107–8; Moundville Roadway excavations, 46
Alabama River phase, renamed, 6
Algonkian-speaking peoples, 76, 79, 91
Alligator gar (*Atractosteus spatula*), *219*
Alligator Incised sherd count, *152*, *154*
Amaranth (*Amaranthus* sp.), 197, 199, 210
Amphibians, *219*
Anatidae (duck, geese, swan), *173*, *218*
Ancestral kin cemeteries (Moundville), 44, 47–53; ancestral affiliation and, 57; detailed plan of, *50*; residential structures superimposed by, *48*
Angel Mounds, southern Indiana, xvii–xviii
Anhaica, Apalachee, 258
Animal remains. *See* Faunal assemblages
Animal spirits, 15
Anna mound site, Lower Mississippi Valley, 128
Asphalt Plant site, *135*, 137, *149*
Axes, nonutilitarian, 38

Ball fields, 257
Barton Incised, *var. Oliver*, 155
Bass (*Micropterus* sp.), *220*
Bayesian analysis, of radiocarbon dates, 6–7
Baytown Plain sherd count, *152*, *154*, 155
Beads, marine shell, 15, 38, 49, 92, 113, *114*; as most common artifact with copper gorgets, 116; as most common artifact with stone pendants, 115
Bead Spitter myth, 84, 92
Bean (*Phaseolus vulgaris*), 197, 199, 210
Bean family (Fabaceae), *198*, *200*, *211*
Bear (*Ursus americanus*), 175, *218*, 226, 227, *227*
Bearsfoot (*Smallanthus uvedalius*), *198*, *200*, *211*
Beaver (*Castor canadensis*), *218*, 226
Beech (*Fagus americana*), 197, *200*, 210
Bell Plain, *var. Hale*: beaded rim pottery, *152*, 152–57, *154*; sherd count, *152*, 153–57, *154*
Beneath World, connection to, 15
Benson Punctated sherd count, *152*, 152–57, *154*
Big Sandy Creek, 136–37
Big Sandy Farms site, *135*, 187, *189*; maize kernel-to-cupule ratio, *206*, 207; Moundville I–II plant assemblages, *188*; Moundville I–II standardized count of plants at, *201*; rural site locations, 162–65, *164*

Binford-Saxe approach, to burial, 99
Birds: bone concentrations at Cahokia, 228; Crested Bird theme, 39, 100, *101*; -effigy bowls, 113; feathered garments and ritual paraphernalia, 172–76, *173*, *176*, 181–82, 230; Gilliam site specimens, *176*; Grady Bobo site specimens, *173*; Grady Bobo site unusual assemblage of, 230; Mound Q specimens, *218–19*; as symbolic referents to cosmology and power, 226–27; as Above World representatives, 229. *See also* Owl effigies
Bison (*Bison* sp.), 36, 227, *227*
Black bear (*Ursus americanus*), *218*, 227
Blackberry/raspberry (*Rubus* sp.), 193, *197*, *200*, 211
Blackbirds (Icteridae), *173*, 174
Black Drink, 229
Black duck (*Anas platyrhynchos, rubripes*), *173*
Black hematite, *See* Psilomelane
Blacktail redhorse (*Moxostoma poecilurum*), 220
Black Warrior Valley, 4; Hammerstedt and Myer survey of, 18–19; historical sequence: 1998 version versus current version, *12*; Moundville I–III plant assemblages, *197–98*; Moundville as place of burial for all towns in, 263; nonmound sites, *135*; sherd counts from the UMMA, BWVS, and MCDF assemblages, *152*; sites with faunal assemblages, *189*; sites with plant assemblages, *189*
Black Warrior Valley Survey (BWVS), 137–39, *138*, *140*, *141*; distance between nonmound sites, 147–48, *148*; distribution of sites by survey area and period, *151*; environmental and social variables interpreted from, 148–49; Moundville, local center, and hamlet sites, *135*, 136–37; nonmound sites by topographic zone, 142, *142*; population trends by, *152*, 152–57; site density index calculation, 161n3; sites by distance to mound, *145*, 145–46; sites by distance to water, 142–43, *143*; sites by soil type, 143–45, *144*

Blue catfish (*Ictalurus furcatus*), 220
Blue/Channel catfish (*I.furcatus/punctatus*), 220
Blue heron (*Egretta caerulea*), *173*, 174, 230
Bobcat (*Lynx rufus*), 175, 226, *227*
Bobwhite (*Colinus virginianus*), *173*
Bone tools, from Grady Bobo site, *174*, 175
Bottle Creek site, Mobile Delta, 228
Bottles, engraved, 33, 100, *101*
Bowfin (*Amia calva*), 219
Bowls: bird-effigy, 90, *96*, 97, 113; ceramic serving vessels, 268; engraved carinated, *170*; flared-rim with scallops, 179; geometric design engraved, 168, 170, *170*, *171*, 172; as most common Hemphill-style artifact, 113, *113*, 114; stylistic analysis of, 100; terraced-rim, 33; with yellow pigment, 114. *See also* Bell Plain, *var. Hale*; Hemphill-style pottery
Box turtle (*Terrapene*), 219
Bronk Ramsey's agreement index, 7
Bundles, sacred medicine, 16–17, 81, 102, 125, 131, 133n3; corporate and personal, 132; manganese-rich black stains, 130, *130*; owl effigies carried in, 90, 92, *96*; palettes included in, 129, 234; war, to heal and to safely cross rivers, 90
BWVS. *See* Black Warrior Valley Survey

Ca'bi'tci (Speck's informant), 39
Caciques (chiefs), 1
Cahaba-Adaton-Ellisville soil series, 143–44, *144*
Cahokia, 23, 26, 30, 70, 76, 174; bird bone concentrations at, 228; Monks Mound, 29

Canada goose (*Branta canadensis*), 173, 218, 227, 230
Cane Creek site, 22n2
Cardinal (*Cardinalis cardinalis*), 173, 174, 230
Carnivore (Carnivora), 36, 218, 226, 228
Carolina Parakeet (*Conuropsis carolinensis*), 174–75
Carpetweed (*Mollugo verticilliata*), 198, 200, 211
Carthage Incised pottery sherds, 152, 154
Carthage phase, 9; as new chronological unit, 6; sherd counts for, 152, 152–57, 154, 156; sherd deposition rates by temporal unit, 157
Carving, fine, 34. *See also* Fine gray sandstone; Stone palettes
Catfish (Ictaluridae), 220, 231
Cemeteries: burials with more than one Hemphill-style genre, 116–17, 117; detailed plan of Residential Group 9, 48, 50; kin-group, 44, 47–53, 48, 50, 260–61; as materialization of inscribed social memory, 57; Moundville as necropolis for Path of Souls, 84–98; Moundville site as place of burial for all towns, 263; residential structures superimposed by, 48
Centering theme, 124, 125, 179
Center Symbols and Bands theme, 100, 101
Central Rayed Circle motif, 105
Centrarchids (Centrarchidae), 220
Ceramic serving vessel production, 168–72, 169, 170, 171
Ceremonial ground: Cahokia as multi-town, 267; Moundville as, 255–56, 261–67; Ohio Hopewell ceremonial center, 70; sacred artifacts indicating, 263–64; Southeastern Ceremonial Complex, 74
Cerrusite, 131
Channel catfish (*Ictalurus punctatus*), 220
Chattahoochee River, 29, 42n2

Chenopod (*Chenopodium berlandieri*), 193, 197, 199, 210
Chequamegon (at southern shore, Lake Superior), 78–79
Cherokee: "structural poses" among, 265; town of Citico, 262
Chert, special imported, 38
Chestnut (*Castanea dentata*), 197, 199, 210
Chickasaw, 28, 39, 256; camp square of, 263
Chiefdom, 1, 3, 5
Chiwere Siouan-speakers, 76
Choctaw, 28, 255, 256
Chronology: 1998 sequence and current sequence, 12; major changes to, 6–13; phase boundaries in Moundville chronology, 8
Citico, 262
Clans: "corporate subclans" compared to, 28; "house groups" compared to, 28; matrilineal, 258–59; Moundville as materialized clan relationships, 263; "social houses" compared to, 28; towns compared to, 20
Claystone, red and yellow ferruginous, 105
Cleaver (*Galium* sp.), 198, 200, 211
Coachwhip/racer (*Coluber Masticophus*), 219
Coarse-ware vessels, 172, 177–79, 178
Community structures, 258–59; civic planning, 47–49; greathouse, 15, 33, 92–94, 93; importance of rural social aggregates, 183; kin-based, 40, 44; special-purpose buildings, 47–49, 48; square grounds, ball fields, public and private buildings, 257. *See also* Ceremonial ground
Composite family (Compositae), 198, 201, 212
Cook site, 135
Cool Branch site, Chattahoochee River, 42n2
Coosa polity, 258, 267
Copper ear discs, 113, 114, 116

308 · Index

Copper gorgets, 105, *106*; age group variable in analysis of, *108*; in amount versus variety of grave goods analysis, *109*; conjectures about, 120; frequency of burials with, by mound versus off-mound, 109–11, *110*; sex variable in analysis of, 107–8, *109*; spatial distribution of excavation areas with, *112*, 116
Copper pendants, 38
Cougar (*Felis concolor*), 226, *227*
Courtyards, 47–49, *48*. *See also* Mound-and-plaza arrangement
Crappie (*Micropterus/Pomoxis*), 220
Cree, 76, 77
Creek, 28, 256
Crested Bird theme, 39, 100, *101*
Crow (Corvidae), 172, *173*, 174–75, 180, *219*; *Corvus brachyrhynchos*, *227*; Grady Bobo site specimens, 230
Cultural memory, 56. *See also* Selective forgetting
Cumberland Valley, 90

Dakota, 76, 77
Damnatio memoriae (condemnation of memory), 59–60; Mound X example of, 68–71
Deer and venison (*Odocoileus virginianus*), 36, 177, 179, 218, *218*, *221*, 230, 231; Grady Bobo site specimens, 230; Mounds G and Q, 226; preferred cuts of, 166–67; Wiggins specimens, 231
Delaware (people), 76, 77
Dhegiha Siouan-speakers, 76
Discoidals (gaming stones), 50, *51*
Diskettes, *235*, *239*, 254n2, 254n3
Dog (Canidae), *227*; domestic (*Canis familiaris*), 218, 227
Dome-shaped roof, at Moundville, 94, *95*
Duck (Anatidae), 172, *173*, 218, *227*, 230

Ear discs, copper-clad, 113, 114, 116
Earthlodge, 15, 94–96, *95*, 257
Earthmoving, 47–49, *48*

Eastern Woodlands, 70, 86, 131
Elderberry, *200*, 211
Elliotts Creek, 142
Etowah site, Georgia, 28, 42n5, 70; copper gorgets at, 105, *106*; palettes at, 102, 122, 128–29, 131, 132, 133n1
Evening primrose (*Oenothera* sp.), 197, *201*, 211

Fabric, impressions on palettes, 129, 234; manganese-rich stains, 130, *130*
Fall Line, at Tuscaloosa, 127–28, 194, 195
Faunal assemblages, 187–92; abundance of deer specimens at Moundville and White sites, *224*; abundance of major faunal taxa, *222*; Black Warrior Valley sites with, *189*; Grady Bobo site 7,000 specimens, 230; at Moundville, *190*; Moundville I–III, *192*; Moundville II–III anatomical units for large mammals, *222*; Moundville II–III assemblages in Mound Q: anatomical units for deer, *221*; Moundville II–III Mound Q specimens, *218–20*; procurement reorganization by late Moundville, 224, *224*; provisions to Moundville from hinterlands, *222*, 223–24. *See also* Foodways
Feasting, communal: importance of rural social aggregates, 183; at Moundville, 36–37; potluck approach to, 183–84, 229
Feathered garments, 172–76, *173*, *176*, 181–82, 230. *See also* Birds
Feline-effigy pipe, 113
Fine gray sandstone, 133n2, 153, 167, 176, 181, 240–43, 248–49; from Pottsville geological formation, 234, 236, 238
Fish: dorsal spines for tattooing, 230, 234; -effigy vessels, 97, 114
Fitts site, *135*
Five-phase ceramic chronology, xvii
Flathead catfish (*Pylodictis olivaris*), 220
Flicker (*Colaptes auratus*), *173*, 230
Flood-plain soils, 145
Florida cooter, *219*

Foodways: animal and plant remains evidencing, 187–92; Black Warrior Valley sites with faunal remains, *189*; meals of Moundville residents, 225–29; Moundville I–II of intensified food production, 193–94; Moundville I–II plant assemblages, *188*; Moundville I–III faunal assemblages, *192*; plant and animal assemblages at Moundville, *190*; provisioning meat, 215, 217, *218–20*, 221, *222*, 223–24, *224*; provisioning nuts, 196, 202, 202–3, 209, 213; ritual integration in outlying communities, 229–31; sacred, indicating ceremonial ground, 263–64

Fortification wall, Moundville, 1–2, *2*, 56, 60, 68

Fosters Ferry Landing site, 18, *135*, 137; 18th century Indian town compared to, *262*; in summary of environmental and social variables, 148–49, *149*

Fox (people), 76, *77*, 90

Fox (*Urocyon cinereoargenteus*), 226, 227, *227*

French contact, 7, *11*

Freshwater drum (*Aplodinotus grunniens*), *220*, 231

Frog effigies, 97

Frogs (*Rana* sp.), *219*

Galena, 33, 127, 129, 131

Gaming stones, 51

Gar: *Atractosteus spatula*, *219*; Lepisosteidae, *220*

Garments: bone needles and awls, *174*, 175; feathered, 172–76, *173*, *176*, 181–82, 230; ritual gear, 33; special emblems and regalia, 39

Geese (Branta Canadensis), *173*, *218*, *227*, 230

Ghost Lodge: medicine lodge as separate history from, 91, 92, 97–98; Midé Society separation/link to, 84–86, *85*; Ojibwa north-south alignment of, 84;

Ojibwa separation of Midewiwin from, 84–86, *85*; owl's role, 87–88, *88*

Gibbs Sampler statistical algorithm, 7, 9

Gilliam site, *135*, 165, 186, *189*; abundance of major faunal taxa at, *222*; bird bones at, *176*; Moundville I–III faunal assemblages, *192*; raptor bones at, 175; rural ceremonialism at, 231; rural site locations, 162–65, *164*

Glass mound site, Lower Mississippi Valley, 128

Glauconite, 127, 131

Gorgets, copper. *See* Copper gorgets

Gourd/squash (*Cucurbita* sp.), 193, *197*, *199*, *210*

Grackles (*Quiscalus sp.*), 172, *173*, 174, 230

Grady Bobo site, 18, *135*, *189*; 7,000 specimen faunal assemblage at, 230; abundance of major faunal taxa at, *222*; bird specimens from, *173*, 230; bone tools from, *174*; communal meals evidence at, 177–79, *178*; deer and venison specimens, 230; engraved beaker with engraved design, *171*, 172; maize kernel-to-cupule ratio, *206*, 207; Moundville I–II plant assemblages, *188*; Moundville I–III faunal assemblages from, *192*; Moundville I–II standardized count of plants at, *201*; passenger pigeon specimens, 230; profile and plan of, *171*; rural site locations, 162–65, *164*

Grants Swamp mound, 161n1

Grape (*Vitis* sp.), 193, *197*, *200*, *211*

Grass family (Poaceae), *198*, *201*, *212*

Graveline Mound, Mississippi, 228

Gray fox (*Urocyon cinereoargenteus*), 226, 227, *227*

Gray's Landing, *135*, 137, *149*

Greater scaup (*Aythya marilla*), *227*

Greathouse, 15, 33, 92–94, *93*

Greenstone, 33, 63, 105, 166

Grinding slab, 238–40, *239*, *243*, 248

Grog-tempered sherds, 6, 22n2, 150–52, *152*, *154*, 155–56

Grooved abraders, 238–39, *239*, 254n1
Ground-stone debris, at Pride Place, *239*, 248

Hackberry (*Celtis* sp.), *197*, *200*, *211*
Hammerstone, 238, *239*, 241; quartzite, 242–43
Hawk (*Buteo* sp.), 226, 227, 231; as potent object, 176; red-tailed, 175, *176*, *177*, *219*, 227
Hazelnut (*Corylus* sp.), *197*, *200*, *211*
Hematite, 131
Hemphill-style artifacts, 16, 75, 97–100; amount versus variety of grave goods, *109*; analysis of, 106–11; burials with, by genre, *113*; co-occurrence of genres in burials, 116–17, *117*; distribution of, 99–100; four genres of, 100–106; frequency of burials with, *107*; sex as variable for burials with, 107–8, *109*
Hemphill-style copper gorgets. *See* Copper gorgets
Hemphill-style palettes. *See* Stone palettes
Hemphill-style pendants. *See* Stone pendants
Hemphill-style pottery: age group variable in analysis of, *108*; in amount versus variety of grave goods analysis, *109*; ceramic serving vessel production, 168–72, *169*, *170*, *171*; conjectures about, 118–19; frequency of burials with, by mound versus off-mound, 109–11, *110*; sex variable in analysis of, 107–8, *109*; spatial distribution of excavation areas with, 111–13, *112*, *113*; two basic vessel shapes, 100, *101*. *See also* Bowls
Heron: bitterns (Ardeidae), *173*; little blue (*Egretta caerulea*), *173*, 174, 230
Hickory (*Carya* sp.), 193, 196, *197*, *200*, *202*, 202–3, 209, *209*, *211*, 213, 215
Hill's Gin Landing site, *135*, 137
Hinterland hamlets: communities, 17–20; encompassing Moundville, *4*; faunal provisions to Moundville from, *222*, 223–24; hickory and acorn shell from Moundville I, 201–3, *202*; maize kernel-to-cupule ratio, *206*, *207*; Moundville I–II plant assemblages, *188*; Moundville I–III faunal assemblages, *192*; Moundville II–III sites, 194–95; provisioning of Moundville from, 166; ritual integration in, 229–31; throughout Black Warrior Valley, *197–98*; two kinds of sites in, 3. *See also* Rural life
Hog Pen site, *135*, 187, *189*, 260; Moundville I hickory and acorn shells, 201–3, *202*; Moundville I–II plant assemblages, *188*; Moundville I–II standardized count of plants at, *201*; Moundville I–III, *197–98*; ritual meals during late Moundville I, 229, 230; in summary of environmental and social variables, 148–49, *149*
Holly (*Ilex* sp.), *198*, *201*, *211*
Hornbeam (*Carpinus* sp.), *198*, *201*, *211*
Hull Lake area, 155

Iconography: diffusion of, 75–78; Hemphill-style pendant, 119–20; in high-status burials, 42n5; medicine lodge, 91, *92*; our incomplete understanding of, 14–17, 163–64; Raptor theme, 39, 100, *101*, 175–76, *176*, 180–81, 228; rural commoners' elaborate, 167; in Weeks' Midewiwin study, 83–84. *See also* Owl effigies
Illinois (people), 76, *77*, 80
Inscribed memory, 56–57
Ioway, 76, *77*

Jays (Corvidae), *173*, 174
Jones Ferry site, 22n2, *135*, 194, 260

Kansa, 76, *77*
Kickapoo, 76, *77*
Kin-based community, 40, 44. *See also* Cemeteries
Kin group, 14
King site, Coosa polity, 258
Kits, palette, 129

Knotweed (*Polygonum erectum*), *197*, *199*, 210
Knudgie balls, 202

Lake George mound site, Lower Mississippi Valley, 128
Landbridge mound, *135*, 136, 137, 161n2, 165
Landrum mound site, Lower Mississippi Valley, 128
Lapidary work, 33, 34, 238, 252. *See also* Stone palettes
Large mammals, *222*
Largemouth bass (*Micropterus salmoides*), *220*
Late Woodland period, 9; nonmound sites by distance to Moundville, *147*, 147–48, *148*; nonmound sites by topographic zone, 142, *142*; population trend, 150–52, *151*; sites by distance to single-mound, *145*, 145–46; sites by distance to water, 142–43, *143*; sites by soil type, 143–45, *144*, 159, 161n3; sites in combined MCDF-BWVS study area, *140*; Terminal Woodland house style, 61
Limonite, 127
Little barley (*Hordeum pusillum*), 193, *197*, *199*, 210
Little blue heron (*Ergretta caerulea*), *173*, 174, 230
Little Egypt site, 258, 267
Lower Mississippi Valley: Moundville palettes transported to, 128; owl-bearing post as temple feature in, 88, 88–89, *89*; St. Louis Mound Group, 26, 267; Winterville site, 26, 226, 267
Lubbub Creek site, west central Alabama, xvii, 174–75, 230
Lucedale-Greenville-Bama soil series, 143–44, *144*

Maize (*Zea mays*), 3, *197*, 199, 210; increased consumption of, 166–67, 179; kernel-to-cupule ratio at Moundville, 203, *204*, *205*–6, 207, *214*, *216*; Moundville history and reliance on, 193–95; as primary agricultural staple, 203–14; status-related consumption of, 196, 203–14; storage of, 203
Mallard (*Anas platyrhynchos*), *173*
Mallow family (Malvaceae), *198*, *201*, *212*
Mandan, 76, *77*
Manganese-rich stains, 130, *130*
Markov Chain Monte Carlo (MCMC) algorithm, 8, *10*
Marr's Spring Creek, 238, 240
Matrilineal clans, 258–59
Maygrass (*Phalaris caroliniana*), 193, *197*, *199*, 210
Maypop (*Passiflora incarnata*), *197*, 200, *211*
MCDF. *See* Moundville Coal Degasification Field
MCMC. *See* Markov Chain Monte Carlo
Meat. *See* Faunal assemblages
Medicine lodge: distribution of, related to Midé Society, 75–77, *77*; Ghost Lodge separate history from, 91, 92, 97–98; Lower Mississippi Valley, *89*; in Wilson's ethnographic survey, 88, 90
Menominee, 76–77, *77*; Owl Dance of, 90
Merlin (*Falco columbarius*), 175
Miami-Illinois medicine society, 80
Mica, 63, 114, 127, 131
Micaceous sandstone, 105
Middle World, 15
Midé (Midewiwin) Society: Acolapissa temple from Lower Mississippi Valley, *89*; characteristics of, 78; dating for creation of, 79–84; Ghost Lodge separation/link to, 84–86, *85*; medicine lodge related to, 15, 76–77, *77*; at Moundville, 91–98; Natchez temple from Lower Mississippi Valley, *89*; Ojibwa medicine society and, 82–91; Ojibwa Red Lake Scroll, *85*, *87*, *88*, *89*; owl effigies in, 86–91, *88*; as revitalization movement versus precolonial, 79–83; shamans of, 76–79, 83, 84, 86–87, *87*, 92; why Moundville iconography compares to, 74–79

Milky Way, as Path of Souls, 84
Mill Creek site, *135*
Mink (*Mustela vison*), *218*, 226, *227*
Minter Creek site, *135*
Mississippian Iconography Workshop, 15
Mississippi period, *140*, 140–42, *141*; Fosters Landing compared with 18th century Indian town, *262*; non-mound components, *143*; nonmound sites by topographic zone, *142*; population decrease during, 159–60; population trend, 150–52, *151*; site density index for, 143, 146, *147*, 150, 161n3; sites in combined MCDF-BWVS study area, *141*, 141–46, 148–50, 155–56; wall-trench construction, 61
Mississippi Plain sherd count, *152*, 152–57, *154*
Monks Mound, 29
Morninglory (*Ipomoea/ Convolvulus*), *198*, *201*, *211*
Mound A, 25, 35, 41, 42n5
Mound-and-plaza arrangement: four readings of, 26–31, *27*; indicating Moundville as ceremonial ground, 255–56; as materialization of inscribed social memory, 57; schematic of, *24*; summary of spatial qualities, 24–26
Mound B, 25, 38, 41, 42n5
Mound C, 42n5, 129, 132
Mound D, 94
Mound E, 15, 33, 92, *93*, 94–95, 97, *188*, *191*, *192*, *201*; ground-stone debris, tools, craft items, *239*; palette manufacture at, 238, 248
Mound F, 42n4, 94, *188*, *191*, *192*, *201*, *205*, *212*
Mound G, 26, 34, 42, *191*, *192*, *205*, *212*, 215, 225–26; unusual animals from, *227*, 227–28, 267
Mound O, 40
Mound Q, 32–34, 42n4, 92, 94, 97, 215–17, 223; bird specimens, 218–19; changing landscape and foodways at, 224–25; deer unit specimens, *221*, *224*; faunal assemblages, 218–20, *221*; large mammals in, *222*; unusual animals from, *227*
Mound R, 34, *45*, 97, 127, *154*, *188*, *191*, *192*, 196, *201*, *212*, 228
Mound U, 40
Mound V, 15, 92, 94, *95*, *96*
Moundville I–II, *8*, *11*; annual sherd deposition rates, *152*, 152–57, *154*, *156*; communal feasting, 184; consolidation of regional polity, 193–94; hickory and acorn shell from, *202*; plant assemblages from, *188*; sherd deposition rates by temporal unit, *157*; standardized count of plants from, *199–201*
Moundville I–III, faunal assemblages, *192*
Moundville II–III, *8*, *11*; annual sherd deposition rates, *152*, 152–57, *154*, *156*; deer specimens at Moundville Mound Q, *221*, *224*; large mammals at Moundville Mound Q, *222*; plant assemblages from, *191*; population exodus from Moundville, 49, 148, 158, 194–95, 261; sherd deposition rates by temporal unit, *157*
Moundville III–IV, *11*, 13, 18–19, 195; end of Moundville IV, *8*; Moundville IV renamed, 6
Moundville Chronology: Phase Boundaries, 7–8, *8*
Moundville Coal Degasification Field (MCDF) Project, 134, *138*, 138–40; BWVS sites combined with sites of, *140*, *141*; distance between nonmound sites, 147–48, *148*; distribution of sites by survey area and period, *151*; environmental and social variables interpreted from, 148–49; nonmound sites by distance to Moundville, 146–47, *147*; nonmound sites by topographic zone, 142, *142*; population trends by, *152*, 152–57; site density index calculation, 161n3; sites by distance to mound,

145, 145–46; sites by distance to water, 142–43, *143*; sites by soil type, 143–45, *144*; surveyed well pads, *139*
Moundville Engraved, *var. Cypress*, 100
Moundville Engraved, *var. Hemphill*, 100, 111, *152, 154*
Moundville Engraved sherd count, *152*, 152–57, *154*
Moundville Incised, *var. Oliver*, 177–78, *178*, 187, 234, 238; contemporarily-crafted incised palette to replicate, *244*; sherd count, *152*, 152–57, *154*
Moundville Incised pottery, *152, 154*
Moundville site: abundance of anatomical units for large mammals: Moundville II and III, *222*; as ceremonial ground, 255–56, 261–67; changing landscape and foodways at, 224–25; chronology, 6–13, 35–36; classic interpretation of, 3; communal feasting evidenced at, 36–37; competing models of monumental space, 37–41; coordinated initial construction, 34–35; deer specimens at Mounds G and Q, *221, 224*, 226; duality of mound categories, 32–34; excavation areas, *44*; hickory and acorn shell from Moundville I, 201–3, *202*; hickory and acorn shell from late Moundville III, *215*; hinterland encompassing, *4*; labor requirements for earthworks of, 37; large mammals in Mound Q, *222*; localities with plant and animal assemblages, *190*; maize kernel-to-cupule ratio, 203, *204, 205, 214, 216*; as materialized clan relationships, 263; meals of residents at, 225–29; Moundville I–III plants identified at, *197–98*; new perspectives on, 20–21; nonmound sites' distances from, *135*, 136–37, 146–47, *147*; palisade wall, 1–2, *2*, 56, 60, 68; as place of burial for all towns, 263; population exodus from, 49, 148, 158, 194–95, 261; rural peoples' importance in polity of, 180–85; settlement and demographic history, 259–61; synopsis of history, 179–95. *See also* Cemeteries, kin-group; Faunal assemblages; Plant assemblages; *specific mounds*
Mound X, 60–64; as *Damnatio memoriae* example, 68–71; decommissioning of, 63, 127, 260, 266; location and projected palisade line, *62*; north profile at western portion of, *67*; palisade wall running through, *68*; plan of excavations at, *65*; study area with location of 2004 excavations, *64*; with palisade lines and refilled 1983 excavation trench, *66*
Mouse (*Peromyscus* sp.), *218*
Mud/musk turtle (*Kinosternon*), *219*
Mulberry Creek Cord Marked, *152, 154*, 154–55
Muskogean-speaking peoples, 28, 76, 256

Neo-evolutionary model, 5, 266
Nightshade (*Solanum* sp.), *198, 201, 211*
Nonmound sites, 18; animal and plant assemblages at mound sites versus, 228–29; in BWVS survey, 134, 137–38, *138*; distance between, 147–48, *148*; distance to Moundville, *135*, 136–37, 146–47, *147*; distance to single-mound sites, *145*, 145–46; distance to water, 142–43, *143*; history of research on, 18, 134–37; Late Woodland and Mississippian landscapes, *140*, 140–42, *141*, 159; in MCDF Project, 134, 138–40, *139*; population trends by, *152*, 152–57, *154*; population trends by period, 150–51, *151*; sites, *135*; in summary of environmental and social variables, 148–49, *149*; topographic zone, 142, *142*
Northwest Riverbank, 187, 196, 233
Nuts: provisioning, 196, *202*, 202–3, 209, 213; status-related consumption of, 196. *See also* Acorn; Foodways; Hickory

Oconee Valley, Georgia, 264
Ohio Hopewell ceremonial center rituals, 70
Oicotypes, 86
Ojibwa: east-west progression depicted on Midé scroll, *95*; Hickerson on Midé Society of, 79–81, 82; Midewiwin society of, 82–91; north-south alignment of Ghost Lodge, 84; Red Lake Scroll, *85, 87, 88, 89*
Okla ("town"), 256
Oliver site, *135, 189*; abundance of major faunal taxa at, *222*; maize kernel-to-cupule ratio, *206*, 207; Moundville I–II plant assemblages, *188*; Moundville I–II standardized count of plants at, *199–201*; Moundville I–III faunal assemblages, *192*; rural site locations, 162–65, *164*. See also Moundville Incised, *var.* Oliver
Omaha, 39, 76, *77*
Opossum (*Didelphis virginianus*), 218
Orioles (Icteridae), *173*, 174
Orpheus quest, 86, 92
Osage, 30, 39, 76, *77*
Otoe, 76, *77*
Ottawa, 76, *77*
Otter pouch and shells rite, shamanic, 78, 83, 84, 92
Overhill Cherokee, 262
Owl (*Otus asio*), *173*, 230
Owl effigies: atop medicine lodge posts, 88, 88–89, *89*; Midé Society, 86–91, *88*; Moundville, 15, 94, *96*, 97; Owl Dance of Menominee, 90; in sacred bundles, 90, 92, *96*
OxCal, 7, 9; phase boundaries in Moundville chronology, *8*; previous versus current sequence using, *12*

Painted turtle (*Chrysemys picta*), 219
Palettes, 33, 38, *103*; age group variable in analysis of, *108*; in amount versus variety of grave goods analysis, *109*; archaeological correlates of sandstone and palette crafting, *243*; conjectures about, 118–20; crafting and distribution of, 127–28; cross sections of typical, *124*; derivation of spiritual qualities of, 252, 253; evidence of use, 128–31, *130*; frequency of burials with, by mound versus off-mound, 109–11, *110*; at Mound E, 238, 248; as portable altars, 16–17, 102; present-day-crafted experimental, *244*; as prestige goods or inalienable possessions, 122–32, *123, 124, 125, 126*; Pride Place, *235,* 236–39, *237, 239*; restricted to religious elites, 181; in sacred bundles, 129, 234; sex variable in analysis of, 107–8, *109*; spatial distribution of excavation areas with, *112, 113*, 113–14; as tangible sign of religious knowledge, 16–17; transported to Lower Mississippi Valley, 128; two ways to restrict ownership of, 249–52, 253. See also Pride Place; *specific palette*
Palisade, Moundville, 1–2, *2*, 56, 60, 68
Paramount center, 255
Partridge (Phasianidae), *173*
Passenger pigeon (*Ectopistes migratorius*), 172, 179; Gilliam site specimens, *176*, 231; Grady Bobo site specimens, *173*, 230; Moundville II–III, *219*; significance of, 227–28
Passerine, 175
Path of Souls: Ghost Lodge north-south axis as, 84; Midé members' right to, 82; Moundville as necropolis for, 84–98; point of entry to, 15
Pawnee, 76, *77*
Peavine/vetch (*Vicia* sp.), *198, 200, 211*
Pebble Society, 76
Pecan (*Carya illinoinensis*), *197, 200, 211*
Peebles, Christopher S., 3, 44, 92, 136; Binford-Saxe approach used by, 99; on hinterland provisioning of Moundville, 166; legacy of, xv, xv–xviii
Pendants, 33, 102–5, *104*; age group

variable in analysis of, *108*; in amount versus variety of grave goods analysis, *109*; conjectures about, 119; copper, 38; frequency of mound versus off-mound specimens, 109–11, *110*; iconograpy, 119–20; sex variable in analysis of, 107–8, *109*; spatial distribution of excavation areas with, *112*, 115

Penobscot, 76, *77*

Peregrine falcon (*Falco peregrinus*), 36, 121, 227, *227*

Persimmon (*Diospyros virginiana*), 193, *197*, *200*, 211

Phase boundaries in Moundville chronology, *8*

Pigments, minerals and, 33, 39

Pink family (Caryophyllaceae), *198*, 201, 212

Pipes, sacred, 39, 263–64; feline-effigy, 113

P. J. site, *135*

Place-based identity politics, 56

Plant assemblages, 187–92, *199–201*; Black Warrior Valley sites with, *189*; mound versus nonmound, 228–29; at Moundville, *190*; Moundville I–II plant assemblages, *188*; Moundville II–III plant assemblages, *191*; Moundville I–III, *197–98*; Moundville I–II standardized count of, *199–201*

Plaza: four models of space around central, 26–29, *143*; hides reference points of prior use, 70–71; as materialization of inscribed social memory, 57; as sociogram, 13–14, 23. *See also* Mound-and-plaza arrangement

Plum/cherry (*Prunus* sp.), 193, *198*, *200*, 211

Poellnitz site, *135*, 137, 194, 260; in summary of environmental and social variables, 148–49, *149*

Pokeweed (*Phytolacca americana*), *198*, 201, 212

Poles, sacred, 39

Political environment, 40–41, 42n5

Ponca, 76, *77*

Population exodus, 49

Portable altars, 16–17, 102, 129, 176

Pottawatomie, 76, *77*

Pottery, Hemphill-style. *See* Hemphill-style pottery

Pottsville geological formation, 234, 236, 238

Powers site, *135*

Pride Place, 18, 127–28, *135*; archaeological correlates of sandstone and palette crafting, *243*; experimentally based evaluation of sandstone assemblage at, 240–49, *244*, *245*, *246–47*; ground-stone debris, tools, craft items, *239*, 248; palette production at, 176; rural site locations, 162–65, *164*; stone palettes at, *235*, 236–39, *237*, *239*

Priests, shamans compared to, 76–77

Psilomelane (black hematite), 131

Purslane (*Portulaca oleracea*), *198*, 201, 212

Quail (Phasianidae), 172, *173*, 230

Quartz cobbles, 33, 240, 241, 242–43

Rabbit sp. (*Sylvilagus* sp.), 177, 225, 226, 230, 231; Eastern cottontail (*Sylvilagus virginianus*), 218; Swamp rabbit (*Sylvilagus aquaticus*), 218

Raccoon (*Procyon lotor*), 177, *218*, 226, 230, 231

Radiocarbon dates, Bayesian analysis of, 6–7

Raptor (Accipitridae), 175–76, *176*, 180, 181, 228

Raptor theme, 39, 100, *101*, 175–76, *176*; symbolic importance of, 180–81, 228

Raspberry. *See* Blackberry/raspberry

Rat (Cricetidae), *218*

Rattlesnake Disk, 124, *126*, 235, 251

Redhead (*Aythya americana*), 227

Redhorse sp. (*Moxostoma* sp.), 220

Red Lake Scroll, 85, *87*, *88*; Lower Mississippi Valley medicine lodge, *89*

Red-tailed hawk (*Buteo jamaicensis*), 175, *176*, *177*, *227*; Moundville II and III, *219*
Regional center, 255
Religious solidarities, 15; Central Plains tribes model of, 29–30, 39, 265–67; monuments as loci sponsored by, 27
Repressive erasure: decommissioning of Mound X, 63, 127, 260, 266; palisade wall through Mound X as, 68–71
Reptiles, *219*, 223
Residential Group 9, 48, *50*
Revitalization movement, 79–83
Rhodes site, 40, 176
Ritual economy, 38–39
Ritual gear, 33
River redhorse (*Moxostoma carinatum*), 220
Robin (*Turdis migratorius*), 173
Rood's Landing site, 29
Rosedale mound site, Lower Mississippi Valley, 128
Rural life: ceramic serving vessel production, 168–72, *169*, *170*, *171*; comestibles production, 166–67; communal meals, 177–79, *178*; feathered garments and ritual paraphernalia, 172–76, *173*, *176*, 181–82, 230; importance of, in Moundville polity, 180–85; mortuary practice, 179–80; population exodus from Moundville, 49, 148, 158, 194–95, 261; possible ritual paraphernalia, 180; production/manufacturing in Moundville polity, 165–66; ritual practices, 177, 182–85; site locations, 162–65, *164*. *See also* Hinterland hamlets

Sacred fire, perpetual, 32
Sandhill crane (*Grus canadensis*), 227
Sandstone: experimentally based evaluation of Pride Place assemblage, 240–49, *244*, *245*, *246–47*; fine gray, 133n2, 153, 167, 176, 181, 234, 236, 238, 240–43, 248–49
Sauk, 76, *77*

Saw, 238, *239*
Scalloped circle motif, 105
Scalp locks, 39
Screech owl (*Otus asio*), *173*, 174, 230
Sedge family (Cyperaceae), *198*, *201*, *212*
Selective forgetting, 14, 54; culture change and social memory, 55–59; Mound X archaeological example of, *64*; palisade wall through Mound X as, 68–71; plazas hide reference points of prior use, 70–71; repressive erasure and, 59–60
Serpents, 15; intertwined, surrounding a hand, 124. *See also* Winged Serpent
Serving vessel production, 168–72, *169*, *170*, *171*
Sex, as variable for burials with Hemphill-style artifacts, 107–8, *109*
Shamans: Hoffman's characterization of, 78–79; initiation by "death," 78, 83, 84, 92; misuse of power, 86–87, *87*; palette ownership by, 249–52; priests compared to, 76–77
Shark (Carcharhinidae), 36, 227, *227*
Shawnee, 76, *77*
Shellfish, 177
Shell (marine) ornaments, 39, 179. *See also* Beads, marine shell
Shells and otter pouch rite, shamanic, 78, 83, 84, 92
Shell Society, 76
Shell-tempered sherd count, *152*
Shooting rite, shamanic, 78, 83, 84, 92
Short-nosed gar (*Lepisosteus platostomus*), 220
Single-mound sites, 18, 195; distance between, *145*, 145–46; maize kernel-to-cupule ratio at, *206*, 207; Moundville I–II plant assemblages, *188*; Moundville I–III faunal assemblages, *192*; Moundville II–III plant assemblages, *191*; rooted in earlier Woodland communities, 266
Siouan-speaking peoples, 76, 91
Site density index, 143, 146, *147*, 150,

161n3; Late Woodland versus Mississippian, 143, 146, *147*, 150, 161n3
Skunk (*Mephitis mephitis*), 227, *227*
Small mammals, *218*; land clearance or forest regrowth indicated by, 223–25
Smallmouth buffalo fish (*Ictiobus bubalus*), *220*
Smartweed (*Polygonum* sp.), *198, 201, 212*
Smithdale-Luverne-Maubila soil series, 143–44, *144*
Snapping turtle (*Chelydra serpentina*), *219*, 239
Snows Bend site, *135*, 195
Social memory, 56; culture change and selective forgetting, 55–59; inscribed in spatial order, 13–14, 23, 57. *See also* Selective forgetting
Sociogram, 13–14, 23, 52, 57–58
Soft-shelled turtle (Trionychidae), *219*
Soil types, 143–45, *144*
Songbirds (Passeriformes), *173, 176,* 180, 231
Southeastern Ceremonial Complex, 74
Spiro, Oklahoma, 105
Spurge family (Euphorbiaceae), *198, 201, 212*
Squash/gourd (*Cucurbita* sp.), 193, *197, 199, 210*
Squirrel sp. (*Sciurus* sp.), 177, *218*, 225, 226, 230; Eastern fox squirrel (*Sciurus niger*), *218*; Eastern gray squirrel (*Sciurus carolinensis*), *218*
Stable-isotope corrections, 6
Stephens Bluff site, *135*
St. Louis Mound Group, 26, 267
Stone diskettes. *See* Diskettes
Stone palettes. *See* Palettes
Stone pendants. *See* Pendants
Striped skunk (*Mephitis mephitis*), 227
Structural amnesia, 71. *See also* Selective forgetting
Structural poses, 265
Sucker (Catostomidae), *220*
Sumac (*Rhus* sp.), *198, 200, 211*

Sumpweed (*Iva annua*), 193, *197, 199, 210*
Sunflower (*Helianthus annuus*), *197, 199, 210*
Swans (*Olor buccinator*), *173,* 174, 180, 230
Swastika (swirl cross), 15, 105

Talwa ("town"), 256
Tattoo, 230, 234
Terminal Woodland house style, 61
Textiles, 129–30, *130, 174,* 175
Thermoluminescence dating, 7
Thunder Beings, 39
Toads (*Bufo* sp.), *219*
Tobacco (*Nicotiana* sp.), *197, 199, 210,* 229, 232; restricted to ritual, elite, or mound-top contexts, 229, 232
Toqua, Tennessee, 230
Touson Lake mound, *135,* 137, 148–49, *149*
Town: affiliation by, 255; Citico, *262*; clan compared to, 20; multi-town gatherings of house groups, 259–63, *262*
Town Creek, 267
Tree-ring calibrations, 6, 7
Trophy theme, 100, *101*
Turkey (*Meleagris gallopavo*), 172, 179, *219,* 227; Gilliam site specimens, *176*; Grady Bobo site specimens, *173,* 230–31; importance of, 36
Turtles, *219*

UMMA. *See* University of Michigan Museum of Anthropology
University of Alabama, 137–38
University of Michigan Museum of Anthropology (UMMA), *152*
Upper Pottsville sandstone, 102, 105

Verbena (*Verbena* sp.), *198, 201, 212*
Viper (Viperidae), *219. See also* Serpents

Walnut (*Juglans nigra*), *197,* 200, *211*
War bundle, to heal and to safely cross rivers, 90
Water Monster, 39

Water privet (*Forestiera angustifolia*), 198, 201, 212
Well pads, 19, 138–40, *139*
West Jefferson phase, 6, *8*, 9–10, *10*, *12*, 159, 260; annual sherd deposition rates, *152*, 152–57, *154*, *156*; communal feasting during, 184; sherd deposition rates by temporal unit, *157*; shortened and shifted, 7–8
White ibis (*Eudocimis alba*), 227
White site, *135*, *189*, 195, *197–98*, 213, 217, 223; abundance of deer specimens, *224*; abundance of major faunal taxa at, *222*; hickory and acorn shell from late Moundville III, *215*; maize kernel-to-cupule ratio, *216*; Moundville I–III, *197–98*; Moundville I–III faunal assemblages, *192*; Moundville II–III plant assemblages, *191*; in summary of environmental and social variables, 148–49, *149*
White-tailed deer. *See* Deer and venison
Wiggins site, 18, *135*, *189*, *201*; communal meals evidence at, 177–79, *178*, 231; engraved carinated bowl from, *170*; maize kernel-to-cupule ratio, *206*, *207*; Moundville I–II plant assemblages, *188*; Moundville I–III faunal assemblages, *192*; Moundville I–II standardized count of plants at, *199–201*; profile and plan of, *169*; rural site locations, 162–65, *164*
Wild bean (*Strophosteles* sp.), *198*, *200*, 211
Wild rice (*Zizania aquatica*), *198*, *201*, *212*; restricted to ritual, elite, or mound-top contexts, 228, 232
Willoughby Disk, 124–25, *126*, *235*, 251, 254n1
Winged Serpent theme, 15, 39, 100–101, *101*
Winnebago, 76, *77*
Winterville site, Lower Mississippi Valley, 26, 226, 267
Witchcraft, 86–87. *See also* Shamans
Wood duck (*Aix sponsa*), *218*, 227
Wood sorrel (*Oxalis* sp.), *198*, *201*, *212*

Yaupon (*Ilex vomitoria*), *198*, *201*, *212*; as Black Drink primary constituent, 229; restricted to ritual, elite, or mound-top contexts, 228, 232
Yellow stargrass (*Hypoxis* sp.), *197*, *201*, *212*
Yuchi, 259

RIPLEY P. BULLEN SERIES
Florida Museum of Natural History

Tacachale: Essays on the Indians of Florida and Southeastern Georgia during the Historic Period, edited by Jerald T. Milanich and Samuel Proctor (1978)
Aboriginal Subsistence Technology on the Southeastern Coastal Plain during the Late Prehistoric Period, by Lewis H. Larson (1980)
Cemochechobee: Archaeology of a Mississippian Ceremonial Center on the Chattahoochee River, by Frank T. Schnell, Vernon J. Knight Jr., and Gail S. Schnell (1981)
Fort Center: An Archaeological Site in the Lake Okeechobee Basin, by William H. Sears, with contributions by Elsie O'R. Sears and Karl T. Steinen (1982)
Perspectives on Gulf Coast Prehistory, edited by Dave D. Davis (1984)
Archaeology of Aboriginal Culture Change in the Interior Southeast: Depopulation during the Early Historic Period, by Marvin T. Smith (1987)
Apalachee: The Land between the Rivers, by John H. Hann (1988)
Key Marco's Buried Treasure: Archaeology and Adventure in the Nineteenth Century, by Marion Spjut Gilliland (1989)
First Encounters: Spanish Explorations in the Caribbean and the United States, 1492–1570, edited by Jerald T. Milanich and Susan Milbrath (1989)
Missions to the Calusa, edited and translated by John H. Hann, with an introduction by William H. Marquardt (1991)
Excavations on the Franciscan Frontier: Archaeology at the Fig Springs Mission, by Brent Richards Weisman (1992)
The People Who Discovered Columbus: The Prehistory of the Bahamas, by William F. Keegan (1992)
Hernando de Soto and the Indians of Florida, by Jerald T. Milanich and Charles Hudson (1993)
Foraging and Farming in the Eastern Woodlands, edited by C. Margaret Scarry (1993)
Puerto Real: The Archaeology of a Sixteenth-Century Spanish Town in Hispaniola, edited by Kathleen Deagan (1995)
Political Structure and Change in the Prehistoric Southeastern United States, edited by John F. Scarry (1996)
Bioarchaeology of Native American Adaptation in the Spanish Borderlands, edited by Brenda J. Baker and Lisa Kealhofer (1996)
A History of the Timucua Indians and Missions, by John H. Hann (1996)
Archaeology of the Mid-Holocene Southeast, edited by Kenneth E. Sassaman and David G. Anderson (1996)
The Indigenous People of the Caribbean, edited by Samuel M. Wilson (1997; first paperback edition, 1999)

Hernando de Soto among the Apalachee: The Archaeology of the First Winter Encampment, by Charles R. Ewen and John H. Hann (1998)
The Timucuan Chiefdoms of Spanish Florida, by John E. Worth: vol. 1, *Assimilation*; vol. 2, *Resistance and Destruction* (1998)
Ancient Earthen Enclosures of the Eastern Woodlands, edited by Robert C. Mainfort Jr. and Lynne P. Sullivan (1998)
An Environmental History of Northeast Florida, by James J. Miller (1998)
Precolumbian Architecture in Eastern North America, by William N. Morgan (1999)
Archaeology of Colonial Pensacola, edited by Judith A. Bense (1999)
Grit-Tempered: Early Women Archaeologists in the Southeastern United States, edited by Nancy Marie White, Lynne P. Sullivan, and Rochelle A. Marrinan (1999; first paperback edition, 2000)
Coosa: The Rise and Fall of a Southeastern Mississippian Chiefdom, by Marvin T. Smith (2000)
Religion, Power, and Politics in Colonial St. Augustine, by Robert L. Kapitzke (2001)
Bioarchaeology of Spanish Florida: The Impact of Colonialism, edited by Clark Spencer Larsen (2001)
Archaeological Studies of Gender in the Southeastern United States, edited by Jane M. Eastman and Christopher B. Rodning (2001)
The Archaeology of Traditions: Agency and History Before and After Columbus, edited by Timothy R. Pauketat (2001)
Foraging, Farming, and Coastal Biocultural Adaptation in Late Prehistoric North Carolina, by Dale L. Hutchinson (2002)
Windover: Multidisciplinary Investigations of an Early Archaic Florida Cemetery, edited by Glen H. Doran (2002)
Archaeology of the Everglades, by John W. Griffin (2002; first paperback edition, 2017)
Pioneer in Space and Time: John Mann Goggin and the Development of Florida Archaeology, by Brent Richards Weisman (2002)
Indians of Central and South Florida, 1513–1763, by John H. Hann (2003)
Presidio Santa María de Galve: A Struggle for Survival in Colonial Spanish Pensacola, edited by Judith A. Bense (2003)
Bioarchaeology of the Florida Gulf Coast: Adaptation, Conflict, and Change, by Dale L. Hutchinson (2004; first paperback edition, 2020)
The Myth of Syphilis: The Natural History of Treponematosis in North America, edited by Mary Lucas Powell and Della Collins Cook (2005)
The Florida Journals of Frank Hamilton Cushing, edited by Phyllis E. Kolianos and Brent R. Weisman (2005)
The Lost Florida Manuscript of Frank Hamilton Cushing, edited by Phyllis E. Kolianos and Brent R. Weisman (2005)

The Native American World Beyond Apalachee: West Florida and the Chattahoochee Valley, by John H. Hann (2006)

Tatham Mound and the Bioarchaeology of European Contact: Disease and Depopulation in Central Gulf Coast Florida, by Dale L. Hutchinson (2006)

Taíno Indian Myth and Practice: The Arrival of the Stranger King, by William F. Keegan (2007)

An Archaeology of Black Markets: Local Ceramics and Economies in Eighteenth-Century Jamaica, by Mark W. Hauser (2008; first paperback edition, 2013)

Mississippian Mortuary Practices: Beyond Hierarchy and the Representationist Perspective, edited by Lynne P. Sullivan and Robert C. Mainfort Jr. (2010; first paperback edition, 2012)

Bioarchaeology of Ethnogenesis in the Colonial Southeast, by Christopher M. Stojanowski (2010; first paperback edition, 2013)

French Colonial Archaeology in the Southeast and Caribbean, edited by Kenneth G. Kelly and Meredith D. Hardy (2011; first paperback edition, 2015)

Late Prehistoric Florida: Archaeology at the Edge of the Mississippian World, edited by Keith Ashley and Nancy Marie White (2012; first paperback edition, 2015)

Early and Middle Woodland Landscapes of the Southeast, edited by Alice P. Wright and Edward R. Henry (2013; first paperback edition, 2019)

Trends and Traditions in Southeastern Zooarchaeology, edited by Tanya M. Peres (2014)

New Histories of Pre-Columbian Florida, edited by Neill J. Wallis and Asa R. Randall (2014; first paperback edition, 2016)

Discovering Florida: First-Contact Narratives from Spanish Expeditions along the Lower Gulf Coast, edited and translated by John E. Worth (2014; first paperback edition, 2016)

Constructing Histories: Archaic Freshwater Shell Mounds and Social Landscapes of the St. Johns River, Florida, by Asa R. Randall (2015)

Archaeology of Early Colonial Interaction at El Chorro de Maíta, Cuba, by Roberto Valcárcel Rojas (2016)

Fort San Juan and the Limits of Empire: Colonialism and Household Practice at the Berry Site, edited by Robin A. Beck, Christopher B. Rodning, and David G. Moore (2016)

Rethinking Moundville and Its Hinterland, edited by Vincas P. Steponaitis and C. Margaret Scarry (2016; first paperback edition, 2019)

Handbook of Ceramic Animal Symbols in the Ancient Lesser Antilles, by Lawrence Waldron (2016)

Paleoindian Societies of the Coastal Southeast, by James S. Dunbar (2016; first paperback edition, 2019)

Gathering at Silver Glen: Community and History in Late Archaic Florida, by Zackary I. Gilmore (2016)

Cuban Archaeology in the Caribbean, edited by Ivan Roksandic (2016)

Archaeologies of Slavery and Freedom in the Caribbean: Exploring the Spaces in Between, edited by Lynsey A. Bates, John M. Chenoweth, and James A. Delle (2016; first paperback edition, 2018)

Setting the Table: Ceramics, Dining, and Cultural Exchange in Andalucía and La Florida, by Kathryn L. Ness (2017)

Simplicity, Equality, and Slavery: An Archaeology of Quakerism in the British Virgin Islands, 1740–1780, by John M. Chenoweth (2017)

Fit for War: Sustenance and Order in the Mid-Eighteenth-Century Catawba Nation, by Mary Elizabeth Fitts (2017)

Water from Stone: Archaeology and Conservation at Florida's Springs, by Jason O'Donoughue (2017)

Mississippian Beginnings, edited by Gregory D. Wilson (2017; first paperback edition, 2019)

Honoring Ancestors in Sacred Space: The Archaeology of an Eighteenth-Century African-Bahamian Cemetery, by Grace Turner (2017)

Investigating the Ordinary: Everyday Matters in Southeast Archaeology, edited by Sarah E. Price and Philip J. Carr (2018)

Harney Flats: A Florida Paleoindian Site, by I. Randolph Daniel Jr. and Michael Wisenbaker (2017)

Early Human Life on the Southeastern Coastal Plain, edited by Albert C. Goodyear and Christopher R. Moore (2018)

New Histories of Village Life at Crystal River, by Thomas J. Pluckhahn and Victor D. Thompson (2018)

The Archaeology of Villages in Eastern North America, edited by Jennifer Birch and Victor D. Thompson (2018)

The Cumberland River Archaic of Middle Tennessee, edited by Tanya M. Peres and Aaron Deter-Wolf (2019)

Pre-Columbian Art of the Caribbean, by Lawrence Waldron (2019)

Iconography and Wetsite Archaeology of Florida's Watery Realms, edited by Ryan Wheeler and Joanna Ostapkowicz (2019)

New Directions in the Search for the First Floridians, edited by David K. Thulman and Ervan G. Garrison (2019)

Cahokia in Context: Hegemony and Diaspora, edited by Charles H. McNutt and Ryan M. Parish (2019)

Archaeology of Domestic Landscapes of the Enslaved in the Caribbean, edited by James A. Delle and Elizabeth C. Clay (2019)

Contact, Colonialism, and Native Communities in the Southeastern United States, edited by Edmond A. Boudreaux III, Maureen Meyers, and Jay K. Johnson (2020)

Bears: Archaeological and Ethnohistorical Perspectives in Native Eastern North America, edited by Heather A. Lapham and Gregory A. Waselkov (2020)

An Archaeology and History of a Caribbean Sugar Plantation on Antigua, edited by Georgia L. Fox (2020)

www.ingramcontent.com/pod-product-compliance
Lightning Source LLC
Chambersburg PA
CBHW052231230426
43666CB00035B/2604